William B. Helmreich

SIMON & SCHUSTER
New York London Toronto
Sydney Tokyo Singapore

AGAINST ALL ODDS

Holocaust Survivors
and the Successful
Lives They Made
in America

Simon & Schuster
Simon & Schuster Building
Rockefeller Center
1230 Avenue of the Americas
New York, New York 10020

SIMON & SCHUSTER and colophon are registered trademarks
of Simon & Schuster Inc.

Designed by Levavi & Levavi
Manufactured in the United States of America

1   3   5   7   9   10   8   6   4   2

Library of Congress Cataloging in Publication Data

Helmreich, William B.
Against all odds : holocaust survivors and the successful lives
they made in America / William B. Helmreich.
p.   cm.
Includes index.
1. Holocaust survivors—United States.   2. Jews—United States.
3. Immigrants—United States.   I. Title.
E184.J5H55   1992
940.53'18'092273—dc20
[B]   92-19790
CIP
ISBN: 0-671-66956-7

Dedication

In Honor of
Menachem Z. Polak and Chana G. Polak, survivors,
in Memory of
Sally (Banach) and Isak Levenstein, survivors,
and
in Memory of
the Stark and Halpern families
from Baberka and Orla, Poland,
and
the Ungar family
of Krasne, Poland,
whose members perished in the Holocaust along with 6,000,000
other Jews, including 1,500,000 children.
May their memories be a source of inspiration for Jewish survival.

Acknowledgments

The following people made this project possible through their generosity. Without their support it could not have been done in the way that it was. Israel and Nechama Polak were there from the beginning and believed in it throughout. Their enthusiasm was infectious and brought in others who played a major role, namely Charles and Rella Feldman and Norman and Helene Stark. William and Jerry Ungar were also crucial in this area. In addition, Melvin Bukiet, who knows from personal experience what writing is all about, and Murray Laulicht provided meaningful assistance. Most important, perhaps, was the total independence I had in carrying out my work and in developing the thesis and conclusions for this book. Credit for the organizational infrastructure and written arrangements that made this possible goes first to Harvey Ishofsky and then to Meyer Bilitsky and Jerry Weinstein.

The idea for this book grew out of discussions with Israel Polak and Joe Berger and I thank them both for having planted the seed. What followed from that is, of course, my own responsibility. In this regard, I am especially grateful to Elie Wiesel for his constant encouragement and stimulation. Similarly, Irving Louis Horowitz, teacher, friend, and colleague, gave advice and support throughout.

My colleagues in the Department of Sociology at City College of New York, as well as certain members of the administration, provided me with an environment conducive to scholarly endeavor, in terms of both time and financial support. Those most helpful included Robert Pfeffer, Jeffrey Rosen, Arline McCord, Marilyn Santomauro, Morris Silberberg, and my longtime friend and colleague Steven Goldberg, who has always stood by me. I am also thankful to Yisrael Gutman, Yehuda Bauer, and Victor Azarya for providing me with a home at Hebrew University while I was doing research in Israel. Since that time period encompassed the Gulf War, it was an especially meaningful and memorable experience.

Among the staff of Simon & Schuster, I am especially grateful to my editor, Dominick Anfuso, whose careful review of my writing greatly improved it, and to Jim Silberman, who acquired this book. Their complete confidence in the importance of the project meant a great deal to me. Many thanks also to Cassie Jones, whose attention to detail and unfailing good cheer made things much easier, and to Fred Chase for his skillful and meticulous copyediting. I am fortunate to have Pam Bernstein of the William Morris Literary Agency as my agent—a consummate professional who knows her business as well as anyone and who, at the same time, understands that books must be treated with care.

Among those who read the manuscript, Nechama Polak, Bernard Rosenberg, Miriam Reinfeld, Steven Goldberg, Lloyd Gartner, Chana Koevary, and Judith Tydor Baumel spent many hours reading most or all of the material. Collectively, they made literally hundreds of suggestions and comments that were of tremendous help. My debt to them cannot be overstated. I was fortunate to have the input of the following individuals who read various chapters and also contributed substantially to what became the final product: Ricki Bernstein, Michael Brown, Joan Downs, Arthur Goren, Yossi Klein Halevi, my father, Leo Helmreich, Simon Herman, Phil and Margie Jacobs, Gaynor Jacobson, Herbert Kalter, Dov Levin, George Linker, William McCord, Barbara Fischman Mevorach, Carol Meyer, Roz Moss, Meir Rotenberg, Michael Silber, Leo Srole, and Roger Waldinger.

The following survivors were interviewed at length for this book but are either not quoted or are quoted anonymously. Nevertheless, all of them, without exception, influenced my conceptualization, thinking, and writing on this subject. They gave unstintingly of their time, and I owe them a profound debt. They are listed here with the caveat that doing so identifies them but cannot do full justice to their actual contributions. I thank them all: Hedy and Terry Auerbach, Ruth Berger, Reva Bernstein, Sharon Blum, Thomas Buergenthal, Al Bukiet, Leon Chadajo, David Chase, Mendel Chulew, Margaret Colb, Jerry Cooper, Rosa Dziewienski, Isadore and Adela Froiman, Esther Geizhals, Regina Goldstein, Betty Goodfriend, Molly Gross, Rosalyn Gross, Shmuel Halpern, Edward Kaswan, Hinda Kibort, Masha Kowalski, Lola Lansky, Yisroel Leifer, Eva Lepold, Margaret Lerner, Helen Nagrodzki, Rose Nass, Sam Natanson, Ilse Nathan, Max Neselrot, Franka Neufeld, Blima Nunberg, Regine Rosenfelder, Hannah Rozen, Benjamin Rubinstein, Edith and Joseph Schlesinger, Helen Schwartz, Jules

Seidenweber, Aron Shampan, Sylvia Spira, Susan Tatum, Sabena Taubenfeld, Fela Urlik, Frieda Wolff, Joshua Wainer.

Marilyn Rosenstein was enormously helpful in transcribing and editing hundreds of tapes. Her dedication to this project was not confined to the mechanics of the work but also extended to the ideas behind it. My debt to her is great. Eva Meyer and Mordechai Granit did excellent jobs of translating key articles on this subject and their own personal reminiscences about the early period after the survivors came to America were both informative and illuminating. I also benefited from my discussions with Hadassah Wachstock on this topic.

Those who did the interviewing and provided research assistance for the quantitative part of this study are deserving of praise for their efforts and diligence. In this regard I want to express my appreciation to my colleague Irvin Schonfeld and to Danqing Ruan, who patiently and skillfully worked with me on the analysis of the data. Special thanks also to Vera Bernstein, Ruth Dienstag, Judith Dori, Rebecca Gris, Mark Jacobs, Beate Kaufman, Minna Kotler, Rhoda Lewin, Jill Lipshie, Brenda Parver, David Raddick, Eric Rasmussen, Phyllis Safdie, Joyce Salomon, Sue-Ann Scherr, Cheryl Sims, Laurie Tansman, Hadassah Wachstock, Sue Weinberg, Judith Wissner-Levy. I am also indebted to Paul Ritterband and Barry Kosmin of the North American Jewish Data Bank and to Jeff Scheckner and Jeff Solomon for making it possible for me to draw upon quantitative data on survivors that appeared in past research sponsored by the New York Federation of Jewish Philanthropies.

No researcher can succeed in a project of this sort without the assistance of archivists, librarians, and other professionals. They are the author's eyes and ears. The following individuals were particularly helpful in guiding me to appropriate sources. They were generous with their time and giving of themselves beyond the call of duty; their affiliations appear in parentheses following their names: Roger Kohn (Yeshiva University); Dina Abramowicz, Fruma Mohrer, Marek Web (YIVO); Iris Berlatsky, Leon Volovici (Yad Vashem); Irma Krentz (Wiener Oral History Library—American Jewish Committee); Judith Kestenberg, Louis Levitan (Child Development Research—Jerome Riker Study); Benjamin Meed (American Gathering of Holocaust Survivors); Yaffa Eliach, Bonnie Gurevitch, Jeshejahu Pery, Betty Weinstein (Center for Holocaust Studies); Dianne Spielmann (Leo Baeck Institute);

Nathan Kaganoff (American Jewish Historical Society); Geoffrey Hartman, Dori Laub, Sandra Rosenstock, Joanne Rudoff (Video Archive for Holocaust Testimonies at Yale University); Benjamin Kahn (private collection of B'nai B'rith Hillel Foundation papers); Denise Gluck (Joint Distribution Committee); Tanya Gross (Ze'ev Jabotinsky Center); Diane Zimmerman (Center for Migration Studies). In addition, Manya Berenholz and Hadassah Wachstock found important archival material.

Other people who provided assistance often defied easy categorization. In some instances they gave me information, access, or leads; in others, they provided encouragement. In all cases, I very much appreciate their involvement and wish to thank them for it: Michael Berenbaum, Randolph Braham, Joseph Brandes, Barbara Burstein, Lucy Dawidowicz, Zachary Dicker, Leonard Dinnerstein, Daniel Elazar, Ellen Epstein, Eve Epstein, Shlomo Fogel, Eva Fogelman, Aviva Fried, Peter B. Friedman, Ricki Garti, Myra Giberovitch, Chaya Gordin, Marc Handelman, Aaron Hass, Leo and Charlotte Helmreich, Alan Helmreich, Jeff Helmreich, Benjamin Hirsch, Helen Ishofsky, Boaz and Eva Kahane, Altie Karper, Roman Kent, Hannah Kliger, Herman Kotler, David Kranzler, Abe and Renee Krieger, Nora Levin, Jerry and Naomi Lippman, Sesil Lissberger, Phil and Tina Machnikoff, Larry Matloss, Vladka Meed, Jacob Mendlovic, Chava and Jeff Miller, Kitty Millet, Gary Mokotoff, Samuel and Pearl Oliner, Abraham Peck, Sonia Pilcer, Garth Potts, David and Harriet Schimel, Fred and Allyne Schwartz, Reuel Shinnar, John Sigal, Martin Sokol, Sigmund Strochlitz, Sue Talansky, Jack Wachstock, Harold Waller, Morton Weinfeld, David Werber, Dorit Whiteman, Miriam Wiener, Avi Zablocki, Zvee Zahavy, Karl Zukerman.

In keeping with the tradition in acknowledgments to save the best for last, I want to express my deepest appreciation and gratitude to my wife, Helaine. Her personal devotion to me and to our children, Jeff, Alan, Joseph, and Deborah, made it possible for me to undertake this long and complex project. Beyond that, however, she read, with a critical eye, every word of the manuscript, and gave invaluable advice on many aspects of the research. No one could ask for more.

Contents

Introduction

Harry Haft is a concentration camp survivor. After the war he became a professional boxer and fought against Rocky Marciano, Roland LaStarza, and other top-ranked fighters. Today, he is retired and lives in Florida. He has many memories of the years spent in the ring, some pleasant, some not, but what gives him the greatest pleasure are his children and grandchildren.

Abe Foxman's life was saved by a Christian nanny who had him baptized as a Catholic. Today, he heads the Anti-Defamation League, where it is his responsibility to combat anti-Semitism wherever it rears its head. It is a job he loves and takes very seriously. "I don't think Jews have the luxury to look at any racist or anti-Semite as a kook," says Foxman. Given his personal background, his attitude is hardly surprising.

Writing in his autobiography about Sam Brach, a Queens, New York, butcher, Governor Mario Cuomo said: "He gave me a lot of good advice." Brach, who survived Auschwitz, is a philanthropist and political activist. More than anything, perhaps, he fights for the dignity of the Holocaust survivor.

Then there is Eva Ebin. Like Brach, she comes from Hungary and was a concentration camp inmate, but her work is of a different sort. She is a psychiatrist with a practice in Great Neck, Long Island. Professionally and personally, she has attained one version of the American dream.

As head of the committee investigating the scandals at the Department of Housing and Urban Development (HUD), Congressman Tom Lantos became a familiar face to millions of TV viewers. His incarceration in labor camps during World War II shaped his worldview and he has, over the years, championed the causes of underdogs, ranging from the Baha'is in Iran and dissidents in China to children exploited in sweatshops.

Five individuals, five stories, all different. Nonetheless, they all share a common history and fate, for they are part of the saga of the estimated 140,000 survivors of the Holocaust who came to the United States in the years immediately following the Second World War. It was their destiny to be catapulted into the vortex of human history during a time and in a place where words like civilization, kindness, and tolerance lost all meaning. That place, of course, was the vast netherworld in which millions of Jews, Gypsies, Slavs, Poles, and others deemed undesirable were ruthlessly murdered by the Nazis. That they lived to tell the tale was, for most, a matter of chance; that they succeeded in rebuilding their lives on American soil was not.

This book is the story of how these people, many of whom emerged sick and emaciated from the concentration camps, learned to live and to hope again. The catastrophe that befell European Jewry conferred upon those who outlived it a special and unique responsibility—to bear witness to what they saw and went through. For some, this translated into writing books about the subject. Others spoke out publicly, and still others built monuments. Regardless of what they did, the war was seared into their consciousness in ways that would remain with them for the rest of their lives even as they struggled to overcome its most deleterious effects.

What emerges here, however, is a portrait that is sharply divergent from the stereotyped images that many have of the survivors as people who are chronically depressed, anxious, and fearful. While it is true that there are indeed survivors who exhibit such traits, this is by no means the norm. It is, when all is said and done, a surprisingly normal and successful community. Their family lives are stable, as are their work patterns. They have a rich and varied social life and they have contributed much to the American Jewish community. Nevertheless, they have forged a distinct identity for themselves as a result of what they endured. This has influenced how they look at life and how they behave. In that sense, they are special.

Those survivors who did well in this country are proof of the human potential for regeneration. At the same time, the survivors' overall achievements must in no way allow us to forget that most of European Jewry was annihilated. Moreover, there were many among those who came to America afterward who were never able to lead normal lives again. A good number of these individuals have already died, but their suffering continues to haunt those who knew them.

Clearly, there were, among the millions of refugees who made their way to these shores both before and after the Holocaust, many others who had known great hardship and privation. However, the experiences of those who survived the Holocaust differed from those of most refugees in very important ways. Few refugees from oppression had undergone a period of sustained torture and brutality carried out in a systematic manner, day in, day out, over such a long period of time. If the survivors' travails did not differ so much in kind, they almost certainly differed in degree, generally lasting for up to five years. Moreover, Holocaust survivors were not persecuted because of what they *did,* but rather because of who they *were.* The terror of being singled out in this manner lay in the utter hopelessness implied by such categorization. There were no re-education camps to be sent to, no prison terms culminating in eventual release, no religions to adopt, and no political stances to take. The Jews were, in short, destined to die and they could do nothing to alter that status. The only questions that remained were when and how.

How do people who have experienced such cataclysmic events pick up the threads of their lives? From where do they obtain the strength to go on and how do they learn to trust others and to have faith in the future again? What about those unable to pick up the pieces who have, nonetheless, survived? What happens to them? In what ways are those with whom the survivors have contact affected? *Most important, perhaps, what lessons can the rest of us learn from the survivors about coping with tragedy and adversity?*

These are some of the questions that this book attempts to answer. One of the major findings is that most survivors who did well possessed in varying degrees ten distinct traits. These are fully discussed and analyzed in the concluding chapter. The book also tells the story of these people as a community, the places they went to, the lives they led, and the impact they had on America. To date, there has been no general history of the community and this volume is therefore a first effort in that direction. The choice between a scholarly tome and a more popular work was decided in favor of the latter because it seemed more important that a topic that has received very little attention be brought before as wide an audience as possible. In truth, much more research can and should be done on this subject and it is hoped that professionals who read this work will do so. There is one problem, however. Unlike their children, about whom a good deal has already been written, the survivors are getting on in years and will soon be gone. In fact, about one third of those who came to the United States after the war have already died. It is, therefore, imperative that such efforts be made now, before the opportunity is irretrievably lost.

The heart of this study is the 170 in-depth interviews conducted with the survivors, each of which averaged approximately two and one half hours in length. I did almost all the interviewing myself, having learned in graduate school that fieldwork is best absorbed and remembered when done by the researcher. In addition, I personally transcribed about half of the interviews, for the same reason. The quotes from interviews that appear in the book were selected, after careful analysis, because they best reflect the experiences and opinions of the survivors in general.

In an attempt to obtain as broad a cross section as possible, I crisscrossed the United States in search of the survivors, from New York to Mississippi, from Florida to Wisconsin. The survivors interviewed in this volume were not chosen arbitrarily, or by coincidence, but because they are representative of the total population of survivors—the famous and the not-so-famous; successes and failures, as well as those in between; atheists, Hasidim, radical socialists, Conservative and Reform Jews; those treated by psychiatrists and those who had never seen anyone for counseling; intellectuals and businesspeople; New Yorkers and those living elsewhere—in short, as many different types as possible.

I also interviewed a number of survivors now living in Israel who had moved there after having spent many years in the United States. In one case I went to Germany, specifically to interview U.S. Army Brigadier General Sidney Shachnow. General Shachnow, a former Green Beret commander in Vietnam, was at the time commander of U.S. forces in Berlin. He survived the Holocaust as a child in Lithuania, where he was incarcerated in a concentration camp.

To round out the picture presented by the survivors, I spoke with social workers and others who assisted the refugees in the early years, those who employed them, some of their teachers, and many of their neighbors and friends.

Besides these interviews, a number of archival collections located in the United States and in Israel were examined for material relating to the survivors. In addition, a large-scale random survey of survivors was carried out. The main results of the survey are interspersed throughout the narrative. Those interested in a more detailed statement regarding this survey may consult the methodological note that appears at the end of the book.

While the survivors suffered together, their prewar backgrounds were frequently dissimilar. There were wealthy, middle-class, and poor Jews; those from both urban and rural environments; and immigrants from over twenty lands, each with its own special history; there were child survivors and those whose trials and tribulations occurred while they were in the prime of their lives; communists and Zionists; blacksmiths, professors, athletes, salesmen—the list is virtually endless. These distinctions are taken into account here, but much more work needs to be done before we can fully understand the implications of all these differences in the postwar adjustment of the survivors.

Finally, a word about the definition of a survivor. The term can and does encompass many categories, including those who escaped from Germany before the war and those who lived in "safe" countries like Switzerland and the Dominican Republic during the Holocaust period. In an attempt to focus on those whose suffering was greatest, the definition has been limited to those who were uprooted by the war and who lived in occupied countries, or in Shanghai or Siberia, during the war years. The definition includes those in the camps and ghettos, those who hid, and those who passed as Gentiles during the war. Whenever possible, real names have been used, but in some cases, where individuals objected or the material was highly sensitive, pseudonyms have been employed or the respondents have remained anonymous. Some minor details have also been changed to preserve anonymity.

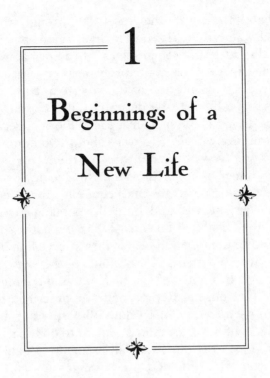

1

Beginnings of a New Life

1

THE SUN SHONE BRIGHT over the calm waters of the Atlantic Ocean, ideal weather for a sea voyage. The passengers on the SS *Ernie Pyle* strolled on deck and exchanged stories, or perhaps simply stared at the horizon and dreamed of what lay ahead. The setting seemed perfect for a luxury cruise. But this was no cruise ship; nor could the passengers have afforded to travel on one. In fact, few were even able to scrape together the $225 fare for the trip and had to rely instead upon the largesse of the organizations sponsoring them.

These were refugees and the *Ernie Pyle* was a refurbished army transport vessel, one of hundreds that regularly crossed the ocean between 1946 and 1953, carrying thousands of Holocaust survivors to the shores of the United States. The names of these boats—*Marine Flasher, Marine Perch, Uruguay, General Gordon,* and *General Ballou*—do not mean anything to the average American. The survivors, however, remember them with a mixture of fondness and anxiety.

On one hand, these were the vessels that brought them to America, the land where they began their lives again, marrying, raising families, and reintegrating themselves into a normal way of life. On the other, the trip itself was not entirely pleasant. Seasickness forced many to spend a good portion of the voyage in bed. The refugees' quarters also left much to be desired. Willy Herskovits, a Czech survivor now living in West Palm Beach, Florida, recalled: "I was separated from my wife. There were about two hundred people in a large room and rows of beds, three of them, one on top of the other. The women, though, slept four to a room."

Food was another problem. Starved almost to the point of death for years during the war and limited, in many cases, to rations afterward in the Displaced Persons (DP) camps, the survivors were unaccustomed to the rich and hearty meals served on board. Some, nonetheless, were unaffected and found the experience delightful. Congressman Tom Lantos of California, the only Holocaust survivor in the U.S. House of Representatives, described his first meal on the *Marine Falcon* as "marvelous. There was a big basket of oranges and one of bananas. And I wanted to do the right thing. So I asked this sailor: 'Should I take an orange or a banana?' And he said: 'Man, you eat all the goddamn oranges and all the goddamn bananas you want.' Then I knew I was in Paradise." Lantos was nineteen years old at the time.

The sailor's response was typical. The crew and officers were, by and large, sympathetic and understanding toward the refugees. For quite a few immigrants, compassion from Americans, especially that of the soldiers who liberated the camps, was crucial. It shaped their view of America in general, one characterized today by intense feelings of loyalty and patriotism.

Paula Gris, who survived the war as a child in the Transnistria area of Ukraine and who now makes her home in Atlanta, Georgia, looked back upon her voyage to New York with affection:

I remember someone playing a guitar, singing "I come from Alabama with my banjo on my knee" and "My bonnie's gone over the ocean." I didn't realize it then but my acculturation process had already begun on the boat. I was hearing the English language as well as that infectious American music! These sounds spoke to me of optimism and trust and exuded a comforting patriotic spirit. It was all so opposite from the suspicion and fear that had dominated my life for so long. For me, a thirteen-year-

old refugee, that boat trip was the physical and emotional and cultural transition from darkness into light. It represented sunshine to me even though I was still suffering the agonies of seasickness.

The affirmation of life by the survivors actually began long before the journey across the ocean. While some were lucky enough to gain admission to the United States soon after the war ended, the majority were compelled to spend years following the war in Europe, usually in Displaced Persons camps, before making the trip. Typically those with visas were taken from the camps to special assembly centers and from there to the port city of Bremerhaven, Germany, where the ships were docked. The majority entered this country after June 1948 when President Truman signed into law a bill allowing 205,000 refugees to enter the United States.

Much has been written about life in the DP camps, the frustration of being in limbo, neither free nor imprisoned. Many had had all they could take of communal living and wanted simply to get on with their lives. But there were few viable options before 1948 outside of Palestine, a hazardous trip that many were physically and mentally incapable of undertaking. As for the lands of their birth, which lay mostly in Eastern Europe, these were unattractive for other reasons. There was first the anti-Semitism in countries such as Poland, Hungary, and Romania. "What, we thought Hitler killed all of you!" was a common refrain when the refugees returned to see what was left of their towns and villages. These fears were reinforced when word spread of the infamous pogrom in Kielce, Poland, on July 4, 1946, in which forty-one Jews were murdered and others wounded. Moreover, the refugees had no desire to be under the rule of communism.

Thus, the survivors reluctantly settled down in the camps where they waited for affidavits to be sent from other countries. Yet even as they did so, they refused to descend into nihilism and to continue to accept the dehumanization that the Nazis had forced upon them during the war. Instead, they set up schools, clubs, and organizations, and they published newspapers. There were many marriages and an extremely high birth rate. There were youth groups, political movements, agricultural settlements, and many different kinds of educational and cultural activities. If the refugees were as passive or selfish as some have claimed, then they could never have achieved all this so soon after liberation.

Even so, these accomplishments occurred for the most part within a highly controlled environment. Once the refugees arrived in the United States, they were, more or less, on their own. True, a vast Jewish organizational apparatus assisted them, not to mention friends and relatives, but the emphasis was now on self-help. These thoughts preoccupied the refugees during the fourteen or so days that they were on the high seas: How would they make out in a strange land? Would they really have the strength and energy to take advantage of the opportunities? What kind of work could they obtain? Did the cousin who made out the affidavit for them really want them or were her actions motivated more by guilt?

Mostly, the survivors passed the time chatting among themselves. There was a library on many ships but no one really had the patience or inclination to read the books found there. It was just another place to talk, plan, and think about what lay ahead. Some made new friends on the boat, others reunited with those they knew in prewar days or in the concentration camps. There were ships whose passengers were almost all Jewish, others whose populations included Christian DPs from countries such as Lithuania, Latvia, and Estonia. Some made no secret of their feelings about Jews and there were, no doubt, among them persons who had actively persecuted Jews during the Nazi occupation. For the most part, Christian and Jewish DPs on the boat kept their distance from each other, interacting only when necessary.

Still, there were incidents. Walter Peltz, a Milwaukee businessman, described to me how one Pole in a uniform assigned the least desirable tasks on the boat to Jews. Moreover, he refused to allow men to visit their sick wives or children. "So I organized a strike in which the Jews on board refused to work. I figured, what could he do to us? Send us back? And when he called me a goddamn Jew, I beat the shit out of him." A journalist wrote of a man who recognized his own suitcase in the hands of a Yugoslav who had taken it from him after sending the man to a camp from his native town.

One incident, reported in the German language weekly *Aufbau,* graphically demonstrated the range and depth of emotions among the immigrants. Titled "A Tribunal on the Immigrant Boat," it recounted how some adolescent passengers aboard the *Marine Perch* discovered that several Jewish "policemen" were traveling with them and accused them of torturing other Jews and turning them over to the Nazis. According to the article "the publicity official, S. L. Schneiderman, also traveling with the group, found it necessary to conduct an immediate investigation to prevent a lynching from taking place." The accused vigorously defended themselves and the case was turned over for further investigation (to whom is not known) after the ship docked. The same article went on to report the presence on the boat of Germans who continued to profess their admiration for Hitler and who admitted to wartime membership in Hitler youth groups.

Today, more than forty years after the war, the memories of the Holocaust continue to play a prominent role in the lives of the survivors and it does not take much to evoke them. A good example of this pattern was that of Elizabeth Gevirtz. In April 1989, she was staying at the Homowack Hotel, a resort in New York's Catskill Mountains. The hotel was filled to capacity with Jews who had come there to celebrate the Passover holiday. Gevirtz, a Czech survivor of Auschwitz, now lives in Bridgeport, Connecticut. A widow, she came to the hotel to relax and, hopefully, meet someone with a "similar background." Without much enthusiasm she agreed to be interviewed, but once we began, a remarkable transformation occurred. Her voice quavered with emotion as she described how she narrowly escaped death during the war:

> When we got to Auschwitz on May 29, 1944, a kapo [concentration camp overseer] said to us that we should mark the date when we came in because that's going to be the date of our death. "You see that chimney?" she said. "You see that smoke, that flame? Those are your parents' bodies going up the chimney." And we thought, how can anybody be so cruel? But later on we understood where we were, what Auschwitz was. Still, I knew that God was with us because one day we went into a very tiny room with space for gas on top, forty of us, like sardines. We stood for twenty minutes and then I heard an SS woman outside say: "We ran out of gas." So we weren't killed. Instead we went to Danzig and we lived.

The memories of last-minute reprieves sustained many of the survivors in the aftermath of the Holocaust. Some attributed it to God, others to fate. Regardless, the belief in a certain destiny gave them courage and hope. Is it any wonder then that Elizabeth Gevirtz could describe her first sight of New York in almost lyrical terms when asked what it was like: "Ohhh, just beautiful! Just beautiful! We started to scream: 'We are in America!' And look at the Statue of Liberty, that we heard about, that we learned about in school. The thought that, Jew or non-Jew, this is ours. We are free in America." Another immigrant noted: "It is such a beautiful statue. It's so symbolic, so meaningful . . . to be greeted firsthand by this great lady."

For some it was the Statue of Liberty, for others, New York's skyline. Luba Bat, the niece of a prominent American labor leader, Sidney Hillman, was "fascinated" by the skyscrapers, observing that in her native Poland they had been referred to as "cloud-scratchers." Judith Traub, now living on Long Island, New York, who survived the harshness of the Siberian wasteland, was reminded of how swiftly the images changed: "That night, when we arrived, everything looked so magnificent and sparkling, with the lights of the highways, bridges, and skyline. It was just incredible, a wonderful, wonderful feeling. And then the next morning, it was bleak and gray and foggy; the piers were dirty and the lights were gone. It was such a disappointment to me. I was crushed."

The excitement and anticipation that enveloped the immigrants was matched and, in some instances, even exceeded, by those who waited by the pier to greet them. Richard Dyck, a reporter for *Aufbau,* wrote of the tension that gripped those on shore as the outline of the gray and white *Marine Flasher* came into view, the small red tugboats guiding it up the Hudson. As Dyck went aboard with other members of the press, a sixty-three-year-old former grain merchant from Cologne pressed a piece of paper into his hand on which was written a poem expressing gratitude to America. Nearby, a woman leaned over a railing, sobbing into her handkerchief. "My husband! My husband!" she wailed. But the most dramatic scenes took place after the passengers had disembarked:

> When the first passengers were allowed onto the gangplank, something akin to an electric shock went through the crowd. A young man ran wildly toward the expectant crowd waiting by the fence. A bone-chilling cry rang out—"My child! My child!" shouted an older man, tears streaming down his cheeks. His daughter, who stood beside him, looked at her brother as he took her in his arms and kissed her. Everyone around them, even the customs officials, was greatly moved. Overcome by emotion, they turned away.

Most of the arrivals were between seventeen and thirty-nine. This was not surprising, since those in this age group were most likely to have survived the camps. They were in reasonably good health, and were able, therefore, to pass the physical examinations required by the American government. Many, however, did not fit this description. There were both the elderly and the very young who had been hidden during the war or who had passed as Christians. Many children were placed in French convents, for example.

Each year thousands of passengers came, but very few of the stories surrounding their arrival were recorded. One ship, whose entry into New York's harbor was described by a journalist, was that of the *General Black*. Its manifest included the first group of people granted visas under the 1948 Displaced Persons Act. As reported by the U.S. Displaced Persons Commission, it received a harbor welcome usually reserved only for "superliners and returning American soldiers." An army tugboat sailed around the ship with a banner reading "Welcome to America." The new immigrants were treated to speeches of welcome from government officials, including one by the U.S. attorney general, who stated: "The President greets you as the Pilgrims of 1948 entering this historic gateway, as did the Pilgrims of 1620." One can only imagine what went through the minds of those on board as they heard these words, if, indeed, they understood them.

While New York was the most common port of entry for the refugees, many other cities received them too. These included San Francisco, New Orleans, Boston, Galveston, and Baltimore. Approximately fifteen thousand Jews survived the war in Shanghai, under the Japanese occupation, living in a specially designated ghetto under miserable conditions. After the war, most emigrated to the United States, with the majority entering via San Francisco. The immigrants spoke of the beauty of the Golden Gate Bridge, the West Coast's equivalent to the Statue of Liberty. Many however had little reaction, their senses numbed by the difficult journey. Still, all felt immense gratitude toward this country for having allowed them in, even as they looked to the future with feelings of both anxiety and hope.

Many who came to San Francisco headed eastward and acquired their initial impressions of America from the windows of a speeding train whose final destination was usually New York. Once there, a second welcome often greeted them. Among these travelers were students and rabbis of the Mirrer Yeshiva, a famed institution of higher Jewish learning whose members had fled across Russia and who had spent the war years in Shanghai. There they kept alive the centuries-old tradition of Talmudic study, living as members of a distinct subculture within the Jewish enclave. Now their goal was to rebuild the school in New York City, home to America's largest Orthodox community.

Whatever their land of origin, port of arrival, or degree of religiosity, all of these refugees had one thing in common—they came ultimately to America. Altogether, they numbered about 140,000 out of about half a million Jewish survivors, with about 37,000 more who entered Canada. The majority of the DPs, two thirds perhaps, eventually settled in Israel, with most coming after 1948 when Israel became an independent nation.

The reasons for choosing America varied. For many it was family. Having lost so many of their loved ones, the refugees eagerly reached out to those who offered a helping hand. Unlike those Jews who came to the *Goldene Medine* (Golden Land) at the turn of the century, the survivors found that America afforded them the opportunity to resume, rather than break off, family ties. This was because in many instances the only members of their families still alive were those who had come to the United States before the war.

Then there were the cumulative effects of the war itself. Many were simply too tired and worn out to take on the challenge of becoming pioneers. They knew, via letters from friends and relatives residing in Israel, that life there was difficult. Getting there was no easy matter either, especially in the years prior to 1948 when the British did their best to prevent Jews from entering Palestine. As Sam Halpern, who became a successful real estate entrepreneur in this country, recalled: "I felt I went through such a terrible war and conditions in Israel were very tough. My uncle here said: 'You can always go to Israel from America.' "

Still, those who opted for the relative security of America often felt ambivalent about that decision. Anna Loewy, a young immigrant, gave eloquent expression to such feelings when she told a reporter for *The Jewish Examiner* that she selected the United States over Palestine "not because I don't love Palestine, but because I *do* love Palestine. But Palestine needs strong people to work and fight for her, and I am no longer strong and I can fight no more. But I have one wish—to see Palestine, just once."

Doubtless, many survivors looked to America because its size, diversity, and separation of church and state offered the promise of being able to fit in, to disappear, and, hopefully, to put the past behind them. Thus, one of the protagonists in Elie Wiesel's novel

The Fifth Son observes that "he is glad that he waited for the American visa, and so is his father. The American way of life suits them; it is easy to blend in with the masses. . . . New York, the most extroverted city in the world, is also the perfect city for loners."

Feelings toward Israel often depended on the prewar lives of the immigrants. Those raised in homes that emphasized Zionism were more apt to experience conflict over not settling in Israel. Even so, there were situations in which one had little choice. Abe Foxman, who is today national director of the Anti-Defamation League, survived the war as a child. Hidden by a Christian family, he came to America in 1950. His father, a journalist, wanted to go to Israel but was discouraged from doing so because his ideological leanings would have severely limited his opportunities there when compared to those available in America. Foxman elaborated: "My father was a Revisionist [the Zionist party opposed to Israel's then-elected leaders]. He edited a Revisionist paper in Europe. My father's brother, who lived in Israel, told him: 'Don't come here because you don't have a profession and because you're a Revisionist.' " Foxman himself recounted at least one instance where his father's political affiliations negatively affected his own professional career.

For Vera Stern, wife of famed violinist Isaac Stern, it was not so much a lack of choice as it was fate that determined where she ultimately settled. While unusual, her story illustrates the conflicts that could—and did—emerge between ideological beliefs and personal considerations. Stern had been a Zionist in Berlin, where she spent the early years of her life, but had not gone to Palestine then because she was too young. After spending the war hidden in Paris until she escaped to neutral Sweden in 1943, she came to the United States.

But the dream of living in Israel refused to die and, in 1951, she moved there to try it out. Interviewed in New York, she talked candidly about her feelings at the time: "From 1948 to 1950 I was thinking of making *aliyah* [a term that describes a move to Israel by a Jew]. . . . I had wanted to go to Israel all my life and now I could go. I felt it was my own country and a wonderful place. I'm saying things that are such platitudes, but they're true." While there, she went to a concert given by Isaac Stern. They were introduced, and in what was obviously a whirlwind courtship, were married only seventeen days later. Isaac had come to America from Russia at the age of ten months and had resided since then in the United States. Vera returned to the States with him and has lived there ever since.

Nonetheless, she retains her strong feelings for Israel, as well as for a host of Jewish causes with which she is involved.

Conversely, those from Hasidic backgrounds spent little time agonizing about their decision to emigrate to America. For many, especially those from the Satmarer sect, Jerusalem was as it always would be, an exalted place whose essence found its deepest expression in the inner core of their hearts and souls and whose promise would be fulfilled only when the Messiah came. One Hasidic Jew, now living in Brooklyn, noted wryly that he was more favorably disposed toward moving to Israel in the years 1945 to 1948, *before* it achieved independence. A second man, who now makes his home in the Hasidic town of New Square, in Rockland County, New York, explained his reason for preferring America to Israel by way of an analogy: "If I see a Jew violating Shabbes [the Sabbath] by smoking on the street, I don't like it but I don't do anything about it. But if I saw my own sons smoking in my house on Shabbes, would I stand for it? Of course not! So this is how I feel about Israel." For him a secular Jewish state where most Jews openly violate God's commandments is intolerable. He also asserted that many who had gone there eventually came to America because life in Israel was very difficult. Obviously, thousands of Hasidic Jews elected to live in Israel regardless of their hostility to the state; nevertheless, reasons such as these were motivating factors for many who did not.

Sometimes, especially right after the war ended, people were unable to go to Israel even if they wanted to because their backgrounds indicated a lack of strong commitment to Zionism. One such individual explained to those in charge that he had always yearned for Jerusalem in his prayers. Nonetheless, he was turned down because he did not belong to any Zionist organization.

Finally, there was the role of chance, a matter of being on a certain list or even being in a particular place at the right time. A perhaps extreme example of this was the case of Edward Blonder, who was in a DP camp when a Zionist group arrived with eight trucks and told everyone to get ready because they would be leaving very shortly for Palestine. He and a friend went into town to buy some items for the trip. When they returned, they discovered to their dismay that the convoy had already left. Efforts to locate the group proved fruitless. Not long afterward, Blonder's name was broadcast over the radio along with those of other refugees. Relatives recognized it and sponsored him and he arrived in the United

States shortly thereafter, in 1946. To this day, he wonders wistfully "how different my life would have been had I gone to Palestine."

It appears that with the passage of time many of those who felt guilty about their decision to emigrate to America rather than Israel have, more or less, come to terms with it. Some are quite blunt in their assessments. Bill Neufeld, a Polish-born survivor who came here in 1949 and now lives in the Midwest, takes great pride in his involvement with Jewish causes, including the local Jewish Federation and the State of Israel. Yet he minced no words when asked if he considered going to Israel after the war:

Of course! And why didn't we go? Because we took the easy way out. Right or wrong I feel pretty guilty about it. I was speaking to a high school class about the Holocaust and 95 percent of the kids were not Jewish and they asked me about it. That's a pretty tough question to answer to a non-Jewish group. But I told them the truth. I thought I was going to live here five years and then go to Israel. But once you get a taste of the good life, you don't want to leave. I took the e-a-s-y way out.

Despite such lingering doubts, these survivors are cushioned by the knowledge that very few American Jews have moved to Israel either, perhaps no more than fifty thousand, or 1 percent, since the state was created. Moreover, of those who have done so, large numbers have returned, unable to adjust to life there, a life considerably easier than it was in the days following World War II.

2 ✳

Once they had passed through customs, the immigrants were generally greeted by a small army of people concerned about their welfare. Those who had relatives or friends were quickly spirited away, but for the others the experience was more trying. Waiting for them were representatives of various Jewish organizations, their colored armbands distinguishing one group from the other. The Hebrew Immigrant Aid Society (HIAS) people had white enamel badges in their buttonholes and navy blue armbands; those with light blue silk armbands with black writing represented the volunteer workers from the National Council of Jewish Women (NCJW);

while those in charge of children wore the blue and yellow armbands that identified them as belonging to the U.S. Committee for Refugees. Other organizations at the pier included the National Catholic Welfare Conference, in charge of Christian DPs, and the Traveler's Aid Society, which concerned itself with all refugees.

For the Jews, however, the two most important such organizations were the HIAS and the United Service for New Americans (USNA). HIAS was founded in 1902 and worked for many years on behalf of immigrants, helping them enter the United States and adjust to life here. The USNA was formed in 1946 by a merger of the National Refugee Service and the National Service to the Foreign Born of the National Council of Jewish Women. These two organizations assumed primary responsibility for getting the immigrants to America and assisting them once they were here. While the refugees were still in Europe, they were helped by the Joint Distribution Committee (JDC).

Both professionals and volunteers worked with the refugees at this point. Regardless, special skills and talents were required of such individuals. They needed to be familiar with the rules and regulations of customs, methods of transportation, baggage handling, first aid, and foreign languages, especially Yiddish. Even more important was a capacity to handle adversity and to respond quickly and efficiently to emergencies. Ships arrived at all hours and in many different locations. Schedules were not always adhered to. The Pier Service Department representatives of the HIAS and those with the USNA's Port and Dock Division were literally on call twenty-four hours a day, 365 days a year. No matter what the weather—snow, rain, heat—the workers knew that being there for the often bewildered refugees was their highest priority. More than anything, perhaps, it was a question of someone making them feel wanted. Irving Goldstein, who became a successful chicken farmer in Swan Lake, New York, reminisced about his reception: "When we came to Boston, everybody got a cardboard box from the HIAS and in it were two eggs, an apple, an orange, and two cookies and a dollar on which they wrote something like, 'Good luck in the U.S.' "

Problems could, and frequently did, occur. A passenger operated on at sea required an ambulance and a stretcher when the ship docked. New York's Great Blizzard of December 1947 necessitated unusual travel arrangements—baggage was taken from the ship to the subway by sled. One immigrant lost his luggage and panicked;

an orphan on her way to relatives in America refused to be separated from the woman who had befriended her on the trip across the ocean. Tact, understanding, and sympathy combined with firmness and common sense were the qualities demanded in such situations. One recurring dilemma was ships arriving on the Sabbath. Some of the passengers refused to leave the ship without reassurances that they wouldn't be asked to travel until after the holiday ended. From all reports it would seem that both agency workers and immigration officials were highly sympathetic to such requests.

From the dock the newcomers were taken to reserved hotel rooms or to the HIAS shelter at 425 Lafayette Street. In New York, this task was usually accomplished by volunteers from the NCJW, which relied upon a pool of about sixty drivers to transport the immigrants. The largest and most frequently used location was the massive, ten-story Hotel Marseilles, situated on Manhattan's Upper West Side, at the intersection of Broadway and 103rd Street. Some remembered it as a "dilapidated halfway house for war refugees" where they, nevertheless, felt at ease. Others identified it as the place where they received their first key ever to a private room.

In 1950, the USNA's executive committee voted unanimously to close its operation at the hotel. Among the reasons given was the hotel's tendency "to perpetuate 'the DP camp atmosphere' of dependent rather than independent living." But this was much later. In the early days the Marseilles was a necessity, serving as the headquarters for the numerous agencies that were coordinating the absorption process. It also contained meeting rooms, recreation halls, medical facilities, offices, and a kosher dining hall. A clothing distribution center was stocked with suits and dresses, all of them provided by manufacturers at substantial discounts. There was simply no better way to efficiently house, feed, and care for the thousands of immigrants who arrived over such a short period of time.

In truth, the Marseilles was far more than a shelter and center for relief agency efforts. Walking around in the lobby and listening to the conversations of immigrants in a dozen tongues gave observers the feeling of being in another world, a world whose inhabitants were unwilling to shed the cultural baggage of the past even as they hesitantly groped their way toward a new life. These perceptions were heightened by the sight of the new immigrants sitting in English classes given at the hotel by the Committee for Refugee Education, as well as attending lectures and films designed to orient them to America. In the lobby hung a large map of the United

States, accompanied by a large, red-lettered sign proclaiming proudly: "This is how America looks." Nearby were photographs of American city scenes with ribbons stretching from the pictures to the cities' locations on the map.

Any doubts that existed about the degree of culture shock experienced by at least some of the immigrants were laid to rest by a variety of incidents. There was the sight of women bursting into tears of joy as they ran their hands over the clean white sheets in the hotel rooms. The well-known philanthropist William Rosenwald recounted how a group of children had arrived at a shelter. The youngest were dispatched to an infants' home. It took a few days before the others gathered enough courage to inquire if the infants had been sent to the gas chambers. They did not believe the social workers' account regarding the infants' whereabouts until taken to see the children. The historian Judith Tydor Baumel has described a similar reaction in her account of refugee children who came to the United States between 1934 and 1945. In one case, a group of children who had arrived in 1941 from the French concentration camp of Gurs hid bread inside their pillowcases at first, refusing to accept reassurances by social workers that they would be fed regularly.

In a lighter vein, one man strenuously objected to resettling in Indianapolis until he was reassured that the city was not a center for Indians. Another survivor recalled how concerned he had been upon learning that the HIAS was sending him to Philadelphia. He had feared that he would be unable to "cross the border" into New York City to visit his relatives there. Such misunderstandings, which were, of course, rapidly cleared up, came about largely because the refugees were not taught in any systematic or uniform fashion about America in the DP camps. Those who lived on their own in postwar Europe had even less information to go on, a book here, a film there, or whatever they knew about the United States from prewar days.

An article in *The New York Times* focused on the telephone as a "symbol of freedom" for the newcomers. It described how the hotel operator "nearly goes crazy" as "the man in room 635 talks for a half hour over the telephone to his neighbor in room 637, although they'd both be more comfortable if one of them walked next door." This was, it seems, a common practice throughout the hotel for people unaccustomed to the luxury of a private phone. Despite such stories, one wonders how representative they really were of the

majority of immigrants, many of whom had lived in urban environments and had been highly educated before the war broke out.
Still, for the younger arrivals, who had spent the years when they
might have been in school either in hiding or in camps, there was
indeed much to learn about everyday life—using a telephone or
ashtray, paying for a magazine, or learning how to hold a knife and
fork, not to mention how to respond to a uniformed police officer
who was actually friendly and helpful.

While for most the reunions in the hotel were pleasant enough,
especially when friends and relatives who had given up hope of ever
seeing their loved ones again met, there were sometimes ugly reminders of the past. Cecilie Klein, an author and a survivor, has
written about her reaction upon recognizing in the Hotel Marseilles
a Jewish woman who had mistreated concentration camp inmates:

*Blood rushed to my head, my first impulse revenge. Lily must
have recognized me too, because she left the table abruptly, followed by her husband. We followed. Upstairs, Lily's husband
came over and begged me not to let his wife come to any harm.
She had locked herself in her room, he said, adding that she was
terrified. I told him that even though she deserves to have her
hands broken, I would not be the one to inform on her. I warned
him, however, that others might not be so forgiving. They left that
very night.*

Frequently, the Marseilles was but a brief first stop for the immigrants. From there they were sent to Jewish communities across
the continent. In fact, the majority of the newcomers did not spend
any time in their port of arrival, instead proceeding directly to their
new homes. Their first encounters varied greatly and it is difficult
to generalize. Some communities were warmer and more hospitable
than others. In Kenosha, Wisconsin, for example, several survivors
said they would never forget how the community gave them furnished apartments and a refrigerator full of food. On the other
hand, one arrival in Pittsburgh described the local Steel City Hotel
where he spent his first few days in terms that made the Marseilles
sound palatial: "Horses should live there, not people," he said. In
many cases, however, these accommodations were temporary, a
place to spend a few days while an apartment was being readied.

Those refugees sent to the HIAS's shelter in lower Manhattan
found themselves in the former home of the Lenox Library, a

building that had been converted into a dormitory able to accommodate four hundred persons. The organization's offices were also located there, and Evelyn Plotsker, who resides today in Brooklyn's heavily Jewish Borough Park section, was one of the workers then. Over the years, she was employed in various capacities, including stenographer, secretary, and head of the complaint department.

"You had to know what it was like," she recalled. "It was a privilege to be part of the history that was being made then." In the beginning things were somewhat chaotic. Appointments were missed, suitcases were lost, relatives were unable to find each other. Part of Plotsker's job was to placate the disappointed and the confused. Her voice dropped as she spoke, assuming a tone of suspense as she tried to re-create the excitement that pervaded the atmosphere when the immigrants first arrived:

There was a synagogue in the building and on that day it was set up with long tables filled with food—eggs, cheese, herring, rolls, really nice. I remember seeing a man sitting in the room with a little valise; he must have been about thirty, but he looked like he was 130. The expression on his face was: "What am I doing here? Do I belong here?" And I started to cry for him, I felt so terrible. Many of the people looked completely bewildered.

Besides the major Jewish organizations, there were other groups interested in bringing over people with whom they shared a special affinity. Several *landsmanschaften* (societies that consisted of natives from a particular town in Europe) supplied affidavits on behalf of their fellow townspeople. Sometimes it was because they recognized a name on a list advertised in a local Jewish paper such as the *Forward;* in other instances they were responding to a written request from a DP who had somehow found the society's address in New York. Members of the Jewish socialist organization, the Bund, were also helped in their efforts to immigrate by the Arbeiter Ring (Workmen's Circle), a cultural Jewish fraternal order here with a socialist orientation.

Elements within the American Orthodox community, most notably Agudath Israel and the Vaad haHatzala, were similarly active in assisting individuals in their attempts to come to the United States. A number of yeshivas that had been established here prior to the war helped refugees come in on student visas. Rabbi Herman

Neuberger, President of Ner Israel Rabbinical College in Baltimore, Maryland, described some of these efforts:

> *The students who came were broken people who had outlived the
> camps. We had faculty and older students counsel them. Among
> the students we brought over was one large group from Sweden.
> I picked them up at Ellis Island and brought them by bus to
> Baltimore. We clothed them and made them feel totally at home,
> something they had not experienced since the beginning of World
> War II. Yiddish, which was the language they knew best, was
> more acceptable to us [than to the average American Jew]. You
> see, our rabbis used Yiddish every day in the classes they taught.*

Once the immigrants entered the United States they soon faced
a new problem—finding a place to live. Most had no desire to
remain in a hotel or the HIAS dormitory any longer than absolutely
necessary. Unfortunately, the late 1940s was a time when the country, in the wake of the war's end, was experiencing a severe apartment shortage. The organizations did their best but these efforts
frequently fell short. As a result, many immigrants took rooms in
other people's apartments. This often put a strain on both tenant
and landlord, especially since the apartments were usually not large
to begin with. The following letter to the famed "Bintel Brief"
("Bundle of Letters") column of the *Forward* in 1949 illustrates the
problem:

> *Worthy Editor:*
> *I'm writing this letter because I would very much appreciate
> your opinion about a problem I have and that I feel would be of
> interest to many of your readers, especially poor women who are
> compelled, because of their impoverished condition, to rent apart-
> ments to strangers through USNA [United Service for New Amer-
> icans] because of the terrible shortage of apartments. The amount
> that USNA pays is not bad. We get $25 a month for one person
> and $45 a month for two persons, but the conditions are very
> difficult. The landlady must pay for gas and electricity. She must
> wash the windows, which costs forty cents a window. She often
> has to wash their underwear. Most of the time they [the immi-
> grants] demand service. You have to wash the floor for them, you
> have to clean and make the beds. . . . Mostly, it is the best room
> that is rented out. I know of a situation where a family of four had*

a three-room apartment. Times were better then. The man made a living. Now that times are worse, the family moved into the dining room and rented out the brighter rooms to New Americans. . . . In the morning when things must be prepared for the husband and children, the New American sits in the kitchen and is very upset that her bed is not made immediately.

The writer, M. Samuelson, cites another similar case of someone she knows and concludes by asking the editor: "What is your opinion about this unacceptable attitude on the part of the New Americans?"

The editor, in his response, assumes a Solomonic posture in his efforts to please both sides:

It is important to know about this situation. Most people are unaware of it. If everything in your letter is true, then it is a real injustice against the poor women who must rent out rooms in their tiny apartments. The immigrants should be able to take care of their own rooms. . . . However, we're not entirely certain that your description is accurate. Such situations are perhaps more the exception than the rule. In any event, it is good that you brought the matter to the public's attention and we hope that things will improve.

The immigrants clearly presented a challenge for the Jewish community in general, straining its resources. There were, no doubt, both good and bad tenants among the survivors, but, under such conditions, the temptation to stereotype was strong. The newcomers often saw the American Jews as cold and unsympathetic to both their present plight and their past suffering. American Jews viewed the immigrants as coarse and demanding, feelings that sometimes masked an effort to conceal their own vague sense of guilt at not having done more to help Europe's Jews during the war. These perceptions time and again were to dominate relations between the two groups over the years. It was a matter that was not easily laid to rest.

In truth, the reception accorded the immigrants was a mixed one. The massive rescue and rehabilitation effort mounted by the JDC in Europe and the HIAS and USNA in this country was widely publicized throughout the Jewish community in the same way that today's Jews are keenly aware of agency work on behalf of Jews from the former Soviet Union. As a result, the sense of responsibility toward the immigrants did filter down to the local level. For example, in a talk given to Jewish farmers at a meeting of a poultry club in Vineland, New Jersey, on September 20, 1945, listeners were urged to contribute toward the support of children orphaned by the war. Vineland was a major Jewish farming community, most of whose members had come as immigrants themselves, and so the appeal must have struck a responsive chord.

On the West Coast, numerous editorials appeared in the *B'nai B'rith Messenger* urging Californians to open up their hearts, not to mention their wallets, to the survivors. When they arrived, the local temples in Los Angeles invited refugees to be their guests at services. At the Ambassador Hotel fashion show there, Pioneer Women auctioned off a shawl brought to the United States by a German émigré who received it from a Jewish woman on her way to a concentration camp. The auction itself was conducted by the Hannah Senesch Club, named after a famous Jewish heroine of World War II.

On an individual level, there was the story of the Hasidic leader in Boston who, on one hour's notice, put up sixty-two guests in the fall of 1946. They had arrived, some observant, others not, on the *Thomas Edison* in Boston's harbor. Because of the approach of the Jewish holiday of Shemini Atzereth, when travel is forbidden, those who were devout were unable to begin their six-hour train ride to New York. They were, therefore, put up in private homes for the duration of the two-day holiday.

It is almost a tradition among Jews that when in need one goes to the local synagogue. Countless immigrant Jews must have received their initial welcome to America there. Sometimes, however, this was of no help. Solomon and Lucy Yehaskel, immigrants from the ancient Sephardic community of Salonika, Greece, lived for a time in the Bronx. A devout Orthodox Jew, Solomon entered a nearby synagogue for Friday night services. He explained what happened: "They started speaking to me in Yiddish and, of course, I couldn't understand them. After all, I was a Greek Jew and my Jewish language was ladino. I didn't know English either and when I couldn't answer their questions, they were thinking, 'Who is this man?' They didn't believe me when I told them where I was from. They thought I was a spy." Eventually the Yehaskels found a

Sephardic synagogue in the area, but it was an unnerving experience for a couple who had been so severely persecuted because of their Jewishness.

Many immigrants told me about the empathy and willingness to help of relatives and friends. These stories were, of course, not newsworthy and the Jewish newspapers of the day hardly mentioned them. Similarly, generosity on the part of family was not the subject of caseworker files. These individuals will probably remain the unsung heroes of that time, occupying a special place only in the memories of those they assisted. At the same time, there were many whose actions ranged from indifferent to callous. Rose Weinreb, a survivor who first settled in New Britain, Connecticut, was shocked when she met a Jewish woman who casually remarked, in Yiddish: " 'Look at her face. She doesn't look so bad. They say she came from a camp. Look at her cheeks. Such a healthy face and such healthy skin.' So I said to her, 'The war is over already five years. What do you want me to do?' "

For some Americans there seemed to be an inability to listen to the tales of woe recounted by the refugees. Most immigrants quickly learned not to talk about the war, often rationalizing their reluctance by saying that the stories were too horrible to be believed. Americans frequently responded to such stories with accounts of how they too had undergone privation during the war, mostly food rationing. Moritz Felberman was told by his aunt: "If you want to have friends here in America, don't keep talking about your experiences. Nobody's interested and if you tell them, they're going to hear it once and then the next time they'll be afraid to come see you. Don't ever speak about it." Felberman followed his aunt's advice, never discussing the war. Only in recent years has he begun to open up about what happened during that terrible period.

What hurt most, perhaps, was the perception of some Americans that those who had come owed their survival to a willingness to be cruel to others in the camps. Frieda Jakubowicz, a Polish concentration camp survivor, reflected bitterly: "I thought, 'You must tell the world about what happened. How else will they know?' But I saw, when we came here, that some people thought, 'How come you're alive and the others are dead? Must be *you* killed them, not Hitler.' And really, no one wanted to know about it. They said: 'We know. We read the paper.' " Still others had the impression that the survivors "came with diamonds and money," as one survivor put it, accumulated in nefarious ways.

Not infrequently refugees experienced difficulties with their relatives. One agency file tells the story of a twenty-year-old woman whose father was killed during the war and who was lured to America by an uncle who promised to help her gain admission to the Juilliard School of Music. He did no such thing. The young woman then accused him of being "very mean" and charged that he made improper advances toward her. The uncle in turn claimed that the USNA had "forced him" to bring the woman over and threatened to report the agency to the State Department. He cited the fact that the young lady had ordered a ham sandwich in a restaurant as evidence that she was not Jewish. When the social worker gently reminded him that "Jewish girls do sometimes order ham sandwiches," he continued to insist that she "just was not Jewish."

The reality was that both the survivors and those who received them ran the gamut from loving, caring, and responsible individuals to those who were selfish, dishonest, and unstable. In another case, a Brooklyn woman almost grudgingly, perhaps out of guilt, sponsored her nephew, acknowledging at the same time that she and her sister, the boy's mother, had always had a strained relationship.

One woman made out an affidavit for a cousin she apparently did not know. The social worker sums up his discussion with her by noting that "she feels that the least she can do is to help one of her own relatives out." The intense loyalty that people felt toward each other during the war frequently carried over into the postwar period. Thus, one person was willing to share his two-room apartment with a wartime friend who had since married and had an eight-month-old baby. "For one's best friend one can never do too much," this person asserted.

These early encounters with Americans often left lasting scars on the survivors. Simon Nagrodzki, a tailor living in Birmingham, Alabama, typified the depth of such feelings. As I entered his home, I did not sense the tension, the uneasiness that seems to grip so many of the survivors, especially when they first meet someone. He was relaxed and talked easily about his family, taking pride in the accomplishments of his children, all of whom have done well by conventional standards. But his voice took on a hard edge as he described how he was treated by his uncle when he first decided to immigrate:

I'm a very independent person and if you don't do right by me, I don't want you anymore. I wrote my uncle in New York that I wanted to come here and it took him a year before he answered.

WILLIAM B. HELMREICH

By then, I had a wife and a child on the way; so I wrote him: "Uncle, I appreciate what you want to do, but I got a wife now and if you want to send papers for all of us, we'll come." Well, he quit writing. So I said, "Forget it." And he was my father's brother. When I came here, I went to see him. I wanted to see what he looked like. He was eating breakfast when I walked in and he started crying and he asked me why I was mad. I told him, "I sent you a telegram from the boat, when I was coming, the date and all, and no one was there to meet us." He cried some more and I said, "Uncle, I didn't come to America to be a burden on you. We'll have lunch and you'll pay for yours and I'll pay for mine. I don't want a penny from you." He lived in the Bronx and when I got up to go back to Brooklyn, where I was staying, he offered to have his son show me the way back. So I said to him, "Uncle, I came through the ocean, so many thousands of miles, and I found your house. Don't you think I'll be able to find Brooklyn?" Later he wanted me to come back to New York, but I didn't. I lost touch with him.

Jack and Millie Werber live in Jamaica Estates, Queens, in a beautiful neighborhood with stately homes, wide streets, and manicured lawns. Jack is a well-to-do real estate developer who owns apartment buildings, shopping centers, and motels. His sons, Martin and David, run the business together with him. Life was not always this good. The Werbers still remember, as if it had happened yesterday, their first impressions of America. Jack received an affidavit from an affluent brother thirty years his senior, who had come to America long before the war and who lived in Beacon, New York.

There was a pained expression on Millie Werber's face as she remembered how uncomfortable her brother-in-law seemed to feel at being seen with them. And then there was the discovery that disinfectant had been put in the tub where they were asked to take a bath. "As though we had lice," she said sarcastically. "We stayed there about three weeks, but it felt like thirty years." Jack recalled how his brother introduced him as " 'my brother from the other side. He cost me four bottles of whiskey already,' meaning he couldn't stand listening to my stories so much. In his family's eyes, we were poor country mice—unfortunate and uncivilized." Millie added, "And then, from the way people looked at us, as if to say, 'How come my brother didn't survive and you did?' I felt as if I had to *apologize* for surviving. So I put a bandage on my number so I wouldn't have to talk about it." Etched indelibly in their minds was the ignorance of their relatives. "My sister-in-law asked me if they gave us orange juice at Auschwitz! On the other hand, she had a whole family in Europe and never even asked us what happened to them. So maybe, I think now, their conscience bothered them," Millie concluded.

Sometimes it was not only the attitudes but the expectations that Americans had of the survivors that was especially disconcerting. One woman was so upset by the way her relatives treated her that she wrote a letter to the "Bintel Brief." The letter demonstrates the loss of status that was often the lot of the survivor. "I had a very good name in Europe. I was known as an important person who was good to everyone." She talked about the "great joy" she felt upon being reunited with her family. "But after two weeks," she continued, "I realized why my relatives brought me here. They brought me here to exploit me. . . . I have to work and become a slave to them. . . . Since I am a very determined person, I have left those who have 'frozen hearts' and do not understand human suffering." She concluded by asking, "Did I do right to leave my relatives?" The *Forward* editor agreed with her decision. "You should not feel guilty. *They* must feel guilty for having forced you to leave and live among strangers." He offered words of comfort to the writer: "Do not despair. Many people are disappointed with their families, because family you do not choose. Good friends, however, you can choose and they therefore become, most of the time, better and more understanding than family."

Taken together, these vignettes provide us with a picture of the human problems involved in resettling the refugees. Even under the best of circumstances, it is difficult for people to accept into their homes relatives they have never even met. When one considers the emotional and physical toll of the war on the survivors, it becomes easy to understand why they expected sympathy and love from their own flesh and blood. On the other hand, viewed from the perspective of the Americans, it is clear that accepting the refugees was an adjustment for them too. American Jews were, as they have always been, an upwardly mobile group, and the greenhorns, as they were called, threatened that mobility. In addition, the nation as a whole was recovering from the war. While their deprivation paled in significance when compared to that of the survivors, in the minds of American Jews it represented unaccustomed hardship. Because the survivors did not look emaciated, because they wore decent, if somewhat shabby clothing, and because they spoke intelligently enough, it was difficult to associate them with the photos of newly liberated, half-dead, and starving camp inmates that flashed across the movie screens on newsreels in theaters throughout the country. Those who fought and were not in camps also presented problems for those who took them in. One researcher who studied orphans brought here after the war succinctly summed up the problem when he asked, "How do you absorb into a family someone who could assemble guns in the dark and who, as a teenager, was in charge of a platoon of men?" It was a challenge indeed.

Along with the adjustment to newfound relatives and Americans in general there was also the matter of acclimating to American life and culture. The first impressions of the survivors when they arrived often depended upon their preconceptions of the country and on specific incidents that occurred when they first came. There were certain fairly common reactions, however, one of which was disappointment with the dirt and noise of New York City. One woman who was taken for a ride through Manhattan streets on her second night in America was asked by her companion, "Isn't it pretty? Isn't it pretty?" Her response: "I did not see anything pretty. The neon lights? My eyes were burning. The streets were full of dirty papers. I was used to Czech towns, where people use wastebaskets and do not litter. Here there were small churches dwarfed by huge, ugly square buildings." In general, however, those accustomed to big-city life were not particularly impressed by America's urban centers, while those from small towns and villages were.

Sometimes the refugees' reactions to the new land surprised their American hosts. Gerda Marcus, who lives today in Jerusalem, survived because she had a knack for languages. She landed a job as a typist in Theresienstadt. After the war, she visited Cleveland, Ohio, where her relatives lived. Soon after she arrived, they took her to a nightclub just outside the city limits to show her how nice life could be in America. Her reaction startled them: "I saw people drinking and having a good time. And I asked: 'Was this open during the war?' And they told me: 'Yes.' And I cannot forget to this day that while so many people perished, they had a nightlife."

Although he laughs about it today, Jack Novin's first encounter with the New York City subway system in 1950 was a traumatic one. He had traveled to Times Square to celebrate New Year's Eve with some wartime friends who had settled in New York a few years earlier. Shortly after midnight, the friends paid his fare, put him on a train heading uptown, and told him to get off at the 103rd Street station since he was staying at the Marseilles Hotel. As luck would have it, he missed his stop and spent the next five hours riding the subway system, thoroughly lost, confused, and frightened. He spoke almost no English and failed to understand the directions people gave when he showed them a slip of paper on which was scrawled the hotel's address:

I didn't know English, half the people were drunk, and by five in the morning I was dizzy and hungry, and I thought, "That's the end of me; I'm going to die right here in the subway." I had never been in a subway in my life. Finally, an older Jewish man walked by and I told him the story in Yiddish. He said, "This is the best country in the world. Come on, I'll take you home." He took me out of the subway, paid for my cab, and said, "America's a golden land. Someday you'll be good to someone else."

America might, indeed, have been a "golden land" for these immigrants, who were, after all, white, but not for black people, especially in the late 1940s. Most of the survivors had had only fleeting contacts with blacks, usually American soldiers. Several had read *Uncle Tom's Cabin,* but most knew nothing about racism. A few mentioned having seen blacks in European circuses where they were exhibited before a public that saw them, at best, as oddities. Sigmund Tobias, now a professor at City College of New York, recalled what was for him a memorable experience shortly after he arrived in the United States. It happened on a train from San Francisco, bound for New York:

I was sitting in a compartment with a black man and in Albuquerque I got off the train briefly. I went into the station and saw, for the first time, "White" and "Colored" signs in the rest rooms. I reacted as if I had been slapped in the face. . . . I had lived in Shanghai for ten years among "colored" people, Chinese people, and seeing this was insulting to me for his sake. And when I returned to the compartment I couldn't face the black man; he obviously knew and that was why he hadn't gotten off to use the facilities.

In the North, the newcomers' curiosity did not last long, but in the South, where discrimination was institutionalized, the encounters were vivid and even shocking. Lola Shtupak, a survivor of various ghettos and camps, spent several months in Houston, where she felt distinctly uncomfortable, both by the way blacks were treated and because of what she believed were anti-Semitic attitudes on the part of people there. On one occasion, she accidentally sat down in the back of the bus, which was then reserved exclusively for blacks:

A man came over, a cowboy, and he grabbed me and threw me off the bus. When I came home, my aunt said: "You're lucky he didn't kill you because they thought you're a troublemaker, fighting for the blacks." My aunt gave her black maid food that we wouldn't eat and made her eat outside, like a dog. When I fought with her, she called me a communist. So I saw this was no life for me and I left for New York.

As often happens when people leave one culture and enter another, there were sometimes comical misunderstandings. Gilbert Metz is the only known survivor living today in the state of Mississippi. Born in Alsace-Lorraine, he survived Auschwitz and Dachau, as well as a death march, during which he refused to stop walking because, as he put it, "After my father was taken, I was not going to give the bastards the satisfaction of killing me." An aunt living in Natchez, Mississippi, sponsored him and he came there after liberation from the camps. His first encounter with bigotry was in his uncle's store:

My uncle had two water fountains in the store; one was marked "Colored" and the other "White." And it was a big mystery to me. I kept looking at the fountains. So one day my uncle said: "Why are you always looking at those fountains?" "Because," I said, "when you press a button, the same color water comes out." He laughed and explained to me: "Well, one is for the schvartzes and one is for the whites." I thought it was the silliest thing I'd ever heard in my life.

Survivors, especially those who were observant, appreciated the sense of religious freedom. While they knew there was prejudice against Jews, it could not compare to the European experience. One

Hasidic Jew related how he immediately began to grow a beard when he stepped off the boat. Another immigrant, a rabbi, was pleasantly surprised to see small children in the Brooklyn neighborhood where he first lived "running around the street with yarmulkes. They were proud of it, or didn't think about it." America was, in fact, entering a period of cultural pluralism, where ethnic differences were more apt to be tolerated than had been the case in the 1930s or 1920s, and this created a favorable environment for those who wanted to preserve their traditions.

In terms of the immigrants' first responses to America, there were often highs and lows, one following quickly upon the heels of the other. Because they had so little on which to base their knowledge of the country, the newcomers tended to magnify in importance anything that happened to them in the early days, hoping that the ability to generalize would make them feel more secure in their newly adopted home. One immigrant's early recollection of America was when his brother took him for a ride in a Cadillac on New York's West Side Highway: "I was sitting in that car, my suitcase in the back, and . . . I felt like we drove up to the moon. You can't explain that feeling." His exhilaration was soon replaced by anger and disbelief when he discovered that a local synagogue in Washington Heights denied him admission to its Yom Kippur services because he had not purchased a ticket even though he explained that he had only recently been liberated from a concentration camp. "I'm in America? Where am I? They call this liberty?" he exclaimed bitterly.

The initial experiences of others were not as emotionally laden, although they were remembered with equal clarity. Sigmund Tobias gorged himself on grapes when he first arrived in San Francisco. "They were so cheap and I would buy two or three pounds of them and eat them in my room in the Uptown Hotel. I was also amazed by the multiplicity of newspapers. I was buying several copies of the same paper in different editions before I realized it. In Shanghai, we were starved for news." Some drew quick conclusions about life in America that, seen through the prism of those who lived through the Nazi era, were perfectly justified. Luba Bat was surprised to see that the working-class relatives with whom she first stayed threw away the fat from the meat instead of using it for seasoning, gravy, or anything else. "America is a land of waste," she decided. The misconceptions were perhaps greatest among the children. One youngster wept because the streets were not paved with gold; others expected, à la Hollywood, to have "long shiny cars at their disposal."

Whatever the perceptions of their new home, the immigrants soon discovered that success in adjusting to life here depended on a willingness to adapt and an ability to sense where the opportunities lay. While support from relatives was important, the trust that anchored relationships established under trying times was more deeply rooted. Thus, the *grine* (pron. "greenah," greenhorns) as they were derisively labeled by many, sought out one another's company, not only to fill the social void in their lives, but also to exchange information and ideas and to renew interrupted ties. Evelyn Plotsker watched it all happen in front of the HIAS headquarters:

> *The streets in the area were thronged with people coming to look for relatives, talking to anyone they could find. "Maybe you heard of this person or that person?" And when people met others from the same city, they kissed and hugged. Gentile people would stand around and watch those scenes. To live through that. . . .*

3 ✦

Help received by immigrants from relatives and friends, and support extended to them by Jewish organizations, could hardly have taken place without a willingness by the United States to accept the refugees. But that scenario was played out on a much larger stage—in various government agencies, in the halls of Congress, and in the White House. It was there that regulations and laws were drafted and passed that made it possible for the survivors to enter this country. Creating a climate favorable to such legislation was a complex and difficult process, one that required a major effort on the part of the American Jewish community.

The majority of the DPs entered the United States after June 1948. Until then, perhaps 50,000 Jewish refugees had passed through U.S. customs officials. Eligibility was based on a quota system for each country. On June 2, 1948, however, the Senate, by a vote of 63–13, passed the Displaced Persons Act, allowing up to 200,000 DPs, both Jewish and non-Jewish, to gain admission over the next two years. Shortly thereafter, the House passed a similar measure by an equally lopsided margin of 289–91. The final version increased the number to be admitted to 205,000 and also granted permanent residence to 15,000 DPs who were already in the United States on a temporary basis.

While a vast improvement over the previous situation, the bill fell short of expectations in the Jewish community because of various measures that favored Christian, over Jewish, DPs. One problem was that only those who were in Germany, Austria, or Italy on or before December 22, 1945, were eligible for admission. This excluded perhaps 150,000 Jews who had entered these lands after fleeing pogroms that occurred in Poland in 1946. Moreover, many, if not most, of those who were in these countries before the December cutoff date had already found refuge in the United States and elsewhere. Another provision of the bill gave preference to applicants from the Baltic countries, most of whom were not Jewish, as well as to persons who were primarily engaged in agricultural pursuits, few of whom were Jewish.

Senator Claude Pepper of Florida gave voice to the Jewish community's dismay when he denounced the bill from the Senate floor, charging that it discriminated against the "most persecuted, most massacred, most butchered of people—the Jews." The final version of the bill, which contained some modifications, was hardly any better and President Truman indicated as much when he asserted, even as he reluctantly signed, that it "discriminates in callous fashion against displaced persons of the Jewish faith. This brutal fact cannot be obscured by the maze of technicalities in the bill or by the protestations of some of its sponsors." Echoing the President's sentiments, *Rescue,* an official organ of the HIAS, noted that the bill "has left a wake of dissent and disappointment in its passage."

While America was on the whole highly sympathetic to the plight of Europe's homeless, there remained nevertheless a strong streak of nativist sentiment, one that had been nurtured between the two world wars. In those years, immigration policy had been characterized by isolationist attitudes. The Johnson Acts, passed in 1921 and 1924, so limited immigration to this country that far fewer than in previous years were able to come. It was therefore not surprising that disparaging comments about the refugees were made by individuals such as Captain Eddie Rickenbacker and Paul Griffith, national commander of the American Legion. In a speech to the Daughters of the American Revolution, Griffith offered the view that refugees were likely to be here for "Trojan Horse purposes." The specter of communism was raised by others too, ironic when one considers that so many of the DPs, Jews and Christians, were fleeing communism as Russia consolidated its hold over Eastern Europe.

Notwithstanding the discriminatory features of the 1948 DP bill, the Jewish community generally supported it as an opportunity to bring more Jews here. At the same time, the community continued to lobby among its friends in the government for an easing of its restrictions. Similar efforts were mounted by Christian organizations, which also sought favorable treatment for their co-religionists stranded on the European continent.

Finally, on June 16, 1950, the campaign waged by those concerned with the refugees' plight bore fruit. On that day, President Truman signed into law an amended version of the 1948 Displaced Persons Act, expanding to 415,744 the number of DPs to be admitted. Most important, the bill wiped out the restrictive provisions of the earlier act. As a result, not only Jews but Catholics, Italians fleeing Fascism, those displaced by a guerrilla war in Northern Greece, five thousand orphans, and various other groups suffering from discrimination were able to enter "The Promised Land." Truman, best known in the Jewish community for supporting the creation of the State of Israel, proved himself an equally devoted friend of the Jewish community through his actions regarding the survivors of the Holocaust. In a ceremonial signing of the bill, Truman used twelve pens, distributing them to those surrounding his desk who had played pivotal roles in supporting and securing passage of the legislation. Summing up the rationale for his actions, the President stated:

The countrymen of these displaced persons have brought to us in the past the best of their labor, their hatred of tyranny and their love of freedom. They have helped our country grow in strength and moral leadership. I have every confidence that the new Americans who will come to our country under the provisions of the present bill will also make a substantial contribution to our national well-being.

The USNA and the HIAS worked side by side through this tumultuous period of Jewish immigration, sometimes cooperating and, at other times, competing with each other. In 1954, they merged together with the JDC Migration Department into one entity known as the United HIAS Service. Typically, applicants were sponsored by the HIAS or the USNA, or by friends or family members. The latter often filled out the applications and made travel arrangements through the organizations. The affidavits affirmed that those signing them were financially capable of supporting the applicants or finding them employment, and that the immigrants would not become public charges.

The organized Jewish community tried in many ways to stir the conscience of American Jewry with regard to the survivors. There were rallies, editorials in newspapers, fashion show benefits, furniture giveaways, and newspaper articles about volunteers assembling care packages for refugees still in Europe. The various Federations of Jewish Philanthropies inserted photos of poor and miserable refugees in every Jewish paper in America. Typical was the following ad that appeared, together with an accompanying photo of small children, perhaps six or seven years old, sleeping on a bare mattress, in *The Jewish Times* of April 25, 1947:

What Shall We Do About Josef?

It's cold in the Displaced Persons Camp. There's not much food . . . nor the right kinds of food for a small boy like Josef and his kid sister, Sarah.

The last time Josef and Sarah saw their parents was when the Nazis bayonetted them. They'd have bayonetted the children too . . . only they ran and hid.

After the flames had stopped crackling, and the smoke no longer blew about the village, Josef crept out of his hiding place, dragging Sarah with him. They were alive and uninjured physically. But what they had seen was not good for children their age.

Josef mutters and tosses at night . . . and sometimes he wakes screaming. In the daytime he mostly just sits and watches Sarah . . . and the look on his face is the look of a bitter old man. What are we going to do about Josef . . . and Sarah? We can feed them. We can clothe them. But what shall we do about the way their lips tremble and their eyes grow bigger every time they see a soldier? These children need to be taken out of the desolation and misery of the DP camp. They need to go to Palestine, or America, or England, or some other place— where they can forget the past.

Josef and his sister need to be shown that there are decent people in the world. They need to be tucked into bed and given a good night kiss . . . to sit in the protective glow of a family dinner table . . . to go to school . . . to learn to play once more . . . to laugh and have treasured little possessions of their own.

That's why it is imperative for you to give to the United Jewish Appeal. When you are asked to give, give generously . . . give sacrificially.

The size of the community's response was evident in the reports by the organizations directly responsible for helping the refugees. In 1950, Edwin Rosenberg, the USNA's president, opened a two-day conference at the Astor Hotel by announcing that American Jewish communities had spent $37 million in the past five years for what he called the "greatest voluntary resettlement program in the history of the United States." An estimated 380 Jewish communities had worked with the USNA to help achieve this goal.

While the majority of private sponsors fulfilled their commitments to support the applicants once they arrived, there were those who backed out, leaving it to the organizations to take over. From the files it appears that some individuals did this knowingly from the start, aware that the USNA or the HIAS were not likely to deny assistance to the refugees once they were here, provided they were able-bodied and could work. Another ruse involved people with the same last names claiming they were brothers or sisters of people living in America. Circumventing the various requirements was possible, in part, because of the overwhelmingly large number of applicants. In one year, 1946, the HIAS alone received 205,097 inquiries. Those who applied were often desperate. Not only had they endured terrible hardships, not only was America considered by them to be the greatest country in the world, but the number of available visas relative to the number applying for them was very small. In that same year, 1946, the quota for Poland was only about two hundred immigrants per month.

Those who survived came from every stratum of society and included criminals, loafers, and people of generally poor character as well as those of unquestionable integrity and those who had accomplished a great deal in their prewar lives. If anything united those who came to these shores it was their wish to gain admission. Some stowed away to achieve that goal. The minutes of the HIAS indicate that when this occurred the organization tried to intercede on their behalf. In one such case, the HIAS arranged for twelve Jews who were apprehended to be rerouted to Ecuador instead of being sent back to Europe. A *New York Times* story in 1947 described a black market operation in which displaced persons bought X-rays of healthy lungs from hospitals in the French zone to improve their chances of admission to the United States.

Embarrassing situations sometimes developed when people applied to relatives in this country, unaware that those to whom they wrote had serious problems of their own. One woman's elderly parents wrote to her, asking for assistance in gaining admission to the United States. What they did not know was that their daughter had recently separated from her husband and had been confined to a mental institution for six months, where she had received shock treatments before being released. At the time that they wrote she was earning twenty-four dollars a week sewing and ironing pieces of pocketbooks. She told her parents nothing of her difficulties, saying only that she could not support them and that it might therefore be better for them to remain in Germany. Feeling guilty, she regularly sent them care packages. The case history reveals nothing about whether her parents were satisfied with this response or felt rejected and abandoned by their child.

Because their support could mean the difference between being allowed to stay here or not, finding one's relatives was often of crucial importance to the survivors. This, however, frequently proved to be a formidable task. Newspapers with large Jewish readerships regularly published extensive lists of survivors as a service to the refugees. The *Aufbau* functioned as a general delivery address for survivors sending letters to unknown relatives in the United States; the following ad appeared in *The Jewish Examiner:* "Mr. J. Rubinstein, now in a DP camp in Austria, is desperately trying to locate his two uncles, Isaac and Yechiel Garfinkle who came to Brooklyn from Dubnow, Poland." Rubinstein's address appeared at the end of the notice.

The anxiety, loneliness, and pathos emerge even more clearly from the following letter, which was enclosed in a message received by an American Jew from his relative in Romania. Clearly, the woman's English was poor, but perhaps she felt that writing in English would increase her chances of gaining a sympathetic ear. It is reprinted here exactly as it was received:

Excuse that as a strange woman I am interrupting you! I should liek to knoa a address from a cousin from me.

> *Mistress Rosy Stein*
> *New York, Brooklyn*

If it is not too heavy for you, I beg you very much to make it for a very unhappy woman. I am also alone here. I have lost my whole family in the lager *[camps].*

> *Many thanks before*
> *My name is* ———

The letter was addressed to the Location Service of the National Council of Jewish Women. It is not known whether the woman ever found her cousin.

Thousands of refugees came here on visitor's visas, transit visas, and temporary visas. Their hope was that once they were in this country they would find ways of remaining. Many succeeded, either through marriage, "connections," legal technicalities, or by going to third countries for short periods and then reapplying from there. Typical of the twists and turns taken by the refugees in their travels was the case of two sisters from Poland who joined their brother in Costa Rica, came to the United States on temporary visas, and then asked to have them extended for medical reasons, noting that those who had paid for their trip here had made no such commitment for the return journey. While here, they were supported by Jewish agencies. In the end, one returned to Costa Rica and the other married a legal resident. Others came on special quotas based on contracts they had received to teach religious studies or to serve as rabbis. In most cases, those offering the positions had never met the prospective employees and there were times, therefore, when things did not work out and the immigrant found himself unemployed. Here again, the organizations frequently intervened, either with funds or job offers.

Sometimes non-Jewish people were also moved by the refugees' plight. There were numerous stories of GIs helping DPs whom they met after the war while still stationed in Europe. In one case, a Gentile GI prevailed upon his parents in the United States to prepare an affidavit for a Polish-born Jewish DP who was a cook in the GI's camp in Austria. The soldier was deeply moved by the man's tales of suffering and horror and threatened not to come home if his parents did not assist the refugee in his efforts to emigrate. The parents reluctantly agreed to sponsor the man. In an ironic twist, that DP turned out to have an uncle in America. The uncle claimed to be very pleased that a relative of his had been found. However, he did nothing to help him and, according to the social worker's report, "evaded" efforts by the GI's family to contact him.

The files clearly show that social workers often went to considerable lengths to assist those who approached them with requests for help. One case worker's entries reveal a total of twenty-one phone calls, as well as several written letters, all part of an effort to locate one person living here. Both the HIAS and the USNA had location services that, together, handled thousands of cases. When their efforts failed, the organizations sometimes turned for assistance to the International Tracing Service, run by the U.S. Army, or to the International Red Cross. In addition, private individuals inserted notices in various newspapers. There was even a coast-to-coast radio program called *Reunion,* which featured dramatic reunifications between refugees and those searching for them.

The involvement of the organizations in the refugees' lives began from the time they applied for emigration in Europe, with the JDC helping them fill out the forms and booking passage for their trip. As soon as they stepped off the boat, those who did not have family or friends waiting for them were welcomed by the port and reception workers. Screening interviews were conducted in rooms adjacent to the pier and decisions made about where to send the immigrants. In cases where their final destinations had already been determined, the workers gave the arrivals a brief orientation as to what they might expect in their new homes, whether in Brownsville, Texas, or Chicago, Illinois, and then saw them off at the train stations.

Once they were safely in their new communities, the agencies assisted newcomers in handling their day-to-day affairs. They found apartments, distributed allowances for furniture, food, and clothing, and attempted to find employment for them. Many were immediately enrolled in night school, where they learned English, basic facts about the United States, where to go for medical services, and how to ask a policeman for directions. In the larger cities, responsibility for these matters was usually assumed by Jewish family service agencies; in smaller communities Jewish leaders formed ad hoc committees to help the immigrants.

American Jewish leaders knew that, in addition to basic needs, the refugees would also have to be socially reintegrated. Thus, arrangements were made for summer camps. A brief article in *The New York Times,* for instance, in June 1945 announced the establishment of a camp for refugee children at Dombek Lodge in Sullivan County, New York. Called Camp Help and Reconstruction, its financial backers included the well-known philanthropists Max Warburg and the Baroness Guy de Rothschild. Centers were set up in most cities where there were concentrations of newcomers, enabling them to meet socially and engage in organized activities.

What held all this together were the thousands of people who worked for the organizations. Of crucial importance were the social workers whose job it was to smooth the way for the immigrants. Recognizing that they were dealing with a population whose experiences were unique, agency heads tried to prepare the workers for what to expect through lectures and training sessions. Even though they were professionals, conventional training methods could not fully prepare them to respond to people who may well have seen their children tortured to death in front of their eyes, some of whom had worked as *sonderkommandos,* burning thousands of bodies, and others who had hidden in attics and cellars for periods of up to four or five years. Here is one social worker's assessment of the initial reaction to the survivors:

We had no sense of the Holocaust as we know now, with a capital H. We really didn't understand what people were telling us. The stories sounded too horrible. We simply did not believe them. They needed help, and we had no idea what they were talking about. We were so incredibly dumb! . . . We thought we saw symptoms of neurotic behavior . . . but our thinking was totally inappropriate. . . . They were grieving, trying to deal with what they had lived through. . . . Beyond that, some of the medical personnel [at the hospital where she worked] had no patience with the survivors. They complained that the DPs were mourning too long, that they were not becoming Americans fast enough, that the war was over; "enough already!" And the survivors felt their impatience. . . . They used to tell me.

Notwithstanding their initial shock and ignorance of what the survivors had lived through, those who worked with them learned soon enough. Perhaps it was a matter of rising to the occasion but, whatever the case, the caseworker files, as well as articles in social work journals of the day, demonstrate conclusively that the majority of those involved with the refugees were indeed familiar with and responsive to the wide array of problems that faced them. There were meetings and conferences held in every part of the country, where professionals came together and shared their experiences with others and this too helped raise the level of knowledge about the survivors.

One organization that was particularly challenged by the circumstances at hand was the nonsectarian Committee for the Care of European Children. Those with whom they dealt were often the most scarred individuals because the horrors they had seen occurred when they were in their formative years. Helping these children, most of them orphans, recover required love, patience, and understanding, qualities that were not always readily available in the period of postwar turmoil. Even carefully laid plans to resettle children sometimes went awry. In one heartbreaking case, a small family consisting of a father and two children, aged seventeen and two, sailed for the United States. While they were at sea the father died. The man's sister in Chicago, who was the sponsor, was contacted as to whether burial should take place at sea or in Chicago. She cabled back that her brother's remains should be interred at sea and that she would be unable to assume responsibility for the now orphaned children. The Committee for the Care of European Children then agreed to receive them. As a result, they were sent to Ellis Island and, after a hearing, turned over to committee personnel.

Besides the establishment organizations, some of the *landsmanschaften* also played a part in helping the DPs. The survivors, especially those who had no family in America, looked to their hometown brethren as people with whom they had an emotional bond and hoped that life in America had only loosened, but not completely broken, the connection. One man, from Ostrowiec, Poland, penned the following appeal to the *landsmanschaft* here, which was reprinted in the *Forward:*

The Jewish town of Ostrowiec is empty and desolated. Can you help us? Can you rebuild the town of our youth? Are you able to bring back to life our fathers, mothers, brothers, sisters, and children? Can you help recreate a family life out of broken shards and

fragments? We do not want money. We want to be rescued. . . .
Only death faces us here. Death hovers over the few children who
have survived. We are not sure of our lives.

Monetarily, the *landsmanschaften*'s contributions were small.
Their donations generally ranged from five hundred to one thousand dollars, a pittance compared to the millions spent by the agencies. But their influence was felt in different ways. They served as
intermediaries between the organizations and the refugees, prodding the organizations to search harder and to provide more assistance for the refugees. They often worked through the JDC
Landsmanschaften Section. Between 1945 and 1947, more than a
thousand societies sent money and packages to Europe. In so doing,
they provided both psychological and financial support to many
survivors in their hour of need.

In 1938, responding to the growing threat of Nazism, Dr. Abram
Leon Sachar, the national director of the B'nai B'rith Hillel Foundation, had created a program to enable academically qualified refugees to study at American universities. Working through the Hillel
organizations on each campus, Sachar, later to become president of
Brandeis University, persuaded Jewish fraternities and sororities to
provide room, board, tuition, and personal expenses, and to welcome the refugees. In that year, thirty-eight young men and women
came to the United States on student visas. By 1940, the number
had grown to sixty-four and had attracted the interest and involvement of prominent figures in the Jewish community, including
Albert Einstein.

This was the model for an expanded version of the program after
World War II. More than a hundred young refugees entered the
United States through the efforts of the Hillel Foundation and
many became highly successful in their chosen fields. One such
person was future congressman Tom Lantos. In a letter to Rabbi
Arthur Lelyveld of Hillel, written shortly after he arrived here in
1947, Lantos expressed his gratitude: "I am so happy and glad that
it is impossible to find the proper words to thank you for everything. Since I am in this country everybody is so kind and good to
me that I simply don't want to believe it." Lantos expressed the
wish that he would be helped in finding "some job for me so I'll be
able to help my aunt and uncle."

Lantos had no idea at the time that he would one day receive a
Ph.D. from the University of California at Berkeley. Nor could he

imagine that one day he would sit in the U.S. House of Representatives as a respected member of Congress. An extreme example of success, no doubt, but not really surprising when considering the success achieved by thousands of other survivors in their personal and professional lives.

In a sense, each of the survivors succeeded. By outlasting the Nazi death machine, they foiled Hitler's dreams of total destruction. When they came here, however, they were at the beginning of a new stage in their lives, one whose outcome they could not predict. Many had not received as warm a welcome as that accorded Lantos, and their apprehension as they faced the future was understandable. Most had waited a long time before they were able to enter this country, some as long as six or seven years, and they prized their precious visas in a way that only stateless people could. For some, a measure of tranquillity was the main objective; for others recovery of lost wealth and status. Some would realize their dreams and ambitions, others would fall short and rail about how life had cheated them once again. At this juncture, however, all realized that they would have to build new lives, solve new problems, and begin the long struggle toward a stable and secure existence.

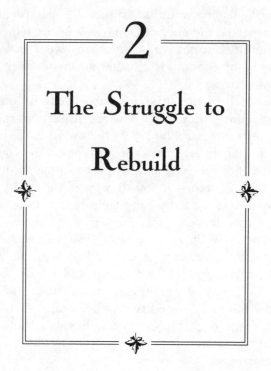

2

The Struggle to

Rebuild

Never shall I forget that night, the first night in camp, which
has turned my life into one long night, seven times cursed and
seven times sealed. Never shall I forget that smoke. Never shall
I forget the little faces of the children, whose bodies I saw
turned into wreaths of smoke beneath a silent blue sky.

ELIE WIESEL, *NIGHT*

AS THE SURVIVORS, carrying their battered suitcases and bulky packages, fanned out across America, the memory of their ordeal was
still fresh in their minds. As they stared out the windows of speeding trains or stood in the crowded subways of New York, their
thoughts turned often to the camps, ghettos, and forests of Europe.
On one hand, it still seemed hard to believe that it had all happened; on the other, the fact that so many of those whom they loved
were gone forever left no doubt about the reality of the horrors
through which they had lived.

Still, the survivors knew that they could not afford to dwell constantly on the past. As Terrence Des Pres has written in *The Survivor*: "Survivors are proof that the desire to live returns." Moreover, Wiesel himself argued that the past, terrible as it was, ought to become a basis for the future. In an address to a United Jewish Appeal conference in 1973 shortly after the Yom Kippur War in Israel, he stated:

> *We owe it to our past not to lose hope. . . . We must show our children that three thousand years of history cannot end with an act of despair on our part. . . . Do not permit the enemy to rob us of our joy and our hope: to give up would be his victory and he does not deserve it.*

Many challenges and problems faced the newcomers. There was, first of all, a different language to learn, an especially difficult task for those who were already adults when they came. In addition, while their friends and relatives were almost all Jewish, they were also Americans. As a result, they thought differently and did things in ways that were new and strange. Added to that was the need to secure employment and the very understandable wish to raise a family. As we shall see, what happened to the immigrants in these early years—the people they met, where they lived, the occupations they entered—was crucial, for it often determined how they were to live out the rest of their lives.

1

A majority of the immigrants, perhaps two thirds, remained in the New York metropolitan area, the rest scattered among hundreds of communities in almost every state. While they tended to concentrate in cities with substantial populations, many settled in smaller towns. In Iowa, for example, some survivors came to Des Moines, but they also made their homes in the smaller communities of Council Bluffs and Mount Pleasant. Similarly, a majority of the refugees in Pennsylvania lived in Philadelphia, but others migrated to places like Hazelton, Stroudsburg, Reading, Wilkes-Barre, Chester, and Easton. Philadelphia, as a seaboard city, was often a starting point for resettlement in the "hinterland."

This pattern of movement was often more than a matter of fate or individual preference. The USNA and HIAS were very concerned with presenting a positive image of the survivors to America in general. They wanted to ensure that they and, by extension, the larger Jewish community would not be viewed negatively and that the flow of immigration would proceed unimpeded. Integrating the refugees smoothly into American culture was, therefore, a priority and, in their view, Jews would assimilate faster in places where they were a small minority. They also wanted to dispel the stereotype that Jews were only capable of dwelling in densely populated urban ghettos.

The agencies' desires were not necessarily shared by the immigrants themselves, many of whom had relatives and friends in New York. Others, who were strictly observant, insisted on putting down roots in the largest cities because they felt that only there could they fully practice the tenets of their faith in terms of Orthodox synagogues, strictly kosher food, and proper religious schools for their children. Rabbi Isaac Trainin, who handled placement for the USNA's Religious Functionary Division, told the story of his efforts to persuade one rabbi to take a position in a small Texas town, all to no avail: "This community needs you; aren't you concerned with your reward in the world to come?" he asked in exasperation. "You worry about this world and I'll worry about the world to come!" the man replied. Then there were those for whom the pace of life in the smaller communities was too slow and dull. Many had lived in Berlin, Prague, Warsaw, or Budapest either before or after the war and had grown accustomed to the cosmopolitan atmosphere and nightlife.

Those who opted for New York probably experienced less trauma in terms of cultural adaptation because they were able to more easily re-create certain aspects of their previous lifestyles. There were many synagogues and yeshivas to choose from, as well as schools that taught Yiddish mixed in with Bundist socialism; bakeries, restaurants, and delicatessens that sold products reminiscent of their homelands. Most important, perhaps, the refugees were able to live in neighborhoods where other survivors resided—Manhattan's Upper West Side (then known as "Midtown" by the survivors), Washington Heights, and the Lower East Side; Brooklyn's Borough Park, Crown Heights, Brownsville, and East New York neighborhoods; and, in the Bronx, the southern and eastern portions of the borough. Some survivors who were relatively well off even ventured into Queens, settling primarily in Forest Hills and Kew Gardens.

In these areas, the refugees generally formed little enclaves, befriending one another and sending their children to the same schools and, when after a few years they could afford to, the same summer camps. Opportunities for social contact were numerous, ranging from gossiping at the local butcher shop and socializing in one another's homes, to meeting in the local parks. As Sandy Mayer recalled:

My parents would pack a meal and go to Riverside Drive with their friends. We'd meet by the grassy area near Grant's Tomb. Europeans, you know, like the outdoors and picnicking. There was no air conditioning then and we enjoyed the nice breeze from the Hudson.

On Saturdays, those who observed the Sabbath would rise from their naps around three or four in the afternoon in their small apartments along the side streets of the Upper West Side between Columbus, Amsterdam, Broadway, and West End avenues. Putting the small children in carriages, they would walk down the stairs and head for their *shpatzir,* or walk, along the upper portion of Riverside Drive, usually between 97th and 105th streets. There they would meet their friends and talk about the daily necessities— finding a job or an apartment, or arranging with someone to take care of their child. They spoke also of the old country, about what was and what could never be again.

Each section of the city had its meeting points, places on a map known only to the local inhabitants. In Brownsville, it was Eastern Parkway and Pitkin Avenue, with stores, movie theaters, and, above all, slatted wooden benches resting on concrete, determining the specific gathering spots. In the Bronx, there was the Grand Concourse and many small parks along the side streets whose names have long since been forgotten except by those who sat in them.

Besides the recreational areas, there were other opportunities for socializing. The hometown societies, many of which had become moribund as this country's Jews became Americanized, were rejuvenated by the immigrants who saw in them the opportunity to retain some vestige of the past. Besides the monthly meetings and various regular activities, there were annual affairs. Survivors from a *landsmanschaft* consisting of those born in the Munkács, Hungary, area, held a ball every year at the Manhattan Center on 34th Street, to which about five hundred guests came. Those who were observant formed or took over existing synagogues in their own neighborhoods. In them, prayer would alternate with shmoozing, and the after-services *kiddush*, or party, would provide the survivors with yet another setting in which they could genuinely feel at home.

The survivors, especially those who were observant, conversed in Yiddish and clung to the old and the familiar, becoming only as American as seemed necessary. As is true of virtually all immigrant groups, the bridge to the new world was crossed by their children. Even those survivors who were well educated and who had thrown off the trappings of Jewish observances and culture before the war remained somewhat apart after their arrival here. Their sentiments were captured in Helen Epstein's book *Children of the Holocaust*: "The assimilationist stream of Judaism that had flourished in Germany, Czechoslovakia and Austria seemed to have evaporated in the passage to America. Its premise, that Jews could participate freely in Christian society while retaining their cultural affiliation, had been dealt a death blow by Nazism."

Initially, residential placements outside New York City were made only in large cities that had professional agencies, for this meant that an infrastructure was already in place that could help the refugees acclimate. Typically, there was a Jewish family service agency, a community center, sometimes a general hospital under Jewish auspices, as well as Jewish schools and temples. When the flow of immigration increased, however, it became necessary to resettle people in smaller towns that were near metropolises or in communities with small Jewish populations that relied only on volunteers.

The results varied considerably. A USNA field report, written in 1952, summed up the results of field visits to a number of medium-sized and small communities. In Montgomery, Alabama, only one of seven immigrants remained; in Savannah, Georgia, only five out of twenty-six were left. This was the general pattern, although there were some happy exceptions, such as Norfolk and Newport News, Virginia, and Columbia, South Carolina. With the help of a USNA advisor, the Jewish community of Columbia, which numbered only 250 families, set up committees to provide housing, employment, hospitality, education, health services, and free legal assistance. A non-Jewish beauty parlor operator became caught up in the mood of giving and offered a free "American up-to-date hairdo to each female newcomer."

More often than not, however, the survivors were lonely and lacking in enthusiasm for their new homes. Thus, many left after short stays that sometimes lasted only a few weeks. Away from the large Jewish communities, they felt isolated, culturally and geographically. In the small towns of New Jersey and Connecticut, they would at least have been able to travel frequently to New York to visit relatives and friends. The report concluded by questioning whether communities without trained social workers, especially those in the South, where cultural differences were greater, could really be used as homes for the DPs.

Still, many survivors put down roots in these smaller cities and still live there today. The interviews conducted with these people suggest that there were many factors responsible for that decision, the most important of which was the existence of a support system. Those who came to the smaller towns because relatives lived there stood the greatest chance of successfully integrating into the community. Finding work suited to their abilities was another consideration. Those who arrived as families also fared better—they had one another's shoulders to cry on. Still others, while disappointed in the lack of opportunity or the quality of Jewish life, never left, largely out of inertia. They had been through too much during the war, or they simply lacked the drive and ambition to change their circumstances. Finally, there were those who were drawn in by the warmth and hospitality shown them by the local natives. This last factor was very much an individual matter. The human chemistry upon which all relationships depend had to be there and this differed from place to place simply because survivors, and people in general, are all different. As a result, survivors often had contradictory opinions about the same communities and even the same people in these communities.

One of the more interesting stories about the postwar migration to America is that of the survivors who became farmers. The image of the farmer raising cows and chickens stands in sharp contrast to the stereotype of the city-dwelling, business-oriented Jew. And yet, approximately 1,500 Holocaust survivors and their families selected farming as an occupation after the war. The pages of the monthly journal that served these communities, Der Yidisher Farmer, present a portrait of a community throbbing with energy and rich in Jewish life and culture. Schools and synagogues linked the residents of these towns to one another, and Yiddish theater, concerts, public lectures, and social gatherings gave meaning and purpose to their lives.

New Jersey, New York, and Connecticut attracted the greatest number of farmer survivors, with some settling also in the Petaluma, California, area. In many cases, such as Vineland, New Jersey, or Liberty, New York, they augmented communities that already had a Jewish farming population. Most had no prior experience in this area. Nor was there a pattern among these would-be farmers in terms of country of origin, religious background, or occupation before the war. Some came because they liked the idea of country living, and others because they thought they could do well financially or as a result of an invitation from friends or relatives. Whatever their reasons, their lifestyles turned out to be quite different from those who stayed in the urban centers.

Israel Goldman, at eighty-eight, is the oldest living Holocaust survivor in Vineland and was one of the first to go there. He lives in the farmhouse he originally moved into together with his son, Louis, single and fifty-six, who returned to Vineland to help his father after Louis's mother died several years ago. The farm runs along a busy highway between restaurants and used-car lots, one of which has leased some of Goldman's property. The rotting hulks of weatherbeaten and boarded-up chicken coops still stand, somewhat unsteadily, in the tall and uncut grass behind the Goldman residence. Israel is quite spry and fit for a man his age. He attends religious services daily and displays a keen sense of humor despite his advanced years. When asked where he was born, he shot back, with a twinkle in his eyes: "This, also, you have to know?"

Goldman spent the war years in Poland, running and hiding. He lived briefly in Williamsburg, Brooklyn, before moving to Vineland: "I was earning thirty-two dollars a week making pocketbooks and wallets in my cousin's factory. We were five in the family and I couldn't make a living. We paid fifty-five dollars a month in rent." His son, Louis, added, "Word got around that Jews were buying farms and you could be your own boss and you didn't have to worry about the language that much." As another farmer jokingly observed, "With the chickens you could talk any language."

Chris and Miles Lerman are also survivors who settled in Vineland. Chris was the name she had adopted in an effort to hide her Jewishness during the war and, after a while, the name stuck. She and her husband are prominent members of the community. Because of their involvement in many national Jewish organizations, especially Miles's position as national campaign chairman of the United States Holocaust Memorial Council, they are well known among survivors in the United States. The Lermans live in a suburban ranch home just outside of Vineland. Hanging over the front door is a large commissioned painting divided into three panels. One depicts Miles standing alone, looking wistful and sad. In the middle panel is a drawing of the crematorium at Auschwitz and in the third is a portrait of the Lermans, together and happy.

The Lermans also stayed in Brooklyn before settling in Vineland. Although they had no experience as farmers, their families had owned flour mills in Europe. They were attracted to the area because of the beautiful countryside and because good friends of theirs lived there. But there was an even more compelling reason that went beyond individual interests. It was a sense of group solidarity and an urge to build something new. As Chris put it:

Eighty percent of the people here were my age, in their early twenties. All of us had stopped attending school in the fifth, sixth, seventh, tops, eleventh grade because of the war. About 20 percent had higher education. Not only were we urban, but we'd been through a terrible experience and we had to start life over again here without any parental supervision or guidance. It wasn't easy but life here was simple and good. We made friends as we went along and we loved it. It was exciting because we were doing things together, helping each other. There was a certain camaraderie; it was a challenge.

Generally, the agencies' assistance to the newcomers fell into two areas—financial aid and counseling. The National Council of Jewish Women (NCJW), with 115 local sections throughout the country, was particularly active. They helped the immigrants find housing, provided furniture, set up hospitality and advisory committees, and gave English classes. Similarly, the New York Association for New Arrivals (NYANA) assisted the refugees with child care, aid to religious functionaries, vocational services, and business loans. Local family service agencies helped them adapt psychologically and socially to their new environment.

One woman interviewed recalled how the Jewish Family Service had given her two sets of dishes to help her keep kosher and money for a bedroom set she still had. Another man wrote a letter to the *Forward* expressing his gratitude for assistance in finding work. Louis Shulman's words succinctly encapsulated one immigrant's experience:

I was born in a small town in Poland, went through all of the concentration camps and was liberated from Theresienstadt. I came to the U.S. through a Jewish community contract and went to Ra-

cine, Wisconsin. . . . But we couldn't find work there and went instead to New York where I found work in a sweater factory. . . . Then my troubles began. After a short time I lost my job, did not have an apartment, and I was forced to sleep in the subway. Fortunately, ORT [a Jewish vocational organization] taught me to become a sewing machine operator and then I was able to find work. Today, we live in a four room apartment. We are happy and joyous, as much as one can be happy after losing one's family.

Research on immigration clearly demonstrates that personal interest on the part of organizational officials greatly eased the adjustment process for immigrants. Besides good intentions, however, there was the problem of adapting theories of social work to the specific backgrounds and experiences of those who came. The agencies abandoned their traditional approach of taking lengthy case histories once it became apparent that many of the DPs were trying to repress their experiences. Another challenge that faced the agencies was the need to mediate between the goals of helping the refugees while at the same time encouraging them to become independent. Personal rapport was of course crucial, but some workers were reported to have overidentified with the often extreme suffering of their clients and this interfered with their general effectiveness. In addition, the attitudes of the refugees to the idea of being helped varied considerably. While some did not object to any level of assistance, others accepted it very reluctantly or not at all, seeing the agencies only as a resource to be used minimally.

While many refugees reported positive experiences, this response was by no means universal. In Pittsburgh, for example, the refugees' reactions to the agencies were mixed. Some praised the social workers, saying they visited them and showed genuine interest, while others described "mean" workers lacking in "warmth." In addition to the human factor, timing may also have played a role. During certain periods, such as 1949, the number of immigrants arriving at once was great and the harried caseworkers felt overwhelmed; this was no doubt reflected in their attitudes and behavior toward the newcomers.

Of particular concern to the agencies was the adjustment of children, especially those orphaned by the war. Numerous special agencies existed to care for and educate them. Their activities included administering private schools, providing scholarships and tutors, and consulting with school boards about individual problems and general policy issues. Certain schools, such as the Rabbi Jacob Joseph School, the Rabbi Solomon Kluger School, and the Mesivta Torah Vodaath, all Orthodox institutions, accepted large numbers of immigrant children who paid nothing or next to nothing in tuition. The Hebrew teachers in these schools were frequently refugees themselves. Often, teaching was a field they entered by default. Other skills were not transferable to America and they were either unable or unwilling to learn new professions. This, plus the havoc that the war had wreaked on their personal lives, often made them poor pedagogues. As a result, they soon became the hapless victims of students whose immigrant parents were similarly unable to control or motivate them to be more assiduous in their studies. True, many of the survivors' children did very well later on, but this was probably not as a result of the education they received in these underfunded and inadequately staffed institutions. In fact, children of survivors who attended these schools, many of whom today are successful professionals, seem to derive considerable delight from telling stories of the mayhem they caused their teachers and principals in those days.

An important contribution to the happiness of these children was the opportunity to leave the city during the hot summer months. Many of the Jewish camps that dotted the countryside in New York's Catskills, Pennsylvania's Poconos, or in the White Mountains of New Hampshire sponsored refugee children. The Orthodox-oriented Camp Agudah and Camp Yeshiva offered free vacations in the late 1940s and early 1950s to those who could not afford to pay. Besides wanting everyone to have a good time, the camps and their Jewish support organizations saw them as an opportunity to teach both Jewish and American values. Thus Camp Agudah proclaimed in an ad: "Just a short time ago . . . these Jewish boys were friendless DPs in Europe. . . . America was a miracle that happened to other people. Now we have the opportunity to help them become healthy, self-reliant American citizens." Indeed, when Louis Goldman was interviewed in Vineland, he retrieved some old black-and-white photos of himself with his bunkmates in Camp Yeshiva and proudly showed them to me. As he spoke about the camp, it was clear that they were mementos of happy childhood days. Survivors who had been active in the Jewish socialist movement in Europe sent their children to Camp Hemshech, sponsored by the Arbeiter Ring, and to Kindervelt, run by the Zionist Arbeiter Farband. Those inclined toward the philoso-

phy of the Zionist Revisionist Movement often opted for Camp
Betar. For the majority of immigrants, however, the religious or
political affiliation of the camp was unimportant; they simply
wanted their children to be in the country for the summer.

The goal of making Americans out of European children was
clearly stated in an *Aufbau* article in which Erna Pollinger, the
executive director of Summer Placement for Emigre Children, explained the organization's philosophy: "The Americanization process is quicker here than on the asphalt of city streets. We don't
send children to camp simply to pamper them but also to acclimate
them rapidly into an English-speaking environment."

A key factor in the survivors' adjustment was the community's
attitude and response to them. Here there was tremendous variation. Denver was described in a 1948 USNA report as "extremely
cooperative" and willing to accept difficult family units, while
Washington, D.C., was portrayed as refusing to do so. Miami declined to accept Sabbath observers (presumably because of employment problems), as did Atlanta, which also stated its opposition to
accepting those with serious medical problems, the aged, artists, or
musicians. Similar reservations were expressed by those living in
Louisville, New Orleans, and Minneapolis. San Antonio was considered a "difficult sell" because of the heat, while Milwaukee and
St. Louis were identified as "cooperative cities" that, nevertheless,
faced periodic staff shortages. Of course, the assessment of these
cities may have changed from year to year.

In those cities with professional agencies, contact between native
residents and survivors was more superficial. In the communities
that had no professional agencies but that nonetheless were willing
to accept refugees, agency professionals met with local leaders and
explained to them what was involved. In this way, jobs and housing
could be found, welcome committees set up, and other preparations
made. A typical announcement distributed in Montgomery, Alabama, on April 26, 1948, read as follows:

THIS IS WHERE YOUR MONEY GOES!:

Mr. and Mrs. JOSEPH RABINOVITZ and CHILDREN May Move
Next Door to You Next Week . . .
THEY SPEAK NO ENGLISH!
THEY SPENT 4 YEARS IN DACHAU!
THEY HAVE NO MONEY, NO JOB
. . . what's to be done for them???

The rest of the flier gave details of a forthcoming meeting to be sponsored by the Jewish Federation of Montgomery at which a USNA representative would speak.

How leaders responded clearly affected the views of the general population, and no one felt this more keenly than the survivors themselves. Thus, one survivor in Pittsburgh recalled bitterly how shocked he was "when a local rabbi of a major congregation announced that, in his opinion, the Jews who survived were collaborators." No rabbi, or anyone else in the Jewish community, would make such a generalization today but in those days it was possible. Historian Barbara Burstin charges in her book on survivors who lived in Pittsburgh that synagogue involvement in the plight of the refugees there was conspicuously absent, whether it was the Orthodox, Conservative, or Reform congregations.

The insensitivity to the survivors, where it occurred, was often a reflection of ignorance regarding the concentration camp experience itself. For example, many Americans were unaware of the meaning of the numbers on the survivors' arms. Ruth Siegler, a survivor who settled in Birmingham, Alabama, remembered: "We went to a dance at Temple Emanuel in New York and I walked into the bathroom. They were all Jewish people and the girl next to me said: 'Oh, I didn't get a number.' Other people thought it was a telephone number." A survivor living in San Francisco attended an alumni dinner dance at her husband's law school and was confronted by a man who asked why she was wearing her "laundry numbers" on her arm. She responded sarcastically that it was her telephone number. Later on, she learned that he was the dean of the law school.

Of course, people knew of the horrors in a general way. But while this engendered sympathy for the survivors, it also had American Jews wondering whether they themselves could have made it through the camps. This led to the next question—what types of people could have survived and how did the dehumanizing experience change them? If the survivors acted cruelly under these circumstances, did that mean that they too would have responded similarly? The reluctance of the survivors to discuss what had happened, based in part on the lack of interest by American Jews, created a "conspiracy of silence" that lasted for many years. This pattern is perhaps best summed up in the following retrospective by a survivor:

I went to stay with my relatives in the Midwest. . . . My cousins were American-born Jews; very Middle-Western, kind, generous people, who also shrank from me a little. You understand, the concentration camp experience is nothing that endears you to people. People who came to my cousin's house used to ask me such things as whether I had been able to survive because, perchance, I had slept with an SS man. And if I had, did they think I could tell them?

Helen Gilmer, a survivor who lives in Atlanta, explained how her child was rejected as a playmate because of such attitudes: "One day my oldest daughter came home crying that a girl didn't invite her to play house with her. The child said that we, her parents, had made ammunition in the camps that killed other Jews. She must have heard her own parents talking."

Still, most Jews in this country empathized with the plight of their fellow Jews and many refugees spoke positively of their reception. Moreover, it seems that volunteers were especially appreciated by the newcomers, who saw them as sensitive and caring individuals. Whenever money was involved, motives were likely to be suspect. One survivor, in recounting his treatment as a "roomer" in the home of an American family, acknowledged that the family had sacrificed because their daughter had been forced to move into her parents' bedroom. He also noted that they were paid to take him in and said he never really felt wanted by the family. This was the main issue and those involved with the refugees did not always grasp it. Thus one representative of a local Jewish organization defended himself against assertions made in a letter to the *Forward* that people in that community were "heartless" by pointing out that $300,000 had been spent on the newcomers. The problem was not money, however, but a need to believe that assistance rendered came from the heart, and not just the pocket.

Even when American Jews extended themselves purely out of kindness, problems sometimes developed. Dora Zaidenweber, a survivor living in Minneapolis, recalled how a woman repeatedly offered her and her husband free tickets to concerts, plays, and the like, all of which she gratefully accepted. "But," she noted, "we had just talked on the phone. . . . So I called her and invited her for lunch, for a Sunday. I thought that would be a nice way to meet." The woman declined her invitations a number of times. "Suddenly it dawned on me," said Zaidenweber, "that I was a charity case as far as she was concerned. I wasn't her equal. She wasn't interested in meeting me."

As newly arrived immigrants, the survivors were highly sensitive to every nuance, every comment, and every slight. Leah Henson laughed as she remembered how her new American neighbors entered her apartment and expressed amazement at how clean it was: "They thought, 'I can't cook, I can't do anything. Who am I?—a *grine!*'" Frieda Kessler, who first lived in Kenosha, Wisconsin, found Americans to be very nice but noted that they viewed the survivors as backward. "They came to see if we knew how to eat. They gave us a banana and they said, 'Oh, they know how to eat a banana.' And they brought us *chulent* [a European Sabbath food]. I guess they thought we had to have *chulent.*" Henry Lindeman, a Kenosha resident, described how, when they first came, several members of the community had brought over cake, fruit, and homemade soup. "But then," he said ruefully, "after the novelty of our arrival wore off, people seemed less and less interested in us. Today, forty years later, we are friendly with perhaps two or three families in the entire community. Our closest friends are the ones who were in camps with us and who now live in the Chicago and Milwaukee areas." In truth, many Americans were simply not ready to commit themselves emotionally to the degree that the survivors were. They already had their own families and close friends.

The survivors were well aware that American Jews lived in relative safety and comfort during the war, but the point was repeatedly reinforced whenever they interacted with them, largely because of the Americans' insensitivity to the issue. One survivor overheard a conversation on a bus in 1949 in which a Jewish woman commented to her friend that now "times are not so good since we can't get any overtime. During the war it was wonderful. My husband was able to buy me a mink coat." The survivor exploded in anger and shouted, "While your husband was earning overtime for a mink coat we were being killed in concentration camps." Marika Abrams, a survivor who was given a scholarship to the University of Washington after the war, found that even when Americans talked about the war in negative terms, they tried to minimize the survivors' suffering by claiming that they too had suffered. The father of one of Marika's sorority friends informed her that Jews in his town had also had a hard time during the war, citing the fact that a window in their synagogue had once been broken.

The survivors often internalized the negative stereotypes that many Americans had of them. Some felt that others looked down upon them and this sometimes made them timid in their relationships with their new neighbors. They were self-conscious about their accents, their lack of education, and their unfamiliarity with American ways. Most kept quiet, but some reacted with anger whenever they felt themselves being unfairly judged. Renia Chadajo was born in Wlocwaczek, Poland, and spent the war years in both labor and concentration camps. A feisty woman, she responded with shrill laughter when asked where she spent the war: "Where do you think? In the resorts, the hotels, in camp!" A resident of Boston, she married a survivor from Salonika, Greece, who has been a barber for the past forty years. The Chadajos are working-class people who have struggled to achieve the American dream. They live in a modest one-family house in one of Boston's suburbs. When asked if there was jealousy against the newcomers when they came, she responded:

Yes. When we bought our house and moved in, our neighbor, I was friendly with her, called someone over and said, "I want you to meet the refugee." I said, "Liz, since when am I a refugee? I have a name. I own a house just like you do. And I'm working. I pay taxes just like you do. I'm an American." And other Americans were also jealous that we were here such a short time and already we owned a house. And I said to them, "I didn't get the money for the house by sitting on my big you-know-what. I worked hard for it."

Generally speaking, those survivors who came after 1948 were not received as enthusiastically as those who arrived earlier. They were no longer a novelty and World War II was beginning to recede from the American-Jewish community's consciousness. Moreover, there were housing shortages and unemployment began to rise as more and more DPs, Jewish and Christian, continued to make their way to these shores. As a result, the agencies found it harder to place refugees.

The attitudes of Americans toward the survivors must be seen in the context of immigration in general. To what extent were Eastern European Jews befriended by German Jews when they immigrated to the United States at the turn of the century? And how many German Jews who came in the 1800s were welcomed by their Sephardic co-religionists? How were the Irish and Italians greeted by those American immigrant groups who were here first? Some will point to the tragic events that the survivors went through and argue that sympathy for them should have been greater as a result. Indeed, the survivors were generally treated better than other groups. Nevertheless, to the extent that they were not, simply demonstrates that even catastrophic suffering is not always sufficient to overcome the traditional hostility and suspicion that incoming groups who are different inevitably face. This is not often readily admitted by those who feel their turf threatened. The candid comments of Arthur Goldhaft, an American who wrote about the survivors in the Vineland farming community, are a refreshing exception:

> On our side there was something of the suspicion that is felt over any influx of newcomers. Sympathetic as we were to them, we could not help being critical. If a hard-pressed new settler ran up a bill with a feed dealer, and then switched and ran up a second bill with another dealer, the story spread like wildfire, and we forgot that most of us, in such straits in the Depression, had resorted to similar expedients. If, on the contrary, one of the new settlers arrived with some money, unfair tales were instantly spread that all the newcomers had grown rich on the black market.

2✴

The survivors have not, as a group, assimilated into mainstream American society. To this day, they identify very strongly as Jews in many ways. This is not due simply to their prewar backgrounds and their experiences during the war. On the contrary, persecution can cause people to deny their heritage. Rather, the survivors' decision to remain active members of the Jewish community can best be understood by examining their experiences in the first few years after their arrival.

The survivors were admitted to America as a group. Although many came as individuals, they received special consideration as victims of Hitler's tyranny. This enhanced their sense of uniqueness and the belief that only other survivors could really understand what they had been through. At the same time, they fully appreciated the fact that their situation had changed drastically, that they were now in a free land where they could look to the future with hope. The well-known journalist Jacob Patt captured the dual nature of the survivors' past and present in the following article in the *Forward*:

> *I went to a hall and there I saw refugees dancing. They turned left and then right, dancing joyously, yet without singing. . . . Several hundred women were dancing, their arms intertwined with those of the men. . . . I stood there and stared. Before my eyes, I saw heads with black hair, blond hair, and burning eyes. Many had the death camp numbers on their arms. All this took place a few minutes before midnight on New Year's Eve at the Hotel Diplomat. About one minute before midnight, Nathan Gurevitch and his klezmer band suddenly became very still as he spoke a few words: "We are all former DPs. We remained alive through miracles. We continue to live and now we are in free America and we are no longer alone." As he finished, the clock struck twelve. The lights were turned off, the various instruments came to life. . . . Everyone began to shout with joy—"The American New Year is here!" Among the dancers I saw the famous Vladka [Meed], the heroine of the Warsaw Ghetto. I also saw Bernard Goldstein, the author of the great book about memories of the ghetto. . . . I could not resist and I joined the dancers. I danced with thousands of them. I danced with a people who were miracle Jews.*

Those who gathered that night probably lived in the same neighborhoods and that too held them together. This was, of course, a matter of choice, but irrespective of that, the outcome was the same—values, beliefs, attitudes, and behavior patterns, the social glue that holds people together, were strengthened. The Lower East Side, where the *Forward* was headquartered, typified such neighborhoods and its residents felt that way. As Lola Shtupak put it: "The East Side was full of refugees, it was the center, it was "Israel" there. You felt, you know, like you were really home." The feeling of warmth was palpable and Abe Foxman's eyes literally glowed as he reminisced about it: "I was lucky in that I was able to experience the "true" East Side when the *Tog, Forward,* and *Morgen Journal* were still publishing. I'd go to the Garden Cafeteria and have lunch and as a kid who spoke Yiddish I met the great Yiddish poets while they were still alive. I would go with my father to book presentations on 14th Street and on 8th Street on Saturday night." In essence, what the survivors did was extend the lifespan of the Yiddish culture that had been brought over from Europe at the turn of the century. The theaters and cabarets and the Yiddish press, which had begun to die out as Jews left the areas of first settlement, were suddenly discovered by a new audience who saw them as the embodiment of that which had been torn apart in Europe only a few years earlier.

While these neighborhoods were indeed home, they were not necessarily safe. Just as previous generations of Jews had found it necessary to defend themselves against hostility from other groups, so did the survivors often have to bear the brunt of anti-Semitism. Their dress, lack of English, and inexperience with American culture made them easy targets. In one such case, five refugee youths were set upon in the Brownsville section of Brooklyn by thirty men who beat them as they shouted anti-Semitic slogans. Given what they had gone through during the war it must have been an especially horrifying experience. Benjamin Hirsch, now a successful architect living in Atlanta, recalled winning a fight against a class bully in public school who ordered him to remove his yarmulke. Later on he was, as he put it, "pulverized" when the bully's gang ambushed him outside of the school. Bias did not always emerge in the form of a physical attack. The survivors learned soon enough that anti-Semitism could be subtly expressed, but equally pernicious. One immigrant remembered how she wanted to go on vacation to a certain resort area. Her friends advised against it, however. "Why?" she asked. "Because if it says 'church nearby' then it means that the hotel doesn't take any Jews."

The range and variety of Jewish cultural organizations available to the newcomers tended to slow down the assimilation process. These included the *landsmanschaften*, the Bund, and the Jewish Labor Committee, as well as establishment organizations. The societies were not only convenient locations where the refugees could mingle; they also served as vehicles for perpetuating the memories of what had happened. Most held annual services commemorating the destruction of their communities. Here is an account of one such event:

I was present at a memorial service of the Pruzhiner Landsmanschaft that took place in the Rand School on 15th Street and Union Square. The hall was packed. . . . It was the seventh memorial of the destruction of the six-hundred-year-old Jewish community of Pruzhin. The memorial began with an excellent cantor chanting a chapter of Psalms. A tenor, he was thin, with dark hair, and he appeared obsessed with his own thoughts. He sang very emotionally. As he sang one could hear the weeping of the five hundred Pruzhiner Jews in the hall. . . . [The cantor] was in the Pruzhin Ghetto and in other camps. And if you believe in the resurrection of souls, you may also believe that in this hall, all of the people from Pruzhin who died, who were burned in Auschwitz, came and joined in commemorating this anniversary. On the platform stood a young Jew who said: "I was with the Pruzhiner people in Auschwitz . . . I saw them, the Pruzhiner children, the little ones, the innocent ones, over there, over there."

The *landsmanschaften* were creations of Eastern European Jewry, but Jews from Germany and Central Europe also had their organizations. Perhaps the most important of these was the New World Club, originally founded by German Jews who had come to the United States before the war. Among their activities were women's organizations, sports teams, stamp clubs, and a physician's training program. They also assisted people in finding jobs and advertised frequently in the *Aufbau*. Other organizations that worked with the immigrants also publicized their programs in the *Aufbau*. There were English language courses given by the American Institute of Modern Languages, as well as parties, folk dancing, and guest speakers, all sponsored by the American Friends Services Committee. Jews from countries lacking formal organizations also found ways to coalesce. Belgian Jews, for example (most were originally from either Poland or Hungary), joined certain synagogues and burial societies. The same held true for Jews from France and Luxembourg.

National Jewish organizations were also involved with the survivors. As early as 1946, there were already stirrings with respect to commemorating the Holocaust. A *New York Times* article reported on a reunion meeting of Bergen-Belsen survivors held in the offices of the United Jewish Appeal. It announced the formation of a committee that would work through the UJA to help relocate the ten thousand Jews that were still in Belsen. Such organizations were particularly useful for people who did not fit in because their towns were gone, they had no relatives or good friends, or they were religiously unaffiliated. A good example of such people who fell between the cracks was Irena Schwarz, a survivor who escaped detection by passing as a member of a sympathetic Polish Christian family.

When the war ended, Irena, then aged fourteen, wanted to convert to Christianity, largely out of a desire to belong, a need she admits is a very strong feature of her personality. But her adoptive family suggested she defer her decision until she reached twenty-one. Irena's aunt and uncle, physicians living in America, learned of her whereabouts and invited her to come live with them. She went, but against her will. In Brooklyn, where her relatives lived, she attended James Madison High School and then went to the University of Michigan, where she first came into contact with Zionism through the campus Hillel Club. She also learned more about her family history, namely that her father, a friend of Ben-Gurion, had been secretary of the Polish Zionist Party. "I started looking for myself," she said, "for my roots. And I began looking only for Jewish contacts. Once I gave up the other [Christian] world, I had to find something for myself." The vehicles for this affirmation of identity were the Zionist clubs in college, where she was an active member, and a summer spent at a Brandeis camp. Her decision to make *aliyah* came on a trip to Israel after the Six Day War in 1967. "I went with my aunt and I fell in love with the country. That's all I remember; that's all I can tell you. I felt that I found my place in the world. This was my home and I felt good."

Even after the Holocaust there was resentment among many American Jews toward those survivors who identified overtly with the faith. This attitude is vividly portrayed in Philip Roth's short story "Eli the Fanatic," which centers around the angst that results when a Jew in Hasidic garb moves into a small town. The story's main protagonist, himself a Jew, observes at one point that had Jews been more willing to play down the ways in which they were different from Gentiles, the Holocaust might never have happened. For most survivors, these concepts were totally alien to their way of thinking. They had seen and shared the fate of assimilated German and Austrian Jewry and harbored no illusions about their ability to disappear into the fabric of Christian society. This realization also affected the degree to which they integrated into American life and culture. They loved America and were proud to share in its vision of a free and open society but they nevertheless viewed themselves as distinct.

Livia Bitton is a professor of Jewish studies at the City University of New York's Herbert Lehman College. Her life was saved at Auschwitz in part because the infamous Dr. Mengele refused to believe that she was Jewish even though she said so. Now married to a Jewish man from Ireland whose last name is Jackson, she is frequently mistaken for a Gentile. As a proud Jew, however, she pointedly lets people know about her background: "When I meet new people I say: 'Oh, I live part of the year in Israel.' I bring it into the conversation. Or I say: 'I teach Jewish studies.' " To emphasize her point, she related the following incident, one that graphically demonstrates how the trauma of the Holocaust can come alive in the daily life of a survivor at any time:

> *Once in the subway, a husky blond woman who was obviously a nurse was sitting next to me. She noticed a pregnant woman standing and she turned to me and said in an undertone: "These Jewish women. They are so brazen. They have no taste or manners. Do you see her? She's pregnant and she's flaunting her pregnancy." So I thought she's crazy and I said, "What are you talking about?" And she answered: "When I was a young woman and pregnant I always wore a coat. We were brought up with good taste, but these Jews . . . heh!" So I looked at her and I said: "How do you know she's Jewish?" And she says: "I can tell a Jew anywhere." And I couldn't tell. So I said: "Would you ever take me for a Jew?" She said: "No." So I pulled up my sleeve and I said: "Do you see this?" She looked and she said: "What is this?" I answered: "This number was put on my arm at Auschwitz by people like you." And by this time I was getting excited and everybody's looking at us. And I said: "Are you a German?" She said: "No. Only my husband is a German. My family came here from Germany many years ago and I was born here." So I replied: "You don't have to be a German to be a Nazi. I don't care whether you are a German or not, but you are a Nazi. People like you put six million Jews to death." And everybody was quiet. And when the train came into the station, she ran out. And everybody was applauding.*

A disproportionate number of survivors identify themselves as religiously observant Orthodox Jews. While only about 10 percent of American Jews in general claim affiliation with the Orthodox community, the survey conducted for this book found that approximately 41 percent* of the survivors identify with Orthodoxy, with most practicing, in varying degrees, the dietary laws and maintaining Sabbath observance. In practical terms, Orthodox Jews are limited in their social contact with the larger society because of certain religious restrictions. Thus, the high level of observance found among survivors also lessened the likelihood that they would assimilate rapidly. Their religious needs dictated that they would have to live among other Jews. Miriam Brach, a survivor presently living in the largely Orthodox community of Kew Gardens Hills, Queens, first went to her uncle's home in Reading, Pennsylvania, when she came to this country. They were lovely people, as she recalled: "They had a completely furnished apartment for us. They gave our family everything we needed; they even polished the doorknobs. Their kindness was incredible. It broke my heart when I realized we weren't going to stay there. We were religious and needed an Orthodox *shul* [synagogue], a *mikveh* [ritualarium], a kosher butcher. I told the rabbi: 'I'm twenty-two; I come from a prominent religious family and I want to remain Jewish.' " Miriam and her husband, Sam, came to New York and accomplished a good deal there. It is clear, however, from her account that she in no way looked down upon her less observant relatives. It was simply a matter of religion having been the central unifying force in her life and that of her family.

Another important factor that encouraged survivors to retain a distinct sense of group identity was the foreign language press. Yiddish newspapers such as the *Forward, Morgen Journal,* and *Der Amerikaner* filled several roles for the newcomers. First, they provided comfort for those who pined for the old way of life, and, in a practical sense, they enabled the survivors to maintain contact with one another through advertisements and stories regarding activities taking place in the community. Second, they were a bridge between the old and the new. While never devaluing Jewish culture, those who published these newspapers recognized that if the immigrants were to succeed, they would have to become adept at making their way in their adopted home. To this end, they published articles that discussed the adjustment of the survivors. A contest sponsored by the *Forward* called "America, My New

*Unless otherwise specified, this and all other figures cited in this book refer to the quantitative survey conducted for this study.

Home" invited readers to send in stories of how they were acclimating to the new land. The titles of winning contributions spoke volumes about the refugees' concerns, hopes, and desires: "She Likes America, a Place Where One Can Even Criticize the President"; "We Do Not Want to Receive Support"; "We Found Good Family and Good Jews in the United States."

Finally, the existence of a vibrant Yiddish and, to a lesser extent, German press strengthened Jewish life. By telling people about events of Jewish interest, it drew attention to and increased the degree of participation in such activities. By printing articles about the experiences of other survivors, it heightened the level of group solidarity. The survivors who had difficulty adjusting did not have to feel alone. They were all going through the same thing and the blame did not necessarily lie with them. If their boss fired them because they were "pushy refs" (refugees), this happened to others too. If family members did not prove to be as welcoming as they had anticipated, so what—many survivors had found this to be the case.

What most slowed down the assimilation process, perhaps, was the immigrants' retention of Yiddish. The language that had nurtured them in their youth remained very much alive, to be used among themselves on a daily basis. They knew that relying on Yiddish would hurt their progress in becoming Americanized, but it was too important a component of their past to be eliminated. To them, the psychic benefits of speaking in the mother tongue, *mamme loshon,* as they referred to it, far outweighed the disadvantages.

Compelling as this argument might have been, however, the survivors recognized that speaking English was a necessity if they were to do well. Most attended night school, where they studied English with a diligence that would have put Leo Rosten's immigrant character, Hyman Kaplan, to shame. But classroom instruction was often insufficient for those with dreams and ambitions. One such individual approached his Italian-American teacher one night after class and said, "I want to open up a printing business. If I learn one word a night, it will take me a hundred years." Her response: "This is not for you. Go into a movie theater. Sit two or three times through the film. The third time I want you to mumble what they're saying." He followed her advice and was soon able to grasp the language. Other refugees learned by listening to radio and watching TV.

If not knowing the language was a problem, learning it introduced another—the accent. Indicative of the seriousness with which this was regarded by the immigrants was an article that appeared in the *Aufbau* in 1945. Written in English by a Professor Jon Whyte, it explained how people could eliminate their accents. As with all immigrants, the accent deprived them of their anonymity. Everyone knew from the moment they spoke that they were foreigners. Sometimes this actually prevented them from speaking in public, especially those child survivors who went to school in America.

Formal education is probably one of the most important factors determining the rate of acculturation. For most of the survivors, the acquisition of such education was unrealistic, if not impossible. They had lost precious years during the war, often the very years in which they would have been students in school, and they did not have the patience to go to school full-time. Even if they had, the necessity of earning a living, particularly for those with families, precluded any serious efforts in this direction. Those who went were a small minority—child survivors who were now teenagers, single men and women whose abilities had been discovered in Europe by the B'nai B'rith Hillel Foundation and who were then awarded scholarships to study in American universities, and those few whose desire to advance in this country so motivated them that they were willing to make the necessary sacrifices to achieve their goals.

Those who did attend school found it to be a positive experience. Generally speaking, they were treated sympathetically by their teachers and socially accepted by their peers. Students were sometimes assigned to guide them through classes and schools, and special educational arrangements were frequently made to accommodate their needs. Most of those interviewed could not recall instances of prejudice. On the contrary, they made friends readily and felt accepted. Teachers of that era substantiated the respondents' claims of having been good students. The following case of a Brooklyn high school student was typical: "I was a leader and I was popular in school. . . . The Jewish kids were really interested in me as a foreigner. . . . I was almost looked upon as a celebrity. . . . And our teachers and counselors, everyone really, I must say, was always extremely kind and understanding and patient with us." Besides the educational function, the schools also provided opportunities for refugees to learn about what it meant to be an American. They were exposed to American music, sports, the latest clothing styles, and so on, and this speeded up the Americanization process.

Another key institution that determined how the newcomers did was family. Those who had family waiting for them had an easier time of it. They had someone to turn to in time of need, someone who could give them a start in business, a place to stay, and, most important, make them feel wanted. Ben Hirsch, who was orphaned during the war and who came here as a young child, did not have a family that could take him in and provide necessary protection from outsiders. His description of what this meant is illuminating:

> *I was always being blamed for everything as a kid. You wouldn't believe the things I got blamed for! And why did I get blamed for all these things? Because I had no parents. Other kids' parents would say: "Now don't you say that about my son, or daughter." And I had a terrible reputation in the Jewish community, a reputation that I got because there was nobody to defend me.*

One study of survivors served by the USNA found that conflict with relatives was the most commonly reported problem. It was also a frequent subject of letters to the *Forward* in the "Bintel Brief" column. The letter below shows how family problems were often intertwined with cultural clashes and generational differences and how having family here did not necessarily guarantee that everything would work out:

> *Worthy Editor:*
>
> We brought over to this country a nephew who is now twenty-two. . . . It took two years to bring him here. It cost us plenty of money and aggravation, but we finally accomplished our goal. . . . All in all, he is a very talented boy and is not lazy. Everything would have been all right, but during his first week here he saw a girl who was a neighbor, a child, sixteen years old, and immediately fell in love with her. The girl too, who incidentally does not understand one word of Yiddish, was overwhelmed by him. . . . I tell him he is here too short a period of time to get involved with a girl. He should first become oysgegrined [ungreened]. . . . But he says the United States is a democratic land and everyone can do as they please. . . . We have signed an agreement that he will remain with us for one year, and afterward he can go wherever he pleases. We will, however, not bring

anyone else to the United States because one bad experience like this spoils it for the others.

Do you feel the boy acted properly after all we did for him? We feel he misled us. . . . He [my husband] thought he'd teach him how to be a butcher with the idea that, after a while, he would work his way up and become, eventually, a partner. . . ."

Your Dedicated Reader
A.L.

Answer:
You should not be embittered against your nephew although we understand your disappointment that he became involved with a young girl. Don't forget that even one's own children run away many times from parents because they have different friends. . . . You could suggest to your nephew that he think about becoming established before he gets married. . . . Many times young people listen to their hearts and not to their minds. And who knows who is right—the heart or the mind? We were also young once and where is the guarantee that the practical plans of the parents are always better than the impractical plans of our young people? Help him become independent. . . . Times are different today and even years ago these things happened.

Most of the difficulties encountered by the survivors fell within the normal boundaries of the struggles common to all immigrants. Some survivors, however, were so scarred by the horrors of what they had lived through that they were unable to function normally. While the instances of severe impairment were not the norm, they happened and are part of the story. In one such instance a couple was sent to Selma, Alabama. Before long it became evident that the woman had what was described by the USNA social worker in charge of the case as "an area of irrationality." She believed that her husband had been dating a Polish Christian woman while they were still in Europe, that he had continued seeing her on the ship that brought them to America, and that she was somewhere in the house in which they now lived. Neighbors told of having seen her looking for such a person in closets and under beds. The woman eventually left for New York, where she was placed under psychiatric care. Correspondence between the USNA and community leaders reveal that this case jeopardized the entire resettlement program in Selma. Until then, Selma, which had several hundred Jews, had accepted

Selma community is definitely not receptive towards accepting any additional displaced families. I must inform you that should one be sent to us, it will be so without our permission. . . ."

Many survivors who were to lead perfectly normal and healthy lives initially had very strong reactions to the concentration camp experience. For one woman, giving birth to her child triggered a traumatic reaction: "When I woke up from the anesthesia I thought that I am back in the camp. . . . And I started to yell and scream: 'Don't kill the baby! This is not a Jewish baby; this is a Christian baby. I swear to you and I have witnesses.' " Fortunately, the doctor understood the situation and told her sister to humor her until she calmed down. This was not always the case, however. In one particularly horrendous instance, a woman who had come to Philadelphia with her father and apparently suffered from a neurosis was hospitalized, mistakenly diagnosed as a psychotic, and given a lobotomy. Her distraught father later told NCJW workers that his daughter had been a "perfectly normal, strong, highly educated girl until she was in a concentration camp where she was called upon to assist in removing bodies from the camp where inmates had died during the night of starvation and disease. [Her] 'hand-washing compulsion' arose as a result of this experience."

For the most part, caseworkers involved with those refugees who needed help in adjusting expressed surprise at the resilience and strength of the survivors. Noting that the survivors were often manipulative and distrustful, they concluded that it was precisely the development of such capabilities that had enabled them to survive the camps. "Unfortunately," observed one article on adolescent survivors, "the mechanism which had served them well in survival before coming to America . . . was self-destructive and actually prevented them from making adjustments satisfactory to themselves." The challenge facing the agencies was to heal the scars of the war by helping the survivors regain trust both in themselves and in others.

Did the survivors succeed in this area? One of the more striking aspects of the postwar generation is the almost complete absence of criminal behavior of the sort that accompanied the arrival of earlier waves of immigration. If the need to survive reduces people to animal-like behavior and if, as some have argued, the best did not make it, how are we to account for the fact that there was relatively animal-like behavior and if, as some have argued, the best did not make it, how are we to account for the fact that there was relatively little crime or juvenile delinquency among both the newcomers and their children? Where are the Lepke Buchalters, Arnold Rothsteins, and Dutch Schultzes among the children of the survivors?

While these questions need to be researched further, the fact that the survivors came to America during a period of relative prosperity and received a great deal of support from Jewish agencies, as well as from relatives and friends, was certainly very important. In any event, it is clear that the Nazis were unable to destroy the survivors' basic value system, one that had been nurtured and developed in the families and communities in which they were raised prior to the war. The best proof of this lies in the way in which they conducted themselves and rebuilt their lives after the war ended. Their adaptation would seem to support the argument advanced by Terrence Des Pres, Eugen Kogon, and others that survival in the camps depended upon the retention of human values and not upon selfishness and cruelty to others.

By 1948, almost no DPs had been deported for any reason. On the average they needed six months to become settled and to secure employment. Their children had excellent school records. Most were not supported by private agencies and none were known to have been on public relief. A follow-up study of survivors in Cleveland found them to have established three goals as priorities—job security, putting down roots in a community, and identifying with America and its democratic ideals. Two to five years after their arrival over 40 percent were fluent in English. Another long-range study of newcomers who settled in San Francisco concluded that 90 percent of those survivors who had encountered difficulties when they first came had succeeded in overcoming them. But these figures tell only part of the story. We need to examine more carefully the type of work they did after liberation, the families they raised, and how they established themselves in their communities.

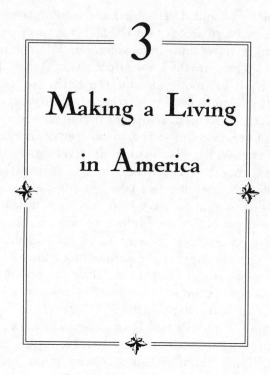

3

Making a Living

in America

Work has always had a special meaning for survivors. During the long years of the war, work became synonymous with survival, especially in the camps. Those who had a trade that their captors needed did best; the unskilled were less fortunate, but even they could usually prolong their existence as long as they were healthy.

The jobs given the inmates varied greatly. Some found employment directly related to their training—electricians, welders, shoemakers, physicians. Others became flexible, fitting into whatever niche was available. Executive secretaries fluent in German became camp typists, while artists were transformed into engravers. Intellectuals fared poorly, not only because their ideas were inimical to those of their masters, but because their skills were useless to the German war machine. Yet even those Jews who were needed knew that their favored position was only temporary. Defined as *untermenschen,* they would be employed only until others could be found to replace them, at which point they would be put to death.

The survivors' encounter with the world of work after the war must be seen against the backdrop of their wartime experiences. In *Working,* Studs Terkel observed that work is "a search . . . for daily meaning as well as daily bread, for recognition as well as cash, for astonishment, rather than torpor." For the survivors, all this, and more, marked their approach to labor. In addition to the normal goals and attitudes that characterize those who work, they greatly appreciated the things that most of us take for granted in this area—payment for work, the right to quit a job, the opportunity to select an occupation, the availability of training programs, fixed hours of work, vacations. In short, for survivors work was a privilege as much as it was a necessity and this often determined what they chose to do as well as how they did it.

1 ✴

Once they had found a place to live, most survivors turned their attention to the challenge of finding suitable employment. Those who had friends or relatives to guide them went to work almost immediately; the others took a bit longer. Some Jewish communities made strenuous efforts in this area while others did little to help. The *B'nai B'rith Messenger* in Los Angeles found it necessary to exhort community members via editorials, one of which stated in part: "Several hundred Jewish émigrés, men and women, the responsibility of the Jewish community of Los Angeles, brought to this community from the DP camps of Europe, are walking the streets daily, looking for work. We cannot and must not let them down." On the other hand, Jews in Pittsburgh quickly established a network to assist their brethren.

The Jewish organizations that had been so helpful in arranging transportation, lodging, and food for the refugees were heavily involved in this area too. For example, the Jewish Agricultural Society (JAS) did much to help survivors who became farmers. Between 1949 and 1953 it lent survivors $1,354,550, almost all of which was eventually repaid, to start and maintain farms. By the end of 1949, it had held at least fourteen thousand individual consultations with approximately six thousand newcomers.

It is difficult to say exactly how many refugees found jobs through the agencies, but the number of cases they handled was quite large. The USNA, the agency most active in this area, reported that 87 percent of those who settled in New York City between 1946 and 1951 applied to them. Of that group, 90 percent, or sixty-one thousand, were referred to the agency's Vocational Services Department. Many of those applying to the organizations were people classified as "hard to place." In 1951, 55 percent of those registered with the New York Association for New Arrivals (NYANA) were in this category.

In many cases, the first job obtained with the agencies' help was merely a stepping-stone to better employment. A common pattern among the newcomers was a series of menial jobs, each one a little better than the previous one, until the immigrant finally succeeded in establishing himself. Consider Willy Herskovits's account of his early days in New York. Although he found work on his own rather than through an organization, the series of jobs he had was typical:

I came in on a Thursday. On Tuesday I went to work. I fixed zippers on pants and got the job through my aunt. I made forty dollars a week. Then my uncle got me a job on Division Street. And this I'll never forget. I met there the boss. And I see he's eating a sandwich—cream cheese and jelly. And I'm thinking to myself—"Only a boss could be so rich." I had never seen this together, with a roll, with everything. And he already gave me sixty dollars a week. It was ladies' coats and men's suits. And then, by Pesach [Passover], I looked for another job. Meanwhile, I had already become educated. I knew where the market was for jobs in suits—on 35th and 37th streets.

Herskovits eventually became an independent entrepreneur in the upholstery business, where he did quite well.

Besides finding jobs for the immigrants, the agencies provided a variety of other services. These included on-the-job training, helping newcomers assess their own abilities, providing start-up tools and equipment for new enterprises, making arrangements for job-related English instruction, vocational rehabilitation for handicapped refugees, and specialized services for musicians, religious functionaries, and other professional groups. One ad in a Jewish publication that appeared in 1950 claimed to have placed religious functionaries such as rabbis, Hebrew teachers, and cantors in more than four hundred communities.

Agency literature prepared for public consumption can, however, only tell us part of the story. To really understand the challenges that faced those who worked in this area, it is necessary to look at the papers delivered by professionals in the field at conferences attended by other professionals. The issues raised in this milieu reflected common concerns shared by all those who served the immigrant population and were presented without regard to what impression their discussions would make on the government, the general public, or the immigrants themselves. For example, at a regional USNA conference held in New York in 1947, the director of the Vocational Adjustment Department, William Karp, made the following remarks:

Reverend L. is a man in his early fifties, married, with a family of six children. He has a long, unruly beard, wears old-fashioned rabbinic garb and is a fanatic chasid. He is also a shochet *[ritual slaughterer] and a* baal tefilah *[cantor, but not for a main service]. His qualifications add up to a minor religious functionary. Planning with him was extremely difficult. Reverend L. rejected several out-of-town referrals, stating categorically that he would rather die than be resettled outside of New York City. Finally, after great effort, the counselor came upon an advertisement in the* Jewish Press *for a minor religious functionary in a city in Pennsylvania. Through investigation of the job, it was discovered that the community contained many Jewish immigrants who came from the town in Poland where Reverend L. lived all of his life prior to his arrival in the United States. After much persuasion, the applicant consented to visit the town for a weekend. After being there one day, the applicant signed an agreement to take the job and indicated he was the happiest person in the world to leave New York and join his own kind. The resettlement was so successful that several of his relatives in New York City have joined him. Reverend L. is typical of the case load of several hundred religious functionaries.*

While the agencies certainly tried hard to satisfy their clients, their biases also emerged as in the words "unruly beard" and "fanatic chasid." Still, it must be remembered that the Orthodox Jews who arrived after the war were, as a rule, far more stringent in their adherence to Jewish law than most of the Orthodox, not to mention general Jewish community members already living here. Thus, for the agencies the initial reaction sometimes amounted to a kind of culture shock. We also see that those who had been respected members of their communities in Europe did not approach the agencies as supplicants. They had demands and priorities and did not hesitate to express them as one might well expect of people who find their status greatly reduced.

Another example of the lengths to which agency officials sometimes went on behalf of applicants was that of a Lithuanian physician, Dr. R., whose university of graduation was completely destroyed during the war. As a result, he had no way of obtaining duplicate medical credentials. The worker and Dr. R. searched the files of Lithuanian medical journals, where some of his articles were discovered. One had been published along with a comment by the Lithuanian Medical Society commending him on his outstanding contribution, while a second piece named him as a member of a specialty board. Looking further, they found a list of graduates from Dr. R.'s university. These materials were used to help the doctor acquire certification in the United States. In addition, the agencies offered refresher courses, loans, and other forms of assistance to all physicians who applied.

Services were by no means limited to professionals. Most skills and trades practiced in Europe differed in certain ways from the way things were done in the United States and necessitated varying degrees of reorientation. A butcher, for instance, needed to become familiar with the American way of dividing meat into steaks, chops, and roasts. The same held true for plumbers, tailors, and electricians. Experts were frequently called in to determine how much and what forms of retraining were necessary in each case. Moreover, those who expressed dissatisfaction with the jobs given them had the option of taking evening courses to advance themselves.

The *landsmanschaften* also tried to help their fellow townspeople, but they did not have the resources to rival the extent or varied forms of the agencies' assistance. Nevertheless they tried, and the help they gave was sometimes the turning point in the successful adaptation of the refugee. Most often, such aid took the form of loans and networking through members to find jobs. One member of the Kurower Society, a manufacturer, personally sponsored ten tailors to work in his factory. Others offered loans anonymously, acts deemed by Jewish tradition to be the highest form of charity. The Dynover Society of Middle Village, Queens, went so far as to sponsor the admission of a Rabbi David Halberstam. They created a position for him as rabbi of the society and promised the USNA that they would find a congregation in New York that he could serve. Each member pledged ten dollars for this purpose.

Not all immigrants were pleased with the efforts made by the organizations on their behalf. One group of handicapped survivors, who felt that the NYANA was not doing enough to help them, responded by forming a group known as the Association of Invalid Survivors of Nazism. Made up of sixty survivors, the group appealed to wealthy Jews to sponsor them. Their stated goal was to set up a co-op for handicraft work. The Jewish Federation, clearly sensitive to such charges of neglect, described them as a "pressure group" that had "threatened to picket the NYANA building with its armless and legless members." The NYANA claimed it wanted to help them but that government rules limited it to providing assistance to individuals only and not to organizations. Another disenchanted group was the Histadrut Rabonim Pleitim, based in Boston, which, along with several other rabbinical groups, complained that the USNA's Religious Functionary Division had not sufficiently helped them. It would, of course, be difficult to substantiate or refute accusations of this sort forty-five years after the fact, but they do indicate that approval for the agencies' work was less than universal.

On a more subtle but broader level, many refugees found it distasteful to depend on the agencies for financial support. The agencies, however, were sometimes reluctant to discontinue such assistance. Simon Nagrodzki recalled how the United Jewish Fund had said to him: "You make a few dollars, put it in the bank in case you need something." After he had found a position that paid him fifty dollars a week, Nagrodzki had responded: "Please, I can live on the fifty dollars and I don't want it [their help], and I hope that next year I'll also be able to give to charity fifty dollars." Ben Geizhals, who survived the Plaszow concentration camp, also expressed his feelings in terms that made it clear that pride was his central concern:

When we came the HIAS wanted to help us. My sisters and I met with the social worker, who said: "We want to support you for about six months, get you clothing and everything." And I said: "But I'd like to get a job while you're doing that." "No," she said, "it's too hard for you now." And this didn't sit well with me. I felt so bad I started to cry. I mean, I cry easily, but I was really upset. I said to her: "Do you want to make welfare cases out of

*us? We don't want to take any money. . . . You know why you
want to do it? Because your future depends on supporting us. All
I want is a job where they speak German or Polish so I can work."
So in a few days they gave me a job as a printer.*

Geizhals's suspicion of the social worker's motives was shared by
other survivors interviewed. In their defense, however, the social
workers may have wanted to be certain that the immigrants were
indeed ready to fend for themselves and were not allowing mere
pride to affect their assumptions. There are discussions in social
work journals regarding the delicate balance that needed to be maintained between the extremes of overdependence and lack of any
assistance whatsoever. What made matters so difficult was that the
survivors had been deprived of their independence not only during
the war, but also in the DP camps, where they had often languished
for years. In many cases, however, this had in no way diminished
their ambition and they were, therefore, eager for an opportunity to
prove themselves.

Agency professionals who worked directly with the refugees
tended to view them as people with a great deal of drive, who took
too much pride in their skills and talents. One agency head observed that "our newcomers of today want to build the America of
tomorrow." On the other hand, it was also noted that a number of
the refugees they saw had emotional problems serious enough to
require treatment. They were especially concerned with young people, but felt that because of their youth the prognosis for them was
more promising than for the older survivors, particularly those who
were unskilled.

Many employers responded negatively at first to what they felt to
be the "aggressiveness and tenaciousness" exhibited by many survivors, but they soon came to appreciate the positive aspect of these
traits—namely, a willingness to work hard. Bill Neufeld, a survivor
living in Milwaukee, agreed with this assessment and related it to
the camp experience: "Some of our people were very aggressive;
they were business-thinking. If a person was in a camp, he had to
be able to read somebody's mind. If I looked at you I knew what
you were thinking." To get a better picture of how the survivors
were thought of as workers, interviews were conducted with a number of individuals who employed survivors. The observations made
by Moses Feuerstein, an owner of Malden Mills, a textiles firm,
were fairly typical. Moses and his brother, Aaron, had made a

commitment in the early 1930s to Rabbi Leo Jung, a prominent American Jewish leader, to employ refugees. As a result, a good number were given jobs, working primarily as laborers and middle-management employees in the company's sweater and fabric divisions. According to Moses:

They were generally good workers who had gone through a lot. As a result they were very serious people. They were easy to deal with if you treated them right. They didn't want to be pampered. They were willing to work hard and they were quite intelligent. When they got a job, they stayed where they were a long time. Maybe this was because they lacked the education.

2✷

Regardless of how they secured employment, through the agencies, sympathetic employers, relatives and friends, or by virtue of their own efforts, the survivors encountered a variety of difficulties and problems at work. Some of them were very common, others rare. Some were related to the fact that they were immigrants and survivors; others constituted difficulties that could have existed for anyone, newcomer or not.

Mostly, the survivors went into business or sales or found work on the blue-collar level. A study published in 1947 noted that out of one thousand survivors, only forty-five were professionals. This contrasts sharply with the occupational profile of German and Austrian Jews who came before World War II and who numbered many professionals among them. Since many of the survivors spent years hiding or in camps during the period in their lives when they would otherwise have been in school, this pattern is not surprising. Moreover, Jews in prewar Austria and Germany had easier access to higher education. Quite a few survivors, however, entered fields that did not conform to this path, among them music, art, teaching, journalism, and politics.

While many survivors raised their level of education after coming to the United States, most did not do so to any appreciable degree. More than half never graduated high school. Of those who did, only about one in five went on to attend college. Of those who went to college, about half earned a degree, with a good number of them continuing on to graduate or professional school. Many survivors voiced regret that the war and the need to earn a living afterward had made the pursuit of higher education impractical. Added to this, of course, were their age upon arrival here and their lack of proficiency in English, which often impeded their job performance and opportunities.

For Czech-born Irene Fishman, this last problem, and the fact that she was a woman, determined her career pattern. Her American uncle laughed when she informed him of her desire to pursue a career in business, telling her that she needed to know the language. "And this was my biggest handicap," said Fishman. "I decided to sell spices, but when I went into a few places they just threw me out. Nobody wanted to buy from me; I didn't know English and I was a woman. Women sold clothing or jewelry, but not spices." Someone advised her to sell to the Yiddish-speaking storeowners in Harlem, which she did. Through hard work and perseverance, she built up her business, learning English at night school and by listening to the radio. Today Irene Fishman heads one of the largest spice companies in America. Located in a 150,000 square foot building in Bayonne, New Jersey, it employs about seventy-five people and has millions of dollars a year in sales. Now past retirement age, Fishman still goes to work every day from her home in Brooklyn's Borough Park. "If I don't do something every day, I'm not happy. Shopping is okay, but only once in a while. I need to work to have satisfaction."

For Ernest Michel, not knowing English constituted an even more serious problem than it did for the average immigrant, for he had resolved to become a journalist in the United States. A German-born Jew who survived Auschwitz and Buchenwald, Michel had been a reporter at the Nuremberg War Crimes Trials. He naively assumed that because of this experience he would have no trouble finding a position on the staff of a large American newspaper. Since his English was only fair, he was turned down everywhere and became discouraged. A turning point for the better came when the UPI chief in Chicago told him: "Michel, if you want to be a newspaperman, learn English. Second, you have to learn about America, what this country is. . . . Find a job in a small town, on a newspaper, because there you might have a chance to learn it." He then recommended Michel to a friend who owned a newspaper in Port Huron, Michigan.

Michel took his advice, was hired, and began writing a column every day, one which was to fascinate Midwestern readers for the year that it ran. Called "My New Home," it described Michel's initial reactions to this country. And, of course, he learned English. He changed professions, becoming a fund-raiser for the United Jewish Appeal (UJA) and eventually rose to the post of executive vice president of UJA/Federation in New York. Even though it had been many years and many jobs since he had worked for *The Port Huron Times Herald,* Michel still takes great pride in this early achievement. Among the many topics covered in his columns were American schools, American slang, the complexities of English, politics, attending a wiener-roast party, and a date with a young lady. Taken together, the columns are an insightful portrait of how an immigrant who was a survivor viewed his new land.

Another serious problem for thousands of newcomers was their health. Starved for years and deprived of the basic necessities such as adequate shelter and clothing, the survivors' physical condition deteriorated, with effects that were frequently long-lasting, or even permanent. In their desire to do well, some accepted jobs that they were physically incapable of handling. They suffered from terrible anxiety about whether they would ever fully recover and how they would be able to regain their lost or atrophied skills. Concerns of this sort often led to confusion, procrastination, and poor judgment in obtaining employment.

Those who attempted to find work in skilled trades learned quickly about unions. Since the survivors usually lacked the connections that those already here possessed, they found it very difficult to enter the unions and serve the apprenticeships that led to better jobs. Those who came into conflict with the unions in those days soon discovered that without their support, life could be very difficult indeed. One new arrival recalled his first encounter:

A man hired me and promised me forty dollars a week. But he only paid me twenty-five. Then I saw a Jewish union organizer who always came into his office. So I went to the main office and I complained to a big man, a Jewish union boss: "What kind of justice is this? This boss puts the money [the extra fifteen dollars] in the organizer's pocket." So this big guy, what did he do? He picked me up by the back of my neck and he threw me out the door! So I wished him dead in Yiddish. And you know something? A year later he died! Because I wished it! Then I worked in sweaters and I joined the union.

Other immigrants faced a different dilemma—circumstances that made it imperative for them to learn new trades and skills. Probably a majority of the survivors changed lines of work after the war. Their willingness to do so in the interests of advancement gave rise to the following joke:

When J.J. registered for a visa to Canada, he called himself a furrier. Two weeks later he received an affidavit from America, certifying that he was a shoemaker. So the question was: "What do you mean, you are a furrier and a shoemaker?" I said: "I used to make shoes from fur."

Willingness was, however, no substitute for experience. Irving Goldstein remembered what it was like when he first learned to milk a cow: "I had more milk in my sleeve than in the pail. My hands swelled up the first couple of days." In a letter to the *Forward*, Paul Levita, a partisan leader whose group operated in the Baranovichi, Russia, area, explained what it was like on his first job in America:

The butcher showed me fifty chickens and told me to clean them. I was sweating because I didn't know what to do, since I had never, in my whole life, held a chicken in my hands. However, I pretended that I knew what to do and I said to myself: "Either I do it and exist or I lose my job." So I began to pluck the chicken. From that first chicken I made ten pieces. I so much tore it apart that one could no longer tell it was a chicken. I was terrified that the boss would fire me. But in this world one can still find good people and, in America, my first boss was a very good man. . . . He taught me how to be a butcher. Thanks to God and thanks to the Jews here, I'm in a good position and I intend shortly to open my own butcher shop.

Judy Rubinstein was not as fortunate as Levita. Settling in Kenosha, Wisconsin, after the war, she traveled four times a week to nearby Racine, where she had a job as a Hebrew teacher that paid fifty dollars a week. Teaching was what she wanted to do, but "the children were terrible. . . . They only went to Hebrew school because their parents wanted them to. . . . When I complained to the parents they said, 'They are all day in school; they have to let off steam.' " After four years, Rubinstein quit in frustration and took a job for seventy-five cents an hour in a dry cleaners. Later she earned more as a nurse, but she never was able to return to her first love—educating and working with young children.

Harry Haft's first love was boxing. He was born in Belchatower, Poland, a little town near Lodz. While a prisoner in various concentration camps, including Birkenau, he fought for his life:

As a youngster in school I was already training to be a boxer. In the camps, however, the fight was to the finish. The loser wound up in the hospital and if he didn't get well after a few days he went out on the next transport to Auschwitz.

After the war, Haft continued boxing and was named European Jewish Champion of the refugees in the DP camps. After arriving in America, he continued his career:

I trained with all the big boys—Cus D'Amato, Whitey Bimstein, and Charlie Goldman, who also trained Marciano. In 1949, I was picked the third-best prospect in the light-heavyweight division; I'd already had nineteen fights. Then I stepped up into the heavyweight division, because of politics, and I lost. I gave up twenty-seven pounds to Marciano and twenty-five to Roland LaStarza.

His fighting career over, Haft, like Rubinstein, was forced to change careers. After drifting from job to job for several years—he worked as a hat blocker and in the wholesale fruit business—he bought a taxicab in New York and drove it until retirement. Despite his pugilistic past, Haft is a gentle man. When asked if he ever speaks about the war to his children, he made a negative gesture with his huge fighter's hands: "No, because I'm very soft. To a stranger I can talk but if I speak to my kids, I'll start crying."

For Abe Foxman's father, the problem was different, but equally exasperating. The Anti-Defamation League head recalled how his father, a respected journalist in Europe, was compelled to take a job cleaning out the garage at Pechter's Bakery headquarters. Later, he ran a chicken farm in Toms River, New Jersey. "My father had it very rough here," said Foxman, himself a survivor. "He wasn't old, but he wasn't young. He was blacklisted here by the Bund, which ran the Yiddish establishment. . . . I was also blacklisted when they found out I was a Betari [the right-wing Zionist-Revisionist organization]." In the end, however, Foxman's father was given a position in his field at the YIVO Institute.

For Isaac Kowalski, the American experience was only partially satisfactory. Kowalski is a war hero. As a partisan in Lithuania, he equipped two secret printing shops, leading the Nazis to post a 100,000 reichsmark reward for his capture. He demonstrated great courage and a penchant for leadership during this period. As we sat and talked in the kitchen in his Brooklyn home, it was clear that nothing that happened in America ever measured up to the excitement of those years. Early in the interview, when it became clear that my focus was on the postwar period, he suddenly declared angrily: "What you want to know about is not important to me. I want to talk about my wartime activities. I could tell you half a book about that."

Kowalski worked for *The Wall Street Journal* and, in later years, the *Daily News,* both of which were good positions but not terribly exciting. Nevertheless, he derives some consolation from the years spent in this country, for he has edited and published several magazines and a massive four-volume encyclopedic work about partisan activities in Europe during the Nazi period.

Some survivors returned to that which had interested them before the war but only after a detour into other types of work. Alexander Petrushka was born into a musical family and music occupied a central place in his life. Even as he and his family were confined to the ghetto during the war, Petrushka continued playing the piano. When asked if there was in the years immediately following the war a reluctance to play because of all the horrors he had gone through, he responded: "On the contrary. It was a feeling of expression, of breathing life. I love music." Nevertheless, he wanted to succeed in America and decided to try his hand at business:

I was told by people that the best business in America is plastics. Of course, I didn't know what plastics was. So three days later I went to work in a plastics factory in Yonkers [New York] on McLean Avenue. Don't ask. I was back in concentration camp all over again. I was cutting cones for ten hours a day for sixty-five cents an hour six days a week—I just didn't believe what was happening—supporting my mother and myself. Then I got a job sorting panties for seventy-five cents an hour and I concluded: "This is not the way." I decided immediately to go to

school. I went to USNA and they were unbelievable. They gave
me a fellowship of twenty-five dollars a week which I repaid years
later, every penny of it, with joy.

Petrushka completed his studies and succeeded in the field of music, but he apparently needed to try his hand at other things before returning to his first love.

Survivors who wished to remain religiously observant were sometimes compelled to change careers in order to do so. Albert Schimel had always wanted to be a musician. He was admitted to the Vienna Conservatory at age eleven and later studied music at Vienna University. When he discovered that American musicians in first-rate orchestras were required to play on the Sabbath, he became a furrier instead. It was not an easy decision. "For me, playing the fiddle is not a hobby," he said. "It's a passion and I must play several hours a day."

Another major employment difficulty for the survivors was something that affected Jews in general—anti-Semitism. James Rapp couldn't find a job as Rappaport, but when he shortened his name he was hired immediately. Some survivors felt that their failure to be hired because they were Sabbath observers masked anti-Jewish bias, but this was difficult to prove. In any event, there was plenty of overt prejudice and most Jews felt its sting one way or another.

Edward Goodman of Minneapolis came to the United States after the war hoping to find work in international trade, his occupation in prewar Czechoslovakia. Wherever he went for interviews—Minnesota Mining, General Mills, Honeywell, Pillsbury—he was warmly received. "Mr. Goodman, it's wonderful. Wonderful experience. We'll hire you." Only no one ever made him a serious offer. Finally, someone in an employment agency told him, "Ed, there isn't a single Jew working in these companies. . . . You'll never get a job there. You might as well forget it." Hungry and unwilling to accept charity, he took a job as a sandwich-maker on the graveyard shift at Hasty Tasty, a fast-food restaurant. His tenure there was very brief:

They asked me if I am a cook. I says yes. In fact, the only thing
I knew how to cook is hot water. But I was making sandwiches
and hamburgers and they promoted me the third night to make
waffles and that was my downfall. [It] was a very busy Friday
night and I forgot to take the waffle out—smoked up the place, lost

their customers. They picked me up and they kicked me out so fast they says I should never come back.

Sometimes, however, it was more a matter of a lack of contact than prejudice. Tom Lewinsohn's wife applied for a teaching position in a Topeka, Kansas, suburb. She returned from the interview visibly upset. Although they offered her the job, the interviewer told her, quite matter-of-factly, that they had never hired a Jewish person in the system. It was, in her view, a very anti-Semitic statement. Nevertheless, she accepted the job and was pleasantly surprised at how warm and friendly people were to her. Her conclusion, after three years at the school, was that it was "primarily a question of ignorance."

Survivors did not necessarily turn the other cheek when confronted with bigotry. Renia Chadajo was quite emphatic when it happened to her:

When I told this woman who works with me "I'm a Jew," she said: "Oh my God! You're not a Jew. How can you be a Jew?" I said: "Listen, you don't have to bother with me if you don't like it. Did I change from yesterday when you just knew I was Polish? If I would be a Polish Catholic instead of a Polish Jew, would I look different to you?" "Oh," she says, "forget it, Renia, forget it." I put everyone in their place. I'm a Jew, but I don't take crap from anybody.

Leon Gross, a survivor of Buchenwald and other camps, took a similar tack with respect to anti-Semitism, but the circumstances were a bit more complex. Gross lives in Tuscaloosa, Alabama. He had come there in 1973 to manage a division of the Jonathan Logan textile corporation:

I once met Bobby Shelton, the grand wizard of the Klan; shook hands with him. My assistant was his sister-in-law. I go fishing with her husband and never, over fifteen years, did I detect any anti-Semitic behavior. But when I first found out who she was, I called her into my office and said: "I happen to be of Jewish belief and I know who your brother-in-law is. If you want to stay on the job, there can be no politics here. There's no room for that kind of nonsense. It's a business." And there never was. I only had trou-

*ble once with someone in this area and I fired him. I had control
over three hundred people.*

Nathan Krieger did not fare as well. Also a survivor of the camps,
he opened up a coat factory in Buchanan, Georgia, in 1981, after a
successful career in the clothing business in New York. Krieger
divided his time between Buchanan and Woodmere, Long Island,
where he lived with his wife and children. One Monday morning he
found a letter in his mail at the factory that said simply: "Jewboy,
go home." This was apparently a response to the policy he had
established of paying employees by piecework rather than an hourly
wage. As a result, salaries had gone up, thus threatening the status
quo in other plants. After numerous threats, he decided to close the
business. His workers opposed the move but, as Krieger told me,
that had little effect on him:

NK: The Ku Klux Klan, which represented the workers, came
to me and said I'm going to get better protection than President
Reagan if I *don't* close down. So I said, "I lived under the gun
already." I was staying at the Holiday Inn and they said they'd
have a twenty-four-hour guard there. So I said: "I'm going to be
afraid to go out?" You know, I used to love nature, to take the car
and go out. If I wanted a kosher meal, I'd have to drive thirty-
five miles to Atlanta and I'd have to come back at night by
myself.
WH: Did you consider staying when they offered you this protection?
NK: No, because my wife got a telephone call in New York.
They said: "If your husband shows his face in Georgia again, I'm
gonna blow his head off."

In general, survivors seemed to have more problems in the Deep
South than in other regions. There was the Atlanta woman who was
told on the phone by a repairman: "I don't work for Jews and
Niggers." Or the Alabama man who encountered hatred from local
schoolchildren. The survivors' accents and unfamiliarity with
American ways made them stand out and they were therefore easier
targets for hostility. Were they also oversensitive because of their
past suffering? Perhaps. Jews and other minorities are often accused of reading too much into what others say and do. Whatever

the case, prejudice and discrimination were a significant part of their acculturation.

3

In what ways did the Holocaust affect how survivors perceived work itself? How did the meaning and sense of purpose they tried to derive from it relate to their past suffering? To begin with, there was what almost amounted to a veneration of labor. As one survivor put it: "Work is a privilege. If you come to another country and you have to shovel shit, plain English, it should be something acceptable to you." Survivors, while they may have regretted the work they were frequently compelled to do, often found it difficult to understand how their own children could say that a particular job was beneath them. For those who equated work with life itself, such attitudes were contemptible.

For many of the newcomers, work took on a therapeutic quality because it gave them little time to think about the past. Building a new life for themselves in America was not only an acceptable goal, it was laudable and required no explanation. Thus, the survivor could rise early in the morning, spend fourteen or sixteen hours a day at work, as many did, and come home too exhausted to think about much of anything. As a way of demonstrating how much they had sacrificed, survivors with whom I spoke often mentioned how few vacations they had taken over the years. Only in unguarded moments did they admit that free time frightened them. Our data, while they do not explain why survivors work, strongly suggest that work was central to their lives. People often stop working because of health problems. The survivors' health was more apt to deteriorate at an earlier point in their life than that of the average American Jew. Yet within the same age group, survivors worked full-time for as long as American Jews did and were no more or less likely to retire than their American counterparts.

Another important issue was independence, both personal and financial. It was basically a matter of controlling one's destiny after having been deprived of all autonomy. There was also a deep feeling in the survivors that, in the final analysis, they could trust only themselves. Even when they entered partnerships, it was usually only with other survivors. Also linked to the need for independence was a profound sense of financial insecurity, the fear that a day might come when money would be needed to save their lives. As a minority without a land of their own, Jews had been perennially vulnerable to attack. Money provided them with a certain degree of security. Even during the Holocaust, Jews had been able on many occasions to save their lives by bribing officials and by paying families in occupied lands to shelter them. It was therefore not surprising that Jews, and in particular the survivors, tended to equate financial security with independence and were willing to work very hard to attain it.

The very structure of life in the camps often led to a strong aversion to being given orders. One woman who lived in Waterbury, Connecticut, found work shortly after her arrival in a garment factory. Although she badly needed the job, she quit after a short while because "the foreman yelled at me and he reminded me of an SS man. He yelled and yelled and I just walked out crying and I did not even go back to get my check." Another man, who became a multimillionaire, asserted: "I didn't want to work for somebody like I'm a slave again. In a factory, with a thousand people working, I felt like I'm a number."

In addition, there was the aggressiveness described earlier by those who employed survivors. This attitude is almost self-explanatory. Those who lived through the camps often attributed it to their strong will to live and their willingness to struggle, a subject to be taken up in the last chapter when the qualities the survivors possessed that enabled them to rebuild their lives in America are discussed. For now, it can be said that such traits characterized at least some survivors and can be traced to the war's effects. But passivity was also observed in survivors, both by employers and by psychologists who have studied them. Some DPs had a sense of being beaten down by life; they approached their work in a resigned manner, and there was a reported dulling of affect, an inability to express emotion.

Finding meaning, let alone gratification, in one's work is important to people in general. Still, for those who lived through the war, a meaningful occupation was not only life-enhancing, it was rejuvenating. For Charlotte Wendel, who spent the war in Shanghai, self-fulfillment came through healing others. A nurse and a medical masseuse, she says: "I love my work and can do it day and night because I feel I do good things for people." Ernest Michel achieved similar gratification in his work for UJA Federation; in his eyes it went far beyond a good salary. "I *love* my job!" he said. "I don't think you could have paid me for the enjoyment that I got out of my forty-two years with Federation." What Wendel and Michel have in common is a feeling of excitement about their work and a zest for life that has not been noticeably dimmed by age or the passage of time.

A large proportion of the survivors started businesses of their own. Most did not become highly successful but quite a few did, and what unites them is involvement with and devotion to Jewish causes. They give generously and participate in the Jewish communities to which they belong. Some survivors, such as Sam Halpern, have been able to combine involvement in Jewish affairs with their work. Halpern, a successful builder, has, together with other survivors, built hotels and factories in Israel. According to him, a venture has to "make business sense," but at the same time he derives deep satisfaction from the fact that his business allows him to employ Israeli citizens.

On the other hand, for Harold Hersh, his business—owning and managing a supermarket—provided him with a unique opportunity to demonstrate a commitment to oppressed people who were not Jewish. Hersh spent several hours recounting his long and close association with Atlanta's black community. He began in a small way with a nondescript mom-and-pop store in the city's black ghetto. It was not easy at first; he was pressured to pay protection money and found it necessary to prove that he was "as tough as the next guy." Eventually, he was able to expand his business. When it became necessary to hire additional employees, Hersh became the first white in the city to hire black cashiers. Moreover, in addition to training them, he sent his employees to a program sponsored by the National Cash Register Company, where they received instruction in the finer points of their work. Hersh became friendly with the civil rights movement leaders in Atlanta, among them the Reverend Martin Luther King, Jr., who was a regular customer, and Stokely Carmichael. Harry Belafonte and Pearl Bailey also shopped there. When riots threatened at the time of King's assassination, instead of closing down out of fear, Hersh stayed open. He knew he would be protected. "In fact," he remembers, "they came to my store to shop because they thought they might not have any food tomorrow if there were riots." Over the years, he helped the black community politically and financially. Hersh takes considerable pride in these activities and they have clearly enriched his life. He traces his empathy for blacks to his own suffering in the ghettos and camps of Europe.

For some survivors, work presented them with an opportunity to perpetuate in a direct way the memory of those who died. Benjamin Hirsch, who came to America at the age of nine, is a man who believes Jews could again be the victims of a Holocaust, even in the United States. One way of minimizing that possibility, in his view, is to perpetuate the memory of what happened. Using his talents as an architect, Hirsch discovered a way of doing that. Holocaust survivors in his city, also Atlanta, had formed an organization, called Hemschech (Continuation), whose main purpose was to build a memorial to the six million Jewish victims of the Holocaust. After seeing an article in the local Jewish newspaper announcing a meeting of the organization, he decided to attend:

I went to the meeting, and afterward I told some of the group's leaders, "Look, you don't know me, but I'm also a survivor and I'm an architect. I want to design a memorial for you. I will not charge a penny." They gave me two weeks to come up with a design. I designed it that night while I was sleeping. It came to me, like in a dream, when I was in a state of semiconsciousness. The next morning I drew it up. I did it because I wanted to do something meaningful. They accepted it.

Hirsch's memorial is internationally acclaimed and has won numerous awards, bringing him both recognition and stature in the community.

Frederick Terna is an artist who was born in Vienna and grew up in Prague. Incarcerated in Theresienstadt, Dachau, and Auschwitz from 1941 until the end of the war, he came to the United States in 1952, having waited seven years for a visa. Today he lives with his wife, a physician, and their young son in a rambling three-story brownstone in the Clinton Hill section of Brooklyn. The Terna home is filled with books on every conceivable subject—art, religion, philosophy, current best-sellers, cookbooks—but it is his paintings, which adorn every room of the house, that immediately catch the eye. His media are acrylic and aggregate, combining colors and shapes with different surfaces.

Terna began drawing in Theresienstadt and never stopped. A good number of his works deal with the Holocaust, and the biblical theme of Abraham's willingness to sacrifice Isaac appears frequently in them. Terna explains its meaning to him:

It is essentially an old theme, that asks: "Why is this happening?" So, in the Middle Ages, Jews used this theme to ask why did so many Jews die in Worms and Troyes during the Crusades. The connection to the Holocaust is that at all times of persecution in the Jewish community the image of the akedah *[sacrifice] was called up, saying, in a way, "You, God, intervened then. Where are you now?"*

There are drawings among Terna's art that evoke thoughts of Auschwitz and the crematoria, but they tend to be subtly presented in a way that allows the viewer to complete the thought.

Other artist-survivors are more direct. Consider, for instance, the following description:

All Valerie's paintings of the KZ [concentration camp] are in grey and black. . . . Figures with swollen heads and stomachs stare emptily at you, standing against a sky dotted with tattoo numbers. There are charcoal drawings of huge-eyed people, split in two; and sculptures: an agonized head split in two; another head, its long neck encircled by barbed wire; an eyeless bust behind a target, pierced by black arrows.

In addition to its cathartic effects, incorporating the Holocaust into one's work becomes a way of remembering and expressing one's innermost feelings, and a way of allowing work to become a framework for life in general.

Isaac Goodfriend's occupation encompasses both art and religion. A cantor in a Conservative synagogue, he was born in Poland and raised in a Hasidic home. Imprisoned in labor camps throughout the war, he is the sole surviving member of his family. Goodfriend is an introspective man and he shared some of the thoughts that occupied him while he was incarcerated:

My friends and I talked about who will be the lucky one to survive. "He'll be placed in a museum," we said. "People won't know anything about Jews in Poland and Russia and they'll come to see what his dress and manner was like. There'll be so few of us left that we'll become museum pieces, antiques." And then we thought about how lucky the birds were who could fly in and out of the camp at will and how it's better to be born a bird than a human being.

Goodfriend was hired as a cantor, in part, because he persuaded the interviewers that his Holocaust experiences would make him more sensitive to the prayers themselves, and indeed, this would appear to be the case. As he explained it: "When I recite the prayers recalling the destruction of the Temple, I have a replay of what happened, not two thousand years ago, but fifty years ago." For someone like Goodfriend, Jewish life assumes a special dimension, for his art allows him to address God with core theological issues relating to what happened to him at the same time as he represents those with questions of their own. Knowing what he went through, others with doubts can derive strength from the knowledge that he has remained a man of faith. All this, and more, goes through Goodfriend's mind whenever he chants the prayers.

Then there are those involved with organizations whose raison d'être is to preserve the memory of the Holocaust. These persons were often capable and talented individuals who treated their work in this area almost as if it were a mission. Sometimes they even gave up lucrative businesses and became salaried employees of such organizations, or, if they could afford to, served as volunteers. Arthur Nunberg, a Bronx resident, actually became involved with the Workmen's Circle even before he acquired American citizenship. He traveled throughout the United States on behalf of the organization on weekends while working as an operator during the week. By the 1960s, he had given up his shop and become a full-time salaried employee of the Circle. He asserts that he could have earned much more money in his shop, but that this was more than compensated for by the meaning derived from his activities, which were to organize survivors all over the country into cohesive social groups.

What about the average survivor whose job was simply a nine-to-five affair—a tailor, candy store owner, or assembly line worker? What deeper meanings could be extracted from this sort of labor? In all likelihood, not much, but it must again be emphasized that for any survivor, work, salary, freedom of movement on the job, and so forth were not taken for granted. In addition, many survivors tended to concentrate in the same occupations. As a result, the work, while perhaps humdrum, gave them an opportunity to be with other survivors and this heightened their sense of group identity, united them, and caused them to interact socially to a greater extent than might otherwise have been the case.

The garment industry and the diamond trade are but two examples of fields that attracted large numbers of survivors. Working in them meant that the survivor continued speaking in Yiddish or whatever European language he had used before. It meant that he maintained social and economic ties with other survivors. In the diamond trade, for instance, Manhattan's 47th Street, between Fifth and Sixth avenues, is the hub of activity. Many survivors belonged to an organization known as the Diamond Dealers Club (its members referred to it simply as "The Kloop"). The workday was usually interrupted by lunch, which was available on the premises. There the members would sit on the red luncheonette-style barstools or at nearby tables and talk. While the conversations generally revolved around business matters, the discussions frequently turned to the war and what had happened, thus reinforcing the feelings of social cohesion. Frequently, awareness of these shared experiences engendered feelings of mutual trust that became the basis of business relationships. In fact, the industry operated for many years on the premise that a handshake accompanied by the words *Mazel ubrocha* (Good luck and blessings) eliminated the necessity of a written contract. Clearly, this could only be done in a situation where people felt they had a great deal in common.

Quite a few of the survivors who entered the diamond trade had been involved in it in Europe prior to the war, most notably in Antwerp, Belgium. In other cases, however, certain forms of work came to be dominated by survivors purely by circumstance. In Atlanta, to take a case in point, many survivors opened up grocery stores simply because other refugees who had preceded them introduced the newcomers to the trade and even assisted them in their efforts to succeed at it. As one survivor noted, "We got to where we got because we helped each other out." In addition, this type of business had numerous advantages for the survivors—low capital investment, little knowledge of English required, and the fact that the entire family could help out.

Irrespective of the original impetus, the net effect of this clustering pattern was to bring the survivors together and, most important, in the larger sense slow down the assimilation process. Patterns of work are therefore a key factor in explaining why survivors still retain such strong ties today as a community. For many refugees, they completely replaced and rendered superfluous the ethnic associations that usually fulfilled the functions of uniting and binding members of a community to one another.

 4

Did the survivors ultimately succeed in their occupations and professions? Success is a difficult concept to measure. How are we to classify, for example, an unhappy millionaire? A homeless man content with his life? Clearly, it is necessary to rely upon standards generally accepted by most members of society. These would include, but not be limited to, financial wealth, promotions in one's job, influence within a community, recognition by others within one's profession, acclaim by the public, pride and satisfaction in one's accomplishments, and the like.

If these form the basis of evaluation, then survivors have, by and large, done quite well. Looking first at the early period, the available evidence points to successful adaptation. By 1953, the USNA could say that, to its knowledge, less than 2 percent of those Jews who had arrived in the United States since 1945 required financial assistance, and, of these, nearly all were either aged, sick, or physically disabled. A study in Cleveland found that while two thirds of the survivors had unskilled jobs upon arrival, that percentage was reduced to one third five years later. They also earned the same amount of money as native Cleveland residents.

The largest number of survivors are clustered in the semiprofessional (business) or managerial categories, followed by the semiskilled, crafts, and sales/clerical categories. There are very few executives or, at the opposite end of the spectrum, unskilled workers among them. American Jews are in the higher-level occupations but not as much as one might expect when considering that they have been here longer. The difference in income, for instance, is not significant. About 41 percent of American Jews earn over fifty thousand dollars a year, as compared to 34 percent among the survivors. On another index of financial well-being, survivors and American Jews are equally likely to own their own homes. Parenthetically, it would seem that survivors invest in real estate whenever possible. Judging from the interviews, the emphasis on home ownership and property appears to be linked to a desire for tangible security.

When one considers that the survivors suffered greatly and came to the United States as immigrants, the figures are truly remarkable. Some will note that immigrant groups often have a strong drive to do well. But this argument fails to take into account that the survivors lacked educational opportunities, and educational attainment is directly related to level of income. Moreover, their privations were often far greater, involving as they did the combined loss of health, wealth, and family. Finally, the survivors' real income may actually be considerably higher than the figures themselves suggest. This is because survivors, naturally cautious because of what they went through, might well be reluctant to reveal their true income to an interviewer.

Although most of the survivors achieved their success in business, some turned to education as a way of moving up the ladder. Robert Diamant, for example, went to school and became an architect. He worked for a prominent firm in Chicago on projects such as the Gateway Center and the Hartford Building. He was also the principal designer for the John Hancock Building. Similarly, Leon Wells, who wrote an important book about his concentration camp experiences, received a Ph.D. in mechanical engineering from Lehigh University in 1950. He went on to teach at NYU's famed Courant Institute for Mathematics and was a research fellow in the Naval Research Office, where he studied shallow-water theory. Wells then entered the business world, becoming president of a company that did research on what became the forerunner of the VCR. Wells's was a distinguished career, made all the more unusual by his horrible experiences while serving as a *sonderkommando* in the Janowska Road camp in what was then Poland.

When Frank Colb, who now lives in Israel, near Netanya, came to the United States, he first worked as a shipping clerk in a dress factory. Fortunately, a volunteer worker for the NCJW came to the rescue. She read Shakespeare with him and encouraged him to attend college. "I realized that I had no trade, no profession," Colb said. "Unless I would get some education, I would be poor the rest of my life." And so Colb, who had survived numerous camps, not to mention a death march from southern Europe to Hungary, graduated from college and eventually became both a CPA and an attorney.

Although Diamant, Wells, and Colb all did well in an economic sense, one does not get the impression that this was ever their primary objective. Respect as a professional and the chance to do

meaningful work were equally important. Cantor Matus Radzivilover was similarly unconcerned about money. He had a beautiful
voice and was engaged by a large and wealthy congregation in New
York almost immediately upon his arrival in the States. However,
he explained, "I never expected . . . great financial achievements;
this was not my main purpose in life. All I was interested in was
spiritual freedom." Success for Radzivilover, therefore, was assured
as soon as he was permitted to lead his congregation in prayer and
song.

How can the apparent success of the survivors be explained?
Would not the terrible hardships the survivors had undergone have
sapped much of their energy and ambitiousness? Certainly cultural
predispositions to succeed as well as ethnic unity and economic
opportunities made it possible for the newcomers to rise. Nevertheless, it was the personality traits they shared that were most
often the deciding factors. The key factors, it seems, were hard
work and determination, skill or intelligence, good fortune, and a
willingness to take risks. Added to this were special circumstances
and certain principles that seemed to work well for some survivors.
In the majority of cases, it was not one factor, but several taken
together that led to the survivors doing as well as they did.

Sam Brach is a survivor who has done very well in America. He
owns a private home in Queens, New York, and is an influential
leader in his community. Born in the Romanian town of Som Cuta-
mari, he was the third oldest of ten children and the only one in his
entire immediate family to survive the war. His parents, Satmarer
Hasidim, were successful businesspeople and leaders in religious
and community affairs. Among other things, they transmitted religious values of faith and practice that continue to play a central
role in his life today.

When asked what it was like when he first arrived in the United
States, Sam responded:

*As soon as I came here I went to work. No one helped me. So I
took the first job I could get, as a butcher's helper for seventy-five
cents an hour. I also cleaned toilets for three months. But eventually I learned to be a butcher. I spoke Italian perfectly [he had
spent some time in Italy after the war] and I asked the butcher,
Luigi, for a job. And he taught me. I'd never done it before. I
didn't even know how to hold a knife, how to sharpen it. He came
to like and trust me. The driver wanted me to steal and I told*

*him, "I don't steal." I worked hard and was not lazy. That's how
I came to be a butcher. I never collected unemployment.*

This idea of working hard, not taking charity, and, of course,
saving, is deeply embedded in the psyche of the survivors. It is a
natural consequence for people whose lives have been marked by
abandonment and extreme deprivation and who constantly fear its
possible recurrence. Almost as though it were an attempt to regain
control over their lives, the survivors invoke the principle that only
by dint of one's own efforts can a person succeed. Sam Silbiger,
who immigrated from Poland after the war, described how a survivor who owned a grocery would live above the store to save money
and would even come downstairs at midnight to make a profit of five
cents. Helen Gilmer, born in Lithuania, reminisced about the time
she walked fifty blocks with her young daughter to save forty cents.
Such individuals were unperturbed about the negative stereotype of
the Jew as someone overly concerned with money. Why did she do
it? "To save, because my husband always had the goal to go into
business."

Sam Brach explained why opening up a business was so important to the survivor:

*I always had the drive, and I guess it's present in every survivor,
or the need to be secure. This is because unfortunately during the
war, in the camps, I had no one to turn to for help. I had no
brother, no father, no family. This creates in a person a tremendous fear, so much so that I can't even explain it to you. There's
a tremendous pressure that makes it very important that you
shouldn't have to come to a person and ask them to help you. To
achieve that, I got up at two or three in the morning and worked
until ten or eleven at night. And I didn't feel that I had to go out
and eat in restaurants; I'm not such a fancy person. I didn't have
to go to hotels. The first sixteen or seventeen years we were here
I didn't even take a vacation for one day.*

Eventually, Brach opened up his own butcher shop in Kew Gardens Hills. He prospered and gradually bought up much of the
property surrounding the store, as well as other real estate.

What separated him from other butchers was, in part, his ability
to sense an opportunity and take advantage of it. He and his wife
had noticed how the large supermarkets had self-service meat de-

partments where steaks, chops, and chicken cutlets were all pre-packaged. This contrasted with the typical kosher butcher shop, a small operation where customers stood on a sawdust-covered floor while the butcher went into "the box" and brought out chickens with the feet still on them and sides of fat-covered beef. So Brach decided to modernize and sold his kosher meat prepackaged. There were the usual nay-sayers who told him, "Our people are not used to this. They want to see it outside the package." But the Brachs persisted, the customers became used to the idea, and, after a while, they even preferred it. Today, almost all kosher butcher shops are self-service.

Clearly Brach was a very hardworking man, but was it Brach's foresight that led to his success, or was it simply luck? He arrived in Kew Gardens Hills just before the neighborhood took off and became home to thousands of Orthodox Jews. How could he know in advance? When asked about the role luck played in his life, Brach was emphatic in his response:

> *I didn't come here out of choice; I came here because it was my destiny. Everything is* bashert *[preordained]; you have to do yours and God will help you. I cry to God and I ask Him to listen to me because He has to listen to me. Because I went through the fire and came out alive. And what was the purpose of saving me?*

What some attributed to mere chance, Brach attributed to God. In either case, it is something beyond an individual's control, and survivors repeatedly cited this to explain what happened to them both during and after the war. Herman Lewinter, for example, worked as a photographer at the Concord Hotel in the Catskills. In the summer, he owned and operated a bungalow colony. By pure coincidence, a major highway was built that ran right through Lewinter's property, thus providing him with an unexpected bonanza. Everyone talks about luck, and many people swear by it, but for those who survived the war and whose lives were often saved for no apparent reason, luck is a phenomenon of great significance.

Joseph Bukiet is a builder. He builds one- and two-family houses, office buildings, and shopping centers. Born and raised in Proszowicz, Poland, not far from Cracow, he is a survivor of Auschwitz, Birkenau, and Buchenwald, and the manner in which he survived was characteristic of the way he conducted his life afterward. Although he credited luck with having helped him make it through those years, it is clear that Bukiet made his own luck and that determination played a major role in what happened to him:

When I came to Birkenau I said: This is a war and I'm going to survive it. It's that simple. The ones who did not say it, died. They went to the wires [the electrically charged wire that surrounded the camp]. When I was sent from Birkenau to the coal mines in Jawiszowice, I survived because I organized. One of my jobs was to collect dirty laundry and I saw that the kapos wrote down and stamped the number of shirts they got. Then they gave me the same number of clean shirts and underwear. So I went to a Pole who worked in the coal mines and said to him: "If you give me a red pencil, I will give you a beautiful shirt." He gave it to me, saying: "And if you don't bring me one, I will kill you." So I carried in 230 shirts, but with my red pencil I changed the number to 280 and received in return an extra 50 clean shirts. I hid these shirts in a hole and used them when necessary. From that day on, my father, my friend Jacob Banach, and I, lived better. For shirts we got a piece of bread, a piece of salami, a cup of soup. Because of this we survived. To survive took cunning, shrewdness, and luck.

We see here that Bukiet cited a combination of factors—determination to live, risk-taking, shrewdness in obtaining the shirts, and the good fortune not to be apprehended. What it came down to was being in a position to take advantage of opportunities and actually doing so. What is interesting is how the pattern repeated itself in America as Bukiet used cunning and determination to prevail in the business world. He and his brother, Al, bought a grocery store in Far Rockaway, Queens. When shortly afterward two survivors acquired a competing store down the block, he went over to wish them good luck, suggesting at the same time that both stores should close on the High Holy Days. They agreed but did not keep their word. "When I found out that they were going to open on the holiday of Rosh Hashanah, I went to see them and said: 'I thought we had a deal.' 'Look mister, you mind your own business and we'll mind ours,' they told me." Furious, he resolved to get even immediately:

I grabbed the truck and ran down to Atlantic Avenue and had forty big signs made up that said things like: "5 Pounds Sugar, 19 cents"; "A Pack of Cigarettes, One Cent"; "One Dozen Eggs, 12 Cents"; "Pound of Butter, 16 Cents"—ridiculously low prices. Then, at night, I put these signs up in my store so everyone could see them the next day and compare them with the other guys who were staying open. Only I kept the store closed. After the holiday, I came in at 4:00 A.M. and took down all the signs and put up the old ones. The first Irishman walks in and says: "I will tell you something. I said to my wife: Never trust a man who's not religious. I admire you because you're religious; you closed the store. Those bastards, those newcomers, those Jews, they didn't close, but they're a bunch of robbers. You should have seen the prices they charged. I saw your prices yesterday. Never again will I go to those thieves! Because you were closed, they charged three times as much for everything."

Jack Werber is yet another immigrant who began with nothing and did very well. Again there is the combination of hard work, business acumen, a willingness to risk capital and luck. The account, while intrinsically interesting, has a familiar ring:

I took my own place on Avenue C [in Manhattan] making trimmings on collars. I borrowed one thousand dollars and my partner put in one thousand. Then we sold earmuffs. I worked twenty-five hours a day. I never saw the children awake. Then came Davy Crockett and we started with the coonskin caps. They came with trucks and they were selling like hot potatoes. We couldn't make them fast enough.

Werber, also known in the business as "The Davy Crockett King," was fortunate in latching on to a tremendous fad, but he also proved to be a talented innovator: "When we ran out of fur, I took plastic tops, made a picture of Davy Crockett, and printed it in gold." When a shortage of raccoons developed, he used raccoon coats that had been lying around in an old warehouse since the 1920s. Eventually, these were used up, and the company, which was producing twenty thousand coonskin caps a week, used rabbits and made the tails from rabbit skins.

Not everything went his way. As happens with all fads, the Davy Crockett one ended abruptly and Werber found himself stuck with thousands of caps. Still, he had made a healthy profit, enough to enter other businesses. Today, as president of a successful real estate firm, Werber can look back upon his early experiences as an entrepreneur, both successes and failures, with pleasure, because he knows how things turned out.

As was true of most newcomers, those who succeeded often had many jobs in different lines of work before they finally found their niche, but there were exceptions to this rule. William Ungar, a Polish-born survivor, worked for a firm that built machinery for manufacturing envelopes when he first came to the United States. After several years he went into business for himself. Today he is one of America's largest producers of envelopes. The company, with plants throughout the nation, has an output of many millions of envelopes each day. Another individual purchased real estate with whatever savings he was able to bring from across the ocean. Within a few years he had parlayed it into a rather substantial fortune and he remained in that field until his retirement.

Noach Rodzinek came here from Poland with nothing. After an initial period of working as a rug cutter, he opened up a luncheonette in Manhattan. He admits to having been afraid to leave the luncheonette because it meant security. Nevertheless, after thirteen years of serving hamburgers and selling candy and soda, friends persuaded him to join them in the home-building industry. After many difficulties, Rodzinek succeeded, at one time owning 160 homes. In part he attributed his achievements to one guiding principle: "You must keep your word. If you say you're going to pay, then you have to pay. That's why the bank lent us a million dollars." For Nathan Krieger, who also did well in business, demonstrating trust in others was the key to becoming successful. "Once you put trust in people, they wouldn't have the heart to steal," he averred.

Other survivors benefited financially from the very fact that they were survivors. It was their adroit use of these relationships that was responsible for the profits they earned. Leon Lepold, a survivor who settled in Milwaukee, went into the insurance industry, taking a job with Mutual of Omaha. He was a super salesman, especially to other survivors in the city: "There's not a *grine* family in Milwaukee that didn't buy from me." Another man took cash from survivors who owned small shops and invested it in real estate properties. He put up no money himself but received a full share because he managed the properties. Those who invested with him did so, in some measure, because he came from the same town as they did and this gave them confidence.

Special circumstances were sometimes responsible for the career patterns followed by survivors—a family business, a move to a certain city, or a particular, limiting injury. The story of Major General Sidney Shachnow, though highly unusual, is an excellent example of how this could occur. When interviewed, the general was the commanding officer of the American troops stationed in Berlin. A Holocaust survivor who was incarcerated in a Lithuanian concentration camp as a child during the war, he was formerly a commander of the Green Berets in Vietnam, where he served two tours of duty. Shachnow was awarded a Purple Heart, the Distinguished Cross, and many other decorations. Asked how he came to decide on a career in the armed forces, he responded:

When I first came to Salem, Massachusetts, there were not that many immigrants there and the Jewish community took great pride in us, and embraced us. There were some families that wanted to finance my way through college. But when the issue came up that I would marry someone not Jewish—we had met in high school—it just didn't sit well with some of them. My parents were also very upset about it. And I must admit there was no great joy on Arlene's side of the family either, which was Catholic. And for a young person who just finished high school, there weren't too many options. So one day I saw a big sign as I walked by the post office: "Join the Tenth Mountain Division. They're shipping out to Germany." And I thought this is about as far away as I can get from Salem and I thought maybe some of those forces and influences would diminish and I'd be able to put my life together. I looked upon it as a kind of temporary relief, but once I got in there, I kind of liked it.

Most survivors seem to have done well and some, as we have seen, rose to great heights. But there were also survivors who fared poorly and the reasons for that are instructive. One factor seems to have been excessive caution, a reluctance to take chances, with a good number of respondents explaining that this had always been part of their nature. "I was never a big shot and I'm not now," said one survivor. Another man did not invest in a stock whose price rose dramatically because his wife, also a survivor, was opposed to it. He clearly blamed himself for having listened to her importunings.

Many of the farms started by the survivors failed after several years. Mostly this was due to the low, ruinous egg prices that prevailed during the mid-1950s, but there were also other causes that had more to do with individual failings. One of these was a tendency toward an extravagant lifestyle, one of several possible reactions to extended deprivation. As one person familiar with the New Jersey farming communities observed: "A lot of the survivors who did well got too cocky. They weren't happy just making a living. This guy wanted a new car, that guy wanted a new mink and furniture." When the economy began affecting the farms' viability, these farmers were unable to scale down their way of living and sank deeper and deeper into debt until they went bankrupt.

Survivors are, of course, not the only ones who fail to do well. People of all backgrounds can and do have financial difficulties. But for the survivors, the experience was perhaps all the more heartbreaking because of their prior hardships. Zalman and Frieda Jakubowicz owned a farm in Parksville, New York, a village high up in the Catskills. Frieda recalled with bitterness how they "stood and slaved in the heat" to clean out the chicken coops, which were filled with manure:

My two daughters were three years old and a few months old then. I had no money to buy regular milk then, so I bought Carnation Milk; we bought old bread. Our life was very difficult and no one helped us. We bought two thousand chickens, but they were not very good chickens because we couldn't afford better ones. One day, the top floor caved in on our chickens. And then the water dried up and we had to get water from a spring on a hill.

Although conditions improved after a while, the operation was never successful. Frieda said she "felt like a hundred years old" on the farm, and Zalman, who frequently rose at 4:00 A.M. to drive to New York City, where he sold eggs, interjected at one point that working a farm was "an eight-day-a-week job." The Jakubowiczes clearly worked very hard, but they were plagued by bad luck. In addition to a downturn in the market for eggs, their equipment broke down, and then Frieda's husband took ill. In the end, they were forced to leave the farm. Sitting in their small apartment in the town of Liberty, New York, all that seemed left were memories and pictures of the children. Near the end of the interview, Frieda stared out the window at the frame house across the street, her thoughts seemingly elsewhere. Suddenly, she turned and said: "You know, when I first came to America I felt like I had left Egypt and was free. Little did I know that I would become a slave again in another Egypt."

The survivors were clearly a hardworking group. Their economic success in America stands on its own merits. Still, it is important to consider that for people who suffered through the camps, simply being able to get up and go to work in the morning would already have been a significant accomplishment. That they did well in their chosen professions and occupations is even more remarkable. The values of perseverance and ambitiousness and the optimism that typified so many survivors were clearly ingrained in them before the war began. What is interesting is how much they remained part of their worldview even after it ended.

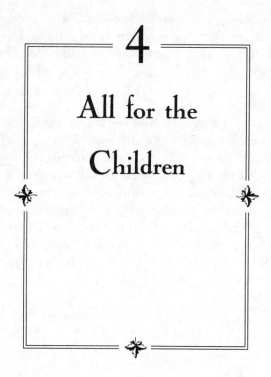

4

All for the

Children

What makes Jews remarkable is not that they believe in God after Auschwitz, but that they have children after Auschwitz. That they affirm life and the future.

RABBI SHLOMO RISKIN

OF ALL THE ACTIVITIES ENGAGED IN by the survivors after the war, nothing required a commitment as great as that of marrying and having children. Work, as we have seen, could be a source of great pleasure and, for some survivors, it was all-encompassing. Belonging to clubs and societies could also occupy one's time. But marriage and children demanded that one genuinely give of oneself to others. They generally involved mutual caring, trust, and love. No doubt, camp inmates, as well as those who hid, met people who possessed these qualities. Sometimes these individuals even saved their lives. But the fact is that betrayal, suspicion, and hatred were far more common traits among those whom the survivors encountered. As the literature on the Holocaust makes amply clear, attacks on the Jews by the Nazis were supported by broad segments of the local population in most of the countries they occupied.

Yet despite seeing neighbors and friends whom they knew for decades turn on them, despite the fact that many in the camps acted selfishly, the survivors were able for the most part to establish and maintain relationships after the war that were based on empathy and concern for others. True, the degree of success they achieved in these areas varied, but this is true of people in general. The horrors they witnessed and experienced often left deep scars, but beneath the scars the capacity to give, to take pleasure in the joy of others, to derive happiness from watching loved ones grow refused to die. As the survivors struggled to come to terms with their past, that past frequently influenced how they related to their loved ones, especially how they raised their children and what they expected of them. Their efforts profoundly influenced the character of the generation that followed them, though here too there was tremendous variation from one person to the next. Understanding the dynamics of family relationships as they occurred within the survivor community can tell us a great deal about how human beings recover, or do not recover, from catastrophic events.

1 ✵

In 1989, about 83 percent of the survivors were married, compared to 62 percent of American Jews in the same, older age group. American Jews were more likely to be divorced or widowed than survivors and they were also more apt to have never married. The high percentage of married survivors forty-five years after the war, most of them to the same partner, clearly indicates that marriage was the dominant trend among the survivors. For younger survivors who married for the first time, doing so was simply part of life. Those a bit older, who had lost spouses, however, faced a different dilemma: to remember those who had perished while at the same time building a future for themselves. It seems that in the overwhelming majority of cases they elected to remarry.

Most survivors, about 80 percent, married other survivors. In many cases, they were "pragmatic marriages," unions based on a sober assessment that living together was mutually beneficial. Some survivors reported that they were afraid to be alone. Said one: "I married him because he had a room, a bed and a blanket." Despite the fact that many of these relationships were entered into rather hastily, they tended to last many years. Some researchers have noted that many of the survivors clung for long periods to unsatisfactory marriages, achieving love only through their children. However, these assessments are based primarily on evaluations of those who came into contact with therapists because they had psychological problems. The interviews done for this project suggest that survivor marriages ran the gamut, with relationships that ranged from excellent to terrible. Although evaluating the quality of the relationship for the average survivor is difficult, it appears that the majority were at least as stable as those in the general population, if not more so.

While Orthodox Jews are, by definition, more insular and less assimilated than other Jews, those belonging to that community were no more likely to have married other survivors than were Conservative, Reform, or unaffiliated Jews. Apparently, being a survivor was the overriding basis for feeling a bond with the other person. In fact, there were several reasons for the high proportion of survivors who married each other. Quite a few survivors wanted to marry as soon as possible after the war ended. Since they were then living in DP camps, the chances were strong that they would meet and marry other survivors. Even those who were single when they arrived in the United States stood a better chance of linking up with a survivor because those were the social circles they traveled in, especially at the beginning. The language barrier made them uncomfortable with other Americans and there was the issue of social status. Being labeled a *griner* by others and treated accordingly often drove the survivors literally into each other's arms.

In addition, the survivors were often, because of shared wartime experiences and a common cultural background, simply more comfortable with each other. As one survivor noted: "We don't have to do a whole lot, or talk a lot; just as long as we are here together." For some the relationship went back even further. Morris Fixler, a Czech survivor who lives in Detroit, stated: "I don't know how I could relate to a wife who *wasn't* a survivor. She's not only a survivor. We know each other's stories from childhood." Still others expressed the view that their survivor spouses could more easily empathize with their nightmares and general fears.

Some survivors married Jewish refugees, that is, persons who came to the United States from Europe before World War II. This was the case with Sandy Mayer. Reflecting on the implications of this difference, she observed:

Well, I looked at Ralph as a survivor, but he didn't because he was very young in 1939, when his family came here. That was something I liked very much about Ralph—he has a greater sense of security. I don't think he has the same sense of impending doom that I experienced when I was living with my parents after the war. And so it just felt more normal living with Ralph.

Fred Terna, the artist who was in several camps during the war, was originally married to a survivor. After she died, he remarried, this time to a child of survivors whom he had met at a survivors' Holocaust rally in 1982. The age difference, twenty-three years, did not seem to have mattered, but the cultural gap might have. His new wife, Rebecca, came from a Hasidic family, whereas he had been raised in an assimilated home in Central Europe. He reacted strongly after attending a reunion of classmates from his wife's Orthodox high school class: "It was like going on an anthropological expedition. I don't run into this kind of a group often enough." Even though he was actually married to a child of survivors, Terna's description points up the difficulties of generalizing about survivors who marry survivors. Other factors, such as country of origin, education, religiosity, socioeconomic status, age, and personality traits must also be taken into account.

Conversations with those whose spouses were American-born demonstrate how having a survivor as a mate was not always viewed as an advantage by other survivors. Several people expressed a desire to avoid reminders of the past. Some, such as Ben Hirsch, denied that this was ever a consideration, simply seeing it as a poor justification by itself for entering into a relationship. Hirsch, who eventually married an American-born woman, recalled:

There was one girl, she was a survivor, and she actually proposed to me on a date. She said that we need each other, that we have something in common. I appreciated what she was saying but I told her: "That's not enough. That's not enough." I mean, it kind of felt almost a little sick to me that we should cling to each other because of our past.

For Judy Traub, there were several factors. She wanted someone "with a normal background," but she also perceived marriage to an American as a step up on the status ladder. She had felt ashamed of being a survivor, "a *grine*," at first, and felt that marriage to an

American was "more sensible, more secure, less problematic." Today she lives in Great Neck, Long Island, with her husband, a dentist. Paradoxically, she now takes great pride in being a survivor. An article of hers on the subject appeared in *The New York Times*. Referring to certain American Jews who snubbed her as a newcomer, she asserted: "I personally feel that my particular family was much more cultured and educated than many of the people that considered themselves superior."

Few survivors married outside the faith, but there were some instances of it, primarily among those who lived in cities with small Jewish communities. Gilbert Metz, for example, who lives in Jackson, Mississippi, married a woman whose family has been in America for several hundred years. "I'm a DAR [Daughter of the American Revolution]," his wife said, laughing. "My grandmother goes back to John Quincy Adams, and on my grandfather's side they go back to Robert E. Lee." Metz's wife converted to Judaism after they were married. She had agreed to raise the children as Jews because she felt this would be best. They have been married for thirty-three years and her Christian background does not seem to have ever been a problem. Alexander Petrushka is another survivor whose wife is not Jewish. It is his second marriage and he describes her as a person who is full of "compassion and understanding." Difficult as it may be for many survivors to have their faith in humanity restored after their experiences, learning to trust someone who is not Jewish would seem to be an even greater challenge.

In the final analysis, however, there are no simple answers as to what type of marriage works best in terms of the survivors' wartime travails. The case of Barbara Davis best exemplifies this, for she was first married to a native-born American Jew and, subsequently, to a survivor. Unfortunately, both unions ended in divorce. Barbara, a former inmate of Auschwitz whose parents died in the war, arrived in America at the age of seventeen, together with her brothers. Shortly thereafter she met and married a young man. Things did not work out for them, however, and the relationship soon turned sour. Her brothers strongly opposed her desire to obtain a divorce, saying, "A Davis doesn't get divorced." And so, because of family pride and obstinacy, she suffered for sixteen years before finally leaving him. "He used to humiliate me. He called me greenie," she recalled. "He and his friends were American."

Soon after her divorce, she met and fell in love with a Jewish professor at a first-rate university. He was Polish and she was Czechoslovakian, but both shared the common bond of having survived the Holocaust. The pain in her voice was palpable as she talked about what happened:

He was an intellectual and I thought I had finally found happiness. Then he hired a young woman from Germany, a graduate student, to be his assistant. She needed a job. And then, after a while, I saw that he was always coming home late. And pretty soon it became clear to me that he was having an affair with her. One time I got so mad that I wanted to go over in the middle of the night and paint swastikas on the door of the place where they were. She wrecked five marriages here before she left.

Barbara soon divorced him too and today she lives alone, her two children grown. In her fifties, she holds a senior position in a large business firm and seems to have recovered, at least on the surface, from her hardships. Still, she is struck by the irony of what happened to her. In fact, Barbara sought me out rather than the other way around because she felt her experience was unique. "Isn't it amazing that first I lost my family to the Germans, in Auschwitz, and then I lost my husband to the Germans, in America?" she mused. "I mean, have you ever heard a story like that?" I confessed I had not and asked her how she saw life today. "I'm looking forward to meeting someone again," she said.

In some instances not being a survivor becomes one of several disadvantages. This was so with an Orthodox survivor who believed that her husband's not having gone through the war was a major problem, and who also felt that his Sephardic background was almost as great a drawback. She was attracted to him because he was a rabbinical scholar, but the fact that he had not gone through the trauma experienced by European Jewry seemed to have made him insensitive to such matters. Even worse, in her view, were the cultural differences: "He had very different ideas about what a wife should do. He didn't want me to go to school, or work, or drive, or talk on the telephone." After fifteen very difficult years, their marriage broke up. "Mentally, it was worse than Auschwitz," she concluded. The woman eventually earned a Ph.D. and is today a successful researcher. She is also happily remarried, this time to a man who clearly respects her intellectual achievements.

Beyond the anecdotal information on divorce, studies by several researchers establish quite clearly that the survivors have a very low divorce rate. One study found the rate to be about 4 percent, another pegged it at 8 percent. Our own results emerged with a number of interesting findings regarding divorce among survivors.

About 11 percent of survivors are divorced, compared to 18 percent for American-raised Jews. Both figures are considerably lower than for U.S. Jews as a whole, but this is not surprising since only people forty-eight years old or older were interviewed, and younger people are more likely to divorce today. On the one hand, it would appear that the turmoil in the Holocaust survivors' lives did not translate into a high divorce rate. On the other hand, they might have been more willing to suffer through bad marriages because of their conservative old-world values.

Do survivor-survivor marriages work out better? Perhaps so, since survivors who married Americans are about twice as likely to divorce as are those who married survivors. Possibly survivors' unions last longer because the couple can better understand each other's problems. It might also mean, however, that those survivors who linked up with Americans were, or became, more Americanized and were therefore more willing to consider divorce as a solution to marital strife.

Of interest too is the fact that the divorce rate among survivor-American couples is the same as the divorce rate among American Jewish couples. Among survivor-American couples, 19 percent were divorced, while among American couples, the rate was 18 percent, almost the same. Thus, having one spouse who is a survivor does not lower the general divorce rate for survivors, but when both are survivors, it does, the divorce rate being only 9 percent.

Finally, divorced survivors were no more or less likely to have seen a psychologist or social worker than those survivors who are not divorced. For American Jews, however, the divorced were more than twice as likely to have seen a professional than those who weren't divorced. This suggests that survivors were much less likely to accept professionals as people to turn to when divorce occurred than were Americans. It also suggests that when survivors did see someone professionally, it was usually because of problems unrelated to marital difficulties.

2 ✳

One of the most striking characteristics of the survivors was the degree to which they were concerned about the welfare of their children. This has long been viewed as a central feature of the Jewish community in general, but it is even more typical of the survivors. However, the average survivor's decision to *have* children was often preceded by a series of contradictory and ambivalent feelings. On the one hand, they were afraid to have children because of apprehension that their offspring might suffer the same fate that befell the survivors themselves. Quite a few admitted having given their children Gentile first names for this reason. Some were even doubtful that they could feel love for children again. On the other hand, they often had a need to replace those who were lost, a need that was frequently accompanied by a belief that having children proved that Hitler's grand design ultimately failed. These two lines of thinking were articulated by many survivors, but they are perhaps best expressed in Elie Wiesel's book *The Fifth Son,* where, in an imaginary dialogue with his son, a father says:

> *Your mother and I told ourselves that not to give life was to hand over yet another victory to the enemy. Why permit him to be the only one to multiply and bear fruit? Abel died a bachelor, Cain did not: it falls to us to correct this injustice. But we did not take into consideration your desires, your judgments, your impulses: and what if one day you tell us, you tell* me; *"You were wrong to take me into this game you seem to be playing with fate and history! Haven't you learned* anything? *Don't you, didn't you know, that this earth and this society are inhospitable toward Jewish children? Didn't you know that the game was rigged? We had no chance of winning! The enemy is too powerful and we are not enough. One thousand children are helpless against one armed assassin! And so, for you, it was a matter of starting over in the purest sense, wasn't it? Well then, couldn't you start over* without me?"

And yet the survivors did decide, by and large, to renew their faith in humanity by bringing into the world a new generation. Moreover, they loved their children as only people who have been reprieved from death can. Together with David Diamond, Wiesel wrote a cantata called "A Song for Hope" that celebrated the survivors' belief in the future. In an essay that appeared in *The New York Times*, Wiesel admitted that he did not know why the survivors felt this way: "I must confess, that of all the mysteries that characterize the Jewish people, its capacity for hope is the one that strikes me most forcibly. How can we think of the past without foundering in the abyss? How can we recall the victims of fire and sword without drowning in our tears?" But the survivors refused to give in to despair. The same capacity for struggle that helped them get through the war may have been responsible for their actions afterward. We see this strength, as well as the effort to put things within a broader perspective, in the words of Paula Gris, who lived through the inferno as a child:

I have five children to replace the Jewish losses. I have five children to fill the world with hope and with the possibilities that were snuffed out with all those other hundreds of thousands of children who never reached adulthood. I have five children because I remember loneliness.

The sense of regeneration that the survivors felt was not always part of their conscious thinking, but it emerged both clearly and forcefully when listening to how they connected events in their lives. There was a definite sense of history that formed a tableau in which what happened to them in the past was tied in to the present. For Samuel Harris the connection was made while he was on a family vacation at a Wisconsin farm resort:

I had my wife and two children with me. I looked out of the window and saw a big barn. I stared at it, meditated for a while, and asked my family to join me for a walk into this barn. The air was misty, drizzly, and very quiet. As we stepped in, I asked my family to climb all the way to the top of the stairs. Once we reached the top I asked them to sit close to me. We covered ourselves with straw entirely. I put my arms around them. We sat quietly in this position for a long while. Raindrops were beating on the roof. In those quiet, peaceful, and precious moments, flashes raced across my mind of another time when I was hiding in a barn covered with straw but it was not so peaceful then. . . . I suddenly heard shooting in Demblin [Poland]. I was seven. We ran down a farm road. I never turned back to see who was doing the shooting. . . . My sisters pushed me through an opening into a barn where we dug ourselves deeply into the straw. The Germans' voices commanded: "Jude heraus!" ["Jew out!"] Then they left. When we came back, we saw piles of dead people. They were all our neighbors.

Philip Bernstein, the U.S. Army Advisor on Jewish Affairs in Europe after the war, reported that the DP camps had the highest birth rate then of any Jewish community in the world. In Zielsheim alone, he noted in a January 1948 article, a new baby was born every day.

The survivors did, in fact, have more children than American Jews. This was due, to a considerable extent, to the presence of more Orthodox Jews among the survivor group; but even when this is taken into consideration, there was still a trend toward larger families. Moreover, Orthodox survivors tended to have bigger families than did Orthodox American Jews. Interestingly, survivors married to American Jews are no more or less likely to have large families than those married to survivors.

A tendency toward overprotectiveness and emphasis on the importance of education typified most survivors in their attitudes toward children. These are of course stereotypes of Jewish parents in general, but like many stereotypes they contain a kernel of truth. They appeared in somewhat exaggerated form among survivor families and were clearly related in most instances to the parents' wartime ordeals. As one mother now living in Los Angeles recalled: "I was always home when they needed me. If they came home at 3:00, I always made it my business to be home. I never went on vacations without them. We cared about them because we had lost everything." Many survivors felt that having been deprived of educational opportunities themselves they would do their best to provide their children with them. Added to this was the traditional respect that Jews as a group have always had for learning. As Dora Neselrot, a Polish-born survivor of the Maidanek concentration camp, put it: "My daughter asked me for a dress. She said all the other kids have nice dresses. I said to her: 'If you ask me for a book, I'll buy it for you because that stays in your brain, but a dress you could rip tomorrow.' "

The majority of the survivors, however, did emphasize material possessions as tangible expressions of love. Barbara Fischman Mevorach, a child of survivors raised in Brooklyn's Borough Park section, vividly remembered her mother's attitude in this regard:

She used to buy me the nicest clothes in Bunnyland [an expensive local shop]. But I didn't want them because no one else in my class had such dresses. It was too much and it embarrassed me. I recall how it was torture for me to go to that store.

Many other children told similar stories of doting parents who said things like "For my darling, nothing is too expensive. I want her to have everything I didn't have."

Given the strong Jewish backgrounds of many survivors, plus the efforts to obliterate their culture during the war, it was not surprising that education often included Jewish education. One survivor summed it up as follows:

For me to have a child when I lost 200 people in my own family is a greater responsibility than is usual. To bring him up and give him not financial wealth but a knowledge of Judaism and the Holocaust. To know what his parents went through and to know why he does not have grandparents when every other child has a grandmother and grandfather coming to graduation.

The importance of this is borne out by the number of survivors who provided their offspring with such education. Even allowing for the existence of a higher number of Orthodox Jews among them, survivors were more than twice as likely as American Jews to have sent their children to Jewish day schools. At the same time, if their children attended public or secular private schools, then survivors' children were no more or less likely than their American counterparts to have attended Sunday or afternoon Hebrew schools. In other words, when it came to Jewish education, once the survivor decided not to send his child to day school, he was no different in his behavior than the average American Jew.

If Holocaust survivors were more protective of their children than other parents, it was not something they were embarrassed about. One study asked survivors to respond to the following statement: "We are often overprotective of our children and seem to attach an exaggerated value and preciousness to them." Two thirds of those responding agreed and only 9 percent disagreed. The in-depth interviews confirmed this attitude and also provided information as to how children were affected by it. Some made a point of not acting disruptively but tried, instead, to please their parents. Some children had difficulty as adults in separating from their parents. In fact, parents had trouble, it seems, viewing the children as adults, and the children had guilt feelings about standing up to their parents and being independent. At the same time there was also an opposite trend, wherein quite a few children of survivors rebelled against what they perceived as their parents' excessive worrying about them by openly opposing them in a variety of ways. Some deliberately put themselves in dangerous situations in a manner that suggested they were trying to prove something to their parents, themselves, or both. Others challenged their parents' values by engaging in conduct directly opposed to those values.

One subject that highlighted this problem was Israel. Holocaust survivors identify very strongly with Israel; they visit there frequently and give generously to causes associated with it. Naturally they want their children to feel similarly, but at the same time they fear exposing their children to danger of any sort and that can include visiting or living in Israel. The paradox is obvious since several hundred thousand survivors and their children reside in Israel, but American Jewish survivors are, in fact, part of the larger U.S. Jewish community, which is generally apprehensive about visiting Israel. The ambivalence on this topic emerged in a number of interviews. Said one woman who lived through Auschwitz and whose daughter had never been to Israel: "Every time she was ready to go, something was always going on there and, as a mother, I was worried. I said: 'Don't go this time. Go next time, all right?' " Today, this woman deeply regrets her efforts in this direction because the daughter married out of the faith. She believes that trips to Israel would have strengthened her Jewish identity and concludes sadly: "Now, when it's too late, I see it was no good."

Other parents, however, put aside their fears and concentrated instead on the positive aspects. Nathan Krieger, for example, was confronted one June day, on the eve of the 1967 Arab-Israeli War, by his son's desire to go there as a volunteer. Krieger, an ardent Zionist, had given his children a strong Jewish background and he felt that to deny his son now would be hypocritical. On the other hand, Abe was his first and only son. Moreover, he was but seventeen years old at the time. After much agonizing, Krieger gave his permission: "Because of his age I had to sign papers for him. I had lost my whole family in the war, but I was a Zionist and in the end I let him go. It was a tough decision." Another parent responded more stoically to his son's decision to volunteer during that time but probably felt just as deeply. The young man, age twenty-one, did not ask for permission but, instead, simply announced his intentions to his parents one evening. They said nothing. A few days later, when he had almost finished packing, the son turned to his father and asked him, in an almost offhand fashion, how he, the father, felt about the son's imminent departure to what was clearly a real danger zone. "I'm not happy that you're going," the father responded, "but I am happy that you *want* to go."

A number of parents lamented the lack of discipline in American families. They blamed it in part on the emphasis on youth that seemed to be part of the culture. As one survivor observed: "Most of them [American children] are spoiled. Everything is done for them and not much expected from them." Perhaps so, but these accusations were often made by immigrant parents in general, and for a very simple reason: the parents lost status in the new country. They were unfamiliar with its ways and customs and often seemed helpless in the eyes of their children, who wished to perceive their parents as people who could protect and care for them. Moreover, with their accents and sometimes odd dress, they stood out and embarrassed their children, who were striving to be "real Americans." Finally, the economic difficulties of the survivors and the unskilled labor that they were often compelled to do, especially when they first arrived, combined to breed a lack of respect for parents who simply could not live up to the expectations of their offspring. In their disappointment and frustration, many children, especially adolescents, lashed out at parents, who, in turn, accused them of being "fresh" and "disrespectful."

The arena of conflict was the clash between generations, but within that framework its focus varied. Sometimes it involved differences over religion, at other times it was their children's choice of friends or job preferences. Whatever the case, the conflict added to the burden of being a survivor. Parents were painfully aware that they lacked the finesse of their American counterparts. This insecurity frequently rose to the surface when they spoke of their children. For one survivor who owned a fabric shop, education was the bone of contention:

> I was talking with my son about investments and he said to me: "How do you know so much? You know all these things and you don't even know how to read English. . . ." Maybe I'm not so

*educated but I know what is going on and I'm interested. The
children think that because I never went to college I don't know
anything. I said to them: "I never went to school here. Can you
imagine how much I'd know if I went through two grades here?"*

Survivors, as a group, are very sensitive about being viewed as
lesser individuals because of a lack of education. They love their
children and are proud of their educational achievements, but at the
same time they want their children to respect them despite their
own failure to achieve a similar level of formal training.

Other children did not feel this way. They understood how the
war had negatively affected their parents' opportunities for higher
learning. Moreover, many of the survivors grew up in religiously
observant communities where education almost always meant Talmudic study in a rabbinical academy for males and in a women's
religious seminary for females, not a B.A. or Ph.D. One child of
such a father observed: "The fact that he was missing a secular
education didn't bother me. He had studied Talmud for many
years. Besides, he wasn't simply 'intelligent'—he had the wisdom of
life."

One of the most difficult issues for the survivors was that of
discussing the Holocaust with their sons and daughters. The majority dealt with it at some point in their children's lives, but usually
only after many years had elapsed. Some, however, were unable to
broach the topic at all. In the early years after the war, the shock
and drama of liberation, combined with the plight of the survivors,
kept the story in the forefront of the news. But then, beginning
perhaps in the mid-1950s, a "curtain of silence" descended on the
subject, allowing people to put what had occurred out of their
minds. The world, so to speak, needed to forget, much as America
needed to forget about Vietnam in the immediate aftermath of that
war. Moreover, the survivors' defense mechanisms enabled them to
repress their own memories. Since their children were not learning
much about the Holocaust in school during those years and were
also not viewing TV programs devoted to the topic, they did not ask
many questions. These circumstances gave the survivors little reason to dwell upon the suffering they wished to put behind them. It
was only when in the 1960s general awareness of the Holocaust
increased that certain issues came to the fore, thus forcing the
survivors to confront and deal with them.

The emotional price of speaking out, even within the family, was sometimes quite high. As one man reflected: "Once I started to talk, the subject of my family came up and I got very depressed and then I couldn't talk about it . . . because sometimes I sat and wondered, 'Did I abandon them, or did they abandon me?' " This individual was the only child out of ten to make it through the conflagration. Another person was fearful of where such a discussion with his child might lead. As opposed to many survivors who feel guilty about what they could have done during the war, he focused on the period after the war's end:

And I said, well, he's going to ask you what happened to the rest of the family sooner or later, and you'll have to tell him that they were killed by the SS, and then he's going to ask you what you did about it after the war; did you do anything to try to track down the murderers of your family? And you will be naked in front of him, because the answer to the question: "What did you do?" is: "I made money."

If it was not their own embarrassment, then it was concern for the children's welfare that made many survivors hesitate to discuss their experiences. "I didn't want to scare her," said one. "I didn't want the Holocaust to take over the children's lives," said a second. "They should live like everyone else in this country does." Others simply did not feel strong enough to talk about their ordeal, at least at first. Regina Altman recalled:

The first few years after I came to the U.S. I was very scared. My dreams were that I was constantly being chased by the Nazis, and I always saw my parents and my sisters being taken away and led to the gas chambers. . . . But, after a while, we started. . . . The children questioned us. . . . We finally had to tell them.

And in some instances the children themselves were unwilling to listen to the stories of those terrible years. Several parents wondered aloud, as we spoke, why their children had never asked much about what had happened. In a few families the reactions varied from one sibling to the next, with one child very curious, almost obsessively so, and another not interested in the least. One respondent, Irena Urdang DeTour, explained why she didn't tell her children much about the Holocaust. "They didn't want to hear. My younger daughter was simply terrified of her graphic imagination. I tried to convince my children to belong to some of these groups that discuss it, like Second Generation, but they didn't want to."

For some survivors talking about the Holocaust, especially after so many years of silence, unleashed a torrent of words and thoughts that found release in public speaking and writing. In addition to discussing it with their loved ones, they volunteered to speak in schools and in synagogues. Others recorded their stories on tape and donated the tapes to Holocaust libraries. These were the survivors for whom speaking about the camps and ghettos was a form of therapy. But it was not simply a matter of releasing pent-up emotions; it was a belief that only by telling the story could a repetition of these horrors be avoided.

Even if they were reluctant to speak out, most survivors wanted their children to know about what happened. They encouraged them to read books and see films on the topic. Several felt that their children had a particular obligation to do so and were deeply disappointed if the second generation failed to show much interest. One survivor felt that a local group of children of survivors ought to do more than simply get together and talk about their uniqueness and the psychological effects of having parents who were survivors. Rather, he felt, they should tape the stories of the survivors. When they declined to do so, he accused them of "dropping the ball. They have a charge to remember and they know it." Other parents took a different approach to the whole topic. Take, for example, Vera Stern, wife of Isaac Stern. Her daughter and son-in-law are both Reform rabbis. She is proud of their Jewish identity and involvement. Her two sons are conductors and are "passionate" in their feelings about music. She noted:

They are much more involved with German musicians than we are, but the younger generation is different and I don't impose my values upon them. I'm not going to make myself into a Nuremberg trial prosecutor. I wouldn't own a Mercedes; instead, I drive a Saab.

Do survivors differ from Jewish parents in general in the expectations they have of their children? As a group, they apparently feel more intensely about the importance of their offspring doing well in life. This usually stems from the need to replace losses suffered during the war. In particular, they are concerned that they attend elite schools. Persons interviewed took great pride in the "Harvard lawyers" and "Yale doctors" they produced.

For the Orthodox, there was the additional emphasis on remaining true to the faith of the forefathers. Joseph Glikman, a Hasidic Jew living in Borough Park, was not enthusiastic when his son decided to pursue a secular career. "I come from a distinguished rabbinical family," he said. The problem was solved when the son became involved with activities sponsored by the "Bostoner Rebbe," a Hasidic leader who has attracted a following among Harvard University students. Today the son is a fully observant Jew and a successful attorney. "Thank God he's religious, which is for me the most important thing," concludes the father. "He lives in Kew Gardens Hills and, while he's not Hasidic, he's religious." Another man, an Orthodox rabbi, was not as fortunate. His daughter completed her studies for an MSW, but his satisfaction with that achievement was completely overshadowed by the fact that she left the Orthodox community: "She got a degree in social work and then she wanted to analyze herself and became irreligious. This was the worst thing that happened to me since the war ended. She was my youngest; I figured I'll get *naches* [pleasure], I'll see a future, and, somehow, she became completely out of her mind." He blames her university education for what happened.

Survivors have other expectations or hopes when it comes to the marriage of their children. On a personal level, probably no other subject is as troubling to survivors as that of interfaith marriage. This is so for several reasons. First, marrying out of the faith is seen as breaking with Jewish tradition and history, or even leaving it altogether. Even when the Christian partner converts, there is a feeling that the identity of the children of such a union will at best be tenuous. Then there is the feeling of personal affront. Survivors often view the decision of their children to intermarry as a personal attack, as a deliberate effort to wound and hurt them. In some cases, this assumption is probably correct. Third, a decision of this nature raises a fundamental question for survivors: Is it really possible to trust a Gentile? Isn't anti-Semitism something that has been with Jews since the beginning of time? Given their own experiences, such suspicion and hostility are quite understandable.

For Orthodox survivors, intermarriage raises questions pertaining to religious law, but it is the emotional hurt that comes through most clearly. Said one such man, a Hungarian survivor who attends synagogue every week and whose own children are quite observant:

If my children had married someone not Jewish, I would have felt terrible, unbelievably terrible. This is how people like me, who suffered so much, feel. A woman in this neighborhood, her son went to medical school and married a shikse *[female Gentile]. Then she became pregnant and his mother said: "I hope she loses the baby. I don't want to have grandchildren who are* Goyim." *For me, it wouldn't help even if they converted. I just couldn't accept, as an in-law, a* John *[slang for Gentile].*

For this individual, there can be no compromise on this issue, it would seem. He is, however, someone to whom this has not happened. Many survivors who are actually faced with the prospect of a non-Jewish in-law become more flexible simply out of love for their son or daughter. At the same time, there are those who sever relations completely.

In any event, survivors whose children intermarry frequently feel a strong sense of failure. After the fact, they bemoan not having given them a sufficiently intensive Jewish education, not having attended synagogue often enough, or not having told their children about the Holocaust. Sometimes they present the argument in more general terms:

There was such a tremendous Jewish community in Europe and if we don't continue our Jewishness, and marry into the Jewish faith, and raise our children as Jews, then actually Hitler did succeed. And I said to my children, "This is what I'm trying to get across to you."

Then there are pragmatic considerations. One survivor voiced his concern about the implications for the family as a whole: "It's not only marrying the person. You actually marry their parents and brothers and sisters and your children go there and they see everyone going to church and having a Christmas tree, and they have other relatives too."

It should not, however, be assumed that such sentiments are universal among the survivors. There are those who feel that a person's faith is not as crucial a criterion as the happiness of the couple in their personal relationship. Moreover, for those who are culturally assimilated, Jewishness is not likely to matter nearly so much as socioeconomic background, country of origin, educational background, and other such factors. Guity Nellhaus responded as follows when asked how she would feel about her children marrying out of the faith:

I would feel they should marry the best, the most intelligent. . . . They should fit together intellectually, in friendship, and in respect. Certainly it would please me if the person would happen to be Jewish; it would avoid, no doubt, some problems that might occur, but, as I look around among the younger married couples, both Jewish, I see more divorces than ever.

For Nellhaus it is not an abstract issue, for her daughter was dating a non-Jewish man at the time of the interview and she stated that "I would feel flattered if he were to marry her."

In several interviews with both parents and children it was apparent that the decision to intermarry caused a permanent rupture between them. In one instance, a woman married a Christian after divorcing her first husband, an observant Jew. Her parents were so angry that they refused to attend the wedding even though the daughter arranged to have the affair in her West Coast hometown instead of the Midwestern city where the Gentile husband was raised. Said the mother: "I was so angry at her that even though they had the local Reform rabbi perform the ceremony, we made sure to leave town. We went to Las Vegas for the weekend. I didn't want to be *near* the wedding."

Five years passed since the wedding and still the parents refused to accept their daughter's decision. She had nothing to do with her parents, not even visiting them once during this period. As for the mother, she subsequently cut the daughter out of her will. Nevertheless, by the time I interviewed the parents, their opposition was beginning to soften and they expressed a desire to reconcile. As we ended our interview, the mother, after asking me to turn off the tape recorder, said: "When my daughter did this to me, she cut me so deep, it just can't heal. But still, I know I'm going to have to see her soon. My ulcer will never heal if I don't get to make peace with her."

Tragically, it was not to be. Two months after our interview I learned that the daughter had been killed in an automobile accident. One can only imagine the despair and heartbreak of the parents, irrespective of their feelings about the man their daughter had married. She was, after all, their only child.

Unusual as such instances are, they demonstrate how interfaith marriage can be used by children to avenge themselves against their parents for real or imagined wrongs. Regardless of the fact that there are legitimate reasons for marrying out of the faith, when it happens in survivor families all parties are acutely aware of both the symbolic and real meaning of the decision. As a result, the consequences, in terms of interpersonal relations, are often far-reaching.

Interfaith marriage among children of survivor families happens in a small minority of cases. Survivors were more concerned about intermarriage than were American Jews, by a 76 to 46 percent margin. Among their children, such unions occurred most frequently in families who lived away from the major Jewish population centers and among those whose level of involvement in Jewish life was weak.

3

What about the attitudes and responses of the children themselves? What does being a child of survivors mean to them? How do they relate to their parents? How do they do as adults? What kinds of problems do they exhibit?

For a good number of children, survivor parents were seen in almost contradictory terms. In one sense, they were regarded as all-powerful, indestructible people who had literally made it through hell, notwithstanding the infirmities they suffered as a result. What counted from this perspective is that they made it. And yet, this view of seeming invincibility was often problematic for the child of such parents, for in their ill-fitting clothes, heavy accents, short height, and unfamiliarity with American culture, they appeared frail and weak. "How did these *shleppers* ever make it?" wondered the child of survivors described in the novel *Summer Long-a-Coming.* Were they once strong and self-confident, these *grine?* For a youngster searching for role models, it was all very difficult to fathom.

Among children of survivors there was often a feeling of embarrassment or shame, especially when they were young, about their parents. It revolved chiefly around their physical appearance, language difficulties and accents, and lack of status within society at large. The fedora hat, the baggy suit, the conservative dress in general, the insistence on wearing a jacket, even on warm summer days, all these remain embedded in the consciousness of the survivors' child long after he or she has reached adulthood. The same is true of the accent, which often caused the child to cringe in embarrassment. Oh, how he wished he could have silenced the father or mother in the playground or as they sat in a restaurant. One child of survivors reported having been so ashamed of the Yiddish spoken by her parents that she "obliterated" her own ability to speak it and insisted that her parents speak only English.

These are, however, only the outward trappings. What may have hurt even more was the poverty of the survivors. To be sure, most had enough to eat, but status, as we know, is a relative matter, and the immigrants entered a Jewish community that was rapidly moving up in the United States, one whose socioeconomic level was already higher than that of the average American. Thus, one child painfully remembered his bar mitzvah in the early 1950s: "It was an open-house party, not in a hall. We borrowed three hundred dollars. We gave back the money. My friends? I couldn't invite my friends. I was embarrassed." In this case, the problem was exacerbated because his parents had been upper-middle-class in prewar Europe:

> My parents were elite, quote, unquote. They came from wealthy homes. My father was a playboy; he dabbled in writing for fun, not to make a living. They had a factory in Warsaw. Who was more likely to have survived? The tailors. They had skills, they were rougher, they were ready to risk. So my parents had no friends. In the DP camps my father was an orator, he was this, he was that. He had a world because people had to run the camp. Then he came to America. And who became the millionaires? Who were the "allrightnickers" among the grine? Those who were smuggling in the camps. My father wouldn't smuggle, God forbid! And I felt so embarrassed [that he wasn't able to succeed here].

The son clearly felt cheated in life. He asserted that his father's honesty cost him. He did not regret the father's decision in this area, only its negative consequences. Interestingly enough, this individual became professionally what could only be described as a crusader for justice. Today he speaks openly of his pain. As a child he was unable to do so.

Another man who rose to the top of his profession had a similar experience. When I met David Brandt, he informed me that he had never spoken to anyone about this subject before but that he now felt it was time he do so. We sat in a spacious office whose furnishings exuded success. Assistants addressed him with great deference and phone calls were fielded by three different secretaries. When in the course of our discussion I asked him what his father had done for a living when he came to America, his voice rose an octave or two: "What did he do?" he repeated. "I'll tell you what he did—he was a janitor. Only he never told *us* that. He said he worked in metals." The father had been an engineer in his native Lithuania but had never been able to adjust in his adopted homeland. Brandt described the pain he felt when he learned the truth:

One day after school I went down there and I was going to pick him up. Only he was not in front of the factory and I went inside looking for him and some people told me where he was. He was late, or maybe I was a little early, and I was shocked when I saw him washing that floor and that latrine. And that was the first time I had an inkling of what he did. I tried to move away, but he, he saw me and. . . . We drove home and he cried . . . a terrible day.

Suddenly, without another word, Brandt got up. Tears welled up in his eyes. He walked over to the window overlooking his plant and began sobbing soundlessly. All I could see were his shoulders heaving. After several moments, he returned to his chair and sat down heavily. "I'm sorry," he said, "but it was one of the worst things that ever happened to me."

Some children expressed shame and even hostility at their parents' passivity. These were the children who felt cheated in a different way. What they missed, needed, and wished for was a father and mother with enough energy and youth to be a pal as well as a parent, someone to play catch with, to run races with them, to take them on a roller-coaster ride. For many of the survivors those days were gone forever, destroyed by the vicissitudes of their lives. Try as they might, laughter did not come easily to them; they had been through too much. But all this could not readily be communicated to small children. "I haven't got a father," said one man to his therapist. "The war killed him. He is a weak and frightened man." Another child of survivors expressed his sentiments in stronger terms:

I used to have to beg him to play ball with me. Just to toss a ball *back and forth. He used to just sit there and fall out. He'd sit there like a fixture, staring at nothing. He read the paper—he read the* Forward, *in Yiddish—and then he'd go to sleep. I used to yell at him, "You're not my father!* You never act like a father to me!*" . . . I saw my friends' fathers do things with their sons. They'd go fishing with them. They'd* talk *to them. I felt as if I never had a father at all. I was ashamed of him. He was like a nebbish. He was completely out of it and I felt myself becoming the same way.*

To prevent himself from "becoming the same way," this individual joined the army and served in Vietnam. "I had the sense that finally, in Vietnam, I could prove that I, too, could be a survivor."

This man's response was extreme, but the theme is shared by other children too, who wonder if they could have survived the camps. Some need to prove it, others don't, but it is something that a child of survivors always thinks about. There are also those who dream of revenge, of finding a Nazi and killing him in retribution for their parents' suffering.

As we have already seen, responses vary within families. In *A Generation After,* a film about survivors' children, resentment is expressed by one son in a family at the "guilt trip" transmitted from parents to children, while a second son views his parents with awe and "forgives them for the pain they have caused him." The idea of the "guilt trip" is a common refrain heard among children of survivors. The weight was too much, it would appear, for some:

Sometimes when my parents recalled the past, puzzling for the thousandth time about why they had come out of the camps when so many of their friends had not, they concluded that the reason was to have us children. When my mother told me that, I shut the words out. I did not argue. But I did not want to hear her say anything more. What she said frightened me. It implied expectations I could never meet.

Another child of survivors complained that everything became an issue of "How can you cause me pain?" while a third charged that it was "emotional blackmail—pure and simple. . . . Everything they did, their bad temper, their nerves, their judgments—everything was justifiable because of the war." Still others tuned out completely whenever their parents discussed the war. As one put it: "In spite of all the injunctions to remember, I am inflicted with selective amnesia when it comes to the 'war business.' . . . No matter how many times I hear these facts, I just can't hold on to them." Some children expressed a desire to suffer too, like their parents.

There were also children who felt guilty about hurting their parents, who genuinely empathized with their suffering without the accompanying ambivalence. One, who dated a non-Jewish woman, never allowed himself to be seen in public with her because of the pain he knew it would give his parents. He expressed no resentment about their apprehension, saying, "I can understand how they feel."

Interest in the problems that faced children of Holocaust survivors became widespread in the late 1970s and much of the early reporting on it encouraged stereotyping and generalization. Menachem Rosensaft, an attorney and founding chairman of the International Network of Children of Jewish Holocaust Survivors, was sharply critical of how such children were portrayed: "There was a lot of amateur pop psychology floating around. There were a lot of people talking about 'transmission trauma' and the like. Neither I nor other Holocaust survivor children recognized the portrait being painted of us."

It is important to keep in mind that many of the studies reporting on the conflicts, resentments, and anxieties of the survivors' children are somewhat selective. The samples on which they are based are often small, ranging from fifty subjects down to as few as three. Often the people were selected because they had already exhibited psychological problems. There are, however, thousands of survivors' children who have never been interviewed on this subject who do not appear to have been traumatized to this extent. In fact, it is precisely for this reason that we do not hear about them.

In the course of doing this project I spoke with many children whose relationships with their parents seemed healthy and normal. Some expressed bewilderment about all of the attention devoted to the subject. "Sure, my parents went through the war," said one. "They discussed it with me. But I don't remember having any particular hang-ups about it." In this vein, it should be remembered that survivors themselves often had very different responses to the war. Some could not stop talking about it, while others could not begin. Some felt guilt-ridden about what they had or had not done during the war, and others were proud of their activities in those years. Clearly, their responses affected their children's development and later attitudes.

Another child of survivors felt that singling out survivors' children for special attention was "good business" for therapists. "My sister gets depressed sometimes, but couldn't that have happened even if she wasn't a child of survivors?" he asked. This last point is important, for, in addition to the small sample size of many studies done to date and the fact that they are based on clinical populations, the root causes of problems such as depression, paranoia, and anxiety are extremely difficult to pinpoint. There might be more than one reason for a person's depressive state and it may have come about even if the person was not a child of survivors. Learning whether psychological problems are hereditary is also hard when so many members of a family have been killed. Clearly, some environmental pathology could be related to the survivor's having been an immigrant and to the parent's personality, which was formed, in essence, before the war. Studies must also take into account the age of the parents during the war; who in their families was murdered; the length and type of incarceration; their prewar life; and many other variables. All this should make the researcher wary of drawing sweeping conclusions based on the present state of research, although there is a basis for detecting trends and tendencies.

Many, if not a majority, of the survivors interviewed in-depth described loving and nurturing relationships with their children. William Ungar showed me a letter written to him by his children and their spouses and read aloud at a dinner held in 1987 to raise money for Israel. It read:

Dearest Always Dad:

Uniting with you in Mind and Heart: We feel the tortures of your existence, the fire that seared your soul, the strength of spirit you mustered to rebuild your life. Your children thrive, and their children too because of your great qualities, faith and compassion, perseverance and courage, brilliance and vision. We proudly stand with you as your progeny, pledging to uphold your values, to follow in the path you have so valiantly cleared before you, before us, for our children, for our people.

With Deepest Love,
Your Children

Until extensive studies of children of survivors are done with truly random nonclinical samples, we will never know the answer to the question of whether their problems as a group have been exaggerated. The work of John Sigal, a psychologist, and Morton Weinfeld, a sociologist, is a noteworthy exception to this pattern. They have relied on properly drawn random samples totaling hundreds of respondents and have used control groups in their studies of the children of Holocaust survivors.

Interestingly, their findings support the position that these children exhibit less pathological disturbance as a group than do the children of other immigrants or native-born parents. They found no differences in terms of guilt, hostility, sadness, and passive-aggressive behavior between survivors' children and the control groups. They did discover that children of survivors were somewhat more rigid and were more apt to feel that their parents were strict. On the other hand, these children assert that their parents did not force them to achieve more and did not worry about them more than the parents of the control groups did. There were also no reported differences in the incidence of depression, anxiety, lack of openness, or difficulty in dealing with death. Sigal and Weinfeld conclude that it is not justified to generalize from those who sought help in other reported studies to those who did not. Still, there is no denying the validity of observations made by various researchers regarding children of survivors that are based on actual cases. Obviously, the experiences of survivors have, in many instances, profoundly affected and traumatized a certain number of survivors' children.

While determining pathology is a difficult matter, measuring how survivors' children do occupationally and educationally is easier. They have, in fact, reached high levels of achievement in these areas. We found no difference between the educational and occupational success of children of survivors and children of American Jews, except for a tendency among survivors' children to enter the helping professions. There is, in some circles, a stereotyped image of children of survivors as driven individuals who do very well. While the quantitative results show no differences between them and other Jews, the in-depth interviews strongly suggest that an unusually high number of survivors' children attended elite institutions and achieved high positions in their chosen professions. Frank Colb, for example, had three children. One finished Harvard Law School, a second completed his studies at the University of

Pennsylvania, with a major in physics, while the third graduated *summa cum laude* from Brown. Another, Alfred Lipson, who, like almost all survivors, said that his children were the most important thing to him, had good reason to take pride in their accomplishments. One is a plastic surgeon and the other received his Ph.D. in nuclear physics from Harvard. Tom and Annette Lantos's two daughters are both Yale graduates and one of them earned her degree at the age of eighteen. These cases were not unusual and occurred both among survivors who did well themselves and among those who did not. Nonetheless, the existence of this tendency should not overshadow the fact that many children of survivors were not especially successful in these areas and some in fact did poorly, just as children in general sometimes do.

Did the suffering of the parents result in offspring who were reluctant to identify as Jews or were even self-hating? It would appear not, from the available research. According to Ilana Kuperstein, who wrote an important review essay summarizing studies of adolescent children of survivors:

> *Many experience conflicts regarding their Jewish identity. The fact that their parents were victimized purely on the basis of their race has many different effects on the parent and the child. Whether the adolescents reject Judaism or not, in most cases they have a very strong sense of being Jewish, because of their parents' experiences, and almost regardless of their religious convictions. These adolescents may rebel against religion, yet they usually come back to see themselves as Jews, and those who are not devoted in the religious sense still retain cultural ties to their heritage. Some become supporters of Zionism and of Israel. It is almost as if Hitler's persecution has singled their families out as Jews, and made them forever aware of being Jewish.*

Overall, what emerges here is a portrait of the survivor family that is surprisingly normal when one considers all that the survivors went through. They marry and seem to have relationships that, for the most part, are stable and enduring. They have great love and affection for their children, as well as high expectations of them. The children themselves do well, but are often affected by the fact that their parents are survivors. It may not result in psychological disturbance, but there is definitely an awareness of their heritage in this regard.

There is a club for survivors in Florida, near Miami Beach. Founded by children of survivors, it is called the Emerald Club. The reason, as stated by one child to her mother, is: "To the rest of the world you were *grine,* but to us, you were like precious jewels."

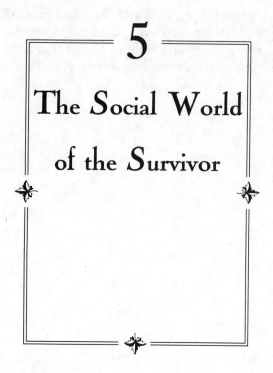

5

The Social World
of the Survivor

A SURVIVOR WAS ONCE ASKED by his small son: "How come you never give a big smile?" "You mean you want me to smile with my teeth?" asked the father. "Yes," the child responded, "with teeth." "Okay," answered the parent and obligingly flashed his teeth, laughing as he did so. Survivors, even today, many years after the war, continue to inhabit a world that is sharply defined and bounded by their experiences. For them, pain, suffering, and fear were what characterized the central events of their lives and the thoughts associated with it can never be banished from their consciousness. They can never let go completely.

Nevertheless, as people who committed themselves to the continuation of life, to a rebirth of sorts, it was imperative that the survivors find a way to counterbalance the horrors of that era, to calm their anxieties, to relieve the sense of desolation they felt when, after their liberation, they discovered the devastation and death that had erased innumerable families and communities from the face of the earth. Because of their common history, there exists, among most of the survivors, a very strong bond, rooted in the events of the past, that ties them to one another in ways that only they can fully appreciate. It surfaces briefly in the knowing glance exchanged by two strangers when they discover that both were in "the camps." It may appear when two survivors look at each other with a shared sense of pain upon hearing an insensitive remark made by an American Jew.

In large part, the survivors seek out one another's company because they feel comfortable among themselves. But there is, over and above that sense of security, a need to find answers to questions that torment them collectively: "Why was this terrible deed done to us?" they ask. "How were we able to survive it?" they wonder, looking at each other and exchanging war stories as if to confirm the fact. It is as if the cumulative rage and fury of twenty centuries of anti-Semitism were unleashed upon them. That they occupied center stage in this upheaval leaves them with a feeling, even as they reminisce, of disbelief. They know it happened, yet they cannot understand how and why they remained alive. That is why they always come back to these questions, over and over.

Despite their feeling of uniqueness in terms of what they had gone through, the survivors had certain needs and desires that typify human beings in general—opportunities for fun and relaxation, the fellowship of others, group affiliations, in short, a social living space in which they could interact with others. Work was important, a necessity for economic survival; family too was basic to their lives; but these were not enough. After their jobs ended, there were free evenings, weekends, summer vacations, and the like. Since the survivors were family-oriented, they expended much energy on their spouses and children, but this apparently did not meet all of their needs. The survivors wanted to be with one another, as a group, and to this end they joined and formed organizations, and also got together informally, simply to enjoy one another's company.

As we shall see shortly, the basis for these friendships was often their common ordeal, and this influenced their choice of friends. Most clung together, but some opted out of that community. Their choice of activities was often mandated by their European background, but there was a broad range of alternatives selected within that framework. They frequently functioned as a separate community within American Jewish life, they perceived themselves as such, and they were seen in this way by outsiders.

1❋

One of the main vehicles for survivors when they sought out one another were the organizations that catered to their needs and that served their interests. Some scholars have argued that such organizations helped refugees acculturate by serving as a bridge between the old world and the new. Others have asserted that they slowed down the process by preventing the newcomers from meeting those outside their community. In truth, the issue is far more complex. Many other considerations impinged upon the survivors, such as their age, socioeconomic background, education, where they settled, marital status, and so on. Their own willingness to adopt new ways also mattered a great deal and this depended on their personalities. The types of organizations they joined made a difference too. Regardless, one thing was clear—these organizations often exerted much influence on the survivors' well-being and the views they had of life in this country.

The most popular organizations were the *landsmanschaften,* the hometown societies that provided, among other things, financial aid, moral support, and fellowship through their many activities. When these societies were first created, usually in the early twentieth century, they became vehicles for the nostalgic reaffirmation of life in the old country. For the survivors, the connection was even more meaningful because these communities had now been totally wiped out. Even if the towns still existed, they were now devoid of any real Jewish life, and the memory of what had once been could only be preserved through the efforts of their former denizens. One member of a society explained: "We don't have graves here in the United States, but all the names are on the monument. And you have to see how when we go over and touch the names on the monument, we feel a connection. We brought over some soil from Auschwitz and put it there." Myra Giberovitch, a social worker who conducted an extensive study of *landsmanschaften* in Montreal, observed that forty years after having settled there many survivors still referred to their European town of birth as their "homes." Often, they had saved voluminous amounts of material pertaining to life in these communities.

Friendship and the preservation of culture were, of course, very important to the refugees, but in the years immediately following the war financial assistance and emotional support were even more crucial. Yitzchak Rybel, executive director of the Bialystoker Society, explained that the society's members sent money, clothing, and food to their European brethren and helped them immigrate to America. Once they arrived in the United States, the society assisted them further, providing medical care, homemakers, loans, and other forms of support. Today the Bialystoker Society remains active, with 1,800 dues-paying members around the world, 1,000 of them in the United States. Many other societies lent assistance to those who came from their hometowns and, coming at a time when the survivors felt abandoned by the world, including American Jewry, such aid was deeply appreciated. In a 1950 letter to the *Forward,* Batya Oplip wrote:

We came here in 1946. We are from Lutsk, Poland. We moved out of a cold-water flat on the Lower East Side after two years and found a good apartment. Thanks to the Lutsker landsleit *[fellow townspeople], we were able to borrow money and open a candy store. We work very long hours, but, thank God, we are able to make a living. My son, sixteen, attends high school and I go to night school. We belong to the Lutsker Society of the Workmen's Circle. We are very happy with our new home.*

The societies were attractive to the refugees, not only because of their hometown affiliation, but also because of the historical tendency of the European arrivals to belong to organizations in general. One survey of survivors found that most of them had belonged to formal organizations prior to the war. And in fact when survivors found themselves in American cities that lacked a hometown society, they invariably set up societies where the common denominator was simply having survived the war. Sometimes former residents of small European communities that had no society in America joined existing societies whose larger towns were located in the same general area as their own villages. Even as they did so, however, the closest ties were with those they had known before the war. One survivor from Minneapolis sketched a loving portrait of how deep these ties went and what they meant to her:

They represent to me my former self. That which my American friends don't know. They only know me as I was here, as a grown up. These people remember me as I was [as] a child. Some of them knew my parents. I am not a nobody to them that suddenly arrived in this country as a refugee. I was not born a refugee. I

was not born an orphan, and I was not born poverty-stricken. I
was a loved child that had a family and parents and belonged.
And these people remember that, and that is very precious to me.
And they represent the remnant of my people and of my culture—
the culture of Polish Jews of which I am immensely proud.

Although the *landsmanschaften* extended a helping hand to the
survivors, their role should not be overly romanticized. Many of the
refugees who joined felt keenly the differences between themselves
and the "old-timers." There was, for example, a view that the
earlier members valued everything American and looked down
upon the *grine* in much the same way as the German Jews perceived
themselves as being above the Eastern Europeans who came to
America after them at the turn of the century. Now, it seemed to
the survivors, these Eastern European Jews were exhibiting the
same behavior toward them. For some, the hostility ran even deeper
because of a belief that many of the societies had not cared enough
about what was happening to their old-country townspeople during
the war. There may have been exceptions, but Hannah Kliger, who
has exhaustively researched the *landsmanschaften,* has written that
they were not "exempt from the inability to recognize the severity
of the situation in Europe. Minute books and meeting protocols of
the time indicate discussions of routine affairs."

Within each society, there were people of varying ages, political
beliefs, and socioeconomic backgrounds, and from different historical periods in terms of when they arrived in the United States. The
last factor was of particular importance because it influenced how
they saw their home community. For example, those who came in
1912 probably remembered their town as a place that, while it was
backward, was characterized by close personal relationships. Those
who came to America after World War II were likely to have seen
the same town as more industrialized and more impersonal. Owing
to the war, they were also apt to recall it as a place where supposedly
good neighbors betrayed them. These differing perceptions often
contributed to a sense that there was little to tie people to one
another beyond the bond rooted in a place of origin. Jack Werber,
the current president of the United Radomer Relief of the United
States and Canada, one of the largest such societies in the United
States, was asked whether he was welcomed by his fellow Radomers
when he first came. His response was revealing:

There were seven Radomer organizations here when we came. There were thirty-five thousand Jews in Radom before the war. Each immigration brought in a new group and each new group couldn't understand the one that came before. Those that were here thought we were less than them because they were here longer. But these people actually didn't know anything. They only knew how to go from their houses on the Lower East Side to work and back. When they saw we were going to Times Square after one week, they said: "Look at the greenhorns. They travel already; they know how to go already." They saw us as upstarts, as being brighter or more intelligent, I don't know what. They didn't really help us either. The relief group gave, maybe, a couple of dollars. But the way we were treated only reinforced our commitment to helping the poor and giving aid to Israel, once we were able to.

Doubtless some societies were more generous than others, but the picture that emerges is one of strong differentiation between the old-timers and the newcomers. The fact that there had been little Jewish immigration from Eastern Europe between 1924 and 1945 widened the gap. Gradually, as the assimilation process continued in the Jewish community at large, the new arrivals replaced the "founding fathers" of these groups and eventually came to control them.

Many of the *landsmanschaften* run by the survivors were characterized by a certain feistiness or combativeness among their members that meeting minutes only hint at. Within them there were disagreements and fights that sometimes reached epic proportions. Often internal politics and personalities were at the center of these conflicts. The subgroups formed among survivors sometimes pitted right- and left-wing Zionists against each other; on other occasions the lines were drawn between intellectuals and working-class types, and sometimes people just disliked each other. To the extent that conflict results in change and improvement in organizations, its existence was a good thing. But the pettiness and bitter animosity that often accompanied their disagreements inflicted considerable pain upon individuals, with damage to people's reputations that could be permanent. Let's look at one such case:

For many years David Nemlitz was an active member of the Beinovich Society. He held important posts within the organization and had numerous friends in it. After twenty-five years, he decided to run for the presidency. Others, however, felt differently. Nemlitz was an intellectual and this did not endear him to certain segments within the society, namely workers or businessmen. Although they belonged to the same organization, the cliques did not socialize. Sometimes they even boycotted events that were supposedly sponsored by the organization. Nemlitz ran for office in the first contested election in over a decade. According to Nemlitz, the incumbent, a wealthy businessman, was infuriated at the idea that anyone would challenge his authority, and together with his supporters vowed to win the election using "whatever means necessary." Here is Nemlitz's account of what happened:

> *Weiss got these three bullies from the garment center; he promised them money and jobs to come down to the election, and they grabbed the ballot boxes and started stuffing them. They brought down twenty or thirty people who weren't even members to vote and nobody could do anything. There was a fight, a fistfight, and we lost. We walked out. I didn't want to get a knife in my stomach. I knew this guy was capable of it. He once hit an old man in the Society, a founder, one of the nicest people, with a broomstick.*

The rough-and-tumble atmosphere of the Beinovich Society was unusual in its intensity but it was not unique. Other societies also had their political infighting, even if it was not as violent. Sadly, the matter did not end with the election. Nemlitz was accused by those he had opposed of having been a *kapo* during the war. Of all the accusations that one survivor can hurl at another, this is probably the most serious. It immediately puts the accused on the defensive and even if the charge is refuted, doubts always linger in people's minds. Nemlitz fought back: "I decided to defend myself against this vicious accusation, against these horrible people who had said to me, like Khrushchev, 'We will bury you.' " His voice trembling with rage, Nemlitz continued:

> *I went to a highly respected man who knew me from Europe. He happened to have worked with me in the stone quarry and I asked him to help me clear my name. He checked with a hundred people and he said: "David Nemlitz was a kapo? What do you mean? He was eighteen then, a kid! There were no kapos there." And I went and got signatures from people who knew me back*

then. I had twenty-seven signatures from Israel alone! I took this document with the signatures and I had it certified by a notary public.

Nemlitz took his accusers to an impartial board. The board had been set up by a Jewish organization to adjudicate disputes between Jews in the community. After hearing the evidence, which included testimony from hometown residents on both sides of the conflict, the board ruled that Nemlitz and the Beinovich Society would, in effect, obtain "a divorce." Moreover, the board threatened to take further action against the society if it persisted in its public accusations and threats against Nemlitz. Subsequent conversations with several members of the society confirm that although they have said nothing publicly, they continue to maintain among themselves that Nemlitz was a *kapo* during the war. As for Nemlitz, his reputation is sullied. It is something that he, his wife, and their three highly successful children will have to live with forever.

Stories of this sort suggest that the long-term ramifications of the Holocaust can make themselves felt in many ways. No one knows how many *kapos* escaped justice after the war, but certainly they do live in America and elsewhere, hoping that their past misdeeds will never catch up with them. Their daily activities, the families they raised, and their involvement in communal life would make a fascinating study. Obviously, it is not likely to ever be written.

In cases where newcomer organizations were founded on the basis of wartime experiences or one's home community, ethnic background frequently played a significant role in who joined and who did not. In cities such as Minneapolis and Pittsburgh, existing immigrant groups made up of German Jews who arrived prior to the war did not encourage the Eastern European postwar arrivals to become members—nor did the newcomers evince any desire to do so. They realized that they had little in common with the more established immigrants. Nor was rejection a one-way street. Ben Hirsch of Atlanta described his efforts as a newly elected president of that city's survivor group to persuade a German-Jewish postwar refugee to join. "It's funny that you want me to join now," said the man. "When I first tried to join, back in 1964, I was told that since I was not Polish, this was not an organization for me." The organization's past presidents stoutly denied this, but Hirsch insists that the story is true because the man's reputation for honesty is well known in the community.

Generally speaking, survivor groups are often either predominantly Polish or Czech-Hungarian. In the smaller communities, however, all Eastern Europeans belong to one organization. It is worth noting in this regard that practically every community in America that has a group of survivors living in it has such an organization. For example, Kansas City, Cleveland, Boston, and Bridgeport, Connecticut, all have such groups, usually with names such as the Newcomers, the Survivors, or the New Americans. Most often, these names have stayed the same throughout the years, but in at least one instance a change was made. Morris Kesselman, a survivor residing in Boston, explained that when he became president of the American Jewish Holocaust Survivors of Greater Boston he called a vote that resulted in the deletion of the word "New" from the organization's name. "I thought it was time to take the word 'New' out after thirty-five years," he said. In New York, which has the largest survivor community, ethnic groups were more apt to form separate associations, with even the Latvians, a relatively small group, creating their own society, a society that, incidentally, attracted fellow Latvians from all over the world.

In some instances, the survivors from a particular place were too few in number or not sufficiently motivated and organized to set up a separate group. This was the case with the Salonika survivors. As a result, survivors like Solomon and Lucy Yehaskel were compelled to join the larger organization of Greek Jews, known as the Jewish Brotherhood of America. This was, of course, similar to the Eastern European *landsmanschaft,* with the only difference being that the survivors who belonged to the Brotherhood were too small a group to influence the direction or activities of the organization. Sometimes a survivors' group was started based solely upon occupation. The furriers in New York's garment center had such an organization, as did the Jewish Poultry Farmers Association in Vineland, New Jersey. In addition to the usual functions of lending money and providing a setting for cultural activities, the farmers' group also set up a court that was comprised of their own peers and that resolved disputes between members.

Survivors who came to the United States as adolescents were too young to join *landsmanschaften* or similar groups. At their age, these organizations, made up almost exclusively of married survivors with families, simply did not appeal to them. Yet even they were organizationally affiliated, largely through youth groups set up for them by the larger Jewish organizations. In Baltimore, to take a case in point, the HIAS worked together with the local YM and YWHA's to sponsor programs. Some of the programming was devoted to films, lectures, and the like. There were also outings, parties, and sightseeing tours. The Y felt that maximum involvement on the part of the refugees was desirable and it tried, whenever possible, to recruit talent from the ranks of the newcomers themselves for its activities.

One of the most popular Jewish organizations among the survivors was B'nai B'rith. In large part this was probably due to the organization's structure. Divided into lodges and with an emphasis on fellowship, it was an American version of the *landsmanschaft,* which gave its members the sense that they were part of a close-knit group of people. Although perhaps most active in Germany, there were before World War II lodges in Romania, Poland, Czechoslovakia, Bulgaria, and other European lands. Even today, B'nai B'rith has lodges in forty-five foreign countries. Commemorating these ties, or origins, the organization held a special reunion in 1982 for European B'nai B'rith members at its national convention.

While the majority of survivors were associated with one or more Jewish groups, there were survivors who had nothing to do with them. These were most often individuals who had assimilated into European society and culture prior to the war. One woman, Irena Urdang DeTour, was actually quite harsh in her criticism of survivors. An antiques dealer, she makes her home in Deep River, a small town in Connecticut, where she is the only Holocaust survivor. She spoke openly and without the slightest hesitation on any topic raised. Of her father, she said: "He was a con artist and that was his occupation. He knew how to repair watches, sometimes, but his idea of making money was to go to the horse races and get dressed to kill, in English-cut jackets. If he lost, he recaptured his money playing poker." On life in general, she observed: "You have to touch at least two thousand lives in order to have any justification for being here." Recalling her early days in America, she complained bitterly about the HIAS's insensitivity to her: "They didn't understand that we were from an old philanthropic and highly educated family." She is scornful of those she feels could not transcend what happened to them, saying: "Most of the survivors are quite boring and provincial and they would never appeal to those belonging to a more heterogeneous society. I myself was raised in Warsaw and, in this country, I was always involved with museums, art galleries, and the literary world."

Andrew Steiner, born in Czechoslovakia in 1908, is a different type of survivor. An architect and city planner, he was responsible for saving the lives of several thousand of his co-religionists. As a Jew, he showed great courage in approaching Nazi leader Dieter Wisliceny and attempting to persuade him to exempt three thousand Jews in Slovakia from deportation, arguing that they would be far more useful to the Third Reich producing furniture and other necessities in Slovakia. After the war, Steiner selected America over Israel because he wanted to resume his professional career rather than live in a land where there were "fighting and wars, shooting and killing."

Steiner joined an architectural firm and specialized in designing university campuses. In his spare time he became involved in various organizations, but they were unrelated to his Jewish origins. He has not attended synagogue services in over twenty-five years and views himself as a totally secular individual. His one passion in life is the future and he belongs to a group whose primary goal is to examine problems that they anticipate will occur in the years to come. In his opinion, the world's three major problems are "race, religion, and nationalism." He wants to find a way of raising people's moral standards without religion. As to the Holocaust, he tells those who ask him: "Stop digging into the past. Look at the future problems that face us, namely getting young Jews and Arabs to stop hating each other. I say young, because the older generation is lost already." He feels alienated from the Jewish community because they seem to show no interest in future-oriented problems. "I was never asked to speak about this by any Jewish organization in Atlanta." As opposed to Irena DeTour, Steiner lives among the survivors. Nevertheless, he is almost completely disengaged from them and their activities.

Orthodox Jews did not, by and large, belong to the *landsmanschaften,* which were often established and controlled by those with a more secular orientation. For them, the synagogue fulfilled a similar purpose. It was a place where they could gather and talk, both during and after services, and a place in which they could engage in political intrigue if they so chose, running for various offices within its organizational structure. Inasmuch as synagogues in general often sponsor trips, lectures, and musical evenings, it provided the survivors with a recreational center as well. Orthodox survivors spoke of their synagogue, or *shtibl,* the name for a smaller, more intimate house of prayer, as a place where they felt totally relaxed. In Willy Herskovits's Brooklyn synagogue: "All the survivors sit in one area. We understand each other better. The rabbi is born in this country so he doesn't always understand things. With my survivor friends I can talk in Yiddish, *mamme loshon* [mother tongue]." In reality, the synagogue represented for the Orthodox a world that was at once both spiritual and temporal. The following description of a small *shul* consisting mostly of refugees on Manhattan's Upper West Side encompasses both of these elements:

> *If one could judge from outward appearances, most of the congregants in the synagogue were unexceptional people. Mr. Rosenbaum was an unskilled laborer in the garment industry. Mr. Pincus owned a small butcher shop, and Mr. Mazer was an order clerk for a Wall Street brokerage firm. But on the Sabbath they were kings. Dressed in their finest clothes, their worn shoes polished to a high gloss, they stood and walked erect. Here in the synagogue they communicated with their Maker, received honors as they were dispensed by the gabbai [an administrative official of the synagogue], talked, sang, argued, and dreamed of a day when all wrongs would be righted, all mistakes forgiven, all misfortunes overcome. A day when they would receive their reward for having shown faith in G-d and for having adhered to the faith of their forefathers.*
>
> *For many of these people, recent immigrants from Hitler's inferno, the* shtetl *still lived. Its way of life continued to influence them as they crowded around the* Kiddush *table after services for a schnapps and some egg* kichel *or herring. They lived in the past despite its recent horrors and turned to the future only for the sake of their children.*

For some survivors, particularly the older ones, the synagogue remained with them even after they discarded other observances. It was a concrete embodiment of the old country that could, at the same time, anchor them in their adopted home. These feelings were clearly what motivated Rachmil Kurlender, an elderly survivor living in Oklahoma City, to be involved:

WH: Are you a religious man?
RK: No. I travel on *Shabbes,* my house is non-kosher, and I eat on Yom Kippur. I have a *mezuzah* on my door only because the

Lubavitcher Hasidim gave it to me for free, but I do go to *shul* every morning.

WH: Why, if you're not religious?

RK: Because that's where Jews are.

2 ✦

The *landsmanschaften* and other organizations provided a framework for many of the activities engaged in by the survivors, especially those of a cultural nature. The refugees had a shared history and culture that they wished to perpetuate, one that was in many ways distinct from that of American Jewry, most of whose members were moving further and further away from their European roots. The following three notices, all of which ran in the February 7, 1950, edition of the *Forward,* were typical of the events that interested them:

> *The New Americans in Syracuse have already organized a society for newcomers. The Farband organized it two months ago. They have 100 members. They gather every Sunday in the Jewish cultural center.*
>
> *The Jewish Camp Organization is preparing to observe the seventh anniversary of the Warsaw Ghetto uprising. They have rented a large hall in New York for this purpose.*
>
> *The Organization of New Arrivals is organizing a literary arts evening in honor of Yonash Turkov in connection with the appearance of his book,* The Struggle for Our Lives, *on Sunday, February 19, at 2:00 P.M. in the Capital Hotel, 51st Street and Eighth Ave. The writer Boruch Chebinsky will speak about the writer and actor Yonash Turkov. The actress Diana Blumenfeld will also appear.*

In essence, the survivors developed a cultural network of their own, replete with plays, lectures, newspapers, and radio programs. In addition to the national Yiddish press, for example, local Yiddish newspapers were published in communities throughout the United States; Yiddish plays were either locally produced or traveled from one city to the next. In New York City, the refugees breathed new life into the Yiddish theater. They constituted the majority of listeners to the Yiddish radio station, WEVD, known as "the station that speaks your language." For Willy Herskovits, the Yiddish paper continues to be essential to this very day:

> *I tell you this. I must read the Jewish paper every week—the* Forward *and the* Algemeiner Journal. *I'll tell you why. It's because I feel at home in these papers. There are stories there I cannot get elsewhere—history that I like and* Chassidishe *[Hasidic] stories that I like. And I can read the Yiddish paper very quickly, while the English paper goes very slowly.*

Though its membership is not what it used to be, the Bialystoker Society still relies on Jewish cultural events to attract members and to raise funds. The names have changed, but the Jewish emphasis has not, with entertainers like Cantor Sol Zim heading the list of offerings. To reinforce the common links, the Bialystoker bought a sixty-family bungalow colony in the Catskills across the road from the Jewish-oriented Pines Hotel. Activities were often scheduled at the same time as Jewish holidays. This provided an opportunity to integrate religion and Jewish history into the lives of even secular members of the community.

Some survivor groups are highly sensitive to their common bond, so much so that they eschew sponsoring parties or balls simply because they feel it would be inappropriate to their image as an organization. This was the position taken, for example, by the Ladies' Auxiliary of the Association of Survivors of Nazi Oppression in Montreal, which substituted lectures on a variety of topics in place of such events. Other survivors have even expressed opposition to dinners held in large hotels to commemorate Holocaust-related events. The average survivor, however, sees the dances, musical shows, and other such events that are held by survivor groups as an opportunity for relaxation and entertainment that he or she would engage in even if it were not offered by these groups.

The survivors' interest in culture was not necessarily limited to Jewish subjects. Many attended plays, concerts, and films of a secular nature, but they did so primarily as individuals. Chris Lerman, who lived in the farming community of Vineland, New Jersey, explained how important such activities were for her and her husband, Miles:

> *Many times we used to finish up on the farm at 5:00 P.M., get a babysitter, go to New York, go to the theater at 8:00 P.M., get out,*

get back into the car, drive to Bordentown, down Route 206. We'd
stop at the diner there, and have breakfast at 2:00 A.M. We came
home, changed into our working clothes, went into the chicken
coops and fed the chickens, and then we'd sleep from 4:00 to 8:00
instead of having to get up at the usual time of 6:00 A.M. We went
to see Porgy and Bess *when it first opened. We went to see* Ma-
dame Butterfly *at the Metropolitan Opera. We went to see* Inherit
the Wind, *with Paul Muni. I went to the Second Avenue Yiddish*
theater once and I promised myself not to go again because I
couldn't stand Menashe Skulnik [the Jewish actor] [she laughs].
We needed to go. We didn't get a television until 1961 or 1962.

What about activities independent of organizations? Can survivors relax in their spare time or must they always keep busy to
crowd out the thoughts that frighten them? What are the things
they enjoy doing? Do they differ markedly from what other people
do? Interviews with survivors unearthed a wide range of leisure
time activities that defy easy classification, both in terms of what
they did when they first arrived on American shores and in the later
years. Of course, survivors spent a great deal of time with their
children, but beyond that there was quite a bit of variation. Andrew
Steiner, for instance, enjoys listening to classical music and has a
collection of thousands of records. Willie Lieberman, a Queens,
New York, tailor, loves freshwater fishing, and Alex Gross, of
Atlanta, is an avid racquetball player, with dozens of league tro-
phies to his name that he keeps in a special room.

On the other hand, certain patterns did emerge. Many survivors
enjoyed reading both fiction and nonfiction. They also read a variety of magazines that included *Time, Newsweek, Reader's Digest,*
as well as the Jewish weekly newspapers and magazines. Few
seemed to have experienced difficulty concentrating or found their
minds wandering to the past. Many read books about the Holocaust
and other Jewish topics, with the Orthodox favoring biblical texts
and commentaries. In most survivor homes I visited there were
large collections of books and these were prominently displayed,
usually in their dens or living rooms. Like 99 percent of the American population, survivors watch TV, but when it comes to Holocaust programs, there is a sharp division between those who
religiously watch everything on the subject and those unable to
stand looking at either documentaries or dramatizations. One survivor, Morris Berkowitz, a furrier living in Brooklyn, stated: "I

don't always watch. What they're showing isn't one percent of what I went through. Even so, I can't stand it, because it tortures me."

Leisure activities are, of course, age related, and when the survivors first came to America they were considerably younger. Thus, Morris Kesselman recalls belonging to a soccer club in Boston. The league to which he belonged was made up of members of other European immigrant groups—Greeks, Italians, Poles, all of whom preferred soccer to American sports. In New York City, there were also numerous locations, usually hotel ballrooms, but sometimes Jewish community centers and temples too, where younger survivors met and "danced the night away." In contrast to the stereotype of the withdrawn and depressed survivor that sometimes predominates in the literature on the subject, these newcomers embraced their newfound freedom with joy. As they repeatedly told me, after the unhappiness of the war they wanted to forget, to start over, "to live again." Many were acutely conscious of how they had lost years of their lives and they therefore regarded each day as precious. The venues for their rendezvous with members of the opposite sex became certain Manhattan cafés and hotels such as the Diplomat and the Broadway Central. Besides enjoyment, these events presented opportunities for learning about the ways of the new land, ways that would allow the survivors to shed the feeling of foreignness that sometimes seemed to weigh so heavily upon them. Sidi Natansohn of Sharon, Massachusetts, remembered it well: "The Diplomat was a place where young Jewish refugee boys and girls tried to become Americanized. They played the samba and the rhumba and the mambo and all the current hit tunes. I never met anyone American there. And we also went to East Broadway, where the Educational Alliance was, where they would have dances too." Nor was New York the only place for such recreation. For example, in Atlanta young survivors began a club that was underwritten by German-Jewish refugees who had come to that city prior to 1939. Besides dancing, there were outings, Ping-Pong tournaments, and barbecues.

In later years there was still dancing, but given the age of the survivors by then, it was more restrained. Survivors went away for vacations to bungalow colonies in the Catskills, where on the weekends there was dancing, mostly waltzes. On one such evening in Sharon Springs, New York, in 1986, couples, most of them survivors, were doing slow dances and their efforts seemed wooden and stilted. But the smiles on their faces and the tenderness with which they held each other as they moved across the large dance floor suggested that this was an activity that they thoroughly enjoyed. Indeed, one elderly woman in a later conversation said, "We always come here, to this hotel, and when I dance with my husband it is as if I am back in Europe, before the war, of course."

Few of the survivors could claim to be well off in the 1950s. They were struggling, trying to carve out a niche for themselves, and their forms of entertainment needed to fit the size of their wallets and pocketbooks. On the West Side, "seeing a Broadway show" typically meant catching a double feature at the Riviera or Riverside theaters on upper Broadway between 96th and 97th streets, followed by "a coffee and a cake" at the Senator Cafeteria, or Bickford's, across the street. Each neighborhood had its "Broadway." In the Bronx, it was Fordham Road, or 170th Street; in Brooklyn, Thirteenth Avenue, Flatbush Avenue, or Pitkin Avenue. An outing with the children on a Saturday or Sunday afternoon might include window shopping, watching a Western at the Loew's Paradise in the Bronx or at Brooklyn's Paramount or Fox theaters, and then hot dogs and french fries at the nearby Zion, Isaac Gellis, or Hebrew National delicatessen. Poor man's entertainment perhaps, but for those who had watched their entire world crumble, it meant everything.

Parks, lakes, and beaches were often important gathering places for the survivor community. Again, it was a cheap form of recreation, a factor that accounts for its popularity among all sorts of immigrant groups. In Brooklyn, there was Prospect Park and in the Bronx the wide expanse of green that ran between Mosholu Parkway East and Mosholu Parkway West, as well as Crotona Park. In Atlanta, there were outings to nearby Calloway Gardens, and in Boston it was the area near the zoo in Franklin Park. While they sat on the benches, or spread their blankets out under the shaded oak, elm, and maple trees, the children played on the monkey bars, or, in the hot summer days, ran underneath the sprinkler systems whose streams of water provided a welcome respite from the heat and humidity. In the Brighton Beach section of Brooklyn, during the summertime survivors gathered every Tuesday evening on the boardwalk and watched the fireworks. There, over kasha and potato knishes, they traded stories about the war and sang Yiddish songs learned in Europe. Even in rural Vineland, picnics in local parks were popular. Louis Goldman fondly remembered those days: "When we had free time, we used to go over to the river in Norma [a small neighboring town], they called it "the Jewish River," and relax. We would speak Yiddish there and the kids would play the jukebox. It was on the Alliance Beach."

For the refugees, the parks were significant in another way too. They reminded them of the happier years before the war. Strolling in parks, as depicted in Isaac Bashevis Singer's portrayal of Warsaw, *The Family Moskat,* was a favorite activity in Europe. The urban sprawl of metropolises like New York, Chicago, and Philadelphia, the very shape of the buildings themselves, was unfamiliar and strange to the newcomers. It was simply not European-looking and made them feel alienated from their environment. The trees, grass, and lakes were far less jarring to the senses. Though the locale might have shifted, the settings themselves were far more conducive to fun and relaxation. Helen Epstein's narrative provides insight into the inner feelings evoked by such places:

My father started the car and pulled away from the crowded street. . . . My brother and I pulled on our jeans in the back seat. In a few minutes we were speeding up the West Side Highway toward the George Washington Bridge and over the Hudson River where there was an open sky.

The space, the absence of enclosure, relaxed my parents like a drug. They began to sing Czech songs, my father first, in a strong, jovial voice, and then my mother. We sang rounds, Czech folksongs, about wild ducks who fell into brooks when they got confused on their flight south, and innkeepers, gardens and old times. My father would recite Czech poetry or intone homilies about the scenery and weather. "Hory, jsou hory," he began to repeat as we left flat ground. "Mountains are mountains."

My brother and I did not have the slightest idea of what these sayings meant, but we warmed to the change in our parents. A sense of well-being pervaded the car; it was like a party, self-contained and happy, flying through the countryside unconstrained. My mother smiled, threw back her head and laughed, even though she often said that she had forgotten how to laugh since the war.

Many of the survivors played dominoes, checkers, chess, and cards in these parks. Poker and bridge were probably the most popular games. As Bella Shampan, a survivor living in Flushing, Queens, explained: "We didn't have opportunities or time to develop hobbies like tennis or golf. We were too busy working day and night." Another survivor, Izzy Raab, pointed out: "We don't have the same interests as Americans. Americans go to a baseball game, they go to a bar, they talk about cars. We're not interested in this." Sometimes, as in Cleveland, where there was a bridge club made up solely of women newcomers, the games were segregated by sex; at other times they were mixed. Whatever the case, since so many survivors seemed to enjoy the game, there may be more to it than the reasons given by Shampan and Raab. Obviously the games, with their breaks for coffee and cake, provided a social setting for the players in which they could chat about business or the war or even, as one person noted, sing songs about the war. But the games might have also had an additional, more subtle function for many survivors. With their emphasis upon winning, chance, courage, bluffing, and simply outsmarting one's opponent, they allowed participants to relive certain key aspects of the war and emerge victorious. This was especially true of poker. Bridge, of course, required far more interaction and cooperation, but, as we know, these traits too were often crucial in terms of surviving the war.

In the 1950s and 1960s survivors flocked to the Catskill Mountains in the summer. Ellenville, Fallsburg, Monticello, Liberty, Woodbourne, Woodridge, and Mountaindale were only a few of the many towns dotting the landscape that became a second home to the newcomers. Originally established by waves of Jewish immigrants, the area's bungalow colonies and hotels appealed to those in search of a relatively inexpensive place to spend the summer or even just a weekend away from the hot city. The names of these colonies—Paradise Acres, Wood Lake, Sunny Hill, Luxor Manor, and Mountainview—conjured up images of peace and quiet, and so they were. Each summer, families would drive up Old Route 17 to the bungalows or *kuchaleyns* (literally: "cook for yourself") they had rented, praying only that they would not get a speeding ticket in Tuxedo or other towns whose local sheriffs seemed to lie in wait for them. Once there, they spent the summer swimming, playing cards, and simply relaxing on the lawn in red or white Adirondack chairs. On the weekends, there were Borscht Belt comedians who came to the casinos of these colonies and told jokes in dialect, followed by over-the-hill singers who specialized in warbling renditions of "Romania, Romania" or "Hava Nagila." Most of the guests had their children with them, but some sent them to camps in the area.

As the survivors grew older, as well as more affluent, the allure of the Catskills decreased. Many retired and moved to Florida, where they also settled in specific areas, such as the Century Villages in the Miami–Boca Raton axis. Survivors still vacation in the Catskills today, dividing their time between "the mountains" in the summertime, and sunny Florida in the winter months, and some even retain their homes in New York City or elsewhere as a base. But they have also branched out, having become more sophisticated and discerning in their tastes, journeying to other parts of the United States, Europe, and even to Africa and Asia.

Although survivors literally travel everywhere, they are distinguished by their solid preference for Israel and by the propensity of at least some of them to return to the places of their youth and birth. Besides the obvious Jewish identification with Israel and its special meaning for those who went through the Holocaust, it is also a place where many survivors have close family, both among those who arrived from Europe prior to World War II and those who came afterward, from 1946 on. Once there, they visit memorial sites and educational centers pertaining to the Holocaust such as Yad Vashem, Beit Hatefutsot and Kibbutz Lochamei Hagetaot, but mostly they travel and visit with relatives in the same way as other American Jewish tourists do.

The return to one's birthplace is often a traumatic experience for the survivor, although for some it has distinctly positive connotations because of certain individuals in these communities who may have saved them from coming to harm during the war. Indeed, there are survivors who regularly send money to Christians in Poland, Hungary, Romania, and other countries out of gratitude to them for their assistance. For most, however, sadness and bitterness are the prevailing emotions. Why then do they go? For some there is a sort of morbid curiosity, the peculiar yet vaguely reassuring feeling that they can walk through their hometown with some semblance of safety, a privilege denied them during those horrible years. For others, there is the additional feeling, more likely a desperate hope, that by returning to their homes again, the place where it all began, they can in some way make their world whole again, even as they know it cannot happen. Judy Traub tried to explain this impulse in the following manner:

I went because I just wanted to convince myself that all these stories and places which I thought about, I truly remembered rather than fabricated. And I was driven to go to all of the ex-

termination places and concentration camps and if I missed out on one I felt as if I hadn't completed my odyssey.

For Judy, as for many other survivors, it was a deeply unsettling experience:

The group my husband and I went with turned out to be all Polish-Americans and Canadian-Americans. And I dislike the Poles! There was only one Jew besides us. When we came to Auschwitz the guide said: "Four million people were murdered here," without even mentioning the Jews. So I asked: "How many Jews?" just to prompt her. So she said: "About 70 percent." And it went on like this throughout the whole trip.

Many others spoke of the hostility and lack of remorse they sensed among the local inhabitants in the towns and villages they visited. Lucy Yehaskel recounted how when they stayed in their native Greece for a brief period, "The Greek at the hotel said: 'Still they come here, these dirty Jews?' I have to hear this word, after the war?" In some instances, there is an aversion not only to visiting their native land but to the entire continent. Moritz Felberman, a Czech survivor of Auschwitz, was unequivocal:

Let me tell you one thing. I go on vacations only to one place on this earth—Israel. I'll go nowhere else for my vacation. I wouldn't enter Europe, not even Switzerland. And when I go to Israel, any plane that stops in any of these countries, I don't take that plane. That's why I go only with El Al. And when I hear that all these Hasidim go to Hungary—to the baths and so on, it eats my insides out.

Sam Brach is an exception. He takes no vacations in the real sense of the word. If he goes away to a hotel for a weekend and takes a dip in the pool, it is only because he has been invited there for a wedding or bar mitzvah. When I inquire as to whether he ever relaxes, he responds: "I wish I could. My mind is always going." As we shall see later, Brach is a man with a mission in life and all his energies are focused on that. Leaning forward in his chair, he jabs a finger at me for emphasis: "Let me ask you this: Do you think if someone would go for a vacation, they would live longer?"

3 ✳

The social world in which the survivors move is highly complex. We have been speaking of the survivors as a group and, in fact, they do represent a distinct subculture. There are, however, many differences among them, both as individuals and in terms of their background. They come from many lands and they identify with a variety of religious, political, and socioeconomic groupings within the Jewish community. When we look more carefully at the survivor community, all sorts of commonalities and distinctions begin to emerge and these often have an impact on how survivors adapt to life in the United States.

Compared to other peoples in America, Jews are a fairly segregated group and survivors are even more so. Based on the interviews and other studies, it would seem that their closest friends are usually other survivors. This often extends beyond their immediate neighborhoods and communities. I found survivors asking me on many occasions whether I knew survivors in other, faraway communities who came from their hometowns or who were in the camps with them. These connections are reinforced when they see each other at national conventions of *landsmanschaften,* through chance, or by deliberate meetings in vacation areas such as Florida or Israel, as well as at weddings, bar mitzvahs, and the like.

The fact that survivors tended to concentrate in certain residential areas when they first came to America strengthened such ties. In her book *New Lives* Dorothy Rabinowitz explained the survivors' decision:

> *The builder of the houses on her street [in Kew Gardens, Queens] was a Polish Jew himself, who had come to America after the war. In addition to the houses in Kew Gardens, he had built in Bayside [Queens] twenty more blocks whose houses were also largely inhabited by Polish Jewish survivors. In part, this had come about because these survivors had reasoned, when they were ready to buy houses, that they were best off dealing with ones like themselves, particularly if there was trouble about repairs or some other problem regarding the house. There still lingered in them, years after 1949 and 1950, when they had arrived, something of the sense they had had then: that the connection between American Jews and themselves was only slightly less remote than the connection between themselves and American Gentiles. . . . In*

buying a house from such a builder, they stood an excellent chance of living next door to, or across the street from, people who had shared their experience, people who could not quite be strangers to them, though they had never laid eyes on them before— neighbors the crucial facts of whose lives they knew before they were even introduced to them.

Naturally, in the early days, as the newcomers were adjusting to life in the United States, they needed one another more. In addition, life in the cities then tended to center far more in the streets, as fewer people owned televisions or automobiles. As a result, the importance of the block and the neighborhood as a social center increased. People as a rule did not even call to say they were coming over—they simply came. As Bill Neufeld, who settled in Milwaukee, put it: "It was European, the way we were raised. Somebody's there? So they walked in and you put down another chair. Today it's very Americanized—call before you come." In reality, many of the refugees were attempting to re-create the type of small village society to which they had been accustomed, and informality was an integral part of that lifestyle. The need to do so was made more urgent because of the abruptness and finality with which it had all ended.

Friendships sometimes developed based on occupation. Earlier arrivals sometimes helped their later compatriots obtain positions in the factories where they worked. Refugees with trades, such as tailors, furriers, printers, assisted one another in gaining entry into unions. Sometimes those involved knew each other from before the war and sometimes not. In any case, one outgrowth of such contacts was social relationships.

Religious preferences also played a role. Orthodox newcomers would meet friends from the old country or make new ones and this would constitute their circle of friends. Sometimes for purely social reasons they joined Hasidic sects with which they had had only a superficial relationship in Europe. Through membership in such sects they often found both jobs and new friends. In a number of cases, however, the opposite happened, with people rejecting groups that they had belonged to in Europe. Moritz Felberman, raised in a strictly Hasidic home in prewar Europe, was brought to Yonkers, New York, by his uncle who lived there and was, therefore, isolated from his Satmarer community, most of whose adherents had settled in Williamsburg, Brooklyn. They rejected him socially and it hurt: "My brother is a Satmarer Hasid. One time I went to a Satmarer wedding and my brother was there too. I had purposely put on a black suit and a black hat for the occasion but even that didn't help. When my brother introduced me to one of his very close friends, saying, 'I'd like you to get to know my brother,' the fellow didn't even look at me. He just asked: 'Where does he live?' 'Yonkers,' said my brother. He didn't say anything else except: 'Shloime, do something with this *Goy.*' To them I was a *sheygetz* [male Gentile] simply because I lived in Yonkers."

Another survivor explained how he had drifted away from his hometown friends over the years because he had gradually grown more observant. As a result, he stopped going to their annual dinners at the Statler Hotel: "I simply didn't have anything in common with them anymore," he said. A third survivor who married a non-Jew in the United States broke off a friendship because the other person had become religiously observant: "I just didn't feel comfortable with him anymore. I knew he condemned me for what I did. It's a shame because we helped each other out so much during the war, but what could I do?" But a fourth survivor, Joseph Eden, now residing in Great Neck, continues to maintain contact, albeit by telephone, with his Hasidic friends from Europe, even though he has long since left that community. Clearly, within the same community, some people are more tolerant than others and some relationships can withstand change and differences more than others.

What is it that drives the survivors to associate almost exclusively with one another in so many cases? Even those who have American friends seem to draw the line at some point in terms of closeness. When I asked one survivor living in Oklahoma City whether American Jews could really comprehend what she had gone through, she retorted: "How could they? To understand me, they had to go through that. People who didn't go through it. . . . My own daughter couldn't understand me." Social workers who had contact with the refugees when they first came also took note of the strength of these bonds. One article made mention of several refugees "who left their old jobs to take on work at a plant where other refugees were already employed. They knew they would not learn a skill in this plant; they knew that they would be the first to be laid off in slack season, but they felt that being together with friends, even for a short period of time, would be more acceptable to them."

So important is maintaining contact with their friends that survivors will sometimes even endure sustained abuse just to be in the company of their peers. One man married a Christian German woman after the war. Behind his back, his survivor friends referred to her as a prostitute, saying he was only interested in "a pretty face." He was publicly taken to task by them because his wife refused to convert to Judaism. "How could he do this?" asked one. "Doesn't he have any pride, any dignity? I called him a Hitler to his face." "What did he say?" I asked. "Nothing. What could he say?" Despite this, the man plays cards with his survivor friends religiously every Saturday night and joins several of them for coffee every morning. Why does he do it? "He feels like a lost soul," says one member of the group. "He doesn't know which way to turn, but he needs the group."

It is not only a question of having endured the same hardships that draws survivors to one another, though this is an important factor. It is the fact that the extreme circumstances of the war gave them an opportunity to forge very close relationships. They had a chance in such situations to discover just who their "true friends" were. Kitty Hart reflected on the nature of camp life and its effects on how she felt about her friends:

> What I missed for some time after the war, improbable as it sounds, was the sort of friendship I had known in Auschwitz. I hadn't realized until I lacked them, just how strong those bonds between staunch friends had been. In our "little families" we were more direct and more honest than in most relationships you find in the outside world.

A shared experience also makes communication easier. There is no need for elaborate explanations about why one feels upset or elated about a particular news story, or why certain topics are taboo. Certain words used require no interpretation and are, in fact, employed to reinforce group solidarity. Norbert Wollheim gave the following example: "Let's say you're eating something nice. One of us will say: 'From this I would like to have *nachschlag.'* Well, nobody else will understand this expression, but in the KZ it meant an extra little helping of food—a bit of bread, a spoonful of soup." The comfort level that exists among survivors when they meet also means that pretensions are unlikely to be tolerated. According to one survivor, a Boston resident: "If somebody I know asks me something about the war, and I say, 'I don't want to talk about it,' he's likely to say to me, 'What do you mean, you're not going to talk about it? I went through it too.' "

Those who have lived through the war often have similar priorities. Jewish identity, fighting anti-Semitism, caring about children, all these and more unite them. Nathan Krieger traced these views directly back to the camp experience: "Coming out of the camps, I thought: 'What's going to happen to the Jewish nation? There's no children.' And so, when a child was born in the DP camps, it was like a *simcha* [celebration] for the whole family." As with most people, the survivors prefer the company of and feel they can most easily trust those who share their value system.

Over and above political alignments and religious philosophy, there are the distinctions made with respect to the intensity of certain wartime traumas and the type of experiences shared. Instances where only a few survivors made it through a particular camp can cement relationships that last for decades. Even when geography, career, or lifestyle creates differences, members of such affinity groups are apt to get together periodically. Herbert Kalter, a retired businessman residing in Great Neck, is part of a circle of eight friends who survived the concentration camps. A soft-spoken, unassuming man, he carefully unwraps a piece of brown soap and shows it to me. It is a memento of the camps that he has saved for fifty years:

> I was in Birkenau and on the death march from Buna to Buchenwald. Every January 18, a group of us go out for dinner to celebrate the day we left Birkenau. We talk mostly about mundane things but sometimes we make references to the camps. We remember, for example, how three fellows who ran away were hung.

In their own quiet and understated way, these individuals are celebrating their triumph over fate. Their repast in the presence of one another's company attests to it.

Where one was and what one did can sometimes determine the choice of friends as well. Survivors sometimes evaluate each other in terms of a hierarchy of suffering. Sonia Pilcer, a novelist who is herself a child of survivors, has described it in an essay:

> Treblinka survivors feel superior to the ones who were in Terezín [Theresienstadt]—summer camp in comparison—who are above those in labor camps, who supersede the escapees to Sweden,

Russia, and South America. The key question is, where did you spend the war? The more dire the circumstances, the more family murdered, the greater the starvation and disease, the higher the rung in this social register.

While this characterization is somewhat harsh, there can be no denying that there is widespread awareness of such categories. Thus, Vera Stern said that she is involved to some extent in Holocaust-related activities, citing as an example her past work for the Warsaw Ghetto Uprising Committee. In the next breath, however, she distanced herself from others: "But you have to remember that, while I'm a survivor, I was never in a camp, although my father died in Auschwitz. I'm grateful I didn't go through it and if you're honest you don't put yourself in that category." Similarly, Sigmund Tobias, who spent the war years in Shanghai, remarked: "I shy away from the term 'survivor' because my experience was really much more benevolent." Conversely, there were those survivors who magnified the horrors they went through, as well as their own supposedly courageous response to them. On occasion, survivors interviewed spoke disparagingly of such individuals. Such tendencies are, perhaps, natural. Here they represented, most typically, an effort at coming to grips with traumatic events, especially the feelings of helplessness, loss of ego, degradation, and humiliation that accompanied them.

American-raised Jews who married survivors sometimes felt estranged from their spouse's circle of friends. They perceived themselves as interlopers, barely tolerated, because they did not go through the war and sometimes they were, in fact, treated that way. For one woman, language was a major problem. She recalled going to *landsmanschaften* meetings and not understanding the Yiddish conversations that swirled around her. "I sat there like an idiot, all night long," she said. Others, however, were able to overcome their "deficiencies" in this area, adjusting quite well in such groups. Clearly, personality was a crucial factor here. Moreover, the reverse occurred as well when survivors encountered difficulty fitting in with their spouse's American friends or, as one survivor called them, "real Yankee Beans."

While the leisure time pursuits of the survivors are not unusual, what makes these pursuits stand out are the things they talk about when they get together. No matter how the conversation begins—children, politics, health—it invariably turns to the war. In the earlier years the focus was on what happened in the camps or in Europe generally, how one's life was saved, which *kapo* was more cruel, who helped them the most. Today, as the survivors age, there is a natural shift to who is ill and who has died. In what is sometimes almost a ritual, survivors will tick off the names of the recently departed. As one survivor, Abraham Kessler, explained, it is more than just another topic of conversation: "We know that it won't be long before all of us are dead and there won't be any witnesses left to tell what happened."

Political involvements and activities in the old country can also be employed as a yardstick by survivors to measure whom they will associate with. In New York this did not present a problem since the survivors were able to find others with similar backgrounds, but in other cities with smaller populations it was not always as easy to find someone. Albert and Naomi Zeder are a good case in point. Before the war they were very active in the Bund, belonging to its youth division, attending lectures, and participating in excursions sponsored by the organization. After the war, they stayed in New York City for a short period before settling in Atlanta, where they ran a grocery store. When I expressed interest in hearing more about the Bund and its activities in Poland and America, I found myself being warmly welcomed, as if I were an old and dear friend. It is a topic that Al was not often asked to discuss. The Zeders wasted no time in telling me that they regret having come to Atlanta. Here, in Al's own words, are the reasons:

We came to Atlanta because a grand-uncle sent us a hundred dollars to come. In New York we had the Bund, friends, theaters, lectures, everything. Here everyone stays in the house, locks the doors, watches TV, and plays cards. Is this a social life? When we came here there was still a Yiddish school from the old-timers, the Americans, but the newcomers weren't interested. They were a raw element; they didn't belong to any party or organization. I considered myself a prisoner here. They came from New York to help us organize a branch of the Arbeiter Ring, but no one was interested. They don't even read Jewish books. They do us a favor when they speak Yiddish. Last week I told a few newcomers that Abba Eban is speaking. We went to hear him. You know what they said? "We heard him already." One time and that's it!

Having interviewed twenty-seven other survivors in Atlanta, I knew that Zeder's characterization of them as ignoramuses who read nothing was exaggerated to say the least. He probably knew it too, but it was his way of articulating his unhappiness at the absence of a particular type of cultural milieu—that of the Yiddish-Bundist-socialist experience. Following our interview, Zeder took me down to his basement. In it were perhaps one thousand Jewish LP records and stacks of Yiddish newspapers. He subscribes to three such papers, as well as numerous other Jewish publications. "This is my only enjoyment," he said. "Every Saturday or Sunday morning I put on the records and listen." His face was glowing as he picked up several albums, examined their covers, and enthusiastically exclaimed over them. He seemed lost in his own world. Suddenly, as if remembering that I was still there, he turned to me. His happy expression began to fade and was replaced by a sad smile: "I live in the past, not in the future," he concluded and began putting the records away.

Zeder's account points up the disadvantages of living apart from those with similar backgrounds. This is so especially because that aspect of his life was so important to him. Moreover, Zeder was born in 1912 and had therefore spent a good portion of his life as an adult in Poland before the war, where his values and attitudes had crystallized. Even New York, with its Jewish socialist organizations, might not have been enough to satisfy him, for, as he put it: "I had such a life in Poland, such a culture. I would give up everything, every material possession that I own, to have it again. I'm alone and can never get it back and that's the real tragedy."

In one sense the Holocaust was the great leveler. Tailors and shoemakers mingled and were on intimate terms with doctors and lawyers. Ethnic distinctions also broke down as German, Polish, and Hungarian Jews found themselves engaged in a common struggle for survival. One wonders if such contact caused any barriers to permanently fall. Perhaps they did for some. Norbert Wollheim, a German-Jewish inmate of Auschwitz, wrote that he now felt closer to Eastern European Jews who survived the camps than to those German Jews who left before the onset of the war. "Whatever prejudices we had against the *Ostjuden* [Eastern European Jews] were burned out at Auschwitz," he declared. "Today we form with them a survivor community based on love and tears."

Beautiful words, and true perhaps of some survivors, but judging from what members of these groups have to say about one another, especially in private, it would not seem to be the case for most of them. I asked one Hungarian survivor, a rabbi, if he had ever been discriminated against by fellow Jews while in the camps. His response:

> *Right! You're bringing up a subject again. The Polish Jews discriminated terribly. They blamed us that we had the privilege of living such a good life in our own homes while they were taken into Auschwitz two years earlier than us. "Now we should suffer!" they said. "We should work and they shouldn't have to work." And they kept constantly picking on us, for no reason. We are Jews too; we didn't send them to Auschwitz.*

The rabbi was referring to the fact that Poland's Jews were deported to the camps far earlier than Hungarian and Czech Jews, who, by and large, arrived in 1944. The attitude of Eastern European and German Jews toward each other after the war was highlighted in a rather vitriolic exchange between writers in the *Aufbau* and the *Forward* that appeared in 1946. Isaac Bashevis Singer, writing under the pen name of Yitzchak Warshawsky, asserted in the *Forward:* "The German Jews still despise Eastern European Jews. . . . Their aim is to assimilate and speak English without an accent. . . . The German refugee's first trait is to try to forget what happened as quickly as possible." Responding in the *Aufbau,* Michael Wurmbrand defended the German-Jewish community: "Warshawsky knows nothing of the great work in Jewish learning done in Germany. . . . One who speaks English with an accent is not necessarily a good Jew."

As is often the case, the truth lies somewhere between these diametrically opposed assessments. There was, and still is, a certain degree of animosity, dislike, and distrust between different ethnic groups of Jews. German Jews often thought of the Polish Jews who entered Germany in the decades before World War II as boors and parvenus. Notwithstanding Wollheim's comments, these opinions were not necessarily altered as a result of the war. One German Jew who has close contact with Polish Jews said to me: "What I'm telling you now is off the record. Even today, there is still a different psychology between German and Polish Jews. I don't really relate to most of them." On the other hand, Polish, German, Hungarian, and Romanian Jews are frequently friendly with one another and many deny making any invidious distinctions on the basis of national origin. They entertain together, vacation in the same resorts, and their children marry each other. Where there is suspicion and a tendency to stay apart it is a result of cultural and linguistic differences stemming from the different countries in which they were born and raised, as well as their encounters with each other in Europe. In most cases, their status as survivors supersedes such considerations.

One common trait among immigrants is a sense of status insecurity. In the case of survivors it is heightened because of their hardships during the war and their having come to the United States as refugees. At times it manifests itself when survivors make negative comments about their own group. One survivor, a farmer, summed up his opinion of survivors, especially those he met from New York, in the following manner:

> *Most of them are show-offs. They just want to play cards. They tried to prove something, but they didn't have the upbringing; they were* prust *[low-class]. But you can't cover up with the jewelry; you can't if there's nothing beneath it. You understand what I mean?*

In one case a man told me that a certain woman lacked culture because she knew nothing of the works of the Yiddish writers Sholem Aleichem and Isaac Leib Peretz. The woman, in turn, observed that this same individual knew nothing of culture because he had never read Dickens or *Uncle Tom's Cabin*. Each person described the other as "a good friend." Obviously, people differ as to what constitutes culture or class, as these terms are popularly used. What matters is not who is correct but that both parties value knowledge and literature and that they need to point to the failings of others in order to raise their own status.

There is in the survivor community a tendency to employ materialistic criteria in judging others. In view of their deprivation, such an emphasis is hardly surprising. For those who lack formal education and degrees, financial success is a necessary substitute for attaining recognition and respect in one's community. The striving, the sensitivity to slights, and the backbiting are well illustrated in the following story related by Joseph Bukiet, a survivor who "made good":

> *I had opened a beautiful large supermarket, so I invited my friends to see it. They came, and, as one woman was leaving, a good friend, I overheard her say to her husband: "If you want to*

live like a pig for two years, you can buy a store like this." We lived in a modest apartment then, so when I heard this, it hurt me. A few years later, my brother and I bought houses in an elegant subdivision in North Woodmere, Long Island. We bought new furniture and carpets and we invited these people for dinner. They were surprised. "Such a gorgeous house," she said. And his son said, "This must be like Rockefeller's mansion." And when he said it, I said, "If you want to live like a pig for two years, you can live in a mansion for the rest of your life."

What about American Jews? Can survivors establish close relationships with them? The general insecurity that most survivors feel as immigrants is heightened when it comes to interacting with outsiders, and they *are* viewed as outsiders in many respects. Coming from a foreign country brings with it certain disadvantages. One survivor, whose children live in an affluent Westchester County community, saw it in terms of schooling: "You won't be socially accepted in today's world without an education. If I would live where my kids live, I would be an outcast there. Even people my own age who live there, the majority went to school." Helen Epstein has written about the linguistic difficulties the survivors have in communicating with other Americans: "The people at the picnic table were voiceless in America. There, in the woods, they spun stories and told jokes and formulated theories, but once back in the world of the city, their voices were stilted and halting. They could not find the right words."

Sam Brach touched on another important issue when he raised the subject of certain traits that many survivors possess because of what happened to them in the war. "I think a survivor will come on stronger and without the finesse of an American Jew. Because of what happened in the war, the survivor sometimes feels more of an obligation to be involved, at the same time as he feels more eager and hungrier." Comments such as "pushy" and "overly aggressive" were often used by American Jews to describe the newcomers and they knew it. In what is a classic response to prejudice and minority status, the survivors sometimes internalized these criticisms and despaired of ever changing the views of their fellow Americans. In what was a self-fulfilling prophecy, they behaved as others expected them to. Another response, less typical of immigrants, was to overcompensate by avoiding mannerisms ascribed to *grine* and shunning association with those of a similar background. Said one such individual:

We are mostly comfortable with American people. We have both Jewish and Gentile friends. We didn't want to listen to all those stories about the war; how everybody was a millionaire; they all came from Cracow or Warsaw and not some small town. I did come from a small town and we were very poor and I went to sleep hungry many nights. Besides, with the refugees there are always jealousies. One has more money and my daughter married this one.

Many respondents recalled bitterly how they had been snubbed socially by other Americans when they first arrived. They acknowledged that when it came to discussing baseball and hot rod automobiles, they had little in common with Americans. Moreover, some of this standoffishness should be seen in a proper historical perspective. The 1950s were a time when Americans in general valued, and even idealized, conformity. Thus, American Jews, as a minority, were especially concerned that the larger society not see them as different in any way. In their view then, friendships with people who had thick accents and dressed poorly would only call attention to their own Jewishness. Survivors understood that they were a social liability, but they felt that the fact that they were Jews and had suffered as Jews ought to have overridden such reasons and were resentful when this did not seem to matter.

Today, survivors seem more comfortable with their place in American society and, especially, in the Jewish community, which is today far more sensitive to the Holocaust in general. Some attribute their acceptance to hard work and the success of their children, others to their involvement in the Jewish community, and still others to the fact that they have been replaced by new Jewish immigrants—Russians and Israelis. But hard feelings remain regarding their past treatment. A survivor who settled in Chicago recalled: "Today, they're interested in us and our money because we've already been here thirty years. But when we needed it, it was very cold; they wouldn't give us a tumble." They are especially unforgiving about the slights and rejection endured by their children as they were growing up in the 1950s. "Why take it out on them?" asked one.

Still, quite a few survivors established strong, if not especially close, relationships with American Jews and even non-Jews. "I wanted to learn English," said one. "All the people in the printing shop were Americans," offered another. The key determinants were age, education, religiosity, and place of residence. The younger and better-educated survivors, as well as those who were religiously less observant and who lived in smaller communities, were more likely to break the circle of survivor exclusivity. People like Ernest Michel, the executive vice president of Federation in New York, and Congressman Tom Lantos, both of whom rose to the top, certainly found it easier to gain social acceptance. Lantos explained how this occurred among his congressional colleagues:

> You see, Congress is a club. We all try to accommodate one another across party lines. It's the last small village in America. And if you're the only Holocaust survivor in Congress and you sit down with them for dinner and they see you have children and grandchildren like them, and you're like them, then the Holocaust becomes very real to them. To say six million Jews perished is like telling them how many fish there are in the ocean. It makes no sense to them on an individual level. But when I say: "You know my younger daughter, and she looks exactly like my mother looked . . . and she was gassed at Auschwitz," then this colleague can understand what happened. I can't think of a single colleague who denies the Holocaust occurred, but it's different when you know someone who has been through it.

There are survivors whose social networks include Gentiles but they are the exceptions to the rule. They see them as "too different" from themselves. Here, age is perhaps the key factor, along with having been raised in an assimilated environment in Europe. Younger survivors with a weak Jewish background were much more likely to include the company of Gentiles, but this whole question requires more research. It would, for instance, be interesting to see if Jews hidden by Gentiles during the war were more apt to have Gentiles as friends after the war.

What we see here, in this examination of the survivors' social patterns, is a community that is quite normal in its activities and interests. At the same time, there is a high degree of consciousness of kind. The survivors are acutely aware of their special status. Even those who had established friendships with American Jews and Gentiles invariably stressed to me that there was a line of understanding that a person who had not been through the war could never cross. Because this experience was the one that was central in their lives it inevitably influences the nature of whatever relationships they have.

6

Reaching Out

There is a need to show our children that we have a
responsibility that goes far beyond simply enjoying
ourselves—to do for the Jewish community and to show those
American Jews who did not go through the Holocaust how
important it is to have helping institutions. And a Jewish
community that is organized politically has real power.

SAM BRACH, HOLOCAUST SURVIVOR AND
POLITICAL ACTIVIST

THE SURVIVORS SUCCEEDED IN THEIR WORK, in the families they raised,
and in forming social relationships. But all of these activities revolved around themselves and those closest to them. What about
the larger Jewish community? Those who went through the war
saw themselves as unique and tended to stay together. Many were
hardened by their suffering. Given that, were they able to transcend their experiences and become involved in activities that benefited the general community? If so, what specifically did they focus

on and what were their priorities? How were their decisions in this area influenced by the Holocaust itself? Furthermore, were they able to transmit to American society the importance of remembering what had transpired in those awful years?

In terms of time, energy, money, and level of commitment, the survivors have compiled an impressive record in the last forty years. Not only did they join many different kinds of Jewish organizations in every community in which they settled, but they frequently rose to leadership positions in them. The survivors could easily have retreated inward and focused primarily on earning enough money to take care of their immediate needs and those of their families. Quite a few survivors did just that. But when the figures assembled for this study are examined carefully, it becomes evident that the dominant trend was in the direction of commitment and involvement and that it was both broad and deep. In doing so, the survivors were emulating the general commitment of American Jews to communal and religious activity. When one considers the tragedies that occurred in the lives of so many of them during the war, their achievements are truly remarkable.

1 ✳

The survivors, with few exceptions, remained marginal to the larger American society. The horrors they had endured and their immigrant status made them feel that they could never really blend in. By contrast, however, they became involved in a wide array of activities dedicated to the preservation of Jewish life and culture. They supported causes such as Israel and Soviet Jewry, became the leaders in ensuring that the lessons of the Holocaust would become part of the Jewish community's agenda, and were active in Jewish organizations and schools, as well as in charitable causes. They even branched out into mainstream politics and secular groups. But with the exception of Holocaust-related projects, no cause touched them as deeply and viscerally as the State of Israel.

About 90 percent of all survivors queried in 1989 had visited Israel once, compared to 54 percent among American Jews. Moreover, survivors were much more likely to have visited Israel than American Jews even after Orthodox affiliation, income, occupation, and family size are taken into account. Depth of commitment to Israel can be better gauged by looking at the number of times people visit. Here the proportion among survivors was far higher. They were more than three times as likely to have gone to Israel twice or more than their American Jewish counterparts. Overall, 57.3 percent of the survivors had been to Israel two or more times, compared to 15.5 percent of the Americans.

Survivors with large families were considerably more apt to have visited Israel than those with smaller families. For example, 64 percent of the survivors with three children had visited Israel more than twice while only 51.5 percent of those with two children had done so. About 75 percent of those with four children had been to Israel two or more times, as compared with 57 percent among those with no children. Even if this pattern stems from the fact that those going more often are Orthodox and the Orthodox generally have more children, it still means that those with larger families identify more strongly with Israel. Furthermore, assuming for the moment that visiting Israel is both associated with and strengthens Jewish identity, these figures then tell us that survivors are passing on such identity to their offspring, and that this is especially true of those survivors who have more children.

Interestingly, among American Jews no such tendency exists. Those with larger families are no more or less apt to have visited Israel more than twice. Perhaps this means that when they have more children they do so not in order to preserve Jewish identity and the Jewish people or because of the Holocaust but rather for personal reasons. Or it may simply tell us that even if they have more children to express a desire to participate in the continuation of the Jewish people, they do not see visits to Israel as an integral way of preserving that identity.

Israelis are fond of telling American Jews, "Bring yourselves, not just your checks," but they do appreciate the vast sums of money donated to Israel by their American co-religionists. According to Leon Lepold, a survivor active in the Milwaukee Jewish community, nearly all of the survivors there, even those who are not well off, purchase Israel bonds. "Even if they don't have any money," he says, "they buy a five-hundred-dollar bond every year." National Jewish leaders in conversations with me confirmed the survivors' generosity in this area. Said one: "Buying a bond is an investment, it's not an outright gift. And we would like the survivors to give more to Federation generally, but I can't deny that they buy a very large number of bonds." Benjamin Meed, president of the American Gathering and Federation of Jewish Holocaust Survivors, estimates that survivors buy about 10 percent of the total number of Israel Bonds sold in the United States. Considering that there are probably less than 100,000 Jewish survivors alive today in America, out of a total population of perhaps 5,500,000 Jews, this is a very high figure.

Survivors assist Israel financially in other ways too. Some have built factories there, based on the principle that it is important to build up the country's economy. Others, such as the members of the Radomer Society, have established health clinics in different Israeli cities. There are survivors living in the United States who own hotels in Israel because, as one put it, "If I'm going to put my money somewhere, why not in Israel?" And then there are the people who feel a deep love for Israel but have no money to build hotels. They too contribute in their own way. As one Bronx resident told me: "I buy Israeli tomatoes, which cost $3.45 a pound; I buy their Elite brand chocolate, things like that. I buy their products when I see them."

For most survivors, support for Israel is something they affirm openly and publicly. But in some cases I found individuals who gave money quietly. They were interested in being fully accepted as Americans and did not want to be thought of as being disloyal in any way to America. Such caution was unusual and may have been a reaction to their wartime experiences. In any case, this was largely true of the more assimilated survivors. In one somewhat bizarre instance, caution may have been the prudent approach, but it was not taken. The case involved a member of the Satmarer Hasidim, a sect virulently opposed to the State of Israel. The story is interesting because it reminds us not to view the Jewish community, Hasidic Jews, or the survivors themselves as monolithic in their attitudes toward Israel.

Moshe Weinstock lives in the Seagate section of Coney Island. The community's inhabitants include a substantial number of Hasidim, most of them members of the anti-Zionist Satmarer sect. Weinstock was born in the town of Fuzesabony, Hungary, in 1922. During the war he was incarcerated in various camps. In 1949 he went to Israel, where he stayed until 1959, when he emigrated to the United States. At first he worked as a laborer in a sweater factory. Then after a brief stint as a sign painter he decided to enroll at Pratt Institute, eventually learning enough to pursue a career as a professional artist. Today he and his wife, who is also an artist, run a successful art gallery in Manhattan from which they sell mats and prints and stage exhibitions for other artists. They have four children, two of whom live in Israel.

Weinstock's problems began when he took a strong pro-Israel stance in a Hungarian-language newspaper that he published. Called *New Horizons,* the paper was aimed at the Hungarian-speaking Hasidic community in New York, most of whom are violently opposed to the existence of the State of Israel, believing instead that Jews ought to wait for the Messiah's arrival before establishing it as an independent country. Weinstock is a proud man who, unlike others in the insular Hasidic community, is not afraid to express his views. A God-fearing individual, he rises each day at 5:00 A.M. for religious services. Weinstock's children are Hasidim too and he considers himself part and parcel of the Orthodox community. At the same time, he is a strong supporter of the State of Israel and because of this, his Hasidic neighbors treat him "as a leper." Since Weinstock's newspaper was popular among the rank and file members of the community, especially the women, a decision was taken to intimidate him:

> *The Satmarer say that the Zionists knew six million Jews would have to die for Israel to be built. I said: "Who could have even dreamed in the 1930s that such a thing would happen?" And I wrote this in my paper and it made them very angry. I also wrote in editorials that they were terrorists. They terrorized other Hasidic groups that are not against Israel, like Belz and Vishnitz.*
>
> *One day they called and said: "We have two hundred Russian paintings. Can you evaluate them? They're in Williamsburg." So I went there and it was nothing. I went into a prayer house and six Hasidic men in their twenties began to beat me. [He pauses momentarily to show a deep scar on his head.] I fell down and was full of blood. They hit me with an iron. And they didn't allow the ambulance to come. Two hundred people were standing there and they knew in advance what would happen. They made a circus out of it. Finally, my wife got me to Coney Island Hospital. They said they did it in the Satmarer Rebbe's honor. Two weeks later the Rebbe passed away.*

I asked Weinstock why, in view of the clear risks involved, he took such a public position regarding Israel. "Because I believed in it and wanted to popularize it," he answered. "I said all the Jews should be in Israel. In fact, I'm going there myself in two years, once my wife and I become eligible for Social Security." When I pressed him as to how he feels being labeled an outcast by his own people, he shrugged his shoulders: "I can't say it's great, but I'm so busy now. I write books about Israel, mythology, novels. I'm working on my fifth book."

Why do the survivors in general support Israel so strongly? Aside from the generally intense feelings shared by millions of Jews for Israel, survivors are motivated by certain considerations related to their experiences. As we have already seen, one of the questions that most disturbs survivors is: Why did the Holocaust happen? The founding of the State of Israel is cited by many as a mitigating factor. They do not, by any means, feel that the creation of a homeland was worth the loss of lives, of loved ones, but as people are often wont to do they try to find something positive in the horrible events they lived through. Thus, I heard many survivors assert: "Well, at least the State of Israel was established." Many believe that the sympathy generated by the Holocaust was what made the world realize that the Jews needed to have a homeland. These feelings about the historical relationship between Israel and the Holocaust, with one following on the heels of the other, create for survivors an emotional linkage to Israel that is very powerful. Just how powerful it is emerges in Sam Brach's comments on the subject: "When the Six Day War broke out in 1967, I cried. I desperately wanted to help even though I'm not a soldier. Without Israel, as rich as Jews may think they are, Jews cannot survive. This is my strong belief."

There was another important consideration. Unlike American Jews who were already in the United States in the late 1940s, the refugees were for the most part stateless. They had no loyalties to the United States, or their countries of birth, which had abandoned them during the war. As a result, they could not reject Israel as a destination by claiming that their home was someplace else. Nevertheless, as has already been seen, many turned down the chance to go to Israel because they were either too tired of war, had relatives in the United States, or for other reasons. Legitimate as these reasons were, many survivors continued to feel guilty about not having gone there when the country was in its infancy and seemed to need them so badly; a number of them said as much when interviewed. For the survivors, giving money became a way of at least partially alleviating such feelings of guilt.

Then there is the pragmatic view of Israel as a refuge from persecution. One of the crucial functions that Israel has served since its inception for Jews around the world is that of a security blanket. Jews may not want to live there and they may show little interest even in visiting it, but the fact that Israel exists is immensely comforting to them. They know they have a place to go to should it become necessary. In fact, one of the more common refrains of the survivors (and many other Jews too) is that the Holocaust might never have occurred if the State of Israel had existed at the time. Whether this is true or not is beside the point. What is important is that many survivors believe it and it causes them to place a high priority on support for Israel as a haven should there be another Holocaust. Parenthetically, it is worth noting that 98 percent of the survivors and 88 percent of American Jews said they were "very concerned" about the State of Israel.

Another factor is the psychological impact of Israel. Its existence is a source of pride for virtually all Jews, but it is especially so for the survivors, who were often required to endure great shame and humiliation because they were identified as Jews. The image of the proud *Sabra* [native-born Israeli] and an independent and militarily powerful state resonates deeply in the minds and hearts of those who knew firsthand what it meant to be defenseless and impotent in the face of an armed and merciless enemy. In many survivors' minds, the Arabs replaced the Nazis in their demonology and they saw Israel's every victory as a replay of history in which the Jews emerge victorious over the oppressor. True, many of the survivors interviewed expressed the view that Israel ought to negotiate with the Arabs if possible. Nevertheless, the idea of a beleaguered land surrounded by hostile neighbors was what predominated, even in the minds of those predisposed to a peaceful resolution of the conflict.

Finally, there is the matter of family. Two thirds of the refugees immigrated to Israel. Many of them are related to survivors who settled in America. Often, families were split up, with some going to Israel and others to America. Sometimes this came about because certain family members were more Zionistically inclined than others. In other cases, it was simply that there were not enough visas to America. Whatever the reason, the result was that close relatives ended up settling on different sides of the ocean and this meant, and continues to mean, frequent visits to Israel and deep concern by Americanized survivors about the personal welfare of brothers, sisters, uncles, and other family members, especially in times of crisis. The net effect is a strengthening of ties to Israel.

For Joseph Bukiet, a fund-raising effort for Israel brought to mind the connection between giving to Israel and another major cause in the Jewish community—Soviet Jewry. Bukiet, who has helped to raise money for Israel over the years, made an appeal for Israel at a synagogue one Yom Kippur evening:

> *Everyone gave, one for twenty thousand dollars and another for one thousand dollars. And then I asked that everyone should give ten dollars so that the entire congregation could participate in the mitzvah [good deed]. So one person, Velvel Beilin, said, "Ten dollars." I stopped, and I started to cry. I don't cry easily; I'm not a crybaby. Since concentration camp, I think this was the second time that I broke down. I just lost my voice; I couldn't talk. Why? Because Velvel Beilin is a Russian Jew. He came from Russia three years prior to that night. He was the man who was collecting from the community. That day he went from being a taker to being a giver: he stopped being a ward of the community. He became a* baal aboos *[a person in his own right].*

For at least some survivors the needs of Soviet Jewry are a reminder of their own situation forty years earlier. Felicia Weingarten, who lives in Minneapolis, recalled how, with the exception of the Jewish Family Service, the Jewish community was not that involved on an individual basis when she first came. Resolving to assist the new immigrants, she helped form a resettlement committee and did some cultural programming. It was, she reported, a gratifying experience. Among the survivors, there were some individuals who complained that Soviet Jews seemed to be receiving more assistance than they themselves had gotten, but most appeared to recognize that this was more a question of there having been fewer resources available then as compared to now.

In July 1990, two Jewish leaders and philanthropists, Albert Reichmann and Dov Wolowitz, co-chaired a meeting whose purpose was to find ways of providing Jewish education for immigrating Soviet Jews. Sam Brach, one of the participants, spoke up, and his comments reflect how survivors connect issues with their own unique past. Like Joseph Bukiet, Brach felt that all members of the Jewish community, rich and poor, should have a sense of personal involvement with the plight of the incoming Russian Jews. In his opinion, Jews as a community could only respond effectively in a crisis if each and every one of them was involved. The cause of Soviet Jewry was important to him because, he declared, "Jews should never again be neglected, physically or spiritually, the way they were in World War II." What we see here is that Holocaust survivors form the latest in a chain of charitable giving whose links are forged anew each time a succeeding immigrant wave arrives in the community. Thus, survivors assist Soviet Jews in the same way that they were helped by American Jews when they first came. Of course, in each instance there are people who refuse to extend themselves, but what matters most is the establishment of the principle and the fact that people in the survivor community act upon it.

2✦

If there was one issue in the Jewish community that the survivors considered crucial it was that of remembering what happened. This was even true in the early years. In 1948, Vladka Meed, who survived the Warsaw Ghetto, published a vivid account of her experiences, one still used today as a basic text in many colleges and high schools. A Warsaw Ghetto commemoration, held in Newark, New Jersey, in 1955, was only one of many such events, and it was survivors who most often spearheaded such efforts. But nothing could match the explosion of interest in the subject that came later, in the 1970s and the 1980s. The passage of time, which covered up some of the raw wounds, the questions and activities of the survivors' children, plus certain events that galvanized the Jewish community, were perhaps most responsible for the awakening. First, there was the Eichmann trial in 1961. His dramatic capture by Israeli agents and the subsequent trial brought back a flood of memories. Then there was the realization, after the 1967 and 1973 wars in Israel, that Jews were still vulnerable to mass murder. The films, courses, meetings, memorials built, and visits to death camp sites were in themselves reinforcing. The more people went, the more others followed in their path.

Nobel Laureate Elie Wiesel has also played an important role. Of course, there are his books, read by millions, but over and above that is the fact that he became the world's best-known spokesman regarding the Holocaust. Perhaps the single most important development that made the Holocaust part of the national consciousness was the establishment by President Jimmy Carter, on November 1, 1978, of the President's Commission on the Holocaust. Wiesel was the chairman of the thirty-four-member Commission and the major guiding force behind its ideas. The establishment of this government-sanctioned body legitimated the Holocaust as an American concern. In addition, the Commission made a number of crucial recommendations, including the focus on living memorials to the Holocaust such as exhibits and museums, rather than monuments, and the establishment of national "days of remembrance" commemorating the Holocaust. The significance of all this was not lost on the American Jewish establishment, which moved swiftly, in a variety of ways, to ensure that the Holocaust would be seen as something that all Jews are deeply concerned with, just as they care about Israel, assimilation, and anti-Semitism. This, in turn, changed the view by American Jews of survivors, from one of people peripheral to the Jewish community, to a perception that what they had gone through is of crucial importance to all Jews. In the words of *New Republic* editor Leon Wieseltier: "Once American Jews decided to make the Holocaust a part of their civic religion, survivors became the American Jewish equivalent of saints and relics."

Wiesel also became a symbol of moral courage and principle to Jews everywhere when he stood up to President Reagan and publicly chastised him for visiting Bitburg. Vladka Meed, a longtime activist in the Jewish community who as a personal friend of Wiesel accompanied him to Oslo, together with her husband and several other survivors, when he received the Nobel Peace Prize, summed up his contributions:

Elie Wiesel's point of view penetrated into the public's mind and he did it in a very convincing way. His Nobel Prize was, in a way, a tribute to all survivors. Going there was one of the high points of my life after the war because I realized that this was for the world. We were in the presence of a most distinguished international audience. What made a very special impression on me was the moment when the chairman of the Nobel Prize Committee, Egil Aavriek, invited Wiesel's son, Elisha, to join him in the ceremony. "This is an exception to the rules," said Mr. Aavriek. "Because Wiesel came from the ashes, his son symbolizes hope for continuity." But what touched me even more was that when Wiesel accepted the Nobel Prize, before he gave his response he put on a yarmulke and said that he was going to say the prayer which his father and grandfather from generations before him had recited on special occasions—Shehecheyanu. The combining of our roots with this unique occasion was for me very moving. It showed that we are proud of who we are.

The event typified Wiesel's capacity to do things in ways that deeply move human beings. To survivors, other Jews, and to people in general, Wiesel symbolized the victory of hope over despair, combined with a determination never to forget what had happened. It was a powerful message and it energized survivors everywhere.

For those who had lived through Hitler's inferno and rebuilt their lives, survival in itself was a tremendous victory. Ernest Michel of Federation felt very strongly that there was a need to honor that accomplishment with a mass gathering of thousands of survivors in one place. Working closely with Benjamin Meed (husband of Vladka) as co-chairmen and with other survivor leaders, he organized a gathering that was held in Israel in 1981 and which attracted more than ten thousand survivors from around the world. Although Michel rose to the top in the Jewish organizational world, a remarkable accomplishment for someone who came to America as a refugee, the 1981 World Gathering was more important to him: "It was probably the greatest personal satisfaction of my life, to create something that I believe will be historically an important event. I also think it was the first time that survivors made a statement, not only to themselves, but to the world."

It was a historic event for the survivor community, but to have a lasting impact it was necessary that individuals come forward whose commitment to the survivors is total. Of all those interviewed here, none epitomized this trait more than Benjamin Meed. Through the organization of which he is president, the American Gathering/Federation of Jewish Holocaust Survivors, Ben Meed played a central role in creating the organizational infrastructure that will help assure the survivors their place in history. Taking the subway from his modest apartment in a cooperative housing development in the Bronx, he arrives each morning at his Manhattan office at 7:30 A.M., where he spends the entire day meeting with people and supervising the work of his staff. He is single-minded in his goal—to ensure that the world will be unable to forget the horrors that befell European Jewry in World War II. Nothing else, with the exception of his family and their well-being, counts.

Meed survived the war by hiding and passing as a Gentile and came to America in 1946, together with his wife, Vladka. They had no relatives in the United States, but they were warmly welcomed by their friends from prewar Poland when they arrived. Meed went into business and like many other survivors did quite well. The Meeds raised two children, both of whom married, had children, and succeeded professionally as physicians.

What makes Benjamin Meed's success story different is that individual achievements were not enough for him. He worried, in an almost paternalistic way, about what would happen, say, one hundred years from now. How would the survivors be remembered? *Would* they be remembered? Rather than simply wondering, he decided to do something about it. Meed had been involved in survivor groups since 1946, but in 1980 he gave up his business to devote all of his time as a volunteer to Holocaust-related activities. "I'm convinced that twenty years from now the world will say it never happened. Some already deny it now," he observed. To prevent that from occurring, Meed undertook a multimillion-dollar project to compile a national registry of Jewish Holocaust survivors and their families. Included in the registry was basic information about the survivors and their families—their place of birth, maiden or original names, and where they were incarcerated. He also asked that people send family photos from before, during, and after the war. In a letter mailed to survivors, Meed emphasized that unlike other documentation centers the registry was not meant to be a record of those who died "but of those who survived and rebuilt their shattered lives." The letter concluded: "Our story must not die with us, but live on forever."

Tracking down the names of survivors throughout North America after so many years is a daunting task, but Meed checks each name and all of the accompanying details before allowing it to be entered into the computer, where it is cross-referenced with other family members' names and people from the same town. He is constantly on the phone with people, dictating correspondence, answering requests for information, and so on. So as to make the information widely available to scholars and institutions seeking to learn more about the topic, the registry and other relevant documents will be permanently housed in the United States Holocaust Memorial Museum.

Meed is also proud of the fact that several doctoral dissertations have been completed, based in part on information provided by the registry. The registry itself, which now contains over seventy thousand files with names and photographs, and is still growing, is partly available in book form. Copies have been sent to synagogues, museums, libraries, and organizations throughout the world.

This project alone would be enough work for most people. But Meed is no ordinary man. He has over the years spoken at countless public events, appeared frequently on TV, often been interviewed by the press, and has organized an annual Holocaust commemoration, where thousands come to honor the memory of those murdered in the war. He also plays a leading role in the Holocaust Memorial Museum, where he heads several important committees. Starting in 1985, he and his wife have, in conjunction with the Educator's Chapter of the Jewish Labor Committee and the American Federation of Teachers, sent hundreds of public school teachers—Jews and non-Jews from throughout the United States—to Israel during the summer months. There they study intensively about the Holocaust and Jewish resistance and visit points of interest. The teachers study at Yad Vashem, Kibbutz Lochamei Hagetaot, and the University of Haifa, returning to their schools better equipped to teach the subject. It is a program that his wife, Vladka, initiated, organized, and directs, spending three weeks in Israel with the teachers. In the past three years, the educators also stopped off in Poland, where they visited various concentration camp sites before continuing on to Israel.

There is little doubt that Benjamin Meed is more closely associated with the survivor community than anyone else, except for Elie Wiesel and famed Nazi-hunter Simon Wiesenthal. True, there are other prominent figures among the survivors, such as Ernest Michel, William Ungar, Miles Lerman, Sigmund Strochlitz, William Lowenberg, Eli Zborowski, and the late Joseph Rosensaft, but Meed's name heads the list. There are people who resent the fact that his name is so often in the limelight, but even they acknowledge his contributions to raising the level of knowledge and awareness about the Holocaust in the United States and elsewhere.

America became even more receptive to hearing about the Holocaust after 1983, the year in which another Holocaust survivors' gathering was held, this time in Washington, D.C. The event, covered by more than six hundred correspondents, attracted the President and Vice President of the United States, as well as hundreds of other major figures in politics and government. The importance of such an occasion is self-evident. It ensures worldwide coverage and brings what happened to everyone's attention. It also tells others and the survivors themselves that they have, so to speak, made it in America, an America that so many of them love. Reflecting on the effect of the gathering, Meed said:

As a result of this national gathering, people began to see survivors in a different light. Their image of survivors was based mostly on the postwar Nazi pictures portrayed often by the media. But when they saw how we organized, how we acted, how we responded to events of the day, and, above all, our concern for humanity and its future, they gained respect for us. And today, whenever something happens, be it David Duke, Saudi Arabia's response to Israel, or whatever, our views are sought out and listened to.

Respect and involvement were the key words and Meed indicated as much when he introduced President Reagan, seen by most Jews as highly sympathetic to them despite his Bitburg visit, to the crowd:

"Who could have imagined that a poor boy from the Warsaw Ghetto, feeling so alone in the world at that time, would be standing here today with the President." And each of the twenty thousand survivors shared that feeling. We can also imagine that every victim who perished had the desire, in the last moments of his or her life, that we who survived should tell the story of what happened to them, and that the lesson of the Holocaust, a unique tragedy of the Jewish people, must become a lesson for the world. Freedom should not be taken for granted. We must always remain vigilant.

When asked if he felt that Reagan had genuine sympathy for the survivors, Meed's answer was unequivocal:

Very much. Not only did I feel that, but standing next to him I saw how moved he was. At certain moments I felt he was shaking. Mrs. Reagan was crying. Someone gave her some tissues. . . . I was praying; I was hoping I'd live up to the importance of the occasion. I was scared. I knew it would not happen again in my lifetime.

The greatest source of pride for Meed is "that I helped to bring the survivors together; that I helped to give them a name and a voice. Survivors were so betrayed by the world that they couldn't trust anyone. To overcome that distrust was the most difficult thing." His primary fear is that the organization he helped build and to which he gave so many years of his life will cease to exist when he and his colleagues are gone. Indeed, survivors provide much of the funding and in general support Meed's various projects. He observed, somewhat wistfully, "Perhaps I assumed too much responsibility." He believes that many people will be working on the Holocaust ten years from now but they will be mostly professionals, since the survivors are aging and many more will be gone by then. His face brightened somewhat when queried as to the future involvement of the survivors' children. "I believe they'll play a very important role ten or fifteen years from now when they no longer have to worry about earning a living and raising their families."

In fact, many children of Holocaust survivors became active in Holocaust-related activities during the 1970s. This frequently caused the survivors themselves to identify more strongly with their children's quests and questions. To what degree such involvement will be long-term is difficult to gauge. Lamenting the sparse turnout at an annual synagogue remembrance in his Bronx neighborhood, Joseph Nass, a survivor who made it through the war by hiding, said: "You see survivors here, but not any young people. They're not interested, even children of survivors. Why don't they come? Maybe they're not interested because they heard it already." Nass's remarks are certainly valid for some of those whose parents are survivors, but perhaps these same individuals will, as Meed has noted, develop an interest in preserving their parents' legacy once their own children have grown up. In any event, thousands of survivors' children have made their presence known and felt—approximately 1,500 children of survivors were in attendance at the 1981 World Gathering and even greater numbers at subsequent gatherings in Washington, Philadelphia, and New York City. Many have also joined organizations such as Second Generation that focus on the concerns of survivors' children. And in recent years, the Jewish community has organized trips for thousands of Jewish teenagers, many of them children or grandchildren of survivors, to vanished Jewish communities and sites of destruction in Europe. Called "the March of the Living" the trip includes a walk from Auschwitz to Birkenau.

Another important development has been the proliferation of museums focusing on the Holocaust. Washington, New York, Los Angeles, Atlanta, and Detroit are only a few of the cities that have built or are presently establishing such institutions. Of them, the most ambitious and far-reaching is clearly the United States Holocaust Memorial Museum in Washington, D.C., first chartered by an act of Congress in 1980. Centrally located on the Washington Mall, its goal is "to educate the living and remember the dead." Scheduled to open in the spring of 1993, it will contain exhibits, a library and archives, and a research institute. Visitors will receive an ID card similar to those carried by many Jews during the Holocaust and will have an opportunity to "relive" some of the victims' experiences, such as walking through an actual boxcar similar to that used to deport Jews to the death camps. While centered around the Holocaust itself, the museum will also portray how the survivors adapted after the war ended.

The choice of Holocaust-related activities engaged in by the survivors was as varied as their positions in American society and their specific talents. Congressman Tom Lantos saw himself as the spokesman for what could also be called, in political terms, an interest group. Shortly after taking office he introduced the Joint Resolution that made Raoul Wallenberg an honorary citizen of the United States. Vladka Meed delivered an address to Polish President Lech Walesa regarding anti-Semitism in that land; Miles Lerman, in his capacity as International Relations Committee Chairman of the Holocaust Memorial Council, participated in negotiations that led to the opening of various governmental archives in Russia and Poland. Isaac Kowalski published numerous anthologies related to resistance during the Holocaust and Sarah Berkowitz wrote two books of her wartime travails. Joseph Eden recorded and published a history of the seven hundred Jews who had lived in his hometown and mailed free copies of the book, at his own expense, to the libraries of hundreds of universities. As an architect, Ben Hirsch designed memorials to the Holocaust that combined his professional abilities with his own unique perspective as a survivor. All of these accomplishments represented an integration of past experiences in a healthy and normal way and they enriched the lives of those around them.

One activity engaged in by more and more survivors in recent years has been speaking out publicly about their experiences. For many it was not easy at first. Alex Gross recollected how Bishop James W. Malone of the Youngstown, Ohio, Catholic diocese helped him overcome his initial hesitation:

He kept telling me how I have to speak about it. One day he picked me up at noon and took me out to his Catholic school and put me in front of the class without telling me in advance. He just took me for a ride and said: "You are going to have to tell these boys about your experiences." It was frightening and painful the first time. I was shaking terribly when he took me home. And then he said, "You're going to have to talk to my other class too." I said, "No I won't. Forget it." And he hugged me and said, "You will." And I did.

Gross eventually became a popular speaker much in demand. He particularly remembers one question asked by a man in a Columbus, Georgia, church, around the time of the trial of John Demjanjuk, who had been charged with murdering Jews at Treblinka:

One guy asked me: "Why do the Jews insist on going after someone forty years after the fact? Isn't it enough?" So I looked at him, it was a packed room, and I said: "Okay, let's assume now, one guy comes in from that door, one from that door, and one from the back. And with machine guns they mow down and kill your son, your wife, and injure your daughter and parents. Suppose that they even cripple you, take everything away from you, and you have to relocate and abandon everything and you suffer for forty years. One day, after forty years, you walk through town and you recognize that man. He's one of the guys that killed your family and crippled you. Would you like to see him go free?" He said nothing. I said, "You asked me a question. Please answer me. Would you say this man deserves to go free?" His wife turned around and gave him a good klop [smack] and said: "Shut up, you dumb jerk."

For most survivors, therefore, speaking is not simply a matter of catharsis. There is also the feeling that they are fulfilling a mission, that they are educating people for the future, and in that way doing their part to prevent another Holocaust from happening. This is why they court the young, choosing primarily to address students of all ages in schools. Not all of them can do it. For example, Fred Terna, the artist, told me: "I've spoken, but I'm slowly stopping because it wipes me out emotionally."

For Rita Kesselman, however, speaking to children is a constant activity and she has addressed thousands of youngsters in the Boston area. When I was in her home, she showed me a thick stack of letters from students who have heard her speak in various schools. These letters are an immense source of gratification to her. Rita read some of them to me and explained what they meant to her:

> *Some write that they are suicidal, but that after listening to me, they'll never complain again. Others write: "You are my hero." I've gotten thousands of letters and I read every one. In fact, there are bad nights when I can't sleep. I go downstairs, take out the letters, and read them. I can sit like that for hours, reading them again and again. I save them all.*

Anti-Semitism is obviously an issue of great concern to the survivors. They were more likely than American Jews to view anti-Semitism as "a very serious problem" by a 43 to 29 percent margin. Moreover, Orthodox survivors and those who are politically conservative felt more strongly about this issue than did other survivors. Interestingly, there seems to be a strong relationship between health and perceptions of anti-Semitism. In both the survivor and American-Jewish samples, the poorer a person's health, the more likely he or she was to see anti-Semitism as a serious problem. Perhaps less-healthy people see the world in more negative terms.

Holocaust survivors were more apt than American Jews to think another Holocaust was possible. About 68 percent of the survivors thought so as opposed to 56 percent of the Americans. About 16 percent of the survivors believed another Holocaust was likely, compared to 8 percent among the American group.

Irrespective of denominational affiliation, those survivors who belonged to a synagogue were more likely to believe another Holocaust was possible. This may be a function of what their rabbis tell them, but among American Jews there was no difference between synagogue and non-synagogue members with respect to believing that a Holocaust was possible. Perhaps rabbis with many survivors in their congregations tell the survivors what they think they want to hear. It may also be due to the activities, like Holocaust remembrance ceremonies that such a synagogue sponsors. Another possibility is that those survivors who are apprehensive and fearful about another Holocaust occurring may turn to religion and, specifically, the synagogue for solace.

How has the Holocaust affected the way in which survivors think about other underprivileged groups? Certainly, in the in-depth interviews, many expressed concern in this area, asserting that a threat to one group was a threat to all, including Jews. Many others were critical of certain groups, especially blacks, charging them with anti-Semitic views. Curious to see what the average survivor in the United States thought, we asked them if "equal rights for minorities, women, and the poor" was something they were "very concerned about" or "not very concerned about." Nearly one half replied that they were "very concerned." This is a fairly high figure when compared to the 36 percent who said that they were "very concerned" about "national defense" and the 46 percent who were "very concerned" about "the economy." The issue was of even greater importance to American Jews, among whom 65 percent stated that they were "very concerned" about the "rights of minorities." For both groups, we might add, Israel, crime, interfaith marriage, and assimilation were of even greater concern to them than this issue.

Among the survivors, the less concerned the person was about anti-Semitism, the more he or she was concerned about equal rights for others. Perhaps those who were worried about anti-Semitism didn't have room to worry about others. Perhaps those who worried about others had concluded that their own group wasn't the only one with problems. Or possibly they were concerned about others because this was simply an important issue for them. Incidentally, the same pattern was found among American Jews.

The specter of a resurgence of Nazism in the world is something that haunts the survivors. It was not surprising then that when neo-Nazis announced their intention to parade through the heavily Jewish Chicago suburb of Skokie, Illinois, the survivors reacted very strongly. Ben Stern, a resident of Skokie and a survivor, was president of the Janusz Korczak Lodge of B'nai B'rith. Together with other Jewish groups, the organization formed a front to fight the proposed march. The lodge itself sent information, petitions, and appeals to communities throughout the United States. Their efforts ultimately succeeded and the survivors felt they had won a significant victory in persuading Jews of the threat such activities posed to the security of Jews everywhere. As is well known, the American Civil Liberties Union disagreed, arguing that even neo-Nazis should not have their freedom curtailed.

Regardless as to whose side one took, what happened in Skokie caused great pain to many survivors and reopened old wounds. The pattern of provocation and response was actually repeated in many communities. In Milwaukee, for instance, Walter Peltz was active in a Jewish self-defense group that formed and took to the streets after synagogue windows were broken and Jews were attacked in the streets. To Peltz, battling anti-Semitism was an act of patriotism, for it meant fighting for the American ideals of freedom and democracy. To emphasize his love for America, Peltz flies a huge American flag on the front lawn of his suburban home.

Gilbert Metz, who survived Auschwitz, lives in Mississippi, a state with less than two thousand Jewish residents. He makes his home in Jackson, the state capital. When the city fathers allowed a cross to be erected on the roof of a state building, Metz decided to fight:

Around Christmas they moved the lights and drapes in a certain way so that you could see the cross from the highway and for miles and miles around. I didn't like it and I decided I would fight against it. The Jews here were afraid. They said: "Why do you want to make trouble?" I have no use for the people in the congregation here. They're all yellow. [Metz's wife, a convert to Judaism, explains that Jews in Mississippi want very much to be accepted because they're such a small minority.] We were on ABC, CBS, and NBC. We got threatening calls at night and three hundred people came out and dumped garbage on our lawn. And the FBI said: "Nothing we can do about it till somebody shoots you." Well, I have a .357 Magnum shotgun, a .38, and an Uzi, and I said: "Somebody shoots me, you're gonna have a dead duck."

Metz won and the cross was removed. When, sometime later, construction workers building a post office placed a cross on that building, Metz protested again just as vociferously. He sent a telegram to the U.S. Postmaster General, reminding him that the building was on federal property, and threatened to fly to Washington to personally deliver a message regarding the lack of justice in America to Mikhail Gorbachev, who was visiting at the time. As before, the cross was taken down. When I asked Metz if he had won friends as a result of his actions, he responded:

Christians yes, Jews no. I'm going to tell you something and I hope I don't step on any toes. I think a lot of Jews come from an eastern Polish background and I think they still hear the stories about how the Cossacks came and all that kind of nonsense. And they still lie down in front of Christians and bow down to them. And

Jews also have a fear of guns. I don't know why! I come from a long-liberated Jewish family in Alsace-Lorraine that fought in the Napoleonic Wars. A lot of Jews came from an environment of pogroms in Poland and they have a different attitude, which is not their fault.

Ben Stern and Walter Peltz, both from Eastern Europe, would certainly disagree with this assessment. So would the thousands of Holocaust survivors from Eastern Europe who fought in the 1948 Arab-Israeli War. Nevertheless, the point made by Metz is both useful and important because it touches on the need of many Holocaust survivors to demonstrate that "Never again!" is not simply an empty slogan, that now that they have the chance they are prepared to fight for their rights and their freedom. This theme of resistance was often expressed in the interviews. It was perhaps best exemplified by the Polish-Jewish survivor who refused to move out with his family from his deteriorating Spanish Harlem neighborhood because: "I ran from the Nazis in Europe and I'm through running. This is America and no one chases me out of my neighborhood."

3

That survivors were active in Holocaust-related causes and organizations is hardly surprising and is not sufficient as a measure of communal involvement. What about participation in other Jewish groups whose goals do not include emphasis on the Holocaust? In other words, have the survivors succeeded in broadening their interests beyond this area? Most important, do they feel a sense of responsibility to the larger Jewish community of which they are a part?

Survivors are both members and leaders in organizations and are more likely to be involved than American Jews. About 67 percent of the survivors belong to Jewish groups versus 48 percent for the American Jews. Moreover, they are just as likely to be leaders in these organizations as their American counterparts, a significant accomplishment for people who, for the most part, came to the United States as impoverished refugees. While survivors living in the New York area are religiously more observant, that is, attend synagogue regularly or keep a kosher home, than those residing in the rest of the country, the reverse is true when it comes to organizational affiliations. By an 81 to 60 percent margin, survivors who live outside of New York are more apt to belong to Jewish organizations. This is probably because there is greater social pressure, as well as more of a need, for Jews in smaller communities to feel they belong somewhere. In the New York area, the large Jewish population, plus the range of cultural offerings, reduces the need for many Jews to formally join organizations.

Newspaper accounts of the survivors that appeared in the years immediately after they arrived suggest that such involvement began early and was often seen as a way of repaying those who had assisted them in their hour of need. In a speech made to leaders of the Baltimore Jewish community on April 18, 1951, Eugene Kaufman, executive director of HIAS-Baltimore, reported that the Newcomers Group had actively participated in the annual campaign to raise money for charity. Noting that the refugees had themselves been charity cases only a year or two earlier, Kaufman concluded: "They have done honor unto Baltimore and honor unto themselves." In that same year, in Linden, New Jersey, twelve DPs wrote, directed, and acted in a four-part Yiddish play before three hundred local Jewish residents. Said one refugee: "We will never forget the warm interest and devotion shown us from the first moment we arrived." A study of newcomers in Pittsburgh found that there were in the early years 111 Jewish organizations of all types in which survivors could be found as members. The same high degree of involvement was found in Montreal and in the farming communities of New Jersey.

In general, the survivors joined organizations that emphasized religious activities, combating anti-Semitism, preserving Yiddish culture, communal work, and Israel—in short, everything that the larger Jewish community was interested in. Some, such as James Rapp, who sponsors large dinners every year on behalf of Russian Jewry, became involved in helping other Jews adapt to life in America. As our figures show, certain types of organizations attracted them more than did others. The largest number belonged to ladies' organizations such as Hadassah, AMIT, WIZO (Women's International Zionist Organization), and Emunah, and, as might be expected, to Holocaust survivor organizations like the American Gathering/Federation of Jewish Holocaust Survivors. The second largest category was Israel, with some 13 percent claiming affiliation with a Zionist organization. B'nai B'rith or the Anti-Defamation League, Yiddish culture organizations such as the Workmen's Circle, and hometown societies were third, with each attracting the loyalties of about 9 percent of the survivors. Orthodox organizations such as Agudath Israel and the Union of Orthodox Jewish Congregations came next at about 6 percent. After that, the figures are too small for statistical significance.

In the in-depth interviews, survivors explained their reasons for such a high level of involvement. Three major considerations emerged—a feeling that communal responsibility had always been a central feature of Jewish culture; a desire to show appreciation for assistance given the refugees when they first set foot on American soil; and an understanding of what it meant to be turned away when requesting help from others. Sam Halpern, a major donor to Jewish causes, elaborated on the first consideration: "Once we began establishing ourselves here, we started asking how we could help the other person who doesn't have money; how can we help the State of Israel? This is the way the Jewish people were taught by Moshe *Rabbenu* [Moses, our teacher] thousands of years ago—that we have to give charity." Sam Brach echoed these sentiments but updated them: "My desire to be involved comes from my European background and from what happened to me during the war. In European communities there were burial societies, *mikveh* [ritualarium] committees, and groups that visited the sick."

When it came to helping the survivors, the picture was mixed. The organized Jewish community did much to ease their adaptation, but among the general Jewish population and in some communities there were those who seemed indifferent to the refugees' plight, as well as others who harbored resentment toward those newcomers who had established themselves quickly. Interestingly, survivors used their encounters with both positive *and negative* responses to account for their organizational involvement. Some responded that they felt gratitude toward those who had helped them and that this had made them recognize the importance of such groups. Bill Neufeld elaborated:

When we came to St. Paul [Minnesota], the people from the Jewish Family Service picked us up and treated us like their own children. They did the best anyone could have done. They gave us an apartment and put food in the refrigerator. It was a small place but it was new, with linens and dishes. A lady took us

*shopping and bought things for us. I didn't even have any clothes
then. In other words, they were there to take me in when I couldn't
even speak English. They cared for me like my mother. So that's
why today I work for Federation or any other kind of Jewish
cause. I think of what HIAS and the Joint [Distribution Commit-
tee] did for me.*

For Sam Brach, the opposite experience in Europe, when the
war ended, led nevertheless to the same conclusion:

*I saw that my family was dead and the Germans were still alive.
And I asked: "If there was a God, how could this happen?" So
many people needed a helping hand then and no one cared. I
think if there had been psychiatrists around in the DP camps right
after the war, it would have been good. People committed suicide;
there was no one to help us adjust. So I decided we can't let this
happen today to Jews who need us.*

Some people, like Ernest Michel and Abe Foxman, became professionally involved with Jewish organizations, seeing it as rewarding work. Foxman recalled his hopes and disappointments when he
first began working at the Anti-Defamation League:

*I wanted to work for the Jewish people. It sounds corny but that's
the way it was. My father was a person who worked for the
community. Maybe it was to make it where he didn't make it
here. He saw some* naches *[pleasure] from this. I've been at ADL
since 1965 and it's still exciting when I get up in the morning. But
when I came to the ADL I was uncomfortable because the ADL
was not a Jewish organization. It was an organization that sometimes worked for Jews. I was the Jewish expert. And I had to
negotiate to go home early on Friday. But it's come a long way.
I remember when people said to me many years ago: "Abe, you
don't have a future here because you're too Jewish." I said: "All
right; so what are you going to do?" Today, we're much more
Jewish. We have people with yarmulkes here, like Jeff Sinensky.*

For Foxman, putting the Holocaust on the ADL's agenda was a
logical outcome since his organization's raison d'être is to battle
anti-Semitism. In Michel's case, interest in this area was only a
small part of UJA/Federation's broader agenda of servicing the

community in terms of education, hospitals, senior-citizen centers, media, and many other programs.

Michel expressed disappointment to me at what he felt was insufficient Federation involvement on the part of most survivors:

They give to Holocaust causes, like Yad Vashem, but to many of them, UJA/Federation is not a priority. Maybe they have a reluctance to part with their money because they suffered a lot. With Israel bonds it's a compromise because they get it back and they're doing something for Israel. I told survivors: "It's time you played a role outside of your immediate group. Give to Jewish education, the Jewish poor." But I've only had limited success.

Survivor leaders disagree sharply, pointing to survivors in communities in the New Jersey and California Federations who give generously. Discussions with Jewish leaders in various communities around the country revealed that in their opinion survivors do contribute more outside of New York but not as much as they could.

More than a question of parting with money is the fact that the survivors feel that Holocaust-related organizations and Israel are, given their own experiences, of greater importance. According to Joseph Bukiet, a major donor to Federation and other causes: "Survivors should have been the biggest givers because they know from what they went through that money doesn't mean anything. But the survivors aren't the biggest givers. Sometimes they have a terrible stinginess because they're afraid of the unknown. They feel they have to make a living. But once you get the survivor to give he gives above and beyond his capacity, especially to Israel."

The gap in understanding between survivors and American Jews is there. It is a belief by many survivors that the average American-raised Jew is sometimes insensitive to what those who came from Europe went through, that for him or her the Holocaust is just another Jewish issue like Israel and Soviet Jewry. Perhaps it is, but not to those who lived through it and lost their families. The feeling that Americans simply do not share the same priorities and are incapable of comprehending what happened cropped up many times in conversations with survivors. Benjamin Hirsch of Atlanta gave perhaps the best example of how this related to Jewish communal involvement, for in his narrative we see the different ways of looking at the same issue and the bitterness evoked by the differing perceptions:

Some survivors give to Federation and some don't and they certainly don't give in the proportion that they could. But one fellow from Federation really annoyed me. He used to berate the survivors for not giving more. So one day I said to him: "Don't berate survivors to me. You don't have the right. Survivors have paid their dues. When you pay your dues like they've paid their dues, then come to me and say what they should or shouldn't do." This is the same guy who called me on the morning of our annual Holocaust remembrance service and said, "We're going to have to call it off, it's raining." And I said, "The hell, you say! Did Hitler call off a death march when it was raining? Did Hitler say you can't go to the showers when it's raining? Did they not shoot Jews when it was raining?" He says, "How can you—we're having this dignitary from Israel come to speak." I said, "Ask him if he doesn't want to speak in the rain. And if he doesn't, I'll find somebody else." And the dignitary had no problem; he was going to speak.

It is clear that the survivors are heavily involved in Jewish organizational life. Besides Holocaust groups, they belong to and support various women's associations, hometown societies, Zionist organizations, B'nai B'rith lodges, and Jewish cultural groups. There are those who would like them to rearrange their priorities and give more to Federation than they do, but no one would deny that the survivors are, on the whole, highly active in the Jewish community. This is clear simply from the fact that they are more apt than American Jews to belong to Jewish organizations in general. Moreover, one can anticipate that their children will probably become more involved in Federation as time goes on and they are assimilated into the mainstream American Jewish community.

What about the 33 percent who belong to no organizations? Judging from the interviews, many of these individuals were simply too exhausted from their trials to become active in communal life. As one put it: "It's enough I had children and raised them." Another one, a tailor, snorted when I brought up the topic: "Organizations? That's for rich people. They can give; they can get honored. I can just lick envelopes. And besides, who will pay my bills?" Yet another survivor criticized the dinners and affairs held by survivors even as he acknowledged the need for them: "I don't think it's appropriate to make dinners and parties when so many people in the world are hungry and it's a show off kind of thing, like, 'I made it big,' but it's necessary to honor people in order to raise the money for important activities, like making sure the Holocaust isn't forgotten."

Still others declared that they were simply not interested in organizations. People become involved with organizations for two basic reasons—a sense of responsibility and because they enjoy it. Perhaps some survivors felt less of an obligation to do volunteer work. In addition, their idea of enjoyment may have tended more toward movies, visiting with children, reading, and talking on the telephone. To put it simply, they were not joiners. Even as we think about the one third who did not link up with Jewish organizations, it is important to remember that a far higher proportion of American Jews, 52 percent, are not members of such organizations. This figure does not bode well for the future vitality of organized Jewry.

Turning to religious identification, among the survivors 84 percent came from observant homes compared to only 62 percent in the case of American Jews. It is therefore not surprising that they are far more likely, by a 73 to 47 percent margin, to belong to a synagogue. American Jews are twice as likely as survivors to never attend synagogue. Survivors are twice as likely to keep a kosher home as American Jews. They are also more apt, though not by a wide margin, to observe the Sabbath. About 41 percent of the survivors identify themselves as Orthodox, 38 percent as Conservative, 5 percent are Reform, and 16 percent are unaffiliated. Among American Jews, 14 percent affiliate with the Orthodox, 40 percent with the Conservatives, 21 percent with the Reform, and 25 percent consider themselves unaffiliated.

It is to be expected that a far higher proportion of survivors living in the New York area are Orthodox. What is interesting is that at the other end of the spectrum, survivors residing in New York are twice as likely as those living in smaller cities to be unaffiliated with any denomination. One possible explanation is that the anonymity afforded by the metropolis places less demands on affiliation than is true of smaller communities. In addition, the larger communities have other outlets for those interested in Jewish activities.

Many of the survivors identify with the Orthodox community because this is the way of life they grew up with, whereas Conservative and certainly Reform Judaism represents something strange and foreign. Nonetheless, even for the most strictly observant Jews, the idea of God permitting a Holocaust to occur was difficult to accept. It seems, however, that many survivors succeeded in coming to terms with it. The point was brought home in an interview with Joseph Glikman:

> When I sit here in Borough Park, by my window, and look out on Shabbes and see all these Jews with shtreimlach and kapotas [Hasidic garb], I say this is the biggest miracle. After the war people questioned God—the Nazis had incinerated their fathers, mothers, brothers, and sisters. And yet, thousands came back to it. I see the hand of God in this.

Doubtless, many Orthodox survivors still retain their faith in God, accepting the Holocaust as an event that, being mere mortals, they simply cannot comprehend. On the other hand, I spoke with quite a few survivors who were observant Jews, praying every day, observing the Sabbath down to the last detail, and so forth, but who nonetheless confided that they no longer had faith in God: "How can I," said one, "after what I saw?" Despite that, they remained in the Orthodox community because that is what they felt most comfortable with.

Among those survivors identifying with the Conservative movement some said that Orthodoxy was too restrictive. Others rejected Orthodoxy because they had associated it in Europe with anti-Zionism but still desired some form of religious affiliation. Still others simply believed in the Conservative point of view. Quite often, those survivors who belong to Conservative temples occupy influential posts in them, not only because they are active and give money but because their strong religious background earns them the respect of their often less knowledgeable fellow members.

Very few survivors belong to Reform temples, but a substantial number are not members of any synagogue. For many it is a reflection of their religious doubts. Sometimes it is related to their distaste for organized religion. In Alexander Petrushka's case, it was a little of both:

> I don't participate in religion because I feel that throughout all the years I found no solace in talking to rabbis. I'll never forget— one day I was at a bar mitzvah in Scarsdale [New York] and a rabbi spoke. He gave one of the most brilliant sermons I ever

heard on the Holocaust. And afterward I came over to him and I said: "You don't know how you touched my heart." And he just went right on shaking my hand and everyone else's—"Gut Shabbes! Gut Shabbes!" So I feel, frankly, more Jewish in my heart, but I don't practice it. . . . I'm still angry at Him.

Among the Orthodox Jews, the postwar immigrants played a prominent role in the establishment of yeshiva day schools, high schools, and post–high school Talmudic academies. In 1945, just as the refugees were beginning to enter the United States, there were only sixty-nine Hebrew day schools. Today there are close to six hundred in the United States alone, not to mention Canada. Similarly, there were nine yeshiva high schools in 1944, while today that number has grown to about two hundred. The pattern of growth for the rabbinical seminaries was similar. It was the postwar European generation that supplied most of the students and the money for these schools because re-creating their religious way of life on American soil was a matter of the highest priority for them. The attitude of Moishe Rubin, who donated $100,000 to a yeshiva, was typical: "I named a yeshiva after my parents, who died in the war. My parents must have led me to this—that I should be religious, and God should help me [financially], and my idea was not to buy a yacht or another condominium, but to put in a lot of money to a yeshiva."

4✳

Politically, survivors, especially the Orthodox, are not as liberal as American-raised Jews. About 23 percent of the survivors identify themselves as liberals versus 39 percent for the American sample. Most are not involved politically beyond voting regularly, a pattern typical of most first-generation immigrants, all of which makes those survivors who did enter politics that much more unusual. In each case, such involvement seemed related to their Holocaust experiences and as such it is worth exploring a bit.

Sam Brach, for example, did very well economically in the United States and in that sense he realized the American dream. But somehow it was not enough. He is a generous man, giving liberally to many different kinds of Jewish causes—schools, Soviet

Jewry, Israel—but he differs from most survivors because he is also very active in American politics. His own family was involved in communal affairs in Hungary and served as a role model for him. In his opinion, many other survivors would have become similarly active were it not for their having been stymied by the American Jewish establishment. He attributes this to a desire on its part to hold on to power, general resentment against the survivors, and to just plain snobbishness. Brach recalled how certain local Jewish leaders in Queens, New York, tried to freeze him out:

If a person like me, a survivor, succeeds financially and the leadership feels threatened by that person, they'll lock him out if they can, they'll make things so difficult for him he'll have to move out, or they'll try to hurt his reputation. This is because they want to dictate to the community what should be done.

I asked Brach if he could specifically point to anything that happened to him of this nature. His response underscored the sensitivity that survivors often feel when they deal with other Jews:

During the time when [Secretary of State George] Shultz and [Secretary of Defense Caspar] Weinberger were criticizing Israel very much for going into Lebanon, I suggested to one of the rabbis that we have a big rally in the neighborhood to show our support for Israel. So the rabbi said to me, "I'll give a speech in the synagogue." And I said: "You need more than simply a speech." He answered, "A businessman, a kosher butcher, should never be involved in politics because they can arrest you [presumably for violations], they can cause you lots of problems." And I told him that it is important for me as a human being, especially as a survivor, that I be involved. Instead of threatening people, they should encourage such involvement. But they kept knocking me to keep me in my place. They said to the politicians: "Who is Sam? Sam is my butcher."

But Brach, who survived Auschwitz and amassed a small fortune in America, was undeterred. He fought to gain recognition in his community as a political activist and he succeeded. First he established a local newspaper called *The Voice of the Hills,* which focused on community issues and problems. He backed politicians, including, at various times, former President Ronald Reagan, Governor

Mario Cuomo, Senator Alfonse D'Amato, and former Mayor Edward Koch. His wife, Miriam, also entered the political arena as a candidate for district leader in the Queens County Democratic Party. A native of Kosice, Hungary, a descendant of a long line of prominent rabbis, and a survivor, she had lost her parents and younger sisters in the war. After coming to the United States she completed night school, receiving a high school diploma, following that up with a La Salle extension course in bookkeeping. Miriam was determined not to let what happened to her destroy her life. Active for many years in her husband's meat business, she only consented to run for public office because "my husband insisted that I do it. My friends supported me, but I'm not the political type."

Sam Brach's efforts did not go unnoticed by the media, and articles recounting his activities and views appeared in various newspapers and magazines, including *The Wall Street Journal*, the *Daily News*, and *New York* magazine. They cited his opinions about Jimmy Carter, Ted Kennedy, and Ronald Reagan, reporting also on the headquarters he had opened in Queens for Reagan's presidential campaign. All this was heady stuff for a refugee who had arrived in America with little more than a visa. Sam explained to me that he wanted to be a member of Governor Cuomo's inner circle so that he could have an impact and related the following conversation that took place between him and the governor:

> *Cuomo asked me when I had a forty-five-minute meeting with him, "Sam, why are you involved with politics?" I said, "May I call you Mario?" "Sure," he said. And I went on: "Mario, some people like to go to bars. I don't. Some people like to go on vacations. I don't. I'm interested in doing something for the Jewish community. You will be the next president." He said, "Sam, you really mean it?" I said, "Sure. . . . But I don't want a job. I want only a dollar-a-year job that would recognize my involvement in the Jewish community."*

Cuomo acknowledged Brach's leadership role and discussed it in his own autobiography. In fact, Brach traveled outside of his own community as well, trying, along with others, to persuade immigrant Hasidic leaders in Brooklyn of the importance of working within the political system, something they have clearly become adept at. Today Brach is a fixture on the Queens political scene and has the grudging respect even of his detractors. Said one: "I don't like his aggressive style but no one can question the man's total commitment and dedication to the Jewish community." His current project is the establishment of a local political action committee. His son is also involved in politics and works for AIPAC (American-Israel Public Affairs Committee). Brach's emphasis remains on the local level and it is a matter of choice because, as he put it, "If you're strong locally you can go further. Look at the Council of Jewish Organizations in Borough Park. They're local but they have tremendous influence." Brach is no longer a young man, but he shows no signs of slowing down. He still puts in a fourteen-hour day. "As long as I can breathe, I'll remain involved in the community," he declared.

Brach's case is important for understanding survivors in general. In it we see the drive and determination that characterized so many of them. We also learn about the slights they often had to endure, especially when they ventured beyond the friendly confines of their own social group. The trek made by Brach within a forty-year span, from refugee to political leader and highly successful businessman, is unusual, but it is indicative of the potential that probably lay within many more survivors had they not been victims of Hitler's atrocities. Certain individuals like Sam Brach were able to rise above the misfortunes that befell them. That a man who lost his parents and all nine of his brothers and sisters could rebuild his life afterward demonstrates that human beings can "come back from the dead." Why this is so remains to be seen.

In a few instances survivors won election as local government officials. One such case was that of Abraham Resnick, vice-mayor of Miami Beach. Resnick was in the Kovno Ghetto for three years before escaping. After a short stay with a partisan group, he joined the Russian army, where he participated in the liberation of Berlin and the Sachsenhausen concentration camp. After the war, he made his way to Cuba, where he lived until Fidel Castro came to power in 1959, resettling once again in Miami. Asked how the Holocaust affected his involvement in politics, Resnick replied: "I entered politics because the Holocaust taught me that Jews cannot be bystanders. We must help those less fortunate than us in every way possible."

Flora Spiegel, a German-born survivor, also entered politics, serving as mayor and City Council member of Corona, California, a city of some seventy thousand residents situated not far from Los

Angeles. Her son Sam, a Corona police lieutenant, in an interview shortly after her death in 1992, described her patriotic feelings about the United States: "She believed in our role as peace leaders in the world and the responsibility each citizen has to maintain that freedom."

There were others too for whom politics was at least an avocation. Fred Terna, the artist who first painted in Terezin, fought the political machine on the Upper East Side and helped to establish a Reform Democratic club. He too traced his decision to participate in politics to the war, saying, "The Holocaust teaches us that you have to get involved." Harold Hersh became active politically partly for business reasons. Since his store was located in Atlanta's black ghetto, good relations with the black community were essential to his economic survival. However, the utilitarian reasons for his involvement were eventually superseded by genuine friendship, when he developed close relationships with people such as the Reverend James Wilborn, leader of the six-thousand-member Union Baptist Church, whom he now has known for over twenty-five years. Moreover, Hersh became involved in the civil rights struggle as a result. Clearly, not all or even most survivors who worked in black ghettos followed this route, but Hersh showed that it could be done. I also encountered other survivors in various cities who in one way or another assisted poor people in the neighborhoods in which they worked. Hersh recounted to me how, in a case that attracted national attention, barricades were put up in the black community by hostile whites who were trying to prevent a black contractor from building homes in an area adjacent to a white area. He sided with the black community and went with them to lodge a strong protest with the mayor. As a result of his efforts and those of others, the barricades were removed.

On the national level there is, of course, the case of Congressman Tom Lantos. He traces his involvement in public affairs to the Holocaust and the lessons it taught him about the importance of preserving freedom and democracy. Moreover, it affects what he chooses to focus on as a congressman:

> I am very strongly underdog oriented. All of my activities are "dangerous activities." For example, I'm chairman of the Labor Oversight Committee. There we deal with OSHA violations in the factories and we deal with child labor violations. Or I'll have a hearing on petrochemical industry violations.

Then, moving on to the hearings on the HUD scandals, over which he presided, Lantos continued:

I've always had a strong social conscience. For instance, it pains me to no end that [former HUD secretary] Samuel Pierce is black. I was the most sympathetic committee chairman he could have had. Moreover, I feel in many ways that in Congress, I'm here, in a sense, for all the survivors. And for this reason I feel particular responsibility for all Jewish issues, whether it's anti-Semitism in the Soviet Union, Syrian or Ethiopian Jews, the failure of Spain to have diplomatic relations with Israel, or whatever. But I do it like breathing, not because it's an obligation. After all, I lost immediate family during the war. I always accept engagements to speak in front of schoolchildren. Many of them are underprivileged, but most had an incredible head start over me. I was a penniless immigrant Jew. I got a Ph.D. [in international economics from the University of California at Berkeley], built a family and a career as a professor of economics, television analyst, and business consultant, and, at the end of my career, was elected to Congress. And I say to them: "Every single one of you can do more than I did. I didn't know a single person in this country when I came." And to see these kids' eyes light up, many of whom come from "the wrong side of the tracks" . . . it's wonderful.

"I do it like breathing" is the operative phrase here. Lantos, like other survivors I met, has taken his ordeal and extracted from it a central lesson—that to help those less fortunate is a moral imperative. Hersh and Brach have acted similarly, as have the thousands of survivors who were able to resist the urge to allow self-pity to dominate and even ruin their lives. As for those unable to do so, they cannot be blamed, for all human beings have different thresholds beyond which they cannot go. Nevertheless, a good case can be made, it seems, for concluding that, on the whole, the survivors were able to overcome the limitations imposed upon them by their own tragic life histories and become both participants and leaders in the larger Jewish community. As a group, the survivors have focused, for the most part, on Jewish issues. Their children, however, have begun to move beyond that sphere, advancing in the corporate world, banking, politics, academia, and the arts.

7

Living with

Memories

"IF YOU'VE BEEN THROUGH AUSCHWITZ and you *don't* have nightmares, then you're not normal," a survivor once remarked to me. Her comment highlighted the importance of evaluating the survivors within the context of their own experience. If by normal we mean a happy, perfectly well-adjusted individual, then many survivors, as well as others who did not go through the Holocaust, could not be so described. But if we are referring to people who get up in the morning, go to work, raise a family, and enjoy a variety of leisure time pursuits, then an overwhelming majority of the survivors would qualify as normal.

Indeed, many survivors did quite well. They achieved financial security, raised families, and were active in community affairs. There is, however, another, more subtle yet crucial, measure of success that has not yet been looked at carefully—how the survivors live with their memories of what happened to them. What do years of incarceration in a world whose very raison d'être was inflicting pain and punishment do to the psyche? What are the long-range psychological effects and how do they influence the individual's outlook on life in general? In short, were the survivors able to resolve the turmoil and conflict that resulted from their ordeals? What insights into life did they gain because of what happened to them?

This criterion of adaptation, the ability to cope with tragedy on an emotional and intellectual level, has important ramifications that go far beyond what happened to those who lived through the hell known as Occupied Europe between 1939 and 1945. For if the survivors could somehow deal with their problems, they may serve as a model for *all* individuals who have gone through crises, be it a life-crippling disease, a debilitating accident, financial ruin, social ostracism, or the loss of loved ones. The mere fact that so many survivors live and function indicates that there are important lessons to be learned from them. To do so, however, it is necessary to look at the world from *their* perspective. This must be combined with an assessment of the research that has been carried out on the survivors. That is the purpose of this chapter and the concluding one that follows.

Before continuing, however, one reminder is in order. Those survivors interviewed are, by definition, only those still alive forty-five years after the war. Perhaps they are special precisely because they have survived for so long and are therefore different from those who died in the 1950s, 1960s, and 1970s. Perhaps the conclusions drawn about the successes and failures of the survivors would have been radically different if those now dead had been interviewed as well. Possibly, but not likely, for there is enough evidence from newspaper accounts, historical documents, and earlier studies to challenge such a notion; we have been citing such evidence throughout this book. Major Abraham S. Hyman was the last Advisor on Jewish Affairs to the Commander in Chief of the U.S. Armed Forces in Germany. Few worked more closely with refugees than he. His summation of what he found among the DPs as early as 1951 strongly supports what we have been saying about the survivors:

The major credit for the amazing comeback made by this remnant of European Jewry, must, of course, go to the people themselves. In evaluating what they achieved in a brief span of a few years, we may err only on the side of understatement. The self-

restraint they exercised during their period of waiting, the resil-
ience they displayed in picking up the threads of their lives, and
the determination they showed in collectively asserting the right
of a Jew to a country of his own, entitle them to a position of honor
in the history of the Jewish people and in the history of mankind.

1 ✳

To understand how the survivors fared psychologically, we need
to take note of their physical condition, since that can have an
impact on a person's state of mind. For those who survived the
camps, poor health often takes on great symbolic importance because in that environment illness ordinarily meant certain death. In
our survey, those survivors who described their health as "poor"
were four times as likely as those who said their health was "excellent" or "good" to have seen a therapist or social worker. Those in
"fair" health were twice as likely to have seen someone as those in
"excellent" or "good" health. One example of the relationship between health and attitudes was anti-Semitism, as discussed in the
previous chapter. Other research has also shown that as survivors
age and their health deteriorates, they are affected psychologically.
Yael Danieli found that many survivors are unable to deal with old
age and frequently suffer from feelings of loneliness and depen-
dence. To some extent such problems are due not only to declining
health, but to the fact that lack of work and the departure of children give the elderly more time in which to reflect and ruminate
about the past.

The problems faced by the aging survivor were present in the
case of Sam Moneta, a nursing home resident, and they are both
physical and psychological. Because he was ninety-three years old,
they were more serious than for most elderly survivors, but the
feelings he expressed were by no means unique. Originally from
Poland, Moneta had spent time in Auschwitz and Treblinka. His
life had been saved in Mauthausen by a doctor who knew him. In
America, he worked as a pharmacist. His wife, also a survivor, had
passed away and now he too wants to die. Over the protests of his
niece and a staff clergyman, Rabbi Esor Ben Sorek, Moneta explained why:

I'm ninety-three, but I'm really five hundred. I survived not only by miracles, but because I had a will to live. Now, however, I have a will to die because I went through so much. The psychiatrist said there's no medication for people with problems like mine. He said what I need is a good social worker. Why do I have to wait till I go completely and they put me on the second floor, the place for senile people? In the past, I belonged to Ben Meed's organization for survivors, the Zionist organization, the UJA. I read the papers, like the Jewish Week. *I have no real complaints. I have colitis, a pacemaker, not bad; but I have no one to talk to. My nieces are here now, but they can't stay long, they don't live in New York.*

Moneta was basically lonely. His wife's death deprived him of someone with whom he could share his life and possibly triggered mourning for losses that occurred during the war as well. Since there was no one who could care for him on the outside, he was forced to live in an institutionalized setting; although the residence is a first-rate establishment, it was still not home. Such dilemmas typically arise among senior citizens but Moneta's wartime incarceration probably exacerbated them. He asserted, "I don't want to be a burden. I have a plot with the Farband and they're waiting for me." "If I had a niece who came to see me from three thousand miles away," argued Rabbi Ben Sorek, "I would hug her and kiss her all the time." But it was all to no avail, as Moneta stared out the window and muttered, "Look, I told you—I don't want to live." His niece clutched her pocketbook tightly and her eyes filled with tears.

Although most survivors did not present a picture of despair like this one, they reported that their physical health suffered in some way because of their wartime experiences. Those surveyed were only half as likely as American-raised Jews to characterize their health as "excellent" and were twice as likely as the American sample to say that it was "poor." At the same time, almost 60 percent claimed that considering what they went through their health was either "good" or "excellent." Another study, conducted by a team of psychologists and sociologists, found a similar percentage of survivors who described their health as "good" or "excellent," adding that those who went through the Holocaust with friends or relatives fared better in terms of long-term health.

One measure of psychological health is whether one feels a need for psychological or psychiatric therapy. Remarkably, our random sample survey discovered that survivors were actually less apt to have seen a psychiatrist, a psychologist, or a social worker (henceforth each referred to as a "professional") than American Jews despite their past ordeals. About 18 percent of the survivors had seen a professional compared to 31 percent for the American sample.

The fact that survivors who sought professional help are a distinct minority presents those trying to understand survivors as a group with a serious dilemma indeed. Since about three quarters of the research to date has sampled only those who have been in treatment, conclusions have too often been based on a type of survivor who represents, at best, 18 percent of the total survivor population. As a result, we know rather little about the average survivor's adjustment. Other samples have been drawn from survivor organizations or from those who requested reparations, but these too are biased since they represent, by definition, a particular type of survivor. This was, in fact, the primary reason why so much care was taken to locate and interview a nationally representative random sample of survivors plus a control group of American Jews.

A number of interesting results emerged regarding what sorts of survivors did and did not seek professional help. In terms of religious affiliation, both Orthodox and Conservative survivors were equally likely to have seen someone (the number of Reform-affiliated survivors was too small for conclusions to be drawn about them), with unaffiliated survivors most likely to have seen someone. There was no relationship among the survivors between synagogue membership and having sought professional help. Among Americans, however, synagogue members were somewhat less likely to have seen a professional. Perhaps for them the synagogue and its rabbi are used as substitutes for therapy. Conversely those who visited a professional may have had less of a need to belong to a synagogue. Or quite possibly those who sought out clinical assistance were not likely to have been synagogue members to begin with. Female survivors were considerably more apt to have seen someone than male survivors. This may or may not be due in part to a feeling that to seek professional help implies weakness in the traditional stereotypical male sense. Whatever the case, among American Jews, males and females were equally likely to have sought out a professional. Among survivors who had seen someone, there was no relationship between that fact and the survivor's age.

Finally, survivors living outside of the New York area were no more or less likely to have had professional guidance than those living in New York.

While use of a random sample may be the most accurate way to study a population, research based on clinical samples is still valid and important with respect to a segment of the survivor community, and the problems reported on in such studies are often related to the Holocaust itself. Moreover, they tell us about the potential problems that could theoretically affect all survivors. Besides, it must be said that many survivors, as is true of people in general, might have experienced psychological difficulties that were not serious enough to warrant their seeking guidance and treatment. Nonetheless, these difficulties may have existed and even bothered them to a degree. In any event, it is worthwhile to assess the work done in this area.

Most of the research on the psychological impact of the Holocaust leads to the conclusion that its effects are long-lasting. Other studies of different types of trauma, such as loss of loved ones through illness, confirm that while people generally recover from the deaths of those who meant a great deal to them, they do not "forget" what happened. It is a loss that can "emerge again and again, in their thoughts and feelings." One survey of survivors whose names were gathered from synagogues, agencies, and survivor organizations found that 65 percent thought that it was "impossible to forget the past." Emphasizing this point, one survivor told me: "The lucky ones died first. Those who survived can never forget seeing the other ones die."

Another survivor described how the terrible fears she felt during the war kept returning in various guises. During the interview we were in a resort hotel that employed Gentile waiters and waitresses. Suddenly, she grabbed my arm and, in a voice filled with anxiety, asked:

Am I crazy to worry about these people? I mean, I was sitting in the dining room and suddenly I became afraid. I thought that these waiters and waitresses will get mad, or jealous, and they'll say: "Look at the Jews! We are only workers here." And they will do something horrible when the hotel will be filled with people. It's terrible to have to live like this. When we have Rosh Hashanah and Yom Kippur, we have to have police outside the temple, watching to see who's coming.

She was visibly relieved when told that such apprehensions are shared, in varying degrees, by other survivors, adding that she was careful in all of her interactions with the hotel staff not to say or do anything that might give them a bad impression of Jews. In her view, the absence of such pressure is the chief advantage to living in Israel. It is a place where Jews are a majority, not a minority. Therefore they need not worry so much about what non-Jews think of them.

This woman's fears, while greater than those of most survivors, were indicative of an acute awareness felt by many survivors vis-à-vis their status as a minority group in America. Its clearest manifestation is a certain cautiousness in proclaiming one's Jewishness. The link between this reluctance and the Holocaust was best expressed in the following observations by a Viennese-born child survivor who is today a college professor:

> *Many of us refuse to display symbols that identify us as Jews right off the bat; so that we will not wear a Star of David, for instance. . . . A few years ago my son, who had joined B'nai B'rith Youth Organization [BBYO], was going to have a simple march in support of the State of Israel . . . but that was the year of the massacres in Sabra and Shatila and I had received a nasty anonymous phone call, accusing me of being responsible for Sabra and Shatila. . . . So I called the regional leader for BBYO and asked him to cancel the march, because I was afraid. I told them I was a survivor . . . so yes, there is some fear. When I moved to this town and the Jewish stores were closed for the High Holidays, my thought was: "The next time they want to throw stones, they'll know exactly which ones are Jewish stores."*

Nightmares are probably the most common symptom of disturbance among survivors. According to one study, more than four out of five survivors experience upsetting dreams. Their frequency and intensity vary from one individual to the next but they are often accompanied by screaming and feelings of anxiety, as depicted in the well-known film *The Pawnbroker.* Most often the survivors dream about what happened to them during the war, but sometimes these memories intermingle with more current fears, such as running and hiding with their children, who were, in fact, born after their liberation. Some survivors awake, are comforted by their spouses, and go back to sleep; others find it necessary to read, walk around the house, or eat something. Most have learned to cope on their own, but a few require regular medication to help them. One man has been taking tranquilizers for almost forty years. Several survivors attributed an increase in nightmares to having read books and seen films on the Holocaust when the topic became very popular in recent years.

Of course, guilt is a normal emotion felt by most people, but among survivors it takes on special meaning when related to the Holocaust. Most feel guilty about the death of loved ones whom they feel they could have, or should have, saved. Even if they could have done nothing to help their friends or relatives, they find themselves asking over and over: "Why did *I* live and not them?" Some feel guilty about situations in which they behaved selfishly even if there was no other way to survive.

Survivors, particularly males, also blame themselves for not having displayed bravery in the face of oppression. As David Jagoda, a survivor living in Minneapolis, put it:

Sometimes I feel like I am really not a survivor. You know why? A lot of times, it came to my mind, like 100 Germans took 10,000 Jews. We could kill them in no time at all. If every one Jew would kill one German, they would be in trouble.

Jagoda makes no mention of the lack of arms, the physical condition of most Jews, or other factors, saying only, "I sometimes feel guilty because I survived; because I did not survive properly. I didn't do anything." In the following example, a survivor described how such guilt was engendered when individuals were forced to make impossible choices between those dear to them:

I remember a man whose wife and son were at the mercy of the Gestapo, and they told him that if he didn't tell them where his parents were in hiding, they would kill his young family. He went to his parents and asked them what he should do, and they said, "You must give us up"; so he did. And he survived the war, as did his wife and child. I have seen him a few times—he lives in New York now—but I can never meet him without thinking of the permanent agony those sadists condemned him to because of what they made him do.

Such agonizing dilemmas cannot ever be forgotten or ignored. In their happiest moments, the survivors remain aware of how human beings can be made to suffer. Moreover, it is an inner misery that remains with them no matter where they are. It affects their daily functioning and, most certainly, their judgments about people, not to mention their worldview. Even as they grapple with the implications of what they were compelled to do, they wonder whether others would have acted less nobly or more nobly were they in a similar situation. The words of a character in Sheila Levin's novel *Simple Truths* bring into sharp focus the horror of having to make such decisions. A father, he is responding to his daughter's question, "What is worse than death?":

> *"Erosion. . . . To be nibbled away at, day after day. Not just from the beatings, the starvation, the fear of death. Worse than that is the mutilation of the spirit. The body can endure what the mind cannot. The brutality was unendurable because it was incomprehensible. . . .*
>
> *The choices that that world allowed were a masterpiece of evil. Civilization was gone. Boundaries, parameters, limits, all canceled. 'Shall we send these hundred-and-fifty boys to the ovens, or these? Tell me, sir, would you prefer us to rape your wife or your daughter? Which twin shall we castrate?' Those were the choices. Madness. Those were the choices. Not once, but every day, every hour, day after day. Every day was the end of the world."*

Guilt, depression, intense feelings of loneliness, withdrawal, anxiety, paranoia, all these formed part of the reaction known as Concentration Camp Survivors Syndrome. Research has shown that such reactions were not necessarily limited to those who did poorly after the war. According to one study of those who came for treatment, successful businessmen and professionals were just as likely to voice complaints about social and personal adjustment as those who were unemployed or marginally adjusted.

Nevertheless, only a minority of survivors found that these problems interfered with their ability to function on a daily basis and that in itself attests to their resiliency as a group. For those unable to cope, the support of friends and family greatly helped to cushion the impact of their suffering and many referred to it as a key factor in their ability to come to terms with what had happened. If the deviant case teaches us about the norm, then much can be learned from the case of Alex Brown, a child survivor who was raised as a

WILLIAM B. HELMREICH

Christian by his survivor parents. Feeling that there was "no place in the world for Jews" after the Holocaust, they told him nothing of his Jewish background. When, at the age of twenty-four, he learned belatedly of his origins, he was so far removed from the Jewish community that there was little he could do to reunite with it. Unlike other survivors, he had no community support system available to guide and comfort him. When we listen to his words, we see how wide was the chasm between him and anything Jewish:

> *I eventually entered a Catholic order, or at least I tried to. They required a history and a dowry, as in classic Canon Law of the Catholic Church. I stayed with the Brothers. But I had personal problems with faith and I suppose I felt a sense of less than joyous support from home. No one ever said no, but no one ever said yes. And I would have had to tell them about my family history. As a result, I never pursued it.*

Still, Brown felt a strong need to relate to his Jewish ancestry, even if he had spent most of his life as a member of the Lithuanian-Christian community. His solution was rather interesting:

> *I had read up on the Nuremberg Trials and so I volunteered to do research for the division in the Justice Department concerned with tracking down Nazi war criminals. I also put on an exhibit at a college where I once taught on what my students had learned interviewing survivors. We had collected photographs of the Holocaust and Israel.*

Such activities were far easier than convincing his parents to relate to the past. They attended the exhibit with misgivings. His father refused to enter the hall, saying he would wait in the lounge for Alex's mother until she had finished looking at the slides and photos. In a desperate attempt to communicate with his parents, Brown rented videos about the Holocaust, featuring films such as *Kitty Returns to Auschwitz, Judgment at Nuremberg,* and *The Man in the Glass Booth.* He selected these films because they were "retrospective, but not graphic." The results were mixed. His father left the room, but his mother generally stayed and watched. In his view, she was unhappy about the life they had chosen while his father was "too repressed to talk about it."

Could Brown have done more to reenter the Jewish community? Perhaps, but he was not especially inclined to do so, for the connections were too tenuous by the time he discovered that part of his life history. He was, after all, a member of a Christian community, had attended church regularly, and had met few Jews in the small midwestern community where he grew up. Still, he felt some sort of vague affinity with Jews. As he put it, "I just seemed to feel comfortable with Jews whenever I met them." To date, Brown has not taken any further steps with respect to linking up with the Jewish community and it is questionable whether he ever will. An extreme case, no doubt, but it points to the important role played by the community as the survivors seek to understand and cope with the aftereffects of the war.

Unlike Brown and other very young survivors, most of those who outlasted the camps and ghettos had already gone through their formative years by the time the war began. Their ability to lead normal lives suggests that even conditions as horrible as those that prevailed in Nazi-occupied Europe could not destroy the effects of positive socialization in the crucial early years of infancy and childhood. By the same token, it is not surprising that those who went through the war as small children were deeply scarred by it. This is corroborated by Sarah Moskovitz's sensitive portrayal in her book *Love Despite Hate* of child survivors of various camps, including Auschwitz, Ravensbruck, and Theresienstadt. Afterward, they were brought to Lingfield House, a children's home in England. The home was run by Alice Goldberger, with Anna Freud serving as an informal consultant. The children ranged in age from three to those who were teenagers.

Many of the children did have problems despite the love extended to them, but as Moskovitz stresses the overwhelming majority were able to find the strength and courage to go on. As a result, she says, we need to rethink "the concept that early deprivation unalterably determines the course of life." Her conclusions about these children after years of intensive observation of their lives are significant because they show that even when children undergo severe trauma, they can, with proper help, recover to some degree:

In spite of the anxiety and fear, and the tortuous detours often used to deflect them, a most striking quality about this diverse group of people is their affirmation of life. They have a quality of stubborn durability. They keep hoping, they keep trying to make the best of their lives. Given all they have endured, this in itself is a kind of heroism; no one has given up. There have been no suicides, only one person out of a whole group who came of age during the sixties had been involved with drugs, and only one lived for a time outside the law. Marta lives alone in a psychiatric hospital. Their hardiness of spirit and their quiet dignity are part of this persistent endurance. And enduring is, after all, most fundamental. This can indeed be regarded as a tribute to Alice [Goldberger] and the milieu she provided, and certainly as a tribute to the parents of the adoptees; but, most of all, it is a tribute to the strength of the survivors themselves.

Equally compelling is Moskovitz's assessment of how these individuals see life:

Despite the severest deprivation in early childhood, these people are neither living a greedy, me-first style of life, nor are they seeking gain at the expense of others. None express the idea that the world owes them a living for all they have suffered. On the contrary, most of their lives are marked by an active compassion for others: Hedi's role in the kibbutz and her recent creation of a kindergarten for neighboring Arab village children; Shana's tender thoughtfulness in planning the process of parting mothers and children on entrance to nursery school; Esther's pleasure in making hot lunches for children; Fritz in his devoted care for the physically disabled; Eva in her synagogue work; Berli's adoption of the orphanage in Vietnam; and Zdenka in the care taken for the mourners' bouquets are but a few examples. Among those who were adopted young the examples are striking: Jack's outing with the London East End children; Judith's commitment to the Israeli war widows; Leah's desire to work in convalescent homes.

What clearly emerges here is the capacity to think of the welfare of others and to give generously of themselves. To be sure, there were survivors who did not fit this image, but judging from the evidence on community involvement, commitment to and love for family, and the almost total absence of criminal behavior, they would seem to be in a distinct minority.

Moskovitz's study is not the only one to arrive at this conclusion. Boaz and Eva Kahana, respectively a psychologist and a sociologist, looked at the lives of several hundred survivors residing in Israel and in America. They concluded that while those interviewed experienced trauma after the war, the extent of it was not nearly so great as some of the literature on the subject would suggest. Gail Sheehy, who examined the effects of trauma on children living in war-torn Southeast Asia, has argued that "the premise that disturbing early childhood experiences inevitably lead to a neurotic adulthood is dangerously uninformed." She notes further that "in the histories of the most satisfied and successful adults I studied, I was struck by one common denominator. Most of them had endured a traumatic period during childhood or adolescence." Is there a positive relationship between stress and success among the survivors? This critical issue will be taken up in the next chapter.

Notwithstanding their resiliency and successful adaptation, many, if not most, survivors view life from a unique perspective that stems from their common experiences. The resulting effect is often one that gives everything a certain tinge, or coloration, that sets them apart despite their heroic and largely successful efforts to be like "everyone else." It is ultimately impossible to expect people to be like everyone else when the central event of their lives did not happen to anyone else and they know it. This perception of self is clearly and eloquently elucidated in a book by Cecilie Klein, a camp survivor currently living on Long Island.

> A survivor will go to a party and feel alone.
> A survivor appears quiet but is screaming within.
> A survivor will make large weddings, with many guests,
> but the ones she wants most will never arrive.
> A survivor will go to a funeral and cry, not for the
> deceased but for the ones that were never buried.
> A survivor will reach out to you but not let you get
> close, for you remind her of what she could have been,
> but will never be.
> A survivor is at ease only with other survivors.

Measuring normality based on unspoken thoughts is exceedingly difficult. It must be based on that which is observable. Survivors manage, for the most part, some better than others. They eat, drink, play, laugh, marry, and have children. If anything is not "normal," in the positive sense, it is that they are still capable of doing so. Far less trauma than what they experienced has been used to justify far more deviant behavior than the survivors exhibited. A man kills fourteen people in a restaurant and we are told how culturally deprived he was as a child. A middle-class father-son team sexually abuse scores of children and stories are written describing how they came from a family that was not "affectionate." Within such a context survivors are by no means bereft of explanations that might account for any deviant behavior on their part. They have, so to speak, "good reason." Seen from this perspective, their history as a community and their contributions to society are remarkable.

What about trust and faith in others? In Sheehy's book *Surviving,* Mohm, a Cambodian child who suffered a great deal during the upheavals that racked that land, says: "You can't tell a thing to anyone . . . because they turn right around and stab you in the back. . . . It happened to me many times." In one survey of Holocaust survivors' attitudes, respondents were asked how they felt about the following statement: "After all that happened, I wonder whether we can really trust others, believe in human worth, have basic confidence, and basic hopes." About 53 percent agreed, 24 percent did not, while the rest were neutral. This result was, however, based on a mailed questionnaire with no opportunity for expanding on one's answers.

Naturally, survivors remember many instances of betrayal and this causes them to be very cautious, but most have also come away from their experiences with a belief that at least certain individuals can be trusted. Notwithstanding the selfishness that existed in the camps as the prisoners struggled to survive, there were also many cases where people cooperated with and helped one another. This has been extensively documented in the work of Shamai Davidson, Terrence Des Pres, Hillel Klein, and others. Crises bring out the worst *and* the best in people. As one survivor put it: "The KZ experience has created a barrier in me, but it taught me about love and understanding my fellow human beings." Such caution influences not only attitudes but behavior as well. Thus, another survivor, when asked how the war affected her, replied: "I don't wait till the last minute. I begin to take action earlier than others usually do." Another said: "I'm much more careful than the average person about telling my last name when I first meet people. I want to know more about them first."

It may be that they want to believe that human beings can be trusted, that this, in a sense, justifies going on with life. Whatever the case, the very high response rate to our survey strongly suggests that survivors trust people more readily than they might admit to others in casual conversation. After all, they were phoned by total strangers who asked a series of personal questions about their age, income, religious observance, children, and other personal matters. Yet over 95 percent cooperated fully. In many cases the interviewers did not even know the names of those whom they contacted, having only a telephone number in front of them. True, most of the interviewers knew some Yiddish and were children of survivors, but this alone cannot account for such a high response rate, one higher than in most random surveys of Americans.

Robert Lifton has explained how people in extreme danger survive through a process he calls "psychic numbing," a diminished capacity to feel. This was true, he notes, of Hiroshima survivors. Lifton adds that in such situations the individual must numb himself but must also retain enough awareness to recognize danger and be able to react appropriately. Many researchers have reported that survivors seem to show little emotion. This may be a residual effect of the war, a fear that to have such feelings, let alone to reveal them to others, is to chance exposing oneself to pain. Dori Laub, a psychiatrist who has studied survivors extensively, has argued that if survivors cling to unhappy marriages, unsatisfying jobs, and unsafe neighborhoods, it may be because they prefer that to the risk of an acute traumatic event.

Other survivors respond emotionally by demonstrating hostility. One researcher found that many adults, profoundly affected by their inability to display aggression in the camps for fear of losing their lives, had a need, especially in the period right after the war, to find "someone to hate." Researchers have noted the fear many survivors have of police officers, but sometimes the survivors' experiences, coupled with their personalities, moved them to respond differently. Shortly after coming to the United States, Moshe Katz, a resident of New York, was confronted by a policeman who charged him with having violated the blue laws by keeping his grocery store open on Sunday. Katz fought back with his fists, shouting, "This isn't Germany!" According to witnesses at the scene, "He gave an excellent account of himself." In the end, the officer, one Francis Tooley, was reprimanded by the desk officer and later came around to apologize. Survivors with whom I spoke recounted similar instances of "un-ghetto-like" responses. In short, survivors were both passive and aggressive after the war, but both reactions were probably strongly related to what they had gone through.

In some instances, survivors are presented with an opportunity to respond openly and forcefully to those who participated in the war. Some are afraid to do so, others are not. The following story, told by a woman who survived Auschwitz, demonstrates how deep the scars can be:

I was shopping in Bloomingdale's and, as I held up a jacket, a man behind me commented that, in his country, the jacket was much more expensive. He kept saying that, so, out of courtesy, I asked: "Where is your country?" "Oh, Germany," he said. "Where are you from?" he asked. "You have an accent." "Hungary," I answered. "I was in Hungary, in 1944," the man said. Then the blood rushed to my head. "In what unit were you, in the Gestapo or the SS?" He said: "No, I wasn't in the Gestapo or the SS. I was in the Wehrmacht." Then I said: "In 1944, in Hungary, there were only SS or Gestapo." And he answered: "No, I wouldn't be ashamed to tell you if I was in the SS unit or the Wehrmacht. I am proud of my Führer. I always was proud. He was a very good man. I am very, very proud of him. He didn't do anything wrong." I started to shake. I started to scream: "You murderer!" And as I was screaming, two salesmen came over and, in the meantime, he ran away down the escalator and disappeared. But in that moment I would have been able to kill him.

Of course, aggressive behavior need not be limited to the physical arena. Another form it took was that of the almost stereotypical, hard-driving survivor who worked long hours and fought tooth and nail to succeed in business. Indeed, many survivors did just that. As Lifton has observed, the roots of this pattern may be found in the need for security. By succeeding, the survivor acquires the very power by which he feels threatened and gains control over his environment. To better understand the motivation involved, we need only consider the opposite of success. To require and receive assistance from others was often viewed by former camp inmates as a sign of weakness, something they could ill afford to have shown during that time. We have only to listen as survivors describe the lessons they feel they gained from going through the Holocaust to grasp the significance of this. Said one person, a woman who sub-sequently did very well in business:

> *I learned how to decide quickly. And that no matter what deci-sion you make in life, you have to be decisive. You go left, you go right. No matter what you do, you have to be pretty much in control of yourself. That I am by myself; I have no one to protect me and guide me and I'm the one who is making the decision and whatever the decision is going to be, it better work.*

The woman's argument is that quick thinking during the war saved her life and indeed the stories about her experiences seem designed to drive home that point. In light of this it seems paradoxical that she also ascribes her survival to luck. In truth, as we shall see in the next chapter when we evaluate why the survivors adapted as well as they did, this is no paradox.

Not long after I began this project, I interviewed an elderly lady who had been in both ghettos and concentration camps. Her adap-tation to life in America had been fairly smooth. She had raised two children and appeared to be happily married. Her demeanor was calm and she smiled often, especially when she spoke about her children and grandchildren. After I finished, her daughter hap-pened to walk in. We spoke briefly about the study I was conduct-ing. Then she called me aside and said, "I suppose you think my mother is well adjusted." "It would seem that way," I replied. "Well, she is, except for one thing. I live in Brooklyn and she lives in the Bronx. Every day she calls me at 3:30 sharp to ask if my kids came home, and if they haven't she goes crazy. One time, when the kids were twenty minutes late, she got into a cab and came over here, all the way from the Bronx, during the rush hour." "Why does she act this way?" I asked. "Because 3:30 is the exact time she was taken away from her parents in the ghetto in Poland and she never saw them again."

This woman's story made me realize early on that survivors can never really banish what happened to them from their minds. Re-sponding to a questionnaire, 72 percent of a large sample of survi-vors agreed with the following statement: "Some rather harmless events can be anxiety-provoking for me; for example: the sight of a uniform, a knock at the door, dogs barking, smoke from a chimney, hearing the German language." Only 11 percent disagreed with this characterization. The events, words, sights, and smells capable of triggering memories and accompanying fears vary considerably from person to person, however. For example, Livia Bitton, a history professor at City University's Lehman College in the Bronx, recounted the following two vignettes to emphasize this point:

> *You never know what will do it. An older student who had been in Occupied Europe came to me because she wanted credit for a book she'd written about her life in the camps. And I looked at the book and helped her. And when I read it I saw that each of her relatives had had some kind of a good job in the camp. Now to you that means nothing. But for me it means that it's very possible that she was one of those "toughies," and then again, maybe she wasn't. I don't know. But to live with that. . . .*
>
> *When I see people pushing, I cry because it brings back memories of pushing in Auschwitz, where your piece of bread was your life. On a tour of the Sinai desert, in Israel, there was this couple—everywhere we went they were always at the head of the line. Then the guide said: "Please save your water because we're going to be in the desert for eight to ten hours." And this woman took her water and she started to clean her shoes and her hands. And I said to her: "What will you do when you run out of water?" And she said: "I'm sure the guide has some more water." I turned to Len, my husband, and I said, "This woman would have done this in the concentration camps and she wouldn't have cared."*

One general feature is that survivors' homes are very clean and neat. This was true of most of those I interviewed. Some researchers have noted that survivor women are compulsive house-cleaners. This seems to be related to life in the camps, where it was extremely difficult to stay clean, both personally and in general. "We had to live with dirt for so long, and every time I see a dirty place I remember those years," observed one former Dachau inmate. For Herbert Kalter, of Great Neck, the reaction was more specific: "I have a terrible reaction to Clorox. I hate it because it reminds me of how they used to pour it on the bodies they stacked, one on top of the other."

Since food was so basic to survival in the camps, survivors hate to see it wasted. Congressman Tom Lantos elaborated on this to me: "I cannot put food on my plate that I don't finish. In a restaurant I always have trouble ordering anything that is more than a reasonable portion because to send food back is a crime." At every dinner that I attended where survivors predominated—an Israel bonds affair or a wedding—those present never failed to comment on the profusion of food and how much of it was thrown away afterward. At home, most survivors freeze food, especially bread, and probably to a far greater extent than the average individual. A good number of survivors' children claim to have inherited this tendency from their parents. Still, this is not true for all survivors. Some have the opposite reaction, though in such instances it is also traceable to the aftereffects of the war. Jack Hirsch, a successful businessman, asserts that he no longer worries about hoarding or saving food because "I don't have to. In those days, when I got that soft drink on the boat to America, I took one swig a day, and it lasted eleven days."

Unease with or fear of authority is another trait shared by many who lived through the war. According to one woman who was hidden during the war, "Just seeing official documents mailed to me, such as a notice about a delayed payment for a parking ticket, causes me an untoward amount of anxiety." Naomi Wilzig, whose husband was in the camps, writes that she has never bought striped garments or clothes with epaulets for her children because of the reaction such items provoke in her spouse. Others prefer to sit in a chair with its back against the wall in a public place, and many have retained the habit of looking around whenever they light up a cigarette, a serious crime in the camps under certain conditions. Most experience only mild discomfort in their daily lives when such things come up, but for a few, even after many years, the reaction is extreme:

I had, and still have, tremendous difficulties with authorities. I cringe and my bladder contracts violently whenever I see a person in uniform and a siren sounds, not only at night, but even during the day when I can check it out. It gets me in a state of panic. Taking orders, especially when they are given in what I perceive as a threatening voice, is almost impossible and I respond to it in an almost unreasonable way.

Fear of helplessness is another apprehension that predominates among the survivors. Herbert Kalter hates to sit in traffic because it means he is no longer in control. "I feel trapped. In general," he adds, "if you follow other people, that's the end. It was that way in the camps." Another woman lamented that she had lost many opportunities to advance her career because of such fears, including a White House dinner that she missed because of her concern that she would be in a place where she could not leave immediately of her own free will if she so desired.

These examples make amply clear the impossibility of forgetting for the survivors. Symbolic of this was the way in which one person who sent in an oral history to Israel's Yad Vashem Testimonies Division in 1981 identified himself as "Schmuel Judkiewitz, PRES-ENTLY SAM BRADIN," and then, beneath it, neatly printed, "#134236, LEFT ARM." Although the camp number can easily be removed, it is not commonly done by survivors, though they may hide it in certain situations. Helen Lewis, a dancer who was imprisoned in Theresienstadt, summed up her feelings about the number as follows:

> *I never wanted to have the tattoo removed—that would have been a kind of betrayal of the past—and it is the Germans' shame, not mine, that I carry. Funnily enough, I am more sensitive about it now than I was then, but I would never show it if I could avoid it, and I still wear long sleeves whenever I can. If I'm anywhere—on holiday in Yugoslavia, for example—and I'm likely to meet Germans, I put a strip of sticking plaster over it. I just don't want them to stare at it. If I'm somewhere where I don't think there will be Germans around, I don't bother, of course.*

The pervasiveness of the war's effects and its indelible nature can also be seen by the way in which the survivors measure time. Their conversations are frequently laced with references such as "before the Nazis came" or "after the war." It is a basic part of their lexicon. Moreover, those who died are not only not forgotten, but are thought of in ways that indicate how conscious the survivor is that the dead have been cheated of life and how the survivor clings to the hope that those who have departed may yet be found, alive and well. Murray Kirschblat, a Polish-born survivor of Dachau and Buchenwald, tried to find his children for five years after the war ended. His daughter, Ricki Bernstein, elaborated on the connection between her father's mourning and his inability to come up with conclusive evidence as to their deaths:

> *Even today, there is a clear sense of loss while he discusses the subject, but never the finality that comes from actual confronta-*

tion with a body or a grave and the working through of grief that normally ensues. I can remember asking my father how old his two children were (meaning when they died) and him answering me with their ages as if they would be alive today—37 and 34. It was as though they were alive somewhere, just irretrievably lost to him.

Bernstein disagreed with the view expressed by one researcher that such behavior stems from a "rebirth fantasy connected with regression to magical thinking." She argued that every survivor knew of cases where people had miraculously been found alive after the war and this made them hopeful that they too would achieve a similar reunification.

2 ✳

Etched into the consciousness of the survivor is an awareness that the events in which he or she was an unwilling participant contain a significance that extends beyond individual suffering, terrible as that was. They know that the sheer horror of the event raises larger questions that man must grapple with if he is to remain human and arrive at an understanding of his role in the cosmos. Chief among these is the question of God and religion. More than anyone, the survivor cannot afford to ignore the implications of the Holocaust vis-à-vis faith. This is because for him the question is twofold—why did it happen and why to him? While the survivors appear to have made a satisfactory adjustment in psychological terms, and function quite well despite the nightmares and apprehensions that are a part of their lives, this is only part of the picture. We need to see how successfully they have assimilated the religious, ethical, philosophical, and intellectual dilemmas posed by the Holocaust. Have they come to grips with these questions and how have they responded to them?

In an attempt to shed light on the religious views of those who went through the war, Reeve Robert Brenner interviewed 708 Israeli survivors and presented those results in a book, *The Faith and Doubt of Holocaust Survivors*. Among the many findings, Brenner discovered that seven out of ten survivors did not change their religious behavior as a result of the Holocaust. There was a decrease from 55 to 34 percent in the proportion of survivors who were observant before the war and in the years immediately following it. Thirty years later, however, 43 percent were observant, meaning that of the 21 percent who had become nonobservant right after the war's end, 9 percent subsequently changed their position and became observant. Parenthetically, the ultra-Orthodox were able to reclaim virtually all of their defectors. About 55 percent of the survivors believed in a "personal God" before the war, meaning a God who took an active interest in their individual lives. This dropped to 36 percent after the war, but many, instead of becoming nonbelievers, shifted their view of God to that of an impersonal supreme being who does not interfere with what takes place in the world. Only 31 percent claimed to be nonbelievers. Another, more general study of survivors who came to America found a similar though somewhat larger drop in religious faith after the war. Interestingly, Brenner also found that 43 percent of survivors who were nonobservant before the war became "favorably disposed" toward Jewish observances after the Holocaust.

The interviews conducted for this book tend to support these conclusions. The majority of believers did not become atheists, but there was a definite decrease in the number of believers. Moreover, for most the Holocaust created grave doubts about the nature of God and His relationship to human beings even as the survivors continued to believe in Him. Most survivors have remained within the Jewish community and their reasons for doing so fall into the following categories: (1) belief in God based on personal experience; (2) general theological explanations; (3) preserving linkages to tradition and to their prior European-Jewish lifestyle; (4) identifying with the contemporary Jewish community; and (5) a richer and more rewarding way of life. Let's examine these reasons a bit more carefully:

For some survivors simply remaining alive during the Holocaust was enough of a miracle to justify continued faith in God. One man extended this view to the period after the war as well, saying: "I got through Auschwitz and nothing happened to me. I went through the Korean War and nothing happened to me, so somebody must be looking after me." Sam Halpern was more specific: "I escaped from camp and didn't know whether to go right or left. Then I saw a pigeon flying and I said: 'I think I'll follow this pigeon.' Well, the pigeon was going to the front and that was the right direction." The proof is presented here in terms of personal survival. However, whenever I pressed respondents to explain why God had not chosen to save others in a similar manner, the response was invariably: "We can't understand God." No one claimed to have been saved because they were more worthy than someone else who died. Most simply asserted that they did not know why God had chosen to save them or why He had decided not to intervene on behalf of those who perished.

Some survivors justified their having been rescued from certain death conditionally, that is, God now expected certain things from them. One wealthy businessman, William Ungar, posed the dilemma in the following terms:

> *Why did I survive and others didn't? Why was I only wounded and others were killed? I survived to be a witness to what took place. And I also think God let me live to see what good I would do. This may be a very primitive way to answer the question but I feel that if I did survive, it was to do some good deeds in my lifetime. Of course, I wouldn't preach about it or advertise it. I'm not trying to elevate myself that I'm the only one who deserved to survive.*

This individual clearly understood that he could not explain why he was, so to speak, "anointed" by God. He is active in the Jewish community and has given generously to charity. It is perhaps the best way for him to justify God's seeming faith in *him*.

On the theological level there are those who refuse to countenance any semblance of doubt in their faith. It is difficult to say to what extent this is due to the strength of their beliefs, for some express a fear that questioning will open the floodgates of doubt and the resultant disaffection will deprive them of their rationale for going on. They are, in short, frightened at the thought of a world without God. To those reared in a community of believers such a world cannot be contemplated because it is a world without meaning. As Lucy Dawidowicz wrote in *The War Against the Jews:* "For believing Jews, the conviction that their sacrifice was required as testimony to Almighty God was more comforting than the supposition that He had abandoned them altogether. To be sure, God's design was concealed from them, but they would remain steadfast in their faith." We can perhaps better comprehend what this meant on an individual level by listening to Paula Gris's candid exposition of her personal struggle with faith and doubt:

I don't know if I believe in God, but the alternative is not having children, not living. I have to believe. I'm too afraid of the alternative. Some survivors came out of the camps not believing in God, but I turned that station off. It wasn't my business to resolve that. There is no other choice. I don't know what happens when you're angry at God and you leave yourself to the mercy of man.

Other survivors' faith seems to be so powerful that it is not rooted in a fear of alternatives but rather in the conviction that their religious beliefs are absolutely true. For Faye Porter, a Lithuanian-born survivor, Jewish history is seen as a series of miracles beginning with the Jewish exodus from Egypt, and culminating in the founding of the State of Israel. She attributed her own survival to divine intervention. Asked if she had any doubts, she answered: "I don't know. I believe. Maybe I'm superstitious. I believe in God and that's all." Dovid Felberbaum, a Hasidic Jew living in the ultra-Orthodox community of New Square, New York, explained how he was able to maintain his faith in God after what he had seen in the camps: "If a father slaps his son, is he no longer his father?" Felberbaum went on to say that the "strength of the slap" did not matter and that it was not for human beings to question God's actions or motives. This is consistent with Brenner's statistical finding that the ultra-Orthodox were the least affected in their beliefs by the Holocaust.

In general, those who professed absolute faith responded to my queries only after considerable prodding, not because they were unsure of their position but because they felt that reasons were unnecessary and even inappropriate. The position of the strictly Orthodox is perhaps best summed up in an article on the subject that appeared in the Orthodox journal published by Agudath Israel of America, *The Jewish Observer*. In it, the author argues that where there is no "answer" silence is the best response. He cites the parable of a European rabbi, the Maggid [storyteller] of Dubnow. It is the tale of a city dweller who saw a farmer plowing up good grass. "Why?" he asked. Six months later, when he passed by again and saw the harvest, he understood. In Messianic times, concludes the author, pointless suffering will be understood and until then faith is all that is required.

For most survivors, however, the questions remain and are not so easily resolved. They believe in varying degrees, but they question, and often they are very angry. Sarah Berkowitz related: "Until this day, we are Sabbath observers and I believe in God, but that does not deny the fact that I question. . . . Why did He allow it? Why did He forsake us?" Another survivor stated: "God, if you felt we had to die, okay . . . but like this? Why?" And sometimes survivors act out their anger directly:

> *A good friend of mine was in Bergen-Belsen and the first thing she did when she got out was she got a sandwich with some kind of meat and put cheese on it [a clear violation of the laws of kashruth]. Then she looked up at God and said, "See? Do me something!" Is that somebody who doesn't believe in God? No. She's mad at God.*

Even those who remain steadfast in their religious observance can engage in behavior of this sort. One woman always places a drop of milk in her chicken soup and says, "This is to punish you, God, for what you have done."

Challenging and questioning God is not an act of heresy according to Jewish law. On the contrary, it is an ancient tradition, one first articulated in the Bible by Abraham when he wondered aloud whether God's desire to destroy Sodom and Gomorrah was just. Jonah defies God when told to go to Nineveh. Elie Wiesel expanded on this idea in *A Jew Today:*

> *Judaism teaches man to overcome despair. What is Jewish history if not an endless quarrel with God . . . and as in every love affair, there are quarrels and reconciliations, more quarrels and more reconciliations, and yet neither God nor the Jews ever gave up on the other. . . . In the endless engagement with God, we proved to Him that we were more patient than He, more compassionate, too. In other words, we did not give up on Him either. For this is the essence of being Jewish: never to give up—never to yield to despair.*

Thus we see that faith is not simply an imperative, it is a way of linking up with the tradition, of guaranteeing its continuity. Moreover, for those who believe, there is the opportunity to question, challenge, and even debate with Him who is responsible for the circumstances in which they find themselves—and to demand answers. But that is only part of the covenant, so to speak. One cannot debate unless one believes, for without faith there is no partner to the debate. Yet how can there be true faith if genuinely felt anger must be repressed? Again, Wiesel, in *The Gates of the Forest*, offers a path through the ashes in the words of a Hasidic *rebbe*:

> *When you come to our celebrations, you'll see how we dance and sing and rejoice. There is joy as well as fury in the* hasid's *dancing. It's his way of proclaiming, "You don't want me to dance; too bad, I'll dance anyhow. You've taken away every reason for singing, but I shall sing. I shall sing of the deceit that walks by day and the truth that walks by night, yes, and of the silence of dusk as well. You didn't expect my joy, but here it is; yes, my joy will rise up; it will submerge you."*

For Jews who adhere to the teachings of the faith there is a causal connection between sin and punishment, even if its precise workings are not known. They read in the Bible of God's threats to the Jews of retribution if they forsake His commandments and they inevitably wonder what transgressions brought about the Holocaust. In Brenner's study 21 percent saw a direct relationship between the death of six million Jews and man's sinfulness. I asked one respondent who felt this way why so many of the Jews who were killed were observant. Her answer: "When it rains, everyone gets wet. On the other hand, the State of Israel was a reward to show the enemy that our Lord is alive." But Wiesel (and others) categorically rejects any linkage between the two events, arguing that both remain mysteries. He adds, "I refuse to give children in tomorrow's Israel such a burden, such guilt."

Some survivors find meaning in the tortures they endured by viewing them as a part of Jewish history, of which the Holocaust is simply the latest and most systematically brutal instance of cruelty to Jews. Hence they do not see it as a unique tragedy. For them, the significance of the event is not diminished but rather heightened by its interconnectedness with the suffering that periodically afflicted Jews through the ages:

> *Out from the depths of my breast, I can feel the same tragedy that befell the ten martyrs that you read about on Yom Kippur, because I was there too. It wasn't much different. The technique may have been different. So Auschwitz gave me a depth of Jewish perspective, whether it was the medieval Crusades, whether it*

was the defenders of York [England], or the Jews of Mainz [Germany], or the Kishinev Pogroms, or the Warsaw Ghetto. I was everywhere. All of a sudden, all the Jews' suffering was internalized and eternalized in me and through me, not by my choice but by the choice of my fellow-being who has so decided.

One woman explained her effort to invest the Holocaust with historical religious meaning by incorporating it into the Passover holiday: "Every year," she said, "when we recite the story of Passover, we also speak about the Holocaust so that our children and grandchildren will know what happened to us and we hope that it will never happen to them."

A substantial number of survivors remain in the community and are observant, largely because it is the only tangible way of continuing in the path of those who died. Nothing else remains except perhaps faded black-and-white photographs and memories. As Noach Rodzinek, a Polish survivor, put it: "I don't believe like I did before the war, but I go to synagogue on Shabbes and keep kosher because that's the way my father did it." Vera Eden, a Hungarian survivor, noted in a similar vein: "We want to re-create the same atmosphere we had at home." One man, now a fully observant Jew, recalled how unhappy he had been when, immediately after the war, he abandoned the faith for a time. "I wasn't happy without that which I was used to and, finally, the needs of the children brought me back." Another added, "We can return easily because we've been brought up that way, and no one is the wiser that we left temporarily."

The importance of the socialization process in motivating the survivor to continue in the tradition should not be underestimated. Those raised in Orthodox surroundings experienced a lifestyle that revolved around the daily rituals of prayer and intensive Talmudic study, a society where all six days of the week were preparatory to the weekly glory of the Sabbath. It was a self-enclosed world where rabbis and scholars were revered and where the joys of the various holidays were the most important events of the year. When they came here, the refugees sought to re-create that world because it was the way of life with which they were most familiar and comfortable. Unlike earlier generations of Jews, they had not come as adventurers in a new land intent upon burying the past. Unfortunately for them, it was others who had attempted to bury both them and that past. Therefore, once they felt secure in their new environment they set out to ensure its survival. Moreover, since they were inextricably tied to European-Jewish culture, preserving it meant that a part of that which had been destroyed could be retrieved. This is why, for example, so many survivors feel at home in small and crowded synagogues. The cacophony of sound, the wooden benches, the long tables upon which the congregants place their prayerbooks and Bibles are all reminiscent of the old country. I spoke with many survivors in the course of this project whose dress and outward level of observance belied the skepticism that lay beneath the image they projected to others. Their oft-stated rationale was always the feeling of "being at home" that was evoked by communal participation and individual observance.

Another consideration was that the religious way of life enabled the survivors to communicate, in an abstract but crucial way, with their parents and others who were close to them. Remaining within the fold was often seen as a verification of that which had been transmitted to them within their families. It meant that though physically dead, those who were gone from this world remained very much alive spiritually. It is an oft-repeated maxim within the observant Jewish community that the great sages such as Maimonides, Rashi, and the ancient rabbis of the Talmud continue to live only when their works are read and studied. For the survivors, ritual observance and cultural involvement became the vehicles for honoring and commemorating those no longer present. Miriam Brach summed it up best in the following words:

I believe that it was my destiny to survive, to come back from the ashes and to be the link from the past that would begin life again and pass it on to future generations. My goal was to remain faithful to the religion into which I was born and to my upbringing. This upbringing gave me the strength to survive the war. When I live this way, I know I am living the kind of life my departed parents would have wanted me to live.

Related to the idea of continuity is the feeling of belonging. Even synagogues that affiliate with the Conservative movement, where men and women sit together, some of the prayers are in English, and the philosophy is far removed from the Orthodox communities of Europe, can attract survivors who wish to be part of the Jewish community. They may believe in Conservative Judaism, they may not; but regardless, it brings them into contact with other Jews and makes them feel that they are part of something. As one man observed: "When I go to synagogue, I feel that I am at one with the Jewish people. And when I look around in the temple, I know that Hitler *yemach shemo* [may his name be erased] did not win." Philosopher Emil Fackenheim has called this "the 614th commandment," namely, that "the authentic Jew of today is forbidden to hand Hitler yet another posthumous victory" by ceasing to identify as a Jew.

Leon Wells is unusual in that he is one of the few survivors who belongs to a Reform temple. For him too the reasons for identifying are the same:

> *I'll tell you the truth. I was raised in a Hasidic family, but I don't believe in God. Even so, I belong to a synagogue, a Reform temple. This [being a Jew] was my background and culture. It's an emotional thing.*

He feels this way even though he entertains serious doubts about the validity of Judaism:

> *But how could there be a God who would allow these things to happen? God said the covenant's symbol is the* bris, *circumcision. And so isn't it ironic that it was the symbol of God's covenant with his people that caused so many Jewish males to perish in the Holocaust because they couldn't hide the fact that they were Jewish?*

People like Wells clearly demonstrate the power of shared history and communal bonds in retaining the allegiance of people, irrespective of their religious beliefs.

Finally, there are those who see remaining Jewish in pragmatic terms. No doubt they feel at ease in the community and they may well enjoy certain aspects of the tradition, but the primary reason is that Judaism "is a good way of life." One such individual, Abraham Kessler, who regularly attends an Orthodox synagogue, was asked if he believed in God. His answer was revealing: "I don't know if He's listening, but my children are going in this direction and I see that it's good." Another survivor based her views on considerations that could easily be applied to many American Jews:

> With all the drugs, AIDS, and crime in the society today, I feel that being religious is just a better way of life. If you are, the chances are much better you won't have these problems. But for my children to be accepted, my husband and I have to be religious too.

When all is said and done, however, there is still a sizable segment of the survivor community whose members have either lost their faith and openly admit it, or who never believed to begin with. One unequivocally asserted: "I don't believe in anything and you wouldn't either if you went through what I went through." They are usually the least affiliated with organized Jewry, though not always. There were also survivors who were atheists but remained within the community by working on behalf of Israel. To them, Israel had little to do with religion or tradition. Its primary function was to serve as a haven for Jews, a need made amply clear by what had happened in World War II.

A number of nonbelieving survivors coupled their assertions with a wish that it could be otherwise. One such individual, who lived through Auschwitz, spoke of her doubts with sincere regret:

> It's easier to believe than not to, but I can't believe. I listened as my granddaughter read the story in synagogue of how the whale spit up Jonah after three days, and of course I couldn't say anything to the children about what a stupidity this is after we were in such a fire, in Auschwitz, where the sky was always black from the flesh of people they burned. There were a few Jews who tried to revolt; so they pushed them into the ovens alive. So I ask, couldn't there have been just one little miracle, something to show that there is justice in the world? I saw how the Nazis learned how to shoot by killing children. So that's why I never believed. There were no miracles. There were no miracles.

Perhaps the most unhappy group of survivors were those who had cut their ties to the community in ways that were irrevocable. Sometimes, especially as they grew older, they yearned to return but found they could not. One man who prided himself on his ability to assimilate confided to me how wrong he had been even as he lamented his inability to reenter the social circle he had so casually dismissed and left years ago. "Now I know I'm still a Jew and I'll always be one, but how can I come back after all these years? I'd be too embarrassed." Another clearly blamed her own desire to assimilate for her son's subsequent interfaith marriage. Her remarks indicated that she would have welcomed a second opportunity to do things differently. The reasons she gave indicate the role of the past in the thinking of the survivor. Speaking of her friends in Europe, she reflected sadly:

> *Somehow I feel I contribute to their total disappearance when I think of my son, who lives in Kentucky with his lovely wife, a Southern Baptist. In all probability, their children will be raised as Baptists—whatever that is. Last year, this did not bother me. Why does it bother me now? I feel a traitor to my childhood friends a second time: for having escaped, and for having future grandchildren who will not be Jewish.*

The Holocaust shook the foundations of the civilized world. After it, there could no longer be any innocence regarding man's enormous potential for evil, least of all among those who directly experienced its horrors. We see here that the survivors have dealt with the theological dilemmas posed by the Holocaust in a variety of ways. The majority have retained some semblance of faith, albeit a faith usually accompanied by serious doubt. Their capacity to think rationally about the event, to discuss it with others, and simply to remain sane in the face of it is an accomplishment that requires no further elaboration. This is the true yardstick against which their successful adaptation must be measured, not the validity or sophistication of the conclusions they have come to. Why this is so has been most eloquently and forcefully presented by the theologian Eliezer Berkovitz:

> *The faith affirmed was superhuman; the loss of faith—in the circumstances—human. . . . Those who were not there and yet, readily accept the holocaust as the will of God that must not be questioned, desecrate the holy disbelief of those whose faith was murdered. And those who were not there, and yet join with self-assurance the rank of the disbelievers, desecrate the holy faith of the believers.*

3✳

As the central event in their lives, the Holocaust has influenced the survivors' outlook on life in a variety of ways, not only theologically, and it is interesting to see how their views have developed since their arrival to these shores. While survivors tended to be less liberal politically than American Jews as a whole, this seems to be more rooted in their concern for Israel's security than anything else. For example, many spoke approvingly of Richard Nixon because of his strong support, in their opinion, for Israel. At the same time, they felt he had antipathy toward Jews as a group and they seemed especially concerned about Watergate, largely because to them it represented a threat to basic freedoms. Nonetheless, the outcome, namely Nixon's forced resignation, appeared to have restored their faith in the United States. As Alex Gross remarked: "It proved we are on the ball." Similarly, Ronald Reagan, perceived by many Jews as the most pro-Israel president in history, received high marks from the survivors. When I raised the matter of his visit to Bitburg and Elie Wiesel's strong criticism of it, they seemed somewhat discomfited, but invariably asserted that Reagan just didn't understand the issues, or that he was misled by his advisors, who were more concerned about good relations with Germany than with anything else.

When it came to attitudes toward minorities, many survivors expressed stereotypical views about various groups, particularly blacks. Nevertheless, these opinions were frequently accompanied by guilt and uncertainty, as well as a conscious attempt to lessen the impact of their negative statements. Often they prefaced their critical observations with disclaimers such as: "I know they suffered a lot and we should understand that, but why should we, who often helped blacks, pay the price for their suffering?" In charging blacks in general with anti-Semitism, quite a few laid the blame on jealousy. Mention of the Reverend Jesse Jackson aroused a great deal of hostility, not only for past remarks but because of his expressive style. The following observation by Helen Schimel, a German-born survivor, was fairly typical: "He makes very nervous. He speaks like Hitler used to speak, with his screaming and angry way of talking." The attitudes of the survivors toward blacks are often a direct result of their unique experiences. First, they themselves feel very vulnerable as a minority, and have a heightened fear of anything that smacks of anti-Semitism. At a time when relations between blacks and Jews are already strained, such apprehensions have increased even more. Second, as impoverished immigrants, the survivors frequently found themselves living in close proximity with blacks (and Hispanics) when they first came to America and this sometimes created tensions.

Despite these mitigating factors, about half of the survivors are concerned about the rights of minorities, according to the figures in our survey. A variety of reasons were given in the interviews, with the fear of how discrimination against one group impinged upon the freedom of all minorities high on the list. Many also thought of it in terms of a moral obligation to help those less fortunate. Survivors living in the South expressed greater sympathy for blacks than survivors in other parts of the country, in part because the racist attacks of organizations like the Klan often also included overt hostility toward Jews. Ruth Siegler, a resident of Birmingham, recalled: "We had policemen protecting our temple from the same people who bombed the church where several black children were killed. In those days, blacks and Jews were one word." Leon Gross, who lives in Tuscaloosa, Alabama, found another outlet for his general concern for minorities. He became active in supporting the resettlement of Vietnamese boat people who had come to the area.

Several respondents also differentiated between blacks and Christians in general, seeing the blacks as people who have been manipulated by others to dislike Jews. Livia Bitton offered the following view:

> As a survivor I have a strong affinity for blacks. Not just because they've suffered, but primarily because I know that blacks did not participate in the Holocaust. I look at them and I know that they or their grandparents couldn't have done it. That is a very important thing for me. The other factor is that blacks don't have a tradition of anti-Semitism the way whites have had for centuries. And I believe that they're being given a lot of propaganda. I think Hispanics have also been misled and I tell my Hispanic students at Lehman College: "You have Jewish blood because in Spain and in places like Recife, Brazil, and Curaçao there were large numbers of Marranos who intermingled—names like Rodríguez or Méndez."

The Arab-Israeli conflict is another subject that has most survivors deeply worried and many of them believe that Israel should try to arrive at an accommodation with the Palestinians. Ina Weiss, who immigrated to Israel from America, does not trust the Arabs a great deal but feels that "we have no right to throw out the Arabs who've been living here for a hundred or more years." Leon Wells, whose home is in Closter, New Jersey, sees the dilemma as one that comes down to what it means to be Jewish, arguing that "if we don't act humane to them, then we're like all the other nations. Unfortunately, I don't think we were ever different." A good number of survivors disagreed with such assessments, taking a more hard-line view. Manny Ragen, who came to Israel from the United States in 1977 and who lives in Netanya, commented: "Israel shouldn't give back the West Bank lands. Before the war in 1967, the Arabs had the West Bank and they started up anyway." Despite their fears of another Holocaust, few survivors connected such views to their perception of Arabs. One possible explanation may be that those who perpetrated the Holocaust were not Arabs, but European and Christian.

Another topic that generated strong, if sometimes ambivalent, reactions was attitudes toward Germans as a people and Germany as a nation. For a sizable segment of survivors, there exists a strong and visceral hatred for Germans, even as they admit that today's Germans cannot, by and large, be blamed for what happened during the war. It manifests itself even in relatively unimportant (though symbolic) areas such as in the case of a man who whenever he sees a golf game or tennis match always hopes the player from Germany is defeated. "I know it's wrong," he tells me, "but I can't help it." Many survivors and their children, as well as, one might add, other Jews, avoid buying German products whenever possible. Some have refused to apply for or accept German reparations payments. "I didn't want to be reminded every month that I'm a Holocaust survivor in need of help from the Germans," asserted one woman, a native Berliner who had been in Dachau. Others disagree, arguing that "the money is better than nothing." This attitude differs sharply from that prevailing in Israel where German products, most noticeably automobiles, are very common, and where the government has accepted large sums of money from Germany. Perhaps a people in their own land do not feel as great a need to take a stand on such an issue. Moreover, Israel's difficult economic situation does not allow it the luxury of cavalierly rejecting offers of assistance.

Jack Tramiel is an exception to the prevailing negative attitudes most survivors have toward Germans. He is a very wealthy man who does quite a bit of business in Europe and that includes Germany. Worth many millions of dollars today, he arrived penniless in America on the *Marine Swallow* in 1947. Feeling an obligation to "give something back to those who liberated me," Tramiel volunteered and served in the U.S. Army before settling down and opening a small typewriter repair shop in Manhattan. Eventually he made it big in the world of computers, founding Commodore International and building it up into one of the world's most successful computer companies. Today he is chairman of the internationally famous Atari Corporation, which he purchased in 1984 from Warner Communications. Tramiel has a reputation as a tough, hard-driving businessman and has, over the years, been the subject of numerous articles in newspapers and magazines such as *The New York Times, Business Week,* and *Maclean's.* "Business is like sex—you have to get involved" is one of his favorite one-liners.

Tramiel is a generous man who gives to many causes, including the United States Holocaust Memorial Museum, the Dalai Lama, Israel, the Red Cross, the Lubavitcher Hasidim, and Chinese student dissidents, among others. Asked how a man who seems to care so much about others in need has acquired a reputation for being so confrontational, even ruthless, in his business dealings (he had once said, "Business is war and you have to be in it to win"), Tramiel replies: "Private life and business are two different things." Even so, the two can sometimes come together in strange ways, shedding light on both. Shortly after he purchased a factory in Germany, he was told by someone there: "Jack, one thing you should not do. Don't tell them you're Jewish. You've got two thousand German employees here and you won't get their loyalty." Tramiel's reaction and response to that warning was rather interesting, to say the least:

So what did I do? I made a speech to them and told them all I was Jewish and that I was a survivor of the concentration camps. And then I said that I wanted everyone who was an SS officer in my office in the next two days. Over twenty of them came in and about six walked out, saying they will never work for a Jew. The others apologized, it wasn't their fault, and all that. I saw it as honesty and that they were looking for forgiveness and I gave it to them. You see, at first, after the war, I had feelings of revenge, but that changed when a priest said to me: "If you are going to treat the Germans the same way they treated you, what's the difference between you and them?" The way he said it just totally changed my outlook.

An exceptional case, perhaps, involving a most unusual person. Nonetheless, it is an example of how certain survivors feel about the futility of continuing to hate all Germans.

A number of respondents took pains to distinguish between older and younger Germans. For Frances Epstein the line was very clear: "I hate to shake hands with him unless I know exactly where he was and what he was doing during the war." David Honig felt that hating the new generation was neither correct nor practical. Still, as he put it: "I cannot forget it and I cannot forgive them either." Most survivors were uneasy about German reunification. I was present when shortly after the Berlin Wall came down a very high-level U.S. government official addressed a gathering of 1,200 survivors. Seemingly oblivious to the sensibilities of the audience he gushed enthusiastically: "Nineteen eighty-nine is a wonderful period in world history. Who would have ever thought that we would live to see the day when the Berlin Wall would come down." Those present sat in shocked silence. Afterward, many were openly critical, even though the speaker lauded the survivors for their achievements in America. Livia Bitton, however, had a different view. "I'm not threatened by it," she averred. "I don't think that being strong and unified gives birth to a Hitler. It was just the other way around in Weimar Germany." In a statistical survey of Canadian survivors, only 26 percent continue to feel hostile toward Germans or other non-Jews. This is not surprising since intellectually most survivors will readily admit that it's wrong to hate someone without knowing his or her views. The problem is that emotionally they often have great difficulty dealing with the problem.

Those who lived through the conflagration were even more hostile, on the whole, toward Poles, often comparing them unfavorably to Germans. One noted, "The German mentality is they do whatever they are told to do." "The Germans at least believed in something—Hitler," added Abraham Krakowski. "The Poles just hate the Jews. What they did to the Jews *after* the war was unbelievable." Noach Rodzinek was saved by a Polish family. He has invited them to America and they have been guests in his home. He feels very close to them but he is, nonetheless, still critical of the Poles as a group: "Most were no good. I lost eight brothers and a sister and also my parents. I'm the only survivor." Moreover, their evaluation of Poles often differed from that of Germans in that they did not see the actions of Poles as a one-generation phenomenon. In their view, Polish anti-Semitism had been a reality for centuries and remains one today. The majority of survivors attributed the primary source for Polish anti-Semitism to the teachings of the Catholic Church in that nation.

Agreement on these points was not, however, unanimous, especially among those who were saved by Poles. Leon Lepold, a survivor and activist in the Jewish community of Milwaukee, claimed:

Speaking from experience, if not for the Poles, none of us would have survived in southeastern Poland. A lot of Polish people were murdered, hung, shot, and had their homes burned because they were hiding Jewish people. One man, Michal Sloniowski, deserves to be remembered forever. He lived in a house, together with his wife and son, that was in the middle of a huge forest. Fourteen young boys and girls survived in this forest thanks to this gentleman who risked his life and the lives of his family, for no payment, just to save our lives. He was an angel sent from God.

What about the future? Do survivors feel safe in the United States? One theme that emerged again and again in the interviews was a belief that wonderful as America was, one could never truly feel secure as a Jew anyplace, except in Israel. The following account of a conversation between a survivor and his friend, which appeared in Dorothy Rabinowitz's *New Lives,* is an excellent portrayal of this stance:

Once, he outlined to a friend all the reasons why it was unlikely that the Jews would ever have to run from America. American democratic tradition was long, its institutions stable; it lacked the entrenched anti-Semitism that had existed in Europe. It was not likely that it would happen here; it was not impossible, either. And though there was no real probability that one would have to become a refugee from America, he could, for argument's sake, list the countries where it would be safest to run. Aside from Israel, there was England. But Sweden was probably safer than England, since Sweden had a more stable economy. By the end of an hour's time he had outlined the flight from America in detail, and in terms that had grown less theoretical by the minute. He did this not for argument's sake but because, like any survivor, he had

thought about the problem of where to run, so that the details were
quite clear in his mind, quite matter-of-fact and practical.

Opinion among the survivors was divided about the effects of the Holocaust on their general outlook on life. Some believed that after what they had gone through their lives were charmed, that it was their destiny to overcome all odds. This attitude was particularly noticeable among those who had achieved financial success in the postwar era. Others came away from the Holocaust with a sense of impending doom that they simply could not shake off. It was, in essence, a feeling that nothing in life could be taken for granted and it was rooted in the knowledge that their whole world had collapsed once before. Sandy Mayer, who had been hidden as a child during the war, remembered reading an article in a newspaper that anti-Semitism in the United States had risen 12 percent between 1986 and 1987. As a result she had given serious consideration to encouraging her children to move to Israel even though she didn't especially identify as a Jew and had never herself visited the country.

Still, a number of survivors seemed to take some comfort in the fact that America is a land with many minorities. As Joseph Eden noted, "In Europe, Jews were a small minority in a large majority. Here you have Polish-Americans, Jewish-Americans, Czech-Americans, and so on." But this view was challenged by Congressman Tom Lantos, who pointed out that Hungary had many minorities—Romanians, Gypsies, Germans, Greeks, and Yugoslavs—living within its borders and that this had not prevented anti-Semitism from proliferating there. And General Sidney Shachnow, who, as an army man, lives and works in a primarily Gentile environment, also felt that Jews always face potential danger in the United States. "Look what happens when the farmers in the Midwest suffer economically," he argued. "Right away they turn around and blame the Jews."

No organization is more directly concerned and involved with the safety of American Jews than the Anti-Defamation League. Their primary task is to monitor and combat anti-Semitism wherever it appears and they are naturally more sensitive to the problem than most people. With this in mind, I asked Abe Foxman, who not only heads the ADL but is a survivor, for his reaction to the apprehension shared by many Jews. His upbeat response was revealing:

We experienced in this country, in a period of twelve to eighteen months, Ivan Boesky, Jonathan Pollard, Irangate, and the crisis with the farmers—four classic situations for anti-Semitism: Boesky—Jewish greed; Pollard—dual loyalty. And our people, not the Gentiles, wrote about dual loyalty. Irangate—a situation where Israel was shlepping [dragging] America into its own interests; the farm crisis—America lives on myths. One of the myths in the farm belt has been that if you work and go to church and you're moral, you'll be rewarded. These people wake up one morning and they're being bankrupted. Guys come in and say, "Hey, the Jews, the Eastern bankers"—it didn't sell. So I say to you, something's different in this country. Thirty, forty years ago, if you had had a confluence of these things, there would have been anti-Semitism. There isn't. In 1973, we saw it coming with the oil crisis, but it didn't. For every bumper sticker to burn Jews, not oil, we got ten thousand phone calls.

Of all the issues that agitate survivors, none is worse than the fact that people, some of them with scholarly credentials, are attempting to persuade the general public that the Holocaust never occurred. The words of Dina Balbien, now living in California, who survived the ghettos and camps and was liberated from Bergen-Belsen, summed up well the anguish felt by all survivors upon hearing such claims:

When I read the papers or see the news that the Holocaust never happened, I just freeze. I just get so ill when I hear this. I feel like my whole body is shaking. I feel like I'm totally helpless. I don't know, I feel like screaming out loud—How can anyone say this! Oh, I'm totally drained of everything.

In an effort to combat such views, Balbien speaks to local groups about the Nazi camps and has had herself videotaped by her local high school.

The State of Israel is what is most important to those who lived through the Holocaust. Invariably, whenever I brought up Israel in conversations with survivors, their faces glowed, as if I were asking them about their children. It is Israel that lightens the weight of their suffering, that seems to make going on in life as a Jew worthwhile. Their voices swell with pride as they speak of the country and its achievements. In it, they see the embodiment of their hopes and dreams that Jews can be a proud and strong people. To better understand the depth and intensity of this feeling and how it is inextricably tied in to their Holocaust experiences, we have only to look at the reactions of Luba Bat, a survivor, when she learned of the founding of the State of Israel on May 14, 1948. Writing in her autobiography, she recalled:

> When I heard the wonderful news announced on the radio, I became for a short while speechless, then I burst into tears, sobbing uncontrollably. . . . I resolved to make a pilgrimage to Israel as soon as I could afford it. . . . Amidst the general excitement . . ., mentally I was transferred to another location, to the death camp Auschwitz, where a hair-raising recollection overpowered me. I saw an aktion. . . . In the severe frost a group of young, barefoot girls, their teeth chattering, their bluish skin covered with goosepimples, proudly walked their last mile to the awaiting truck; amid deafening shrills, they landed on the top of the "human" mountain of crushed bodies. As the truck started, the young girls broke into loud singing of the Hatikvah. The Jews had a national hymn long before their dream country had come into being. The unbelievable courage and heroic singing on their way to the gas chamber was to me the most heartbreaking pain that will forever gnaw my heart. At the time I said to myself that beyond any shadow of doubt, this singing like a passionate prayer had reached heaven, and that someday it would be answered.

The survivors express a wide-ranging variety of views and attitudes about matters such as anti-Semitism, Germany, American politics, and Israel, and these views are often directly related to the Holocaust itself. What about their perceptions of human beings? What have their experiences in extreme circumstances taught them about what people are like? Here, as in the case of religion, we see differing opinions, reflecting as much the personalities and predilections of those expressing them as the different experiences they had.

The general view was that on many occasions camp life brought out the worst in people and that this was due to man's basic desire to survive and his consequent willingness to engage in questionable behavior to achieve that goal. Viktor Frankl, a psychiatrist who survived Auschwitz, has written: "We who have come back, by the aid of many lucky chances or miracles . . . we know: the best of us did not return." In the interviews, comments such as "I learned that people are selfish and have to be to survive" and "There's a thin line between being a human being and becoming an atrocious beast" were typical.

On the other hand, many told stories of how bread was shared in the camps and how people helped one another. This was especially true among relatives, people who came from the same towns and were friends, and those who belonged to various ideological groups, such as Zionists or communists. Terrence Des Pres's book *The Survivor* cites numerous cases where people assisted each other, drawing extensively from the literature on the subject. Des Pres concludes that "the survivor's experience is evidence that the need *to* help is as basic as the need *for* help." One man explained how the war had taught him that "when you have an opportunity to help someone, it's your responsibility to do so. If people hadn't helped me during the war at various points, I wouldn't be here."

For our purposes here, what is important is not so much what happened during the war, but afterward. In other words, how did the survivors' experiences affect their current thinking and behavior? All 170 respondents were asked this question and what is interesting is that even as most of the survivors condemned human excess and cruelty in the camps, they asserted that such behavior was "to be expected because everyone wants to live" and that regardless of how people acted toward one another in camp, to behave in this manner after the war was morally wrong. On this point, some may argue that the altruistic behavior of survivors after the war may in part be motivated by guilt. Even if true in certain cases, it does not change the reality of such behavior. Moreover, people of all backgrounds can be, and often are, motivated to do good deeds out of guilt.

Whatever the case, many of those interviewed saw a basic dichotomy between behavior in the camps and later on. The following story, recounted by Esther Peterseil, a survivor currently living in Lawrence, New York, illustrates the point:

I was in camp with my best friend, who grew up with me. Yet she would never share her bread with me. I wouldn't say she was mean, but she wasn't especially nice either. Yet after the war, I helped this woman by sending her money and care packages every month. In this way, she survived the hard economic situation in Israel. Why did she act this way? Because this was natural behavior in those times. Everyone wants to live and she was afraid she wouldn't have enough.

4

Overall, survivors seemed to be reasonably satisfied with their lives. One study asked whether they agreed with the following statement: "I have such a feeling of emptiness, can experience neither love nor hate, pleasure or pain, and can hardly get any enjoyment out of life." About 52 percent disagreed and 25 percent agreed, with the rest having no opinion. They were also asked for their views about the following statement: "I sometimes doubt whether I have actually found new meaning and purpose in life." Almost 44 percent of those responding disagreed with this charac- terization, 28 percent agreed, and the rest were neutral. Thus, things were far from perfect, with many survivors clearly affected. When queried about their position regarding the following state- ment: "I feel as if the spark has gone out of my life," a slight majority, 42 percent, agreed, about 35 percent did not, and the rest expressed no opinion. It must be remembered that these are people in an age bracket when "the spark" is often lost. In a case study of one community, Pittsburgh, fifty-three out of fifty-eight survivors interviewed felt that they had achieved a good deal in life.

What did "achieving a good deal" actually mean to survivors? For most the response was couched in terms of what might have been had they not been liberated. As Dora Zaidenweber, now living in Minneapolis, put it: "I've certainly been grateful for every day that was granted to me, and I still am." Esther Raab, one of the few survivors of Sobibor (she later helped make a film about it, *Escape from Sobibor*), said: "What has helped me is that I never feel sorry for myself. I feel very fortunate and I never let myself forget it." Achievement is, of course, a relative term and some showed an acute appreciation of just how relative the word was. One such individual, Marcus Tepper, observed: "My biggest achievement is that I managed to survive." Having said that, he then dutifully listed other aspects of his life, such as financial security and a good relationship with his wife.

Most survivors, rich or poor, religious or irreligious, educated or not educated, famous or anonymous, identified raising a nice family as their chief accomplishment. That this was of primary importance can be seen from the story of Herman Lewinter, who lives in Monticello, New York. Lewinter had an unusual job during the war. He was a photographer for the Nazis in the infamous Janowska Road camp. In fact, he was the last photographer of the camp. Unbeknownst to the Nazis, Lewinter risked his life almost every day by secretly snapping pictures of Nazi atrocities such as hangings and mass graves and by hiding the film afterward. Had he been caught, he would have been executed on the spot. But he eventually escaped from the camp, taking with him to freedom sixteen other inmates. After the war, the photographs, all 530 of them, were submitted as evidence at the Nuremberg war crimes trials. Many are still in his house and he showed me a number of them. Their graphic nature makes clear the chance he took in hiding them from the Nazis. Yet despite these clear acts of heroism, he told me that what he was most proud of is "that I raised a nice family." He was also pleased with the fact that he has enough money on which to live comfortably, and that he was able to give to charity. "Weren't you also proud of the pictures you smuggled out of the camp?" I asked him. "Oh yes," he replied, "but you wouldn't find me talking about that. This is between me and God."

Given the reality that there is probably a bit of self-hatred in virtually every member of a minority group, it might be reasonable to assume that many of the survivors, especially those who were more assimilated, took a negative view of their Jewishness, which was, after all, the cause of their troubles. This did not turn out to be the case. Very few of those interviewed expressed regret about being Jewish. Of course, no one knows how many survivors left the Jewish community entirely in the years following the war, but it would seem to be a small minority. In any case, the social psychologists Simon Herman and Uri Farago recently carried out a large-scale survey of American Jewry. Included in the representative sample were Holocaust survivors and one of the questions asked was: "If you were born all over again, would you wish to be born a Jew?" Holocaust survivors were *more likely* than any other group of Jews to answer in the affirmative, with 69 percent saying, "Yes, I would very much wish to be born a Jew." An additional 14 percent stated simply: "Yes, I would wish to be born a Jew," and 9 percent said, "It would not matter one way or another." Only 8 percent took the position of "No, I would not wish to be born a Jew." Judging from this survey, it would appear that most survivors have not internalized the sense of inferiority that the Nazis, who constantly referred to the Jews as *untermenschen,* wished to confer upon them.

A number of survivors who had moved to Israel after first settling in America were also interviewed. Most had emigrated in the late 1960s or 1970s and lived in either Jerusalem, Tel Aviv, or Netanya. Primarily I was curious to know if, in hindsight, they regretted not having come to Israel in the first place, right after the war ended. Most did not, arguing that they would have fared poorly in an economic sense and that coming later with a nest egg meant they could spend their remaining years in relative comfort.

More than anything, I was struck by the happiness of this group. They seemed more at peace with themselves, and the interviews suggested that this was often not the case when they lived in America. Several typologies of survivors emerged when I asked about their reasons for going. One was that of the survivor who emigrated to be with his children who had already made *aliyah.* A second decided that the money received from Social Security and a pension could go further in Israel than, say, in Florida. A third type wanted to live in Israel simply because it was a Jewish country. Many, if not most, of those who moved to Israel are Orthodox, but this alone would not explain their motivation since hundreds of thousands of Orthodox Jews continue to live in the United States. Rather, it was a desire to be part of the majority, a wish finally to belong in the fullest sense of the word. Shirley Ragen, a survivor who lived in the Canarsie section of Brooklyn before moving to Netanya, explained the feeling with an example: "Recently I had to go to the hospital several times. And whenever I got off, the bus driver would say to everyone, *'Refuah shelemah! Refuah shelemah!'* [Have a complete recovery!]. You know, the bus driver." Irena Schwarz, a secular Jew, said, "It sounds a little bit idiotic, but this is my place. I feel like I'm a member of a great family. I feel closer to the people here than anywhere else in the world."

A fourth category was the survivor who had always been a Zionist and saw this as the culmination of the Zionist dream. Why was he or she not content, as are so many American Jews, including survivors, with visiting Israel and buying Israel bonds? Answering such a question would require hundreds of interviews, but one thing is clear—for some people, occasional visits and donations are simply not enough. There was, in any event, a strong undercurrent of apprehension about anti-Semitism among those who responded with affirmations of Zionist ideology. Maury Spira, formerly of Cleveland, best summed up the mélange of sentiments that characterized most of these interviews:

> *I was in the slipcover business and came here in 1972. I began to be excited about Israel when the state was created in 1948. I think that although we appreciated what America had done for us, we couldn't completely shake off the war's effects. It's not that we wanted to leave America. It's that we wanted to come here.*

Finally, there were those who simply preferred the Israeli lifestyle. As Jack Goldreich, currently a Tel Aviv resident, observed: "People here are friendly; you get together with them all the time." Others concurred with the view that Israelis are warmer and more down-to-earth people, adding that life in that land was much simpler and more informal.

Clearly, not all survivors achieved a high degree of satisfaction in their lives. Many were unable to adjust; the psychiatric literature has provided us with more than a few harrowing tales of the postwar traumas of survivors. Even their normal functioning cannot obscure the real pain that continues to haunt them. As one woman says:

> *It is so strange that I could be stronger during the war; that I could even function normally and now I am rather forlorn and sad, though I am rather successful in putting on an act of being okay. There is a sadness in me bordering often with an overbearing feeling of depression and resolve to finish it all. Nights most often are so terrible that I scream and have to be awakened by my husband, also a survivor, who has his own problems to contend with, without my adding to them.*

Not the average case, one hastens to add, based on this study and on numerous others cited here. Most survivors have made a better adaptation, but for this individual and others like her, that is small comfort. They are suffering and will in all likelihood continue to do so until the day they die. And then there are those who, perhaps not so visibly scarred, speak regretfully of opportunities denied them by the capriciousness of events that swept them up and changed their lives forever, and of people dear to them whom they will never see again. When I asked Dovid Felberbaum of New Square, New York, what he was proudest of, he said: "My children and grandchildren of course." But then his half smile gave way to a pensive look as he continued:

> *But you have to remember that I always look back into the past, what I went through. And when I look at the past, I can't really be happy. I think about what might have been, what more I might have been able to do with my life, with scholarly activity, and I am sad.*

We have seen in this chapter how the survivors have, as a group, come to grips with certain psychological effects of the Holocaust. They have also attempted to come to terms with the theological dilemmas posed by the event and have done so rather well. Their attitudes on a host of topics and issues, while clearly influenced by their horrendous experiences, reveal an ability to assimilate information and to emerge with a worldview that is both cogent and well thought out. Their experiences appear also to have made them far more reflective than the average individual.

The success of the survivors in coping, such as it is, should in no way minimize the extent of the horrors they witnessed and were subjected to. On the other hand, and most important, the fact that their ordeals were often terrible, worse in real life than anything the imagination could conjure up, makes their successful adaptation, even to a limited degree, all the more amazing.

8

Overcoming

Tragedy

THE STORIES, EXAMPLES, AND STATISTICS presented until now raise a very important issue: How do we account for the fact that the survivors did as well as they did? Was it due to certain personality traits possessed by those who emerged from the inferno? If so, can we isolate those traits for the benefit of helping others who experience crises? What about the survivors' postwar environment—their families, their communities, and the organizations with which they had contact? Could these have been the key elements that led to successful recovery? When people emerge from a lengthy period of incarceration under conditions of extreme deprivation and unspeakable brutality, and yet more than four out of five do not seek out professional help, it is a phenomenon surely worthy of close examination.

Before proceeding, however, it is necessary to recapitulate the evidence that has been marshaled in support of the thesis that survivors fared quite well after the war. In doing so, the magnitude of what the survivors accomplished in the United States becomes obvious. Their achievements have come in a number of areas, both personal and communal. As we shall see, many factors were involved. But first, let's review what has been said until now.

1✳

The survivors came to America under less than ideal conditions. Besides their ordeals during the war, many languished for years in the DP camps before gaining entry to the United States. Although they were, for the most part, delighted to have gained admission to America, they did not always receive a warm welcome. In some cases, even relatives were not anxious to extend themselves on behalf of their often newly discovered kin, and Americans in general frequently resented the *grine*, as they were derisively called. The Jewish organizations, such as the Hebrew Immigrant Aid Society and the United Service for New Americans, labored mightily on behalf of the newcomers and, in fact, greatly eased their burden, but no organization could substitute for the warmth and genuine acceptance that these homeless people so desperately wanted and sought. Still, the refugees came, anxious to pick up the pieces and start over again. By 1953, about 140,000 Jewish refugees had made it to the United States, fanning out all over the country.

The majority of the new arrivals remained in New York, but a substantial number settled elsewhere, in major cities such as Boston, Cleveland, and Chicago, as well as in smaller communities. The results were mixed. Those who lived in areas with large Jewish population centers generally remained there, but in the smaller communities many left, unable to adjust to both the slow pace of life and the dearth of Jewish culture. In these early years, the survivors were helped along the road to Americanization by friends and relatives, people in the community they met after coming here, and the social agencies set up to help them. They learned about America in night school, through the then vibrant Yiddish press, and by means of television and movies. Despite their wartime suffering, the scars did not translate into social disorganization once they came here. By way of interviews, direct examination of archival material, and perusal of newspapers, a portrait emerges of a group with an almost nonexistent crime rate and with little juvenile delinquency among their children.

The majority of survivors found jobs in sales, business, and blue-collar occupations. Owing largely to the war, more than half have never graduated from high school, though they did succeed, to some extent, in raising their level of education. The need to earn a living upon arrival in the United States and language difficulties made advanced learning something that most could only dream about. Despite the lack of higher education, the survivors did quite well economically. By 1953, according to the USNA, less than 2 percent required financial assistance, and in 1989 about 34 percent of the survivors reported earning over $50,000 annually. A number of them became multimillionaires and some went on to highly successful careers in the professions. The key factors that explain the financial success of the survivors, where they achieved it, were hard work and determination, skill and intelligence, luck, and a willingness to take risks.

Although there was, and still is, pathology within survivor families, the overall picture is one of great love, commitment, and caring. Considering what they went through, the decision by the survivors to bring children into the world was impressive. When compared to American Jews, survivors were less likely to be divorced and they also had more children. There was, among them, a strong tendency to marry other survivors, and these marriages seem to have worked out better than did those between survivors and American Jews. Very few married out of the faith, although their children sometimes did. The survivors displayed great interest in their offspring and were often concerned about them to the point of overprotectiveness. These children have, on the whole, done very well in life by conventional standards and, as adults, generally view their parents with sympathy and understanding. Although some survivors' children have developed psychological problems that appear to be related to the Holocaust, most have adjusted well while retaining a strong awareness of this particular heritage.

The survivors' social world is characterized by strong friendships and loyalties. They are a close-knit group and, while many have American friends, they are clearly more comfortable in their own circle. The *landsmanschaften,* survivor organizations, and synagogues were the principal places where the survivors interacted with one another in a formal sense. In addition, they predominated in certain neighborhoods within the cities they lived in, generally patronizing the same resorts and other vacation spots. The survivors had a shared history and culture that they frequently wished to perpetuate. To do so they developed a network of their own that produced or sponsored plays, lectures, newspapers, and radio programs. Parallel to this, they also participated in activities that exposed and accustomed them to American life and culture. The survivors' ability to create a social living space for themselves in a land that was unfamiliar to them, while at the same time becoming part of American society, demonstrates further that these people were determined not to allow their past tragedies to defeat them.

The contributions of the survivors to the American Jewish community have been impressive, particularly for a group of people who came here as refugees. For a variety of reasons, they have not moved very far along the continuum of assimilation; they are also heavily involved in activities relating to Israel, preserving the memory of the Holocaust, supporting Jewish education, and to a lesser extent helping Soviet Jewry. They are also involved in Jewish communal affairs on a local level. With respect to Israel, survivors are more than three times as likely as American-raised Jews to have visited there twice or more. As first-generation Americans, survivors did not branch out into American politics and secular organizations to any appreciable extent, though there have been notable exceptions. This is to be expected, given the language barrier and the need first to establish themselves financially. It will be interesting to see to what degree their children become active in these areas. The available evidence to date suggests that such involvement is already taking place.

Not only have the survivors done well economically, socially, and communally; they have also come to terms with the Holocaust psychologically and in religious terms. Taking into account their past suffering, the survivors' ability to think rationally about the event and to analyze it in a way that permits them to go on living with themselves and with others is noteworthy. Although they cannot forget the horrors they endured and have been scarred by them, they function well and seem to require less professional counseling and assistance than one would suspect from what has been written about them to date.

In various ways, the survivors have also attempted to confront the religious implications of a world in which these things could happen to them. The majority have retained their belief in God, although their faith is marked by a good deal of doubt and questioning. Remaining sane after emerging from the Holocaust is a significant achievement in itself. To also engage in efforts to understand its deeper meaning and to allow its lessons to become guidelines for life as a whole is truly extraordinary.

2

This book has looked at the survivors as they are today and as they have functioned since their arrival in the United States. It has examined the personality traits they exhibit and the different factors in their environment that may have assisted or impeded them in their adjustment to American life. Before examining those factors which were most responsible for their successful adaptation to life in America, one precaution is in order: the success or failure of the survivors in coping after the war was affected by their different wartime experiences. These included where they were incarcerated, for example death camp or labor camp; the length of time spent in the camps; their specific working conditions in the camps, a job sorting clothing as opposed to one as a *sonderkommando* for example; where they were during the war—camp, hiding, Siberia, Shanghai, and so forth; their treatment as individuals by those who ran the camps or ghettos; the presence of friends or relatives to help them get through the most difficult periods; their age during the war; and a host of other factors. Concerning such criteria, there has been considerable research about their influence on postwar adaptation.

Regardless of the effects of these circumstances, it must also be understood that not all individuals are endowed with the same capacity to withstand suffering. Some committed suicide as soon as they learned of the death of a sibling while others were able to stoically bear the loss of an entire family. Therefore simply comparing wartime experiences without considering that the threshold of tolerance for pain and punishment varies greatly from one individual to the next would be a serious mistake. Bearing in mind these qualifications, let us begin by looking at some of the more striking individual characteristics of the survivors.

The evidence from this project, combined with that gleaned from other studies, suggests that there are ten general traits, or qualities, that were present in those survivors who were able to lead positive and useful lives following the war. These are (1) flexibility (2) assertiveness (3) tenacity (4) optimism (5) intelligence (6) distancing ability (7) group consciousness (8) assimilating the knowledge that they survived (9) finding meaning in one's life (10) courage. Not all of these traits were present in each individual, nor did all people who succeeded possess most of these attributes. What can be said, however, is that based on an analysis of the interviews, at least some of these features were present in a majority of those survivors who did well in their postwar lives. Moreover, the greater the number of these traits present within an individual, the greater the likelihood of successful adjustment. As has already been noted, the criteria used to define and measure success are those conventionally accepted by society in general.

Flexibility was an essential requirement for success in America. The refugees found it necessary to change in a myriad of ways when they came here. They needed to learn a new language, different customs, another set of values and norms. In addition, they often had to be willing to accept types of work in which they had no previous experience or knowledge. In looking at the job histories of the survivors, it quickly became apparent that those who entered new businesses and who changed their ways of doing business to conform with the demands and opportunities that existed in the new land succeeded. Those incapable of or unwilling to adjust failed, or achieved only modest success. Adaptability was also imperative in terms of one's personal life. Those who had lost their spouses in the war had to be willing to remarry and not necessarily to the man or woman of their dreams. An ability to make new friends was also important because these friends were often the people who helped them advance both economically and socially in the new land. The stories presented in this book make amply clear that those capable of changing in these and other areas succeeded.

A second very important trait was *assertiveness*. The survivors quickly realized after coming here that despite widespread sympathy for their suffering they were on their own. It was therefore incumbent upon them to take the initiative in securing adequate housing, opening businesses, and ensuring that their needs in general were met. The agencies with whom the survivors dealt took note of their drive and ambition. Sometimes they praised it and at other times they described the newcomers as pushy. Generally, those who worked very hard and were not embarrassed to say that they could do a job best were given opportunities that they might not otherwise have received had they not been willing to "sell themselves."

Related to assertiveness was *tenacity,* the refusal to take no for an answer. Many of the survivors failed initially in their efforts to establish themselves. Yet their stubbornness ultimately paid off. Some switched careers several times and many went from one business to the next for years before eventually finding their niche. This attitude emerged in ways both small and large. For example, one woman related how she went to the King Tut exhibit in New York after being told it was completely sold out. Yet she simply waited outside until someone sold her a ticket. "I never take no for an answer," she said. Those survivors who did well seemed to have an almost mystical belief that if they persisted they would eventually achieve their goals.

A fourth attribute was *optimism.* Commenting about the contents of a collection of periodicals published by the DPs in their camps that was released by YIVO, the well-known historian and theologian Arthur Hertzberg observed: "The survivors did not dwell on death, they rebuilt life. This was the lesson they were teaching." This future-oriented approach typified those survivors who succeeded. When I asked Elias Epstein, a well-to-do survivor from Radomsko, Poland, what his postwar approach to life had been, he replied, "I made up my mind never to look back, only forward." Similarly, I recall remarking to Atari head Jack Tramiel as I was leaving his Park Avenue apartment, "You've certainly done very well." "You see that bridge out the window, the 59th Street Bridge?" he asked. "I just looked straight ahead, went over the bridge, and never turned back." It was a sentiment echoed and re-echoed by the survivors. The Holocaust was never far from the survivors' minds, but to the extent that they could transcend it and focus their energies on the tasks at hand they did well in life.

Optimism meant more, however, than not thinking about the past horrors. It reflected a certain mind-set about life in general. Alex Gross, who survived Auschwitz, Buchenwald, and other camps, lost his only son, aged fourteen, in a farming accident. When he saw the mangled body, he resolved never to reveal the details of the death to his wife. "That was the same age when I was taken to Auschwitz," he reflected, with great sadness. "To see him like that, I couldn't bear to tell my wife about it. And I said, I was blessed with a wonderful wife, and I loved my three daughters and our son-in-law, and I realized how lucky I was, to have such wonderful, healthy children." Alas, that was not the end of Gross's woes. Nine years later his wife was raped and murdered. To date, the perpetrator has not been apprehended. Despite this double tragedy, Alex Gross functions and lives for the present and the future. He loves and worries about his children and he has remarried. He works hard and is very active in his community, but still finds time to play racquetball several times a week and even takes an occasional vacation. Although his postwar travails were greater than those experienced by most survivors, his response to them epitomizes an attitude shared by many survivors—a determination to go on living despite adversity.

Intelligence, or professional skill, was a fifth factor that influenced the survivors' ability to rebuild their lives in America. Intelligence, as used here, does not refer to intellectual ability so much as what is commonly known as street-smarts. Perhaps such individuals would have done well in university settings had they had the opportunity or inclination to do so after the war. Since they did not, by and large, choose this option, we can only judge them on the basis of how they acted in their areas, which were usually businesses or trades. What emerged in the interviews was a widespread ability to think quickly, to analyze a situation, break down its more complex elements, and make an intelligent decision. The stories presented in Chapter 3, of Jack Werber, "The Davy Crockett King," and of Joseph Bukiet, who outsmarted his competitors in the grocery business, are good examples of this talent.

Sixth was the capability of the survivors after the war to *distance* themselves from what had happened. It came down to the belief that anyone who had gone through the Holocaust and who behaved in certain ways at that time was in a unique situation. Survivors did this, not necessarily out of guilt, but because by distancing themselves from that terrible period in their lives they were able to remove it from their consciousness so that it did not constantly intrude on their thinking.

One example of this phenomenon was Joseph Wind, a seventy-seven-year-old Polish survivor whose job it was to dispose of the dead bodies in the Janowska Road camp in the Ukraine. Wind burned thousands of corpses, picked up the bones from the ground afterward, removed the teeth, and participated in many other gruesome tasks. After the war, he worked as a grocer in Atlanta. He received me in a friendly manner and proceeded to describe in graphic detail, over a two-hour period, his activities as a member of the "Death Brigade." Throughout, he and his wife, a survivor who had passed as a Gentile, plied me with cookies, cake, and tea. When asked if he ever dreamed about the war, his answer was unequiv-ocal: "No. I don't even think about it. Life has to go on. Only one time, I thought about it; I saw *War and Remembrance* on TV." The psychic numbing described by Robert Lifton could be dis-cerned from the emotionless tone in which he talked about the war.

Yet when Wind spoke about the way he had been slighted, in his view, by other survivors in the community, he became quite ani-mated. Similarly, when he showed me photographs of his children, his face brightened considerably. As he stroked the family dog that lay curled in his lap, I commented on how much he seemed to like his pet. My remark reminded him of the dog they had owned before this one. Wind's voice suddenly became husky with emotion as he reminisced about the love he had felt for the animal: "They had to take him to a place where they put him to sleep. I couldn't go. I couldn't kill a fly." When one considers what happened to Wind, it is clear that his ability to raise a family and function on a day-to-day level was a tremendous achievement.

Although Wind's ordeal was exceptionally difficult, the principle is the same. Survivors often felt a need to repress their experiences, whatever they were, to a certain extent. Simply put, those who could, functioned better than those who constantly obsessed about it. People sometimes found unusual ways to close off the most painful aspects of their experience. Livia Bitton, who went through Auschwitz as a teenager, has written books about the Holocaust and taught courses on the subject for many years. Paradoxically, this has created distance. Bitton explains why: "By writing and teaching about the Holocaust, I became more of a spectator than a survivor. In this way I distanced myself from the experience." Intellectual-izing can become a way of dealing with emotions that are too strong to confront openly.

Group consciousness, the seventh important trait, was helpful for many survivors as they struggled to come to terms with their suf-fering. Aaron Antonovsky, who has conducted extensive research into the question of who does well in life and why, has concluded that one important factor is an awareness of belonging to a partic-ular group. As we saw in the discussion of the social world created by the newcomers, they are highly conscious of their status as survivors. This common bond of suffering gave them strength as they faced new hardships and challenges. On the whole, those who disaffiliated from the group frequently had a harder time adjusting because of it. It was, as we have seen, this sense of having endured something unique that was in part responsible for the fact that so many survivors married other survivors. As they did so, the connection to the past was reinforced. In interview after interview, survivors expressed appreciation that their spouses could understand their own sense of loss and their anxieties.

Assimilating the knowledge that they survived was a crucial determinant of how the survivors did after the Holocaust. Erik Erikson has observed that over a person's life cycle he or she gradually accumulates coping capabilities commensurate with each crisis. Lifton has referred to it as having "crossed over to the other side" and Gail Sheehy has coined the term "survival merit." Put simply, what they mean is that while most people do not look forward to going through a crisis, it is part of human nature to reflect upon traumatic events. Many survivors gained confidence and self-respect simply from the knowledge that they had lived through a terrible time. In discussing problems that came up in their lives after the war and how they approached them, many respondents began their explanations with "And I knew if I could survive the war, I could certainly . . ." It is, of course, far from axiomatic that people are strengthened by adversity and, indeed, more than a few survivors were broken by it and went through life apathetic and even despairing. On the other hand, for many other survivors, rising up out of the ashes gave them a sense of invulnerability that prevented them from succumbing to future crises.

Associated with the knowledge that they had prevailed was an ability to translate this awareness of their good fortune into a concrete reason for going on. This is the ninth trait that played a role in the survivors' successful adaptation—*finding meaning in one's life*. Antonovsky found that this was one of the key traits identified with those who had a high "sense of coherence" in their lives. This is also a major goal of logotherapy, as developed by Viktor Frankl—to help people find a purpose in their existence.

Some survivors found happiness in their work. This was especially true of people in the arts and in the professions. In some instances, their gratification stemmed entirely from the work itself and in other cases it was combined with their personal life histories. For example, Sarah Berkowitz wrote two books on the Holocaust because, as she relates, "I committed myself to tell the world about the German atrocities." This commitment to educate and to inform carried her through some very difficult periods in her life.

For a majority, other family members were a primary reason for going on. It meant that someone needed and loved them. For example, Alex Gross explained that one reason for not giving up after his wife's tragic death was "I had to be strong for my three daughters, because if something had happened to me, they would have definitely fallen apart." Other survivors found that living on in the name of family that had perished in the Holocaust gave them sustenance.

Community participation was another way in which survivors justified their place on this earth. Through it they came to be seen by others as socially valued individuals and this gave them deep satisfaction. We have seen that large numbers of survivors were active in local schools and synagogues, indeed, in numerous organizations. Others found solace in religion, which gave them both structure and a sense of higher purpose. Regardless of whether their strong principles were based on a general philosophy of life or rooted in religious beliefs, those who had these strong principles did well in their post-Holocaust lives. Some discovered that the State of Israel meant the most to them and threw themselves wholeheartedly into activities on its behalf. Whatever the case, be it family, work, religion, or community, those who were involved did considerably better than those who were not.

The tenth and final attribute was *courage*. In its broadest sense this was manifested by the survivors' ability to go on living after the war. Beyond that, it was clearly discernible in how different survivors shaped and responded to their postwar experiences. In business, many of those who succeeded were people willing to take financial risks. For some, the choice of a profession told the story. General Sidney Shachnow, for instance, chose a military career. Moreover, he received many decorations, including a Purple Heart and the Vietnamese Cross of Gallantry.

Bravery, however, can take many forms. Moshe Weinstock displayed it when he stood up to elements in the Hasidic community that tried to prevent him from writing favorably about the State of Israel. Gilbert Metz took on the power structure of Jackson, Mississippi, when its leaders refused to remove a large cross from public property. Rita Kesselman and other survivors found the strength to speak publicly about their wartime traumas. Still others fought back from debilitating physical diseases or struggled to overcome the demons that haunted their memories.

Besides these ten traits, to make it in America the survivors had to have both good health and a healthy dose of good luck. The ability to work hard often meant the difference between success and failure. Having a wealthy brother or uncle who was willing to help was simply a fortunate circumstance, but it could make or break the newcomer who came to these shores in need of an opportunity. The refugees also benefited from the fact that the Jewish community and its organizations geared up and mounted a large-scale operation to assist them in many ways once they arrived in the United States. As opposed to the characteristics we have so far identified, however, the survivors obviously had no control over health, luck, and their reception in the new land, crucial as these factors were.

Based on the interviews, the personality features described above were present in quite a few survivors from early childhood on, but in others they were not. Can traits such as optimism and tenacity be taught later on in life? There is a good deal of research which suggests that they can. Drawing on many sources, including his own work, Jerome Kagan, a prominent Harvard University psychologist, has argued persuasively in his book *The Nature of the Child* that human beings are not only influenced by their environment but retain a lifelong capacity for change.

The evidence gathered here strongly supports Kagan's conclusion. When the survivors emerged from the camps, their condition had so deteriorated that those who liberated them often had trouble seeing them as human beings. And yet within a few years these people who had been so debilitated, both physically and psychologically, reconstructed themselves and their lives and became useful and productive members of society. To do so necessitated significant changes on their part, both in terms of behavior and in their outlook. Their former world, the one they grew up in, was now gone forever. Moreover, the long years of hiding and imprisonment had forced them to adapt in ways that were not appropriate to life in a free and open society. That they were able to accommodate to their new condition demonstrates that the process of learning and growth in humans does not end with adulthood, but can and does continue throughout the life cycle.

It may have occurred to the reader by now that the ten attributes cited to explain the survivors' postwar success may have been precisely those that allowed them to endure the camps themselves. And if that is the case, are these survivors then an example of what is popularly known as the theory of survival of the fittest? Put another way, were they stronger or smarter than those who died?

Hardly, for the two situations were radically different. While some may have escaped because of their individual ingenuity, chance played a far greater role than skill simply because in most instances *the survivors were not in control of their destiny*. They were swept up and hurled to their deaths by a giant killing machine that indiscriminately annihilated millions of them. That they acted to enhance their chances of survival on those relatively few occasions when opportunities presented themselves simply proves that human beings will, when given the chance to determine their fate, make every effort to do so. In such situations, having the traits listed here may have made the difference between life and death. However, to assume that those who died would not have done likewise is an untenable position, since their deaths were, in the overwhelming number of cases, completely arbitrary. In any event, we cannot interview them and compare their personalities with those who lived. To better understand the role of "luck," or "coincidence," it is worthwhile to look at some examples as they were depicted by those interviewed.

Willy Herskovits seized the initiative by escaping from a camp. Once out, he came across some people who assisted him. Had that stroke of good fortune not occurred, he would have died, as did others who also escaped but encountered people who turned them over to the Nazis. While in Auschwitz Joseph Bukiet hit a German with a shovel, an offense for which he would surely have been executed. As luck would have it, however, a thick fog enveloped the camp shortly after the incident and in the confusion he was able to make his getaway. Several months later, Bukiet saw the same man with a bandage wrapped around his head. He did not recognize Bukiet. Ernest Michel secured a coveted job in camp, writing down diagnoses in the hospital. He was selected because of superior penmanship acquired as a result of calligraphy lessons his father had forced him to take as a child.

But in most instances survivors did not have the slightest opportunity to influence their destiny. In some camps those in the back of the line were killed, in others those in the front, and in some death greeted those who stood in the center. Most often, no one could be sure where it was best to stand. Similarly, no one knew when volunteering for a transport meant life and when it did not. Leah Henson told of her desperate efforts to join a group of people in her ghetto who were told that they were being taken to Israel. Although the truck was full, she tried to squeeze in. A German noticed this and threw her off. Two hours later all those who had gone were executed in a nearby forest. Sandy Mayer's life was saved because the Christians who hid her interpreted an air raid siren as a sign from God. They had decided to drown her but the noise frightened them and caused them to change their minds. Jack Perry tried to commit suicide on two separate occasions. He felt he had suffered enough. He was thwarted by other inmates both times and is alive and well today. Stories of this sort abound in the literature.

Most survivors stated unequivocally that chance was the most important factor in their survival. "There were others in the camps who were smarter, tougher, and stronger than me. I was just lucky" is typical of the observations made regarding this point. In one quantitative study hundreds of survivors were asked what they felt was the primary reason they outlasted the camps. Luck was the main factor for 74 percent of those responding, while only 27 percent credited coping skills as having played a role in their survival.

Fate was not in their hands during the war, but after the war it was to a far greater extent, and from what we can tell many survivors made the most of it. The ten factors identified here may be seen as applicable to other instances of trauma and crisis as well. The survivors were not supermen; they were ordinary individuals before the war, chosen by sheer accident of history to bear witness to one of its most awful periods. Therefore, the way in which they succeeded in rebuilding their lives contains valuable lessons for all those who suffer through adversity and tragedy.

The story of the survivors is one of courage and strength, of people who are living proof of the indomitable will of human beings to survive and of their tremendous capacity for hope. It is not a story of remarkable people. It is a story of just how remarkable people can be.

Methodological Note

This project took almost six years to complete. It is based on over 15,000 pages of raw data, much of which consisted of the 170 in-depth interviews discussed in the Introduction. Many of the interviews were edited for grammar and general clarity, and in some instances to protect the confidentiality of respondents who spoke about highly sensitive issues relating to their personal lives. In all cases, however, their essential meaning remains unchanged. Full transcripts and/or tapes have been donated to the United States Holocaust Memorial Museum, the Museum of Jewish Heritage, Yad Vashem, and Hebrew University's Oral History Library in the Institute of Contemporary Jewry, where they can be seen by bona fide researchers and other qualified parties.

Of the archives consulted, that of the National Council of Jewish Women, housed at Yeshiva University, was of crucial significance. It contains approximately 60,000 interviews, conducted by social workers and volunteers with refugees when they first came to the United States. Because of time constraints, it was only possible to examine a portion of the more than 200,000 typewritten pages of information. They are a treasure trove that should be of great interest in the years to come as historians become more interested in the topic. The archives of the United Service for New Americans and the Hebrew Immigrant Aid Society, located at the YIVO Institute, were also extremely useful and important.

The quantitative survey of survivors was a key aspect of this project because of the relatively large size of the sample, its randomness, and the use of a control group. Although there have been many studies of survivors that have used questionnaires, few have been based on true random samples. The names have usually been culled from those who have been treated by therapists, restitution claimants, survivor groups, or from membership lists of Jewish organizations or synagogues. All of these categories have inherent biases. Researchers generally agree that the best way to obtain a truly random sample is by a method known as random digit dialing. What this involves is dialing telephone numbers within different telephone exchanges. The method is often modified according to the population being studied. For example, if one were doing a survey of housewives, one would not use telephone exchanges located in areas where places of business predominated.

Obviously, it would have been ludicrous to dial telephone numbers at random in the hope of obtaining a random sample of survivors since almost all of those answering the telephone in such cases would not have qualified. Fortunately, an ideal solution presented itself. Several surveys of Jews in general had been completed over the years using random digit dialing, one carried out by the New York Federation of Jewish Philanthropies and two by myself for a political polling project. By looking at some of the questions asked in these studies, place and year of birth, age, and so forth, I was able to narrow down who among the respondents might be survivors. These individuals were contacted, and over 90 percent, 211 survivors, responded to the questions. A control group of 295 similarly selected American Jews was interviewed in the same fashion for purposes of comparison, with an equally high response rate. Since the questionnaire contained thirty-eight items, it generated a great deal of data, much of which are still being analyzed as this book goes to press. These findings will be reported in scholarly journals.

Abbreviations

Used in

Source Notes

AJHS	American Jewish Historical Society, Waltham, Massachusetts.
MA	Oral Histories, Minneapolis Archives, American Jewish Committee, Minneapolis, Minnesota.
NCJW Papers	National Council of Jewish Women Papers, Yeshiva University Archives, New York, New York.
WOHL	Wiener Oral History Library, American Jewish Committee, New York, New York.
YIVO	YIVO Institute for Jewish Research, New York, New York.
YVA	Oral Histories, Yad Vashem Archives, Jerusalem, Israel.

Unless otherwise stated, all interviews were conducted by the author.

Source Notes

Chapter One
Beginnings of a New Life

20 Willy Herskovits: Interview, December 8, 1987.

20 Congressman Tom Lantos: Interview, May 10, 1990.

20 For quite a few immigrants: As described in George James, "Nazi Survivors Reunite with Black Liberators," *New York Times*, October 7, 1991, p. B1. See also "Warmhearted GIs Helping Displaced Persons Locate Relatives," *Rescue*, October 1945, p. 7.

20 especially that of the soldiers who liberated: There exists a substantial body of research that suggests that the U.S. Army's response to the DPs was, at best, mixed. See Leonard Dinnerstein, *America and the Survivors of the Holocaust* (New York: Columbia University Press, 1982), pp. 9–38. The passage of time, and gratitude to America in general for providing them with a safe haven, may have influenced the survivors in their recollections and assessments of the U.S. military. On the other hand, one cannot deny the validity of the individual positive experiences recalled by many survivors. Certainly American Jewish chaplains did much to ease the pain and suffering of the survivors. See Alex Grobman, "The American Jewish Chaplain and the Remnants of European Jewry, 1944–48." Ph.D. diss., Hebrew University, 1981.

20 Paula Gris: Interview, May 17, 1989.

21 usually in Displaced Persons camps: Substantial numbers also came from Sweden, France, Belgium, and other European countries. These lands had no DP camps and Jews simply lived there as residents. Even in those countries where DP camps were located, namely Germany, Austria, and Italy, thousands of DPs lived on their own, in cities and towns.

21 Typically those with visas: Ilya Dijour, "Step by Step, from DP Camps to the Ships at Bremerhaven," *Rescue*, May 1946, pp. 1–2.

21 Much has been written: For comprehensive discussions of the DP camps, see Leonard Dinnerstein, *America and the Survivors of the*

Holocaust; Yehuda Bauer, *Out of the Ashes: The Impact of American Jews on Post-Holocaust European Jewry* (Oxford, England: Pergamon Press, 1989); Abram L. Sachar, *Redemption of the Unwanted* (New York: St. Martin's/Marek, 1983), pp. 146–73; Leo Schwarcz, *The Redeemers* (New York: Farrar, Straus and Young, 1953); Philip S. Bernstein, "Displaced Persons," *American Jewish Yearbook, 1947–48,* vol. 49 (Philadelphia: Jewish Publication Society, 1947), pp. 520–32.

21 the infamous pogrom: See Yehuda Bauer, *Flight and Rescue: BRICHAH* (New York: Random House, 1970), pp. 206–11.

21 they refused to descend: Ze'ev Mankowitz, "The Affirmation of Life in She'erith Hapleita," in Yehuda Bauer, ed., *Remembering for the Future: Jews and Christians During and After the Holocaust,* vol. 1 (Oxford, England: Pergamon Press, 1988), pp. 1114–22.

22 Walter Peltz: Interview, July 24, 1989.

22 A journalist wrote: Theodore Jacobs, "Anti-Semitism of DP Transports," *Jewish Life,* August 1952, pp. 7–8.

22 One incident: "Gericht auf dem Immigrantenschiff" ("A Tribunal on the Immigrant Boat"), *Aufbau,* September 6, 1946, p. 12. It is not known whether the "policemen" described in the article referred to camp *kapos* or ghetto policemen, though the term "turning them over" implies that it was probably the latter.

23 Elizabeth Gevirtz: Interview, April 23, 1989.

24 Another immigrant noted: Celia Wangrow, WOHL.

24 Luba Bat, the niece of: Luba Bat, *Phoenix* (Jerusalem: Yad Vashem Archives, n.d. Mimeographed), n.p.

24 Judith Traub: Interview, June 27, 1989.

24 Richard Dyck, a reporter: Richard Dyck, "Die Ankunft des *Marine Flasher*" ("The Arrival of the *Marine Flasher*"), *Aufbau,* May 24, 1946, p. 2. In terms of boats containing large groups of refugees, the *Marine Flasher* was probably the first one to arrive in the United States. The first recorded arrival of individual survivors was probably that of the Leitner sisters, who came on the *Brand Whitlock,* which docked in Newport News, Virginia, on May 8, 1945. See Isabella Leitner, *Saving the Fragments: From Auschwitz to New York* (New York: New American Library, 1985).

24 Most of the arrivals: Albert L. Harris, "Communities in Midwest Told of HIAS' Growth," *Rescue,* December 1947, p. 7.

25 One ship, whose entry: *Memo to America. The DP Story: The Final Report of the U.S. Displaced Persons Commission* (Washington, D.C.: U.S. Government Printing Office, 1952), pp. 64–65.

25 These included San Francisco: Lyman Cromwell White, *300,000
New Americans: The Epic of a Modern Immigrant-Aid Service* (New
York: Harper & Bros., 1957), p. 147. For the full story of the Jewish
experience in Shanghai, see David Kranzler, *Japanese, Nazis, and
Jews: The Refugee Community of Shanghai, 1938–1945* (New York:
Yeshiva University Press, 1976).

26 about 140,000:

POSTWAR JEWISH IMMIGRATION TO THE UNITED STATES: MAY 1945–JUNE 1953

Date	Total	DPs	Non-DPs	To NYC Area	Elsewhere in U.S.
1945 (May–Dec.)	4,000			2,800	1,200
1946	15,535			10,870	4,665
1947	25,885			18,116	7,769
1948	15,982			11,187	4,795
1949	37,700	31,381	6,319	20,571	17,129
1950	14,139	10,245	3,894	8,861	5,278
1951	16,973	13,580	3,393	8,416	8,557
1952	7,236	3,508	3,728	4,307	2,929
1953 (Jan.–June)	2,383	765	1,618	1,571	812
TOTAL:	139,833	59,479	18,952	86,699 (63%)	53,134 (37%)

Sources: "Third Annual Report: New York Association for New Americans Inc.," Kurt
Grossman mss., Box 55, Folder 9, Leo Baeck Institute, New York City; "USNA Correspondence, Misc., 1944–1955, Budget Reports," Council of Jewish Federation and Welfare
Funds (CJFWF) Papers: Agency Files, Box 148, AJHS. According to statistics compiled
by the Joint Distribution Committee, the total might have been higher. See Yehuda
Bauer, *Out of the Ashes*, p. 285n. This table differs slightly from an earlier version
that appeared in Leonard Dinnerstein's *America and the Survivors of the Holocaust*,
p. 288.

26 about 37,000 more who entered Canada: Here is the Canadian breakdown:

1946	2,100
1947	2,424
1948	9,892
1949	5,047
1950	3,006
1951	7,167
1952	5,177
1953 (Jan.–June)	2,055
TOTAL:	36,868

Source: Joseph Kage, "Canadian Immigration: Facts, Figures and Trends," *Rescue,* Fall
1953, p. 8. For more on Jewish immigration to Canada see Harold Troper, "Canada and the
Survivors of the Holocaust," in Yisrael Gutman and Avital Saf, eds., *She'erit Hapletah,
1944–1948: Proceedings of the Sixth Yad Vashem International Historical Conference* (Jerusalem: Yad Vashem, 1990), pp. 261–85.

26 The reasons for choosing America varied: To understand fully why some survivors selected America or Canada while others opted for Israel, much research is required, particularly a full demographic breakdown of those who entered each country, comparing factors such as age, health, religious affiliation, country of origin, socioeco-. nomic status, and how they spent the war years. We would need to know whether they were positively influenced by Zionist ideas before the war, whether they had relatives in Israel, Europe, and America, where in Europe they were after the war, and so forth. All of this would have to be done for each year of the postwar era. Ideally, this breakdown would have to be supplemented with in-depth interviews that would seek to determine the precise basis for the decisions made. Only then could general conclusions be drawn about the survivor communities in Israel and the West. Such work has not as yet been undertaken.

26 Many were simply too tired: Those that did go to Israel underwent an experience that would of necessity shape their worldview and identity in a manner quite different from those who did not. First, there was the cathartic effect of fighting the enemy instead of the running, cowering in fear, and humiliation that typified the wartime experi- ences of most survivors. Second, survivors in Israel immediately be- came members of a majority, as opposed to a minority, culture. Finally, even as new arrivals, they were not seen as an intrinsically different group because large numbers of Jewish immigrants both preceded and followed them. Crucial as these factors were, a propor- tion of survivors exhibited problems related to their unique experi- ences. For examples of research in this area, see Shamai Davidson, "The Clinical Effects of Massive Psychic Trauma in Families of Ho- locaust Survivors," *Journal of Marital and Family Therapy,* January 1980, pp. 11–21; Aaron Antonovsky *et al.,* "Twenty-Five Years Later: A Limited Study of Sequelae of the Concentration Camp Experience," *Social Psychiatry,* vol. 6, no. 4 (1971), pp. 186–93. A full range of studies is reported on in the *Israel Annals of Psychiatry and Related Disciplines.*

26 Sam Halpern: Interview, February 14, 1988.

26 "not because I don't love Palestine": Cited in Shirley S. Rosenberg, "Refugee from Horror Works for Her People," *Jewish Examiner,* December 5, 1947, p. 13.

26 Thus, one of the protagonists: Elie Wiesel, *The Fifth Son* (New York: Warner Books, 1985), p. 181.

27 Abe Foxman: Interview, January 10, 1990.

27 Hidden by a Christian family: In May 1991 a conference focusing on and reuniting children hidden during the war was held in New York City. See Frank J. Prial, "Coming Out of Hiding: Childhoods as Non-Jews," *New York Times*, May 5, 1991, p. 45.

27 Vera Stern: Interview, February 13, 1990.

28 One Hasidic Jew: Joseph Hirsch, interview, January 26, 1988.

28 A second man: Dovid Felberbaum, interview, March 8, 1990.

28 Nonetheless, he was turned down: Yehuda Bauer has estimated that perhaps one third of the 250,000 people who used the Brichah escape route to Israel were Zionists. See Yehuda Bauer, "The Brichah," in Gutman and Saf, eds., *She'erit Hapletah, 1944–1948*, p. 55.

28 A perhaps extreme example: Edward Blonder, YVA, 406.

29 Bill Neufeld: Interview, July 25, 1989.

29 Despite such lingering doubts: For more on this see Calvin Goldscheider and Alan S. Zuckerman, *The Transformation of the Jews* (Chicago: University of Chicago Press, 1984), pp. 175–76.

29 Waiting for them: Richard Dyck, "Die Ankunft des *Marine Flasher*," p. 2.

30 the HIAS and the United Service for New Americans: The HIAS, the National Refugee Service (NRS), and the National Council of Jewish Women (NCJW) first worked together on behalf of postwar refugees when they provided financial backing and other services to the approximately one thousand refugees who were housed at Fort Ontario, in Oswego, New York, between 1944 and 1946. The refugees came from Italy and were admitted by the Roosevelt administration. For the full story of this group see Ruth Gruber, *Haven: The Unknown Story of 1,000 World War Two Refugees* (New York: Coward-McCann, 1983) and Sharon R. Lowenstein, *Token Refuge: The Story of the Jewish Refugee Shelter at Oswego, 1944–1946* (Bloomington, Ind.: Indiana University Press, 1986).

30 Joint Distribution Committee: Through an organization called Supplies for Overseas Survivors, sixteen New York women's organizations sent 26 million pounds of relief supplies, including food, clothing, and medicine. In addition, thousands of voluntary workers from 419 different communities were involved in helping European Jews. All of these efforts were channeled through the JDC. See Yehuda Bauer, *Out of the Ashes*, p. xxi.

30 Regardless, special skills and talents: Lyman White, *300,000 New Americans*, pp. 134–35; Jack Shafer, "HIAS Pier Representatives Welcome Immigrants Here," *Rescue*, January-February 1947, pp. 4–5.

30 Irving Goldstein: Interview, July 2, 1989.

30 Problems could, and frequently did, occur.: Lyman White, *300,000 New Americans,* p. 134.

31 One recurring dilemma: Jack Shafer, "HIAS Pier Representatives," p. 5; Lyman White, *300,000 New Americans,* p. 134.

31 ten-story Hotel Marseilles: The account of the Hotel Marseilles is drawn largely from the following sources: "New Yorkers Seit Acht Tagen" ("They Have Been New Yorkers for Eight Days"), *Aufbau,* May 31, 1946, p. 1; Lyman White, *300,000 New Americans,* pp. 143–47; Charles Grutzner, "Phone Is a Symbol of Freedom to DP's," *New York Times,* June 18, 1949, p. 15.

31 "to perpetuate": Lyman White, *300,000 New Americans,* p. 147.

32 The historian: Judith Tydor Baumel, *Unfulfilled Promise: Rescue and Resettlement of Jewish Refugee Children in the United States, 1934–1945* (Juneau, Alaska: The Denali Press, 1990), p. 99.

32 An article in *The New York Times:* Charles Grutzner, "Phone Is a Symbol," p. 15.

33 "Blood rushed to my head": Cecilie Klein, *Sentenced to Live* (New York: Holocaust Library, 1988), p. 124.

33 "Horses should live there": Cited in Barbara Stern Burstin, *After the Holocaust: The Migration of Polish Jews and Christians to Pittsburgh* (Pittsburgh: University of Pittsburgh Press, 1989), p. 121.

33 Those refugees sent: Jack Shafer, "How HIAS Shelters Homeless Immigrants," *Rescue,* February-March 1947, p. 9.

34 Evelyn Plotsker: Interview, September 4, 1989.

34 Rabbi Herman Neuberger: Interview, December 21, 1988.

35 The following letter: "Bintel Brief," *Forward,* February 20, 1949, p. 5. For a representative selection of these letters through the years and the responses to them, see Isaac Metzker, *A Bintel Brief* (New York: Doubleday, 1971).

37 For example, in a talk given: "South Jersey Poultrymen Meet," *Jewish Farmer,* October 1945, p. 120.

37 On the West Coast: "The New DP Bill," Editorial, *B'nai B'rith Messenger,* October 14, 1949, p. 4.

37 the local temples: "Émigrés Invited to Synagogues for Holy Day Services," *B'nai B'rith Messenger,* October 7, 1949, p. 11.

37 At the Ambassador Hotel: "Yesteryear Fashion Show to Benefit DP Children," *B'nai B'rith Messenger,* November 4, 1949, p. 7.

37 On an individual level: Hanoch Teller, *Souled!* (New York: New York City Publishing, 1986), pp. 71–82.

37 Solomon and Lucy Yehaskel: Interview, May 29, 1989.

38 Rose Weinreb: Interview, January 19, 1989.

38 Moritz Felberman: Interview, April 25, 1989.

38 Frieda Jakubowicz: Interview, April 16, 1988.

39 a twenty-year-old-woman: NCJW Papers, Box 230, File 622.

39 A Brooklyn woman almost grudgingly: NCJW Papers, Box 230, File 621.

39 "For one's best friend": NCJW Papers, Box 56, File 49-143.

39 Simon Nagrodzki: Interview, May 22, 1989.

40 Jack and Millie Werber: Interview, December 6, 1989.

41 One woman was so upset: "Bintel Brief," *Forward,* February 8, 1950, p. 5.

41 American Jews were: For more on the Americanized Jews who greeted the immigrants, see Deborah Dash Moore, *At Home in America: Second Generation New York Jews* (New York: Columbia University Press, 1981).

42 "How do you absorb": Elaine Mishkin, "Some Common Behavior Patterns of Recently Arrived Adolescent Refugees Living with Substitute Parents" (MSW thesis, New York School of Social Work, Columbia University, 1947), p. 10. For a detailed discussion of how teenage survivors adapted to life here, see also Carol H. Meyer, "Till Human Voices Wake Us" (MSW thesis, New York School of Social Work, Columbia University, 1948).

42 It was a challenge indeed: Judith Baumel, *Unfulfilled Promise.* Although its focus is the 1934–45 period, Baumel's book contains much important material on children's adaptation in the United States that is relevant to the postwar period. See especially pp. 89–110.

42 The first impressions: Ibid., pp. 95–96.

42 One woman who was taken: Zdenka Weinberg, WOHL.

42 Gerda Marcus: Interview, August 17, 1989.

42 Jack Novin's: Interview, July 19, 1989.

43 Sigmund Tobias: Interview, March 1, 1990.

44 Lola Shtupak: Interview, April 28, 1989.

44 Gilbert Metz: Interview, May 14, 1989.

45 Another immigrant, a rabbi: Abraham Feffer, WOHL.

45 more apt to be tolerated: See Milton Gordon, *Assimilation in American Life* (New York: Oxford University Press, 1964).

45 One immigrant's early recollection: Arthur Herz, WOHL.

45 Sigmund Tobias: Interview, March 1, 1990.

45 Luba Bat: Luba Bat, *Phoenix.* See also Judith Baumel, *Unfulfilled Promise,* p. 96.

45 One youngster wept: Kathryn Close, *Transplanted Children: A His-*

tory (New York: The U.S. Committee for the Care of European Children, 1953), pp. 49–51.

46 Evelyn Plotsker: Interview, September 4, 1989.

46 Until then, perhaps 50,000 Jewish refugees: The difficulty in ascertaining the precise number is complicated by the fact that many who entered did so from third countries, especially Canada and various Latin American lands. As a result, they did not always appear in the official statistics kept by Jewish organizations concerned with the immigrants. In addition, the U.S. government did not, at that time, list the religious affiliation of immigrants. The approximations are based on the figures assembled by the United Service for New Americans.

46 On June 2, 1948: Walter H. Waggoner, "DP Admission of 200,000 Is Voted by Senate 63 to 13," *New York Times,* June 3, 1948, pp. 1–2.

47 Senator Claude Pepper: Ibid., p. 2.

47 The final version: Anthony Leviero, "President Scores DP Bill, but Signs," *New York Times,* June 26, 1948, p. 1; "The DP Bill," *Rescue,* June 1948, p. 6.

47 President Truman indicated as much: "Truman's Statement on Refugee Bill," *New York Times,* January 26, 1948, p.1.

47 Echoing the President's sentiments: "The DP Bill," *Rescue,* p. 6.

47 disparaging comments about the refugees: "Captain Eddie Says 'Bar Immigrants,' "*Jewish Examiner,* March 7, 1947, p. 9; "Immigration Is 'Racket of Racial, Religious Groups,' American Legion Commander Tells D.A.R.," *Jewish Times,* May 30, 1947, p. 8.

48 Similar efforts were mounted by Christian organizations: The majority of DP entrants were Christians. See Leonard Dinnerstein, *America and the Survivors of the Holocaust* and Jacques Vernant, *The Refugees in the Post-War World* (London: Allen & Unwin, 1953). The number of Jews admitted in proportion to the total number of Jewish and Christian DPs who applied was thought to be considerably higher than the number of Christians allowed in. According to G. J. Haering, chief of the State Department's visa division, this was because the Jewish agencies worked faster, many applicants were orphans entitled to special consideration, and because the Jews could more easily prove Nazi persecution. See Maurice R. Davie, "Refugee Aid," *American Jewish Yearbook, 1947–48,* vol. 49 (Philadelphia: Jewish Publication Society, 1947), p. 215.

48 On that day, President Truman: Anthony Leviero, "Truman Signs Bill Easing DP Entries: 415,744 Get Refuge," *New York Times,* June 17, 1950, p. 1.

48 "The countrymen of these displaced persons": Ibid.

48 competing with each other: This was true of most of the organizations involved in resettlement. Thus, HIAS officials wrote at one point, "HIAS notes with satisfaction that the Jewish Colonization Association will not join with any other organization to do work in the migration field." HIAS Minutes, November 13, 1946, YIVO.

49 Typically, applicants were sponsored: On December 22, 1945, President Truman issued a directive that allowed voluntary agencies to supply corporate or group affidavits for refugees who had no relatives or friends willing and able to sign for them. This type of affidavit had been used before, but only for children. The USNA and HIAS sponsored the largest number of immigrants. There were, however, other organizations approved by the State Department that also sponsored applicants, such as the U.S. Committee for the Care of European Children, the Vaad haHatzalah, and various yeshivas. For example, Yeshiva Chaim Berlin received approval from the State Department in 1946 for corporate affidavits to bring over 150 students, 50 from Shanghai, 50 from Czechoslovakia, and another 50 from other parts of Europe. See "Rabbi Chaim Berlin Yeshiva and Mesivta, Correspondence," Council of Jewish Federation and Welfare Funds Papers (CJFWF), Agency Files, Box 84, AJHS.

49 tried in many ways: One prominent Jewish leader, Emma Schaver, presented DP songs that she had collected as part of a six-month tour of the DP camps. Schaver reported that they sang despite their suffering. "Emma Schaver to Offer Displaced Persons Songs," *Jewish Examiner,* March 14, 1947, p. 10. In New York's Garment District, the Needle Trades Committee to Combat Anti-Semitism organized a center devoted to helping people locate refugees in Europe, helped prepare affidavits, and donated food and clothing for the DPs. "Center Aids Immigrants," *Jewish Examiner,* August 16, 1946, p. 2.

50 In 1950, Edwin Rosenberg: "$37,000,000 Spent to Resettle D.P.'s," *New York Times,* January 15, 1950, p. 30.

50 to help achieve this goal: The arrival of this wave of Jews to the United States inevitably affected developments surrounding the creation of the State of Israel in 1948. Passage of the DP Act in that same year clearly influenced worldwide immigration patterns. No one knows how many thousands of Jews would have opted for newly independent and more easily accessible Israel had America kept its restrictive policies intact. The same holds true for the amended DP Act of 1950, which opened the gates to the United States even wider. Another important issue was the effect of Israel's emergence as an independent nation with respect to fund-raising on behalf of the survivors in America. The Jewish community was not as well endowed then as it is today and these twin emergencies strained resources to the breaking point. There were complaints from supporters of each cause that what they considered to be priorities were not being adequately funded. Clearly it was in the Zionists' interests to keep the DPs in Europe, while those not so inclined tended to support the opposite approach. Which position prevailed, in which communities and why, is a subject that needs to be fully investigated by historians. For brief discussions of this topic see Yehuda Bauer, "The Brichah," in Gutman and Saf, eds., *She'erit Hapletah, 1944–1948,* p. 55; David Wyman, "Refugees and Survivors: Reception in the New World," *Simon Wiesenthal Center Annual,* vol. 2 (1985), pp. 193–203; Leonard Dinnerstein, *America and the Survivors of the Holocaust,* p. 115.

50 there were those who backed out: NCJW Papers, Box 56, File 48-1159; Box 141, File 140.

50 In one year, 1946: Jack Shafer, "How HIAS Consultants Help Hundreds Each Day to Solve Their Urgent Immigration Problems," *Rescue,* September 1946, pp. 7–8.

50 The minutes of the HIAS: HIAS Minutes, January 7, 1947, and February 25, 1947, YIVO.

51 A *New York Times* story: "X-Rays of Healthy Lungs Join Berlin Black Market," *New York Times,* November 26, 1947, p. 2.

51 One woman's elderly parents: NCJW Papers, Box 255, File 431.

51 the following ad appeared: "Address Unknown," *Jewish Examiner,* June 20, 1947, p. 13.

52 "Excuse that as a strange woman": NCJW Papers, Location Files, April 7, 1947.

52 the case of two sisters: NCJW Papers, Box 56, File 50-288.

52 [Others came on special quotas: NCJW Papers, Box 257, Files 635 [and 652; Box 56, Files 47 and 48.

52 There were numerous stories: NCJW Papers, Box 56, File 47-1025. See also "Ex-GI Fulfills Vow; Brings Orphans to United States," *Jewish Examiner,* February 7, 1947, p. 8.

53 One case worker's entries: NCJW Papers, Box 55, File 48L854.

53 Both the HIAS and the USNA: Jack Shafer, "How HIAS Location Service Finds the Lost," *Rescue,* October 1946, pp. 3–4; Lyman White, *300,000 New Americans,* pp. 112–15.

53 As soon as they stepped off the boat: While Jews were being met by the HIAS and the USNA, a parallel response was taking place among

non-Jewish organizations on behalf of Christian DPs. For example, the United Relief Fund of America met 148 Lithuanian refugees who came to New York aboard the *General Black* on October 30, 1948. Algirdas M. Budreckis, "Reluctant Immigrants: The Lithuanian Displaced Persons," in Dennis Lawrence Cuddy, ed., *Contemporary American Immigration: Interpretive Essays* (Boston: Twayne Publishers, 1982), p. 183. Unlike the Jews, Lithuanians, Latvians, Estonians, and Ukrainians all felt a great sense of loss as they were leaving their homelands. While Jews also lost their communities, those communities could never be resurrected and the Jews knew it. This may account in part for the eagerness of the Jews to adapt to their new homeland. Nonetheless, there were similar experiences among all of the DPs in terms of their acculturation in the United States. The Christian DPs suffered, as did many Jews, when their sponsors would "patronizingly demonstrate how to use light switches, light gas stoves, and use toilet facilities." Moreover, some sponsors were unfriendly to their compatriots and exploited them. Dennis Cuddy, *Contemporary American Immigration,* p. 190.

54 arrangements were made for summer camps: Judith Baumel, *Unfulfilled Promise,* p. 99.

54 A brief article: "Camp for Refugee Children," *New York Times,* June 28, 1945, p. 28.

54 through lectures and training sessions: The New School for Social Research offered a free course for social workers whose focus was the problems of DPs. It was prepared under the direction of the well-known dean of the graduate faculty there, Professor Horace M. Kallen. "New School-Relief Work," *New York Times,* March 18, 1945, Section 4, p. 9.

54 "We had no sense": Cited in Barbara Burstin, *After the Holocaust,* p. 112. Numerous articles written by caseworkers and directors of Jewish agencies on the problems of the immigrants appeared in *Jewish Social Service Quarterly* and the *Journal of Jewish Communal Service.* Other information about the interaction between social workers and their clients can be gleaned from looking at the NCJW files and from masters theses written at the time, especially at Columbia University.

55 One organization: European Jewish Children's Aid was another organization that worked with children, all of them Jewish. They worked together with large city agencies and operated temporary reception centers. Kathryn Close, *Transplanted Children,* p. 55.

55 In one heartbreaking case: HIAS Minutes, December 22, 1949, YIVO.

55 One man, from Ostrowiec: Jacob Lestchinsky, "Balance Sheet of Extermination," as cited in *Jewish Affairs,* February 1, 1946, p. 6.

56 Their donations generally ranged: Michael R. Weisser, *A Brotherhood of Memory: Jewish Landsmanshaftn in the New World* (New York: Basic Books, 1985), pp. 185–89. Their postwar response was in contrast to their tepid reaction during the war, which was, of course, no different than that of American Jewry in general. See Hannah Kliger, "A Home Away from Home: Participation in Jewish Immigrant Associations in America," in Walter P. Zenner, ed., *Persistence and Flexibility: Anthropological Perspectives on the American Jewish Experience* (Albany: State University of New York Press, 1988), p. 156.

56 In 1938: B'nai B'rith Hillel Foundation Papers, private collection of Rabbi Benjamin Kahn, American University, Washington, D.C.

56 In a letter: Ibid. The letter was dated September 2, 1947. See also Judith Sloan Deutsch, "The 'Simple Peasant Mind' of Congressman Tom Lantos," *Long Island Jewish World,* October 27, 1989, pp. 8–11.

Chapter Two
The Struggle to Rebuild

58 "Never shall I forget": Elie Wiesel, *Night* (New York: Avon/Discus, 1969), p. 44.

59 As Terrence Des Pres has written: Terrence Des Pres, *The Survivor: An Anatomy of Life in the Death Camps* (New York: Oxford University Press, 1976), p. 81.

59 In an address: Elie Wiesel, "Against Despair" (First Annual Louis A. Pincus Memorial Lecture, United Jewish Appeal 1974 National Conference, December 8, 1973), pp. 14–15.

59 the rest scattered: For example, by the end of July 1949, 7,716 arrivals under the 1948 DP Act had been settled in 334 communities in 43 states. Morris Zelditch, "Immigrant Aid," *American Jewish Yearbook, 1950,* vol. 51 (Philadelphia: Jewish Publication Society, 1950), p. 195. See also Maurice R. Davie, "Immigration and Naturalization," *American Jewish Yearbook, 1950,* vol. 51 (Philadelphia: Jewish Publication Society, 1950), pp. 129–30; "Papers Read at Regional USNA Conferences, 1948," USNA Papers, File 15, YIVO; Charles Grutzner, "DP's are Resettled All Through U.S.," *New York Times,* May 25, 1949, p. 1. Christian DPs were dispersed throughout the United States in a different pattern. See Danuta Mostwin, "The

Transplanted Family: A Study of Social Adjustment of the Polish Immigrant Family to the United States After the Second War" (DSW diss., Columbia University, 1971), p. 160.

59 This pattern of movement: As a point of interest, our quantitative study of the survivors indicates no differences between New York and out-of-town survivors in terms of country of birth.

59 The USNA and HIAS were very concerned: Leonard Dinnerstein, *America and the Survivors of the Holocaust,* p. 203.

60 Rabbi Isaac Trainin: Isaac N. Trainin, *In My People's Service,* vol. 3, *Communal Diary* (New York: Commission on Synagogue Relations, 1981), p. 28.

61 Sandy Mayer: Interview, January 26, 1988.

61 On Saturdays: For a description of the postwar community in this area, see William B. Helmreich, *Wake Up, Wake Up, to Do the Work of the Creator* (New York: Harper & Row, 1976).

62 "The assimilationist stream of Judaism": Helen Epstein, *Children of the Holocaust: Conversations with Sons and Daughters of Survivors* (New York: Putnam, 1979), p. 231.

62 Initially, residential placements: See Lyman White, *300,000 New Americans,* p. 347.

62 resettle people in smaller towns: Kurt G. Herz, "Patterns in Community Services to Recent Jewish Immigrants," *Jewish Social Service Quarterly* 26 (March 1950), pp. 367–68.

62 A USNA field report: "USNA Correspondence, 1952, USNA Folder," CJFWF Papers, Agency Files, Box 148, AJHS.

62 Columbia, South Carolina: Lyman White, *300,000 New Americans,* p. 79.

63 a community throbbing with energy: See for example Yaakov Bieber, "Chanukah Fayerungen in di Yidisher Farm Yishuvim" ("Chanukah Celebrations in the Jewish Farm Settlements"), *Der Yidisher Farmer,* January 1954, p. 14; Alfred Rosinek, "Groyser Yontef in Dorothy, N.J." ("Big Celebration in Dorothy, New Jersey"), *Der Yidisher Farmer,* November 1956, p. 168; Herman J. Levine, "Dedication of Jewish Center in Mays Landing, New Jersey," *Jewish Farmer,* November 1957, p. 148.

63 New Jersey, New York, and Connecticut: See Arthur Goldhaft, *The Golden Egg* (New York: Horizon Press, 1957); Herman J. Levine and Benjamin Miller, *The American Jewish Farmer in Changing Times* (New York: Jewish Agricultural Society, 1966); Benjamin Miller, "Jewish Farmers in Connecticut," *Jewish Farmer,* May 1958, pp. 77–81; Shlomo Zecktser, "Der Nayer Yidisher Yishuv in Daniel-

son, Connecticut" ("The New Jewish Settlement in Danielson, Connecticut"), *Der Yidisher Farmer,* May 1958, p. 96; Jacob M. Maze, "Petaluma—Oldest Jewish Farm Settlement in California," *Jewish Farmer,* September 1957, p. 121.

63 they augmented communities: For more on these communities see Joseph Brandes, *Immigrants to Freedom: Jewish Communities in Rural New Jersey Since 1882* (Philadelphia: Jewish Publication Society, 1971) and Herman Levine and Benjamin Miller, *The American Jewish Farmer.*

64 their lifestyles turned out: For a novel describing what it meant to start over again in rural America, see Barbara Finkelstein, *Summer Long-a-Coming* (New York: Harper & Row, 1987).

64 Israel Goldman: Interview, June 12, 1990.

64 Chris and Miles Lerman: Interview, June 12, 1990.

65 their families had owned flour mills: Although a number of farmers had previously been engaged in Europe in pursuits related to agriculture such as selling milk or grain, the majority were not.

65 The National Council of Jewish Women: Morris Zelditch, "Immigrant Aid," pp. 196–99. The most active local chapters were New York City, Boston and Worcester, Massachusetts, Philadelphia, Los Angeles, San Francisco, Miami, and Baltimore. The group within the NCJW that coordinated such assistance was called the Foreign Born Advisory Committee. The Brooklyn Section of the NCJW also sponsored meetings in neighborhoods such as Williamsburg and Brownsville that were designed to help people get to know one another and to integrate better into daily life. There were discussions about "nutrition, home economics, health insurance, social security, trade unionism, the public school system, child care, and trips to places of historical and special interest." See "D.P. Strangers Brought Together to Hurdle Barriers to Assimilation," *New York Times,* January 9, 1951, p. 31.

65 One woman interviewed: Bronia Roslawowski, WOHL.

65 Louis Shulman's words: "One Should Always Live with Hope," *Forward,* May 24, 1950, p. 5.

66 personal interest on the part of organizational officials: S. N. Eisenstadt, *The Absorption of Immigrants* (London: Routledge & Kegan Paul, 1954), p. 174.

66 abandoned their traditional approach: Helen L. Glassman, *Adjustment in Freedom: A Follow-up Study of One Hundred Jewish Displaced Families* (Cleveland, Ohio: United HIAS Service and Jewish Family Service Association, 1956), p. 40.

66 Another challenge: These issues are discussed in the following articles: Fred Berl, "The Immigrant Situation as Focus of the Helping Process," *Jewish Social Service Quarterly* 26 (March 1950), pp. 362–72; Isadora Berman and Solomon Shapiro, "Psychological Problems Met in Counseling and Placement of Refugees," *Journal of Jewish Communal Service* 26 (December 1949), pp. 277–85; Sidney S. Eisenberg, "Phases in the Resettlement Process and Their Significance for Casework with New Americans," *Jewish Social Service Quarterly* 27 (September 1950), pp. 86–96; Beatrice Frankel and Ruth Michaels, "A Changing Focus in Work with Young Unattached DP's," *Journal of Jewish Communal Service* 27 (March 1951), pp. 321–31; Mary Russak, "Helping the New Immigrant Achieve His Own Beginning in the U.S.," *Journal of Jewish Communal Service* 26 (December 1949), pp. 239–54.

66 In Pittsburgh, for example: Barbara Burstin, *After the Holocaust,* pp. 119–20.

66 Their activities included: Deborah S. Portnoy, "The Adolescent Immigrant," *Jewish Social Service Quarterly* 24 (December 1948), p. 271.

67 Certain schools: "Rabbi Jacob Joseph School and Mesivta: Reports," CJFWF: Agency Files, Box 121, AJHS. While most of the schools were in New York City, some were in other cities. See "Los Angeles Jewish Academy," CJFWF: Agency Files, Box 84, AJHS.

67 Camp Agudah and Camp Yeshiva: "Camp Agudah 1942–1962," CJFWF: Agency Files, Box 31, "New York: Rabbi Solomon Kluger School," "Memo, 1948," Box 121, AJHS.

67 Those inclined toward: "United States," Betar File, 16B, Ze'ev Jabotinsky Institute, Tel Aviv.

68 in an *Aufbau* article: Vera Craener, "Paradies Amerika: Kinderglück in Sommercamp" ("Paradise in America: The Happiness of Children in Summer Camp"), *Aufbau,* August 9, 1946, p. 23.

68 Denver was described: "Displaced Persons Program/Communities/Quotas: Community Quota Status Report for General Settlement, 9/30/48, USNA Folder," CJFWF: Agency Files, Box 20, AJHS.

68 A typical announcement: "Alabama," USNA Papers, File 613, YIVO.

69 Thus, one survivor in Pittsburgh: Cited in Barbara Burstin, *After the Holocaust,* p. 123.

69 that synagogue involvement: Ibid., p. 113.

69 Ruth Siegler: Interview, May 22, 1989.

69 A survivor living in San Francisco: Dorothy Rabinowitz, *New Lives:*

Survivors of the Holocaust Living in America (New York: Avon, 1976), p. 196.

69 "I went to stay": Cited in Ibid., p. 66.

70 Helen Gilmer: Interview, May 21, 1989.

70 volunteers were especially appreciated: Research on this topic strongly suggests that informal-voluntaristic agencies do best when it comes to absorbing immigrants. See S. N. Eisenstadt, *The Absorption of Immigrants;* Elihu Katz and S. N. Eisenstadt, "Some Sociological Observations on the Response of Israeli Organizations to New Immigrants," in Moshe Lissak et al., eds., *Immigrants in Israel: A Reader* (Jerusalem: Academon Press, 1969), pp. 395–417; Reuven Kahane, "Informal Agencies of Socialization and the Integration of Immigrant Youth into Society: An Example from Israel," *International Migration Review,* vol. 20, no. 1 (1986), pp. 21–39.

70 Thus one representative: "Bintel Brief," *Forward,* March 4, 1950, p. 5.

70 Dora Zaidenweber: MA.

71 Leah Henson: Interview, March 23, 1989.

71 Frieda Kessler: Interview, August 1, 1989.

71 Henry Lindeman: Interview, July 26, 1989.

71 One survivor overheard: Samuel Halpern, interview, February 14, 1988.

71 Marika Abrams: WOHL.

72 Renia Chadajo: Interview, July 21, 1989.

72 those survivors who came after 1948: "Displaced Persons Program/ Communities/Quotas, 9/5/49, USNA Folder," CJFWF: Agency Files, Box 20, AJHS.

72 To what extent were Eastern European Jews: On this see Irving Howe, *World of Our Fathers* (New York: Harcourt Brace Jovanovich, 1976).

73 The candid comments of Arthur Goldhaft: Arthur Goldhaft, *The Golden Egg,* pp. 263–64.

74 "I went to a hall": Jacob Patt, "Akht un Draysik Toyznt Yidisher D.P.s Zeynen Gekumen in Amerika" ("Thirty-Eight Thousand Jews Have Come to America"), *Forward,* February 10, 1950, p. 4.

74 Lola Shtupak: Interview, April 28, 1989.

74 Abe Foxman's: Interview, January 10, 1990.

75 five refugee youths: "Five Refugee Youths Reported Attacked by Anti-Semites," *The Jewish Examiner,* September 15, 1950, p. 1.

75 Benjamin Hirsch: Interview, May 20, 1989.

75 One immigrant remembered: Ilse Rothchild, WOHL.

75 The range and variety: The more institutionalized the community, the less assimilated the group. Raymond Breton, "Institutional Completeness of Ethnic Communities and the Personal Relations of Immigrants," *American Journal of Sociology,* vol. 70, no. 2 (1964), pp. 202–3.

75 the *landsmanschaften*: For an excellent discussion of the role of the *landsmanschaften* see Myra Giberovitch, "The Contributions of Montreal Holocaust Survivor Organizations to Jewish Communal Life" (MSW thesis, McGill University School of Social Work, 1988); Hannah Kliger, "Traditions of Grass-Roots Organization and Leadership: The Continuity of Landsmanschaftn in New York," *American Jewish History,* vol. 76, no. 1 (1986), pp. 25–39; Hannah Kliger, "A Home Away From Home," in Zenner, ed., *Persistence and Flexibility,* pp. 143–64; Hannah Kliger, "In Support of Their Society: The Organizational Dynamics of Immigrant Life in the United States and in Israel," *American Jewish Archives,* vol. 42, no. 2 (1990), pp. 33–53.

75 "I was present at a memorial service": Jacob Patt, "Akht un Draysik Toyznt Yidisher D.P.s" ("38 Thousand Jewish D.P.s"), *Forward,* February 10, 1950, p. 4.

76 the New World Club: "Die Gruppenarbeit des New World Club" ("The Group Work of the New World Club"), *Aufbau,* June 20, 1947, pp. 25–26.

76 A *New York Times* article: "Survivors of Belsen Mark Liberation Day," *New York Times,* April 16, 1946, p. 20.

76 Irena Schwarz: Interview, August 23, 1989.

77 in Philip Roth's short story: Philip Roth, "Eli, the Fanatic," *Commentary* (April 1959), pp. 292–309.

77 Livia Bitton: Interview, March 9, 1990.

78 A disproportionate number of survivors: This may not be the pattern among survivors living in Israel.

79 dietary laws and maintaining Sabbath observance: There are also smaller numbers of survivors identified with Judaism's Conservative movement who follow these religious laws.

79 Miriam Brach: Interview, February 19, 1990.

79 the foreign language press: See Samuel L. Baily, "The Adjustment of Italian Immigrants in Buenos Aires and New York, 1870–1914," *American Historical Review,* vol. 88, no. 2 (1983), pp. 281–305.

80 recognized that speaking English: Raymond Breton, "Institutional Completeness of Ethnic Communities," p. 204.

80 Hyman Kaplan: The main character in a book about Jewish immigration. In it, Kaplan is depicted as a person who makes strenuous efforts to learn the English language in night school, with often hilarious results. See Leo Rosten, *The Education of H*Y*M*A*N* K*A*P*L*A*N** (New York: Harcourt Brace, 1937).

80 One such individual approached: Ben Geizhals, interview, December 25, 1989.

80 Other refugees learned by listening: Raphael Steiglitz, YVA.

81 that appeared in the *Aufbau:* Jon Whyte, "Wie Lernt Man in English" ("English as a Spoken Language"), *Aufbau,* November 9, 1945, p. 2.

81 a Brooklyn high school student: Sylvia Gross, interview, November 27, 1983, Brooklyn Center for Holocaust Studies Archives.

82 Ben Hirsch: Interview, May 20, 1989.

82 One study of survivors: Carol Meyer, "Till Human Voices Wake Us."

82 The letter below: "Bintel Brief," *Forward,* March 11, 1950, p. 5.

83 of what they had lived through: On this, see Martin Bergmann and Milton E. Jucovy, eds., *Generations of the Holocaust* (New York: Basic Books, 1982); Joel E. Dimsdale, ed., *Survivors, Victims and Perpetrators* (Washington: Hemisphere Publishing, 1980); Henry Krystal, ed., *Massive Psychic Trauma* (New York: International Universities Press, 1968); Peter Ostwald and Egon Bittner, "Life Adjustment After Severe Persecution," *American Journal of Psychiatry,* vol. 124, no. 10 (1968), pp. 1393–1400.

83 a couple was sent to Selma, Alabama: "Alabama," USNA Papers, File 613, YIVO.

84 "When I woke up from the anesthesia": Sally Grubman, WOHL.

84 In one particularly horrendous instance: "Pennsylvania," USNA Papers, File 469, YIVO.

84 manipulative and distrustful: Callman Rawley, "The Adjustment of Jewish Displaced Persons," *Journal of Social Casework,* October 1948, p. 318.

84 "Unfortunately," observed one article: Beatrice Frankel and Ruth Michaels, "A Changing Focus," p. 214.

84 almost complete absence of criminal behavior: Contrast this to the situation around the turn of the century. As Jenna Weissman Joselit has pointed out, crime flourished on New York City's Lower East Side and Jewish immigrants were heavily involved in it. According to the New York County district attorney's office, about three quarters of the Jews brought before the courts prior to World War I were born in Europe. Incidentally, 85 percent of the crimes committed by Jews were of the nonviolent sort, such as theft and prostitution. On this, see Joselit's book, *Jewish Crime and the New York Jewish Commu-*

nity, 1900–1940 (Bloomington, Ind.: Indiana University Press, 1983), pp. 5–6, 19, 43 and Irving Howe, *World of Our Fathers,* pp. 96–101.

85 Where are the Lepke Buchalters: See Jenna Joselit, *Jewish Crime,* p. 122. These individuals were second-generation Jews and the parallel here is to survivors' children. The interviews conducted for this book, plus an examination of the files and scholarly literature, reveal no evidence of a pattern of criminal behavior among either parents or their children. Those Americans who were hostile to the idea of immigration after the war, and there were many, would have liked nothing better than to find evidence that the immigrants were ne'er-do-wells. The newspapers and magazines of the period mention almost nothing about maladjustment or pathological behavior among the survivors or their offspring. Moreover, studies done in recent years of survivors and adult children of survivors similarly make no mention of criminal activity by such persons.

85 advanced by Terrence Des Pres: Terrence Des Pres, *The Survivor;* Eugen Kogon, *The Theory and Practice of Hell,* trans. Heinz Norden (New York: Farrar Straus, 1953). This challenges, of course, the position of Bruno Bettelheim. See Bettelheim, *The Informed Heart* (Glencoe, Ill.: The Free Press, 1960).

85 By 1948, almost no DPs: We are forced to rely, for the most part, upon studies carried out by agencies and professionals involved with the DPs. See Maurice R. Davie, "Immigration and Refugee Aid," *American Jewish Yearbook, 1947–48,* vol. 49 (Philadelphia: Jewish Publication Society, 1947), pp. 212–22; Maurice Davie, "Immigration and Naturalization," pp. 127–33.

85 A follow-up study of survivors: Helen Glassman, *Adjustment in Freedom,* pp. 41, 62.

85 Another long-range study: David Crystal, *The Displaced Person and the Social Agency* (New York: United HIAS Service, 1958).

Chapter Three
Making a Living in America

87 In *Working:* Studs Terkel, *Working: People Talk About What They Do All Day and How They Feel About What They Do* (New York: Pantheon, 1972), p. xi.

87 The *B'nai B'rith Messenger:* "Émigrés Need Jobs," Editorial, *B'nai B'rith Messenger,* November 11, 1949, p. 4; "Growing Émigré Pop-

ulation Calls for Emergency Meeting," *B'nai B'rith Messenger,* April 28, 1950, p. 2.

87 Jews in Pittsburgh: Barbara Burstin, *After the Holocaust,* p. 111.

87 the Jewish Agricultural Society: Theodore Norman, *Annual Report of the General Manager* (New York: Jewish Agricultural Society, 1951), p. 11; *Jews in American Agriculture* (New York: Jewish Agricultural Society, 1954), p. 58; Gabriel Davidson, *Report of the Managing Director for the Period 1900–1949* (New York: Jewish Agricultural Society, 1949), p. 37; Gabriel Davidson, *Annual Report of the Managing Director* (New York: Jewish Agricultural Society, 1950), p. 22.

88 The USNA, the agency most active in this area: Smaller organizations were also active. For example, in 1945 the New World Club, which was part of the organization known as Self Help, announced in an ad in the *Aufbau* the creation of an employment service to help newly arrived refugees obtain employment (November 16, 1945). An article in the *Aufbau* that ran in its November 23, 1945, issue described the work of the Veteran's Forum, a group that conducted job searches for both Jewish veterans and survivors.

88 reported that 87 percent: Lyman White, *300,000 New Americans,* pp. 159–60. An important organization funded by various Jewish agencies was the Jewish Occupational Council (JOC), founded in 1939 to help refugees in guidance, placement, and vocational training. It assisted communities around the nation in finding employment for refugees. "JOC: Minutes and Memoranda, 1941–48," CJFWF Papers: Agency Files, Box 73, AJHS.

88 Willy Herskovits's: Interview, December 8, 1987.

88 Besides finding jobs: Lyman White, *300,000 New Americans,* p. 158.

88 One ad: It appeared in *Jewish Life,* April 1950, p. 97. The USNA's Religious Functionary Division worked with other organizations too, such as Young Israel and Torah Umesorah.

89 For example, at a regional USNA conference: William Karp, "Vocational Adjustment Services for Newcomers" (paper delivered at the USNA, Greater New York City Regional Conference, October 29, 1947), pp. 2, 4, 13, 16.

89 certainly tried hard: Under the leadership of Rabbi Isaac Trainin, the USNA's Religious Functionary Division tried hard to give refugee rabbis, ritual slaughterers, and teachers the skills necessary to be effective in their chosen fields in America. With the cooperation of Yeshiva University, it established a homiletics class there given by

Rabbi Joseph Lookstein. There were also pedagogical courses under the noted Jewish educator Pinchas Churgin and the university's president, Samuel Belkin. The division also negotiated with the Young Israel organization to set up a community relations course that would teach synagogue administration and the nature of the rabbi's role in the American Jewish community. See Isaac N. Trainin, "New Americans on the Religious Scene," *Jewish Life*, June 1948, pp. 41–42.

90 was that of a Lithuanian physician: While the physicians assisted by the agencies in Hitler's time were mostly Jewish, arriving in the United States as part of the wave of German and Austrian Jews, those who came after the war were far more likely to be non-Jewish DPs. Therefore, the agencies received funding from non-Jewish sources as well to assist such people. Probably four out of five physicians entering after World War II were Christian. This was because their populations had not been decimated as were those of the Jewish communities. See Lyman White, *300,000 New Americans,* p. 165. The USNA was also involved in helping immigrant dentists secure positions and gave them loans for additional schooling. See "Material of the Policy Committee on Retraining of Foreign Trained: Memorandum from Phil Soskis," USNA Papers, File 8, YIVO.

90 One member of the Kurower Society: Myra Giberovitch, "The Contributions of Montreal Holocaust Survivor Organizations," p. 80.

90 Others offered loans anonymously: Ibid., p. 84.

90 The Dynover Society: NCJW Papers, Box 255, File 416.

91 One group of handicapped survivors: "Memo, October 19, 1950," CJFWF Papers: Agency Files, Box 4, AJHS.

91 Another disenchanted group: Other groups that expressed similar complaints were the Ichud Rabbonim Pleitim, Ezras Rabbonim Pleitim, and the Rabbi's Union of the Association of New Americans. See "Histadrut Rabbonim Pleitim," CJFWF Papers: Agency Files, Box 55; "Rabbi's Union of the Association of New Americans," CJFWF: Agency Files, Box 127; "Ezras Rabbonim Pleitim," CJFWF: Box 53, AJHS.

91 Simon Nagrodzki: Interview, May 22, 1989.

91 Ben Geizhals: Interview, December 25, 1989.

92 was shared by other survivors: This view is also presented by a survivor in Dorothy Rabinowitz, *New Lives,* p. 223, who angrily states: "God had taken mercy on them [social workers] and given them these fat jobs where they had nothing to do but sit there behind the fat desks lording it over people who had no choice but to take it."

92 Agency professionals who worked: William Karp, "Vocational Adjustment Services for Newcomers," pp. 3–4, 7. As director of Vocational Services for the USNA, Karp supervised many caseworkers and was in an excellent position to make generalizations about the survivors.

92 "aggressiveness and tenaciousness": Helen Glassman, *Adjustment in Freedom,* p. 47.

92 Bill Neufeld: Interview, July 25, 1989.

92 Moses Feuerstein: Interview, December 18, 1988.

93 Mostly, the survivors went into: According to the USNA, there were job shortages in many categories, including machine operators, stenographers, dictaphone operators, pharmacists, architectural draftsmen, professors with Ph.D.'s, textile designers, manicurists, chambermaids, and various needle trade occupations. See "Displaced Persons Program: Job Assurances for Professionals, Occupational Shortages," CJFWF: USNA Files, Box 20, AJHS.

93 A study published in 1947: Maurice R. Davie et al., *Refugees in America: Report of the Committee for the Study of Recent Immigration from Europe* (New York: Harper, 1947), pp. 217–18.

93 This contrasts sharply with: On the prewar group, see Steven M. Lowenstein, *Frankfurt on the Hudson: The German Jewish Community of Washington Heights, 1935–1983* (Detroit: Wayne State University Press, 1988); Herbert A. Strauss, ed., *Jewish Immigrants of the Nazi Period in the U.S.A.,* vols. 1–3 (New York: K. G. Saur, 1978, 1981, 1982); Donald Fleming and Bernard Bailyn, eds., *The Intellectual Migration: Europe and America, 1930–1960* (Cambridge, Mass.: Harvard University Press, 1969); Dorit B. Whiteman, *The Uprooted: From Hitler to the Present* (New York: Insight Books, forthcoming).

93 Since many of the survivors: Compare this with the profile of the far less traumatized Christian DPs, who were often resented as intellectual snobs by their compatriots when they came to America. The occupational distribution among a sample of Slovenian immigrants who came to the United States after World War II was as follows: manual—38 percent; semiprofessional—14 percent; professional—41 percent; students—7 percent. See Edward G. Gobetz, "Adjustment and Assimilation of Slovenian Refugees" (Ph.D. diss., Ohio State University, 1962), p. 156. In a study of Polish immigrants, higher executives constituted the single largest category among the arrivals. See Danuta Mostwin, "The Transplanted Family" (DSW diss., Columbia University, 1971), p. 153.

93 only about one in five: There were also no differences in the occupational patterns of New York and out-of-town survivors. Another
follow-up study of survivors identified a similar configuration of only
a small percentage of professionals. See Lore Shelley, "Jewish Holocaust Survivors' Attitudes Toward Contemporary Beliefs About
Themselves" (Ph.D. diss., Fielding Institute, 1984), p. 94.

94 the need to earn a living: See Harold Faber, "DPs Are Quick to Catch
Tempo of America, Survey Shows," *New York Times,* January 19,
1950, p. 1.

94 Irene Fishman: Interview, March 25, 1990.

94 Ernest Michel: Interview, December 27, 1989.

95 Among the many topics covered: *Port Huron Times Herald,* January
6, 1947, p. 1; January 21, 1947, p. 5; January 30, 1947, p. 2; January
31, 1947, p. 4; February 25, 1947, p. 7.

95 the survivors' physical condition deteriorated: Lyman White, *300,000
New Americans,* pp. 157–58; Deborah Portnoy, "The Adolescent
Immigrant," p. 272.

95 learned quickly about unions: Deborah Portnoy, "The Adolescent
Immigrant," p. 271.

95 One new arrival: Joseph Bukiet, interview, December 5, 1989.

96 Probably a majority: Helen Epstein, "A Study in American Pluralism
Through Oral Histories of Holocaust Survivors" (New York: William
E. Wiener Oral History Library of the American Jewish Committee,
1975, unpublished report), p. 24.

96 "When J.J. registered": Cited in Helen Epstein, *A Study in American
Pluralism,* p. 24.

96 Irving Goldstein: Interview, July 2, 1989.

96 In a letter to the *Forward:* Paul Levita, "Er Vet Keynmol nyt Fargesn
zayn Erstn Gutn Bos" ("He Will Never Forget His First Good
Boss"), *Forward,* May 28, 1950, p. 2.

96 Judy Rubinstein: Interview, July 24, 1989.

97 Harry Haft's: Interview, June 28, 1990.

97 Abe Foxman's: Interview, January 10, 1990.

98 he equipped two secret printing shops: Isaac Kowalski, *A Secret
Press in Nazi Europe* (New York: Shengold Books, 1978).

98 As we sat and talked: Isaac Kowalski, interview, December 13, 1989.

98 he has edited and published: The newsletter is called *Jewish Combatants of World War Two* and the anthology is *Anthology on Armed
Resistance, 1939–1945* (Brooklyn, N.Y.: Jewish Combatants Pub-
lisher's House, 1988, 1990).

98 Alexander Petrushka: Interview, March 26, 1990.

99 Albert Schimel: Interview, December 13, 1989.

99 James Rapp: Interview, March 9, 1989.

99 Edward Goodman: Interview, MA.

100 Tom Lewinsohn's wife: Tom Lewinsohn, WOHL.

100 Renia Chadajo: Interview, July 21, 1989.

100 Leon Gross: Interview, May 23, 1989.

101 Nathan Krieger: Interview, June 25, 1989.

101 the Atlanta woman: Paula Gris, interview, May 17, 1989.

102 "Work is a privilege": Joseph Bukiet, interview, December 5, 1989.

103 One woman who lived in Waterbury: Helen Sperling, YVA.

103 In addition, there was: There is a vast literature on the psychological effects of the Holocaust. See for example S. A. Luel and P. Marcus, eds., *Psychoanalytic Reflections on the Holocaust* (Denver and New York: Holocaust Awareness Institute and KTAV Publishing, 1984); Callman Rawley, "The Adjustment of Jewish Displaced Persons," pp. 316–21; Gertrude Schneider, "Survival and Guilt Feelings of Jewish Concentration Camp Victims," *Jewish Social Studies,* Winter 1975, pp. 74–83.

103 Charlotte Wendel: Interview, April 24, 1989.

103 Ernest Michel: Interview, December 27, 1989.

104 Sam Halpern: Interview, February 14, 1988.

104 Harold Hersh: Interview, May 17, 1989.

105 Benjamin Hirsch: Interview, May 20, 1989.

105 Frederick Terna: Interview, February 15, 1990.

106 "All Valerie's paintings": Anton Gill, *Journey Back from Hell: Conversations with Concentration Camp Survivors* (New York: William Morrow/Grafton Books, 1988), p. 432.

106 Isaac Goodfriend's: Interview, May 19, 1989.

107 For someone like Goodfriend: For a book-length account of a survivor-cantor's experiences, see Matus Radzivilover, *Now or Never: A Time for Survival* (New York: Frederick Fell, 1979).

107 Arthur Nunberg: Interview, December 18, 1989.

108 Clearly, this could only be done: Today the Club has quite a few non-Jewish members, as well as many Jews who are not Holocaust survivors; the passing of the earlier era is widely lamented by survivors.

108 "We got to where we got": For a case study of what happens when a group does *not* have such networks at its disposal, see Barry M. Stein, "Occupational Adjustment of Refugees: The Vietnamese in the

United States," *International Migration Review,* vol. 13, no. 1 (1979), pp. 25–45.

108 Patterns of work: On the unifying effect of occupations, see the following study of Iraqi-Americans in Detroit: Mary C. Sengstock, "Developing an Index of Ethnic Community Participation," *International Migration Review,* vol. 12, no. 1 (1978), pp. 55–69.

108 For many refugees: In discussing assimilation, the distinction between refugees and immigrants is important. Since they came voluntarily, immigrants tended to more or less accept assimilation as part of the price of success. Refugees, on the other hand, were less inclined to do so since they generally came only because they were fleeing persecution. They did not, therefore, make a calculated decision about such things as opportunities in a new land and willingness to cease identifying with the original group.

109 the ethnic associations: See Raymond Breton, "Institutional Completeness," pp. 193–205.

109 By 1953, the USNA could say that: "USNA Correspondence to CJFWF, 1953," CJFWF: Agency Files, USNA Folder, AJHS. Lutheran and Catholic officials also reported that Christian DPs had adapted well during this initial period. See Harold Faber, "DPs Quick to Catch Tempo of America." No doubt some DPs who came here, Jewish and Christian, were on welfare, but judging from the absence of any discussion on this in the literature, the number must have been small.

109 A study in Cleveland: Helen Glassman, *Adjustment in Freedom,* pp. 45–46. A study of Canadian survivors cited by Myra Giberovitch found that most immigrants became self-sufficient within six months. Of 441 people seen by the Jewish Immigrant Aid Service, only 9 percent returned for additional assistance. See Myra Giberovitch, "The Contributions of Montreal Holocaust Survivor Organizations," pp. 3–4.

109 in the semiprofessional (business): Jewish immigrants who immigrated to the United States between 1882 and 1917 were far more likely to be working-class, as opposed to small-business entrepreneurs. Why this was so had to do both with opportunities then available in the United States and with the nature and composition of the immigrant generation at the time. To better comprehend this issue requires a closer examination of which classes and religious groupings within the European Jewish community chose to emigrate at that time, as compared to those who arrived after World War II. For general information on this topic see Ilja Dijour, "Jews in the Russian Economy," in Jacob Frumkin et al., eds., *Russian Jewry, 1860–1917* (New York: Thomas Yosseloff, 1966), pp. 120–43; Thomas Kessner, *The Golden Door* (New York: Oxford University Press, 1977).

109 but not as much as one might expect: See Morton Weinfeld et al., "Long Term Effects of the Holocaust on Selected Social Attitudes and Behaviors of Survivors: A Cautionary Note," *Social Forces,* vol. 60, no. 6 (1981), pp. 9–11.

109 survivors invest in real estate: In her book Dorothy Rabinowitz also asserts that "survivors in considerable numbers involved themselves in building and construction careers—immensely successful ones, as it turned out, for some of them." As an example, she mentions the Shapell brothers, who survived Auschwitz and are among the leading manufacturers of prefabricated homes. She notes that real estate, besides providing opportunity, may have served as a strategy against destructiveness or as a symbolic statement about the renewal of life. See Dorothy Rabinowitz, *New Lives,* p. 19. These reasons are plausible, but there were also practical considerations. It was a logical area to enter for survivors who lacked education and language facility and had capital to invest.

110 Some will note that: On this see Illsoo Kim, *The New Urban Immigrants: The Korean Community in New York* (Princeton: Princeton University Press, 1981); Roger Waldinger, *Through the Eye of the Needle: Immigrants and Enterprise in New York's Garment Trades* (New York: New York University Press, 1986).

110 Robert Diamant: WOHL.

110 Leon Wells: Leon Wells, *The Janowska Road* (New York: Macmillan, 1963); and interview, January 8, 1990.

110 Frank Colb: Interview, August 23, 1989.

111 Cantor Matus Radzivilover: As reported in his book *Now or Never,* p. 99.

111 Certainly cultural predispositions to succeed: The cultural position emanates from the classic argument advanced by Max Weber that the discipline and the value placed on work, as embodied in the Protestant ethic, enabled various groups to do better than others. In later years, Nathan Glazer applied this to Jews. Most recently, Ivan Light has argued that it was ethnic resources, not individualism, that accounted for the success of certain groups. See Max Weber, *The Protestant Ethic and the Spirit of Capitalism* (New York: Scribner's, 1958); Nathan Glazer, "Social Characteristics of American Jews,

1654–1954," *American Jewish Yearbook, 1955,* vol. 56 (Philadelphia: Jewish Publication Society, 1955), pp. 3–43; Ivan Light, "Immigrant and Ethnic Business in America," *Ethnic and Racial Studies* 7 (1984), pp. 196–216.

111 ethnic unity and economic opportunities: This approach has been well presented by Howard Aldrich, who stresses the importance of entering fields where access is easily gained. He also points out that these are usually the occupations where the risk of failure is greatest and where the status associated with the job is low. Aldrich also observes that such success often depends on whether the immigrants can expand their market beyond that of consumers belonging to the group. Roger Waldinger has argued that scholars should concentrate on the interaction between culture and opportunity and that both play a crucial role. His framework can be applied to our case. Interviews conducted with survivors in Atlanta, for instance, indicate that it was limited opportunities that propelled the survivors into ownership of mom-and-pop stores there. Once that decision was taken, however, ethnic solidarity, resulting in part because of hostility encountered from the American Jewish population, encouraged closer cooperation. Many of the survivors spoke with resentment of being labeled *grine* and of facing social exclusion. See Howard Aldrich and Albert Reiss, Jr., "Continuities in the Study of Ecological Succession: Changes in the Race Composition of Neighborhoods and Their Businesses," *American Journal of Sociology* 81 (1976), pp. 846–66; Roger Waldinger, *Through the Eye of the Needle,* chapters 1 and 2.

111 Sam Brach: Interview, February 19, 1990.

112 Sam Silbiger: Interview, May 21, 1989.

112 Helen Gilmer: Interview, May 21, 1989.

112 as someone overly concerned with money: See William B. Helmreich, *The Things They Say Behind Your Back: Stereotypes and the Myths Behind Them* (New Brunswick, N.J.: Transaction Books, 1984) pp. 13–16, 24–30.

113 Herman Lewinter: Interview, July 3, 1989.

113 Joseph Bukiet: Interview, December 5, 1989.

115 Jack Werber: Interview, December 6, 1989.

116 William Ungar: Interview, February 21, 1990.

116 Noach Rodzinek: Interview, September 8, 1989.

116 Nathan Krieger: Interview, June 25, 1989.

116 Leon Lepold: Interview, July 25, 1989.

117 Major General Sidney Shachnow: Interview, March 22, 1990.

118 Zalman and Frieda Jakubowicz: Interview, April 16, 1988.

Chapter Four
All for the Children

120 "What makes Jews remarkable": Rabbi Shlomo Riskin (Address given at the Israel Center, Jerusalem, Israel, April 25, 1987).

121 about 83 percent of the survivors: Other studies report similar high percentages of married survivors. See Boaz Kahana et al., "Predictors of Psychological Well-Being Among Survivors of the Holocaust," in John P. Wilson et al., eds., *Human Adaptation to Extreme Stress: From the Holocaust to Vietnam* (New York: Plenum Press, 1988), p. 177; Lore Shelley, "Jewish Holocaust Survivors' Attitudes." Parenthetically, the same trend (88 percent) exists among Christian Polish DPs who came to the United States. See Danuta Mostwin, "The Transplanted Family," p. 161.

121 building a future: Remarrying is a way of asserting vitality. See Robert J. Lifton, *Death in Life: Survivors of Hiroshima* (New York: Random House, 1967), p. 505.

121 Most survivors, about 80 percent: This is supported by other findings. See Boaz Kahana et al., "Predictors of Psychological Well-Being," in Wilson, ed., *Human Adaptation,* p. 177. This tendency is not unique to Holocaust survivors. Among the group of Jewish refugees who came to America between 1931 and 1944, 62.4 percent of the males and 71.4 percent of the females married other refugees. This is not as high as the survivors, but it is still a fairly substantial number. Maurice R. Davie et al., *Refugees in America,* p. 164.

121 "I married him because": Cited in Shamai Davidson, "The Clinical Effects of Massive Psychic Trauma in Families of Holocaust Survivors," *Journal of Marital and Family Therapy,* January 1980, p. 12.

122 Some researchers have noted: Ibid., p. 12.

122 Morris Fixler: Interview, May 16, 1989.

122 Sandy Mayer: Interview, January 26, 1988.

123 Fred Terna: Interview, February 15, 1990.

123 reminders of the past: For a description of such an individual see Dorothy Rabinowitz, *New Lives,* p. 104.

123 Ben Hirsch: Interview, May 20, 1989.

123 Judy Traub: Interview, June 27, 1989.

124 appeared in *The New York Times:* Judith Traub, "The Obligations of a Survivor," *New York Times,* September 11, 1983, Long Island Section, p. 26.

124 Gilbert Metz: Interview, May 14, 1989.

124 Alexander Petrushka: Interview, March 26, 1990.

124 Barbara Davis: Pseudonym, interview, May 19, 1989.

126 about 4 percent: Lore Shelley, "Jewish Holocaust Survivors' Attitudes," p. 93.

126 another pegged it at 8 percent: Boaz Kahana et al., "Predictors of Psychological Well-Being," in Wilson, ed., *Human Adaptation,* p. 177.

126 About 11 percent: The different figures ought not to be surprising. First, the methods and sample sizes varied. Second, the margin of error in studies with less than six hundred respondents is about 5 percent.

127 central feature of the Jewish community: See Marshall Sklare, *America's Jews* (New York: Random House, 1971).

127 they were afraid to have children: On this general point, see Robert Lifton, *Death in Life,* p. 505.

127 having given their children Gentile first names: See Dorothy Rabinowitz, *New Lives,* p. 143.

127 doubtful that they could feel love: Ibid., p. 104.

127 Elie Wiesel's book: Elie Wiesel, *The Fifth Son,* p. 41.

127 Together with David Diamond: Elie Wiesel, "Elie Wiesel on Hope," *New York Times,* June 7, 1987, Section 4, p. 5.

128 in the words of Paula Gris: YVA, 387.

128 For Samuel Harris: YVA, 10.

129 Philip Bernstein: Philip Bernstein, "Fifteen Months as . . . Jewish Advisor," *American Jewish Times,* January 1948, p. 9.

129 have more children than American Jews: The rate was 2.14 versus 1.88, and is statistically significant.

129 stereotypes of Jewish parents in general: See William Helmreich, *The Things They Say Behind Your Back,* pp. 8–11.

129 Added to this was the traditional respect: Christian Lithuanians and Ukrainians who came here after the war also emphasized education. See Algirdas M. Budreckis, "Reluctant Immigrants," in Cuddy, ed., *Contemporary American Immigration,* pp. 197–98; Myron Kuropas, *The Ukrainians in America* (Minneapolis: Lerner Publications, 1972), pp. 39–40. Both groups were far more educated than those of their countrymen who were already in the United States at the time of their arrival.

129 Dora Neselrot: Interview, May 22, 1989.

129 Barbara Fischman Mevorach: Interview, December 18, 1990.

130 One survivor summed it up: Cited in Helen Epstein, "A Study in American Pluralism," p. 33.

130 One study asked survivors: Lore Shelley, "Jewish Holocaust Survivors' Attitudes," p. 174.

131 Nathan Krieger: Interview, June 25, 1989.

132 the lack of discipline: One study that noted this perception among survivors is Doris Kirschmann and Sylvia Savin, "Refugee Adjustment—Five Years Later," *Jewish Social Service Quarterly,* Winter 1953, pp. 197–201.

132 As one survivor observed: Zdenka Weinberg, WOHL.

133 In the early years: On this, see Martin Bergmann and Milton Jucovy, eds., *Generations of the Holocaust,* pp. 5–6.

134 As one man reflected: Nathan Krieger, Interview, June 25, 1989.

134 Another person was fearful: Cited in Anton Gill, *Journey Back from Hell,* p. 223.

134 "I didn't want to scare her": Elizabeth Gevirtz, interview, April 23, 1989.

134 "I didn't want the Holocaust": Willy Herskovits, interview, December 8, 1987.

134 Regina Altman: YVA, 227.

134 why their children had never asked: Some researchers have found that survivors' children are generally unaware of their parents' specific experiences and are also not especially knowledgeable about the history of the Holocaust period. This topic needs to be more fully researched. See Aaron Hass, *In the Shadow of the Holocaust: The Second Generation* (Ithaca, N.Y.: Cornell University Press, 1990), p. 85.

134 Irena Urdang DeTour: Interview, February 19, 1988.

135 One survivor felt: Benjamin Hirsch, interview, May 20, 1989.

135 Vera Stern: Interview, February 13, 1990.

135 apparently feel more intensely: See Judith Kestenberg, "Psychoanalytic Contributions to the Problems of Children of Survivors from Nazi Persecution," *Israel Annals of Psychiatry and Related Disciplines,* vol. 10, no. 4 (1972), pp. 311–25.

135 This usually stems from: In *Children of the Holocaust,* pp. 181–82, Helen Epstein quotes researcher Vivian Rakoff's observations on this question: "It is almost as if the parents, in an attempt to justify their survival, demanded qualities of the children which were the accumulation of their expectations of all the dead who were murdered. The love and ambitions of whole families were resurrected in memory and imposed as hopes on the children, who were expected to supply the gratifications normally coming from mothers, fathers, brothers, sisters, cousins, uncles, and aunts, and to live out in their lifetimes those truncated lives."

136 Joseph Glikman: Interview, May 25, 1990.

136 as that of interfaith marriage: The best work on this subject is Egon Mayer, *Love and Tradition: Marriage Between Christians and Jews* (New York: Plenum Press, 1985).

137 Sometimes they present the argument: Rochella Velt Meekcoms, WOHL.

137 One survivor voiced: Interview, Bill Neufeld, July 25, 1989.

137 Guity Nellhaus: WOHL.

139 "How did these *shleppers*": As described in Barbara Finkelstein, *Summer Long-a-Coming,* p. 247.

139 language difficulties: Helen Epstein has described it beautifully in *Children of the Holocaust* (p. 146): "They could not find the right words. The wide, bright, sprawling fan of their experience snapped shut among people who spoke English. They were forced into a groping that changed the nature of what they had to say, that made them appear helpless, that distorted what they were. They became outsiders."

140 One child of survivors reported: Miriam Greenspan, "Responses to the Holocaust," *Jewish Currents,* October 1980, pp. 20–25, 37–39.

140 painfully remembered his bar mitzvah: Those children born right after the war were perhaps more apt to have suffered in this way. By the time the second or third child was born, the parents had been here longer and could afford a nicer affair.

140 David Brandt: Pseudonym, interview, spring 1990.

141 "I haven't got a father,": Cited in Helen Epstein, *Children of the Holocaust,* p. 184.

141 Another child of survivors: Cited in ibid., p. 199.

142 *A Generation After:* Peggy Kaganoff, "The Second Generation Comes of Age," *National Jewish Monthly,* April 1985, p. 22.

142 "Sometimes when my parents recalled": Cited in Helen Epstein, *Children of the Holocaust,* p. 148.

142 "How can you cause me": Ibid., p. 273; see also Aaron Hass, *In the Shadow of the Holocaust,* pp. 51–52.

143 "In spite of all the injunctions": Sonia Pilcer, "2G," *7 Days,* March 28, 1990, p. 22; see also Helen Epstein, *Children of the Holocaust,* p. 143.

143 There were also children: One group with particular difficulties were orphaned child survivors adopted by families. According to Sarah Moskovitz, who wrote a book about them, these adoptees were especially insecure because they not only were adoptees, but had also known their biological parents. Moreover, these were not parents who had voluntarily given up the children for adoption, but who had been, along with siblings, cruelly taken away from them. "Even as adults, they dare not risk shaking their only real ties of belonging by seeming disloyal or ungrateful. . . ." *Love Despite Hate: Child Survivors of the Holocaust and Their Adult Lives* (New York: Schocken Books, 1983), p. 227.

143 Menachem Rosensaft: Judith Miller, *One, by One, by One* (New York: Simon & Schuster, 1990), p. 225.

143 many of the studies: For an excellent summary and critique of these works, see Norman Solkoff, "Children of the Nazi Holocaust: A Critical Review of the Literature," *American Journal of Orthopsychiatry*, vol. 51, no. 1 (1981), pp. 29–42; also Aaron Hass, *In the Shadow of the Holocaust*, pp. 32–36.

144 William Ungar: Interview, February 21, 1990.

145 The work of John Sigal: See John J. Sigal and Morton Weinfeld, *Trauma and Rebirth: Intergenerational Effects of the Holocaust* (New York: Praeger, 1989); Morton Weinfeld and John J. Sigal, "The Effect of the Holocaust on Selected Socio-Political Attitudes of Adult Children of Survivors," *Canadian Review of Sociology and Anthropology*, vol. 23, no. 3 (1986), pp. 365–82.

145 Obviously, the experiences of survivors: For some examples of research on the problems of such children see Norman Linzer, *The Jewish Family: Authority and Tradition in Modern Perspective* (New York: Human Sciences Press, 1984), pp. 186–87; Steven Greenblatt, "The Influence of Survival Guilt on Chronic Family Crises," *Journal of Psychology and Judaism*, vol. 2, no. 2 (Spring 1978), pp. 19–28; Stanley Schneider, "Attitudes Toward Death in Adolescent Offspring of Holocaust Survivors," *Adolescence*, vol. 13 (1978), pp. 575–84; S. L. Rustin and F. S. Lipsig, "Psychotherapy with Children of Concentration Camp Survivors," *Journal of Contemporary Psychotherapy* 4 (1972), pp. 87–94; Hillel Klein, "Children of the Holocaust: Mourning and Bereavement," in E. J. Anthony and C. Koupernik, eds., *The Child in His Family: The Impact of Disease and Death* (New York: John Wiley, 1973), pp. 393–409; Henry Krystal, ed., *Massive Psychic Trauma*.

145 While determining pathology is a difficult matter: See Martin Bergmann and Bernard Jucovy, eds., *Generations of the Holocaust*, p. 19.

145 They have, in fact, reached high levels: This was also true of

Lithuanian refugees' children. Algirdas Budreckis, "Reluctant Immigrants," in Cuddy, ed., *Contemporary American Immigration,* pp. 197–98.

145 We found no difference: Sigal and Weinfeld reached a similar conclusion in their research. See *Trauma and Rebirth,* pp. 120–27.

145 to enter the helping professions: For more on the reasons for this, see Aaron Hass, *In the Shadow of the Holocaust,* p. 45.

146 According to Ilana Kuperstein: Ilana Kuperstein, "Adolescents of Parent Survivors of Concentration Camps: A Review of Literature," *Journal of Psychology and Judaism,* vol. 6, no. 1 (1981), pp. 7–22. A study of Christian immigrants from Estonia also found a high level of ethnic identification among the immigrants' children that came about because the parents made a conscious effort to instill pride of heritage in their offspring. See Mary Ann Walko, "A Sociological Study of the Estonian Community of Lakewood, New Jersey: Patterns and Ethnic Maintenance Between Parents" (Ed.D. diss., Rutgers University, 1983), p. iii.

146 an awareness of their heritage in this regard: Over the years, various organizations consisting of children of survivors have sprung up. The best known of these is Second Generation. Myra Giberovitch, a researcher who is herself very involved with such organizations around the world, has written: "Over the years, I have spoken with many daughters and sons of survivor parents. Many of my peers have expressed apprehension about openly identifying with our group. A major reason given was the fear of stereotyped behaviour being attributed to them. The fear of a 'children of survivors syndrome' label has served as a deterrent to membership." See "The Contributions of Montreal Holocaust Survivor Organizations," p. 55.

Chapter Five
The Social World of the Survivor

150 the issue is far more complex: Raymond Breton, "Institutional Completeness," pp. 193–205.

150 The types of organizations: Ulrike Schoeneberg, "Participation in Ethnic Associations: The Case of Immigrants in West Germany," *International Migration Review,* vol. 19, no. 3 (1985), pp. 416–37.

150 One member of a society: Millie Werber, Interview, December 6, 1989.

150 Myra Giberovitch: "The Contributions of Montreal Holocaust Survivor Organizations," pp. 59–60.

150 were even more crucial: Samuel Baily, "The Adjustment of Italian Immigrants," pp. 292–93.

150 Yitzchak Rybel: Interview, April 24, 1990.

151 Many other societies: Steven Lowenstein, *Frankfurt on the Hudson,* p. 55.

151 In a 1950 letter to the *Forward:* Batya Oplip, "Zey Arbeten do Shver, es iz zey ober Lib di Arbet." ("Work Here Is Difficult, but It's Very Wonderful to Work"), a letter in the "My New Home" contest, *Forward,* May 14, 1950, p. 2.

151 historical tendency of the European arrivals: Like the Jews, the Christian Latvian DPs who came to the United States established cultural organizations, theaters, and choruses. They also published ethnic newspapers and books. See Juris Veidemanis, "Social Change: Major Value Systems of Latvians as Refugees and as Immigrants" (Ph.D. diss., University of Wisconsin, 1961), pp. 399–418.

151 One survivor from Minneapolis: Felicia Weingarten, MA.

152 in much the same way: See Charles E. Silberman, *A Certain People: American Jews and Their Lives Today* (New York: Summit, 1985), p. 50.

152 Hannah Kliger: "A Home Away from Home," in Zenner, ed., *Persistence and Flexibility,* p. 156.

152 Jack Werber: Interview, December 6, 1989.

153 To the extent that conflict results: See Lewis Coser, *The Social Functions of Conflict* (Glencoe, Ill.: The Free Press, 1956).

153 David Nemlitz: Pseudonym, interview, fall 1989. The Beinovich Society is also a fictitious name, as is Weiss.

155 had been set up by a Jewish organization: It was not the first case to be handled in this manner. See Landon S. Wainwright, "You Are the Man Who Killed my Brother," *Life,* December 11, 1950, pp. 132–50. In that case, the matter was judged by the American Jewish Congress (Krieger vs. Mitleman).

155 like Minneapolis and Pittsburgh: Dora Zaidenweber, MA; Barbara Burstin, *After the Holocaust,* p. 122.

155 Ben Hirsch: Interview, May 20, 1989.

156 Morris Kesselman: Interview, July 19, 1989.

156 with even the Latvians: Operating under the name of Jewish Survivors of Latvia, the organization has members throughout the world. It runs dinners, convenes meetings, and publishes a monthly newsletter.

156 Solomon and Lucy Yehaskel: Interview, May 29, 1989.

156 Jewish Poultry Farmers Association: Joseph Brandes, *Immigrants to*

Freedom: Jewish Communities in Rural New Jersey Since 1882 (Philadelphia: Jewish Publication Society, 1971), pp. 330–31.

156 Yet even they were organizationally affiliated: Milton and Judith Kestenberg have noted that young survivors had a great need to belong because they were excluded from groups at a crucial time in their development, a time when they were forming and building stable relationships. All this was interrupted by the war. See their article on this, "The Sense of Belonging and Altruism in Children Who Survived the Holocaust," *Psychoanalytic Review,* vol. 75, no. 4 (Winter 1988), pp. 619–40.

156 In Baltimore: Eugene Kaufman, "A Social, Educational, and Recreational Program in the Adjustment of Adult Newcomers," *Jewish Social Service Quarterly,* March 1950, p. 407.

157 was B'nai B'rith: This was confirmed by our survey as well as one done on Cleveland survivors. See Helen Glassman, *Adjustment in Freedom,* pp. 64–69. See also Deborah Dash Moore, *B'nai B'rith and the Challenge of Ethnic Leadership* (Albany, New York: State University of New York Press, 1981).

157 held a special reunion: "Reunion," *National Jewish Monthly,* December 1982, pp. 40–41.

157 Irena Urdang DeTour: Interview, February 19, 1988.

158 Andrew Steiner: Interview, May 18, 1989.

158 he showed great courage: Jim Auchmutey, "Deals with the Devil: Ransom Plan Is a Footnote to Holocaust," *Atlanta Constitution,* September 20, 1988, Section E, p. 1.

159 Willy Herskovits's: Interview, December 8, 1987.

159 The following description: William Helmreich, *Wake Up, Wake Up,* p. 17.

159 Rachmil Kurlender: Interview, March 23, 1989.

160 especially those of a cultural nature: Sometimes the organizations supported different types of activities. Carol Meyer studied a Y group made up of young survivors who met once a month. Their ages were between eighteen and twenty-four and anywhere from forty-five to a hundred people came. The programs dealt with discussions of Israel and other world problems, life in America, movies, and job opportunities. In addition to lectures, there was also social dancing. There were conflicts between one group that had been in Buchenwald and a second one that had not and there were also cliques based upon land of origin. The survivors experienced difficulties integrating socially with the American Jewish Y members. See "Till Human Voices Wake Us," p. 67.

160 February 7, 1950, edition: *Forward,* February 7, 1950, p. 10.

160 developed a cultural network: See Joseph Brandes, *Immigrants to Freedom,* for information on the cultural life of the survivors in southern New Jersey.

160 In addition to the national Yiddish press: Ethnic newspapers are very important in preserving cultural life. They keep alive the culture and interpret events in the new land, with special attention to the interests of ethnic groups. See Raymond Breton, "Institutional Completeness," p. 201.

161 Willy Herskovits: Interview, December 8, 1987.

161 the Bialystoker Society: Yitzchak Rybel, interview, April 24, 1990.

161 at the same time as Jewish holidays: Myra Giberovitch, "The Contributions of Montreal Holocaust Survivor Organizations," p. 83.

161 Chris Lerman: Interview, June 12, 1990.

162 Andrew Steiner: Interview, May 18, 1989.

162 Willie Lieberman: Interview, January 5, 1988.

162 Alex Gross: Interview, May 17, 1989.

162 Morris Berkowitz: Interview, September 18, 1989.

163 Morris Kesselman: Interview, July 19, 1989.

163 Sidi Natansohn: Interview, July 20, 1989.

164 Louis Goldman: June 12, 1990.

165 Helen Epstein's narrative: Helen Epstein, *Children of the Holocaust,* pp. 137–38.

165 Bella Shampan: Interview, June 29, 1989.

166 Izzy Raab: Interview, June 12, 1990.

166 as in Cleveland: Helen Glassman, *Adjustment in Freedom,* pp. 64–69.

166 With their emphasis upon winning: I am indebted to Helen Ishofsky for clarifying my thinking on this matter.

166 the Catskill Mountains: For a general history of this period, see Stefan Kanfer, *A Summer World* (New York: Farrar, Straus & Giroux, 1989), pp. 199–256.

167 Judy Traub: Interview, June 27, 1989.

168 Lucy Yehaskel: Interview, May 29, 1989.

168 Moritz Felberman: Interview, April 25, 1989.

168 Sam Brach: Interview, February 19, 1990.

169 interviews and other studies: See John Sigal and Morton Weinfeld, *Trauma and Rebirth,* p. 79. This is due not only to their status as survivors but also to the fact that they are immigrants. A study of Polish-Christian DPs who immigrated to the United States found a similarly high rate of in-group friendships. See Danuta Mostwin, "The Transplanted Family," p. 217.

169 strengthened such ties: Mary Sengstock has noted that geographical proximity brings the group closer together. See "Developing an Index of Ethnic Community Participation," *International Migration Review,* vol. 12, no. 1 (1978), pp. 55–69.

169 Dorothy Rabinowitz: Dorothy Rabinowitz, *New Lives,* pp. 138–39.

170 they simply came: By way of contrast, a study of Latvian-Christian DPs living in Milwaukee found that they did not drop in on each other. Nor did they cluster in the same neighborhoods. Juris Veidemanis, "Social Change," p. 428.

170 Bill Neufeld: Interview, July 25, 1989.

170 Moritz Felberman: Interview, April 25, 1989.

171 Another survivor explained: Willy Herskovits, interview, December 8, 1987.

171 Joseph Eden: Interview, June 22, 1989.

171 One article made mention: Isadora Berman and Solomon Shapiro, "Psychological Problems Met in Counseling and Placement of Refugees," *Journal of Jewish Communal Service* 26 (December 1949), p. 282.

172 Kitty Hart: *Return to Auschwitz* (New York: Atheneum, 1982), p. 169.

172 Norbert Wollheim: Cited in Anton Gill, *Journey Back from Hell,* p. 297.

173 Nathan Krieger: Interview, June 25, 1989.

173 Herbert Kalter: Interview, September 1, 1989.

173 Sonia Pilcer: Sonia Pilcer, "2G," p. 22.

174 Vera Stern: Interview, February 13, 1990.

174 Sigmund Tobias: Interview, March 1, 1990.

175 Abraham Kessler: Interview, August 1, 1989.

175 Albert and Naomi Zeder: Interview, May 24, 1989.

176 "Whatever prejudices we had": Norbert Wollheim, "The German-Jewish Legacy After Auschwitz," *American Jewish Archives,* vol. 40, no. 2 (November 1988), p. 234.

177 a rather vitriolic exchange: As cited in Michael Wurmbrand, "Kampf gegen Windmühlen in U.S.A.: Ein Angriff auf die Deutschsprachigen Juden" ("Tilting Against Windmills in the U.S.A.: An Attack on German-Speaking Jews"), *Aufbau,* August 9, 1946, pp. 21–22; Michael Wurmbrand, "Ostjuden und Westjuden: Yitzchak Warshawsky Antwortet" ("Eastern Jews and Western Jews: Yitzchak Warshawsky Responds"), *Aufbau,* September 6, 1946, p. 17. See also Benny Kraut, *German-Jewish Orthodoxy in an Immigrant Synagogue: Cincinnati's New Hope Congregation and the Ambi-*

guities of Ethnic Religion (New York: Markus Wiener Publishing, 1988).

178 Joseph Bukiet: Interview, December 15, 1989.

179 Helen Epstein: Helen Epstein, *Children of the Holocaust,* pp. 145–46.

179 Sam Brach: Interview, February 19, 1990.

180 endured by their children: The effort to send children to camps stressing American values was a conscious one on the part of large numbers of survivors. For a description of one such camp, Camp Tranquillity, in Earlton, New York, see "E. A. Cohen Dies in Jerusalem," *Rescue,* Fall 1952, p. 13.

180 "I wanted to learn": Sandy Mayer, interview, January 26, 1988.

180 "All the people": Ben Geizhals, interview, December 25, 1989.

181 Lantos explained: Interview, May 10, 1990.

Chapter Six
Reaching Out

183 "There is a need": Sam Brach, interview, July 7, 1990.

184 Israel and Soviet Jewry: Other knowledgeable researchers have also cited these as the two main issues. See for example Jack Nusan Porter, "Is There a Survivor Syndrome? Psychological and Sociopolitical Implications," *Journal of Psychology and Judaism,* vol. 6, no. 1 (1981), pp. 33–52.

184 About 90 percent of all survivors: According to the 1990 National Jewish Population Study, slightly more than one in four Jewish adults have visited Israel at least once. Tom Tugend, "Counting U.S. Jews," *Jerusalem Post,* November 27, 1990, p. 8. The high figures for visits in this study are due to the fact that our samples of survivors and American Jews are drawn from people at least forty-five years old (to be survivors they have to have been born before 1945).

185 identify more strongly with Israel: In some cases, one or more of their children may even live there.

185 Leon Lepold: Interview, July 25, 1989.

185 Benjamin Meed: Interview, November 29, 1989.

186 sold in the United States: A study of survivors living in Montreal reported a similarly high level of involvement. Myra Giberovitch, "The Contributions of Montreal Holocaust Survivor Organizations," p. 68.

186 "I buy Israeli": Sandy Mayer, interview, January 26, 1988.

186 Moshe Weinstock: Interview, December 6, 1989.

188 Sam Brach's: Interview, February 19, 1990. For more on how the Six Day War affected the survivors, see Judith Miller, *One, by One, by One,* pp. 222–23.

189 Joseph Bukiet: Interview, December 15, 1989.

190 Felicia Weingarten: MA.

190 In July 1990: Sam Brach, interview, July 7, 1990.

191 in the early years: See Breina Goldman, "Hazkore zum Elftn Yortog Noch di 6 Million Kdoyshim" ("Remembrance in the Eleventh Year Since the Annihilation of the Six Million Martyrs"), *Der Yidisher Farmer,* May 1954, p. 74; Breina Goldman, "Hazkore Noch di Umgekumene Kdoyshim" ("Memorial for the Slaughtered Martyrs"), *Der Yidisher Farmer,* May 1956, p. 75.

191 In 1948: Vladka Meed (Miedzyrzecki), *Fun Beyde Zaytn Geto-Moyer* (New York: Educational Committee of the Workmen's Circle, 1948). It was later translated into English and appeared as *On Both Sides of the Wall* (Israel: Ghetto Fighters' House and Hakibbutz Hameuchad Publishing House, 1973).

191 in Newark, New Jersey: More than three hundred persons attended the commemoration, which was held at the local YMHA. There was also an organization in the community, called the Association of Refugee Jews/European Refugees of New Jersey. The group organized weekends at places like the Farband Unser Camp in Highland Mills, New York. See Josef Butterman, *Jewish Displaced Persons in Germany and in the United States of America, 1945–1960: A Report* (Jerusalem: Yad Vashem Archives, 1960).

191 Of course, there are his books: See Alvin H. Rosenberg and Irving Greenberg, eds., *Confronting the Holocaust: The Impact of Elie Wiesel* (Bloomington, Indiana: Indiana University Press, 1978).

192 which moved swiftly: For a detailed account of how this was done, see Judith Miller, *One, by One, by One.*

192 Leon Wieseltier: Cited in ibid, p. 231.

192 Vladka Meed: Interview, January 5, 1990.

193 Ernest Michel: Cited in Anton Gill, *Journey Back from Hell,* p. 290.

193 which attracted more than ten thousand survivors: Ruth Seligman, "Unto the Second Generation," *Hadassah,* August-September 1981, pp. 4–6. One observer has noted that "these ceremonies have many functions, but on the psychological level they help to actualize mourning, bring a sense of healing, and perhaps even restore a sense of order and justice in the world." Ricki Bernstein, "Research and Methodology in the Study of Nazi Holocaust Survivors and Their

Children: A Critique" (unpublished paper, Hunter College, 1982), p. 10.

193 "It was probably the greatest": Ernest Michel, interview, December 27, 1989.

194 "I'm convinced that twenty years": Benjamin Meed, interview, November 29, 1989.

196 made it in America: Actually, a group of six survivors, led by Ernest Michel and Haskel Tydor, had already met with a U.S. president, but it was a private encounter. They had journeyed to Washington in 1960, at the invitation of then President Dwight D. Eisenhower, to present him with a scroll expressing gratitude and loyalty to the United States. Ernest W. Michel, "My Long Journey to Eisenhower," *Reader's Digest,* December 1960, pp. 135–39.

196 an America that so many of them love: See Masha Leon, "Together at Brown's Hotel," *Forward* (English ed.), October 6, 1989, p. 10. In our own study, survivors were asked: "Is America really the land of opportunity for all, regardless of race, religion, or ethnic group?" About 90 percent replied yes, compared to 76 percent among American Jews.

197 Joseph Nass: Interview, May 28, 1989.

197 approximately 1,500 children of survivors: Ruth Seligman, "Unto the Second Generation," pp. 4–6.

197 Another important development: For a full and critical discussion of the commercialization of these museums and the internal politics surrounding them, see Judith Miller, *One, by One, by One.*

198 Sarah Berkowitz: Sarah Bick Berkowitz, *Where Are My Brothers?* (New York: Helios Books, 1965); *In Search of Ashes* (New York: Shengold Books, 1984).

198 Joseph Eden: Interview, June 22, 1989.

198 Alex Gross: Interview, May 17, 1989.

199 they court the young: Suzy Lampert, "How Students Perceive the Holocaust," *Midstream,* April 1984, pp. 29–31; William B. Helmreich, "How Jewish Students View the Holocaust: A Preliminary Appraisal," *Response,* vol. 9, no. 1 (1975), pp. 101–14.

199 Fred Terna: Interview, February 15, 1990.

199 Rita Kesselman: Interview, July 19, 1989.

200 to view anti-Semitism as "a very serious problem": This is corroborated by another study of anti-Semitism that compared the two groups. See Simon N. Herman and Uri Farago, "Reactions of Jews to Anti-Semitism" (American Jewish Committee, forthcoming). There is, incidentally, no difference in perceptions of how serious a problem anti-Semitism is between survivors living in New York and elsewhere.

200 How has the Holocaust affected: For a discussion of the idea that previous victims sympathize with the plight of other victims, see Lawrence Fuchs, "Sources of Jewish Individualism and Liberalism," in Marshall Sklare, ed., *The Jews: Social Patterns of an American Group* (Glencoe, Ill.: The Free Press, 1958), pp. 595–613.

201 This is a fairly high figure: In a study of tolerance among children of survivors, almost two thirds of those responding said that a person wishing to make a speech in their community about the genetic inferiority of blacks should not be allowed to do so. See Morton Weinfeld and John Sigal, "The Effect of the Holocaust," p. 375.

201 Ben Stern: YVA.

201 Walter Peltz: Interview, July 24, 1989.

202 Gilbert Metz: Interview, May 14, 1989.

203 now that they have the chance: The underlying basis for this attitude is perceptively analyzed in Abraham J. Peck, "The Lost Legacy of Holocaust Survivors," *SHOAH,* vol. 3, nos. 2–3, pp. 33–37.

203 are both members and leaders: Other studies corroborate this. See Lore Shelley, "Jewish Holocaust Survivors' Attitudes," p. 122; Barbara Burstin, *After the Holocaust,* p. 167.

204 In a speech made: "Baltimore Newcomers Group Participates in Campaign," *Rescue,* April-May 1951, p. 5.

204 In that same year: "Twelve DP's Enact Drama Based on Memories of Their Own Lives," *Jewish Examiner,* June 1, 1951, p. 9.

204 newcomers in Pittsburgh: Barbara Burstin, *After the Holocaust,* p. 167.

204 in Montreal: Myra Giberovitch, "The Contributions of Montreal Holocaust Survivor Organizations," p. 17.

204 in the farming communities: I. Harry Levin, "Vineland—A Haven for Refugees," *The Jewish Poultry Farmers Association of South Jersey: 10th Anniversary Journal,* 1962, p. 5.

204 helping other Jews adapt to life: Some survivors are currently involved in efforts to assist Iranian Jews.

205 Sam Halpern: Interview, February 14, 1988.

205 Sam Brach: Interview, February 19, 1990.

205 Bill Neufeld: Interview, July 25, 1989. Neufeld later moved to Milwaukee, where he settled permanently, after fourteen months in St. Paul.

206 Sam Brach: Interview, February 19, 1990.

206 Abe Foxman: Interview, January 10, 1990.

207 Michel expressed disappointment: Interview, December 27, 1989.

207 of greater importance: For more on why these issues are so important to them, see Ragnar Kvam, "Among Two Hundred Survivors From Auschwitz," trans. Otto Reinert, *Judaism,* vol. 28, no. 3 (Summer 1979), pp. 283–92.

207 Joseph Bukiet: Interview, December 15, 1989.

207 Benjamin Hirsch: Interview, May 20, 1989.

210 God permitting a Holocaust to occur: For a full discussion of survivors and their religious beliefs, see Reeve Robert Brenner, *The Faith and Doubt of Holocaust Survivors* (New York: The Free Press, 1980).

210 Joseph Glikman: Interview, May 25, 1990.

210 Alexander Petrushka's: Interview, March 26, 1990.

211 the postwar immigrants: William B. Helmreich, *The World of the Yeshiva: An Intimate Portrait of Orthodox Jewry* (New York: The Free Press, 1982), pp. 302–4, 307–8.

211 Moishe Rubin: Interview, June 25, 1989.

211 Sam Brach: Interview, February 19, 1990.

213 "my husband insisted": Miriam Brach, interview, February 19, 1990.

213 various newspapers and magazines: Albert R. Hunt, "Estranged Friends: Pivotal Jewish Voters Are Down on Carter Because of Israeli Policy," *Wall Street Journal,* September 22, 1980, p. 1; John Toscano, "Special at Butcher's: Koch for Governor," *New York Daily News,* February 21, 1982, p. B6; Joe Klein and Michael Kramer, "Primary Time: Of Kennedy, Carter, Jews, and the Money Gap," *New York,* March 24, 1980, pp. 6–8.

214 Abraham Resnick: Interview, March 25, 1992.

214 Flora Spiegel: Craig Van Rooyen, "City Mourns Death of Flora Spiegel," *Corona Independent,* March 11, 1992, p. 1.

215 Fred Terna: Interview, February 15, 1990.

215 Harold Hersh: Interview, May 17, 1989.

216 Tom Lantos: Interview, May 10, 1990.

Chapter Seven
Living with Memories

218 His summation: "DP Problem Near Finale, Report Shows," *Jewish Examiner,* October 16, 1951, p. 6. The historian Yehuda Bauer drew the same conclusion, observing in 1989 that "the real heroes of the story were the survivors. . . . Had it not been for the determination of the survivors, no JDC [Joint Distribution Committee] would have made any difference." *Out of the Ashes,* p. xxv; also pp. 38–39.

219 Other research has also shown: Miriam J. Hirschfeld, "Care of the Aging Survivor," *American Journal of Nursing,* July 1977, pp. 1187–89.

219 Yael Danieli found: Yael Danieli, "On the Achievement of Integration in Aging Survivors of the Nazi Holocaust," *Journal of Geriatric Psychiatry,* vol. 14, no. 2 (1982), pp. 191–210.

219 Sam Moneta: Interview, January 11, 1990.

220 Another study: Eva Kahana et al., "Coping with Extreme Trauma," in Wilson et al., eds., *Human Adaptation,* p. 70. A second study found that survivors, when compared to various control groups, were no more or less likely to have visited physicians. See John Sigal and Morton Weinfeld, *Trauma and Rebirth,* pp. 53–54. For more on this topic, see Leo Eitinger, *Concentration Camp Survivors in Norway and Israel* (London: Allen & Unwin, 1961); Paul Matussek, *Internment in Concentration Camps and Its Consequences* (New York: Springer-Verlag, 1975).

220 long-term health: Today there are organizations such as Blue Card that help survivors with health (and financial) problems. See Diane Zorcik, "Blue Card Still Helping Holocaust Survivors," *Jewish Week,* May 4, 1990, p. 33.

221 About 18 percent of the survivors: Since this question was asked as part of a questionnaire, rather than in an in-depth interview, it was not possible to probe into the conditions under which the survivors had seen someone. Clearly a person who went because he was required to in order to receive reparations or because the HIAS asked him to when he arrived in this country is not in the same category as a person in therapy for serious psychological problems. If those in the former category were taken out of the yes column, the 18 percent figure would surely be lower. On the other hand, as Norman Linzer has pointed out, survivors may resist seeing someone because they do not want to admit that they need to, or that the Nazis were able to inflict such damage against them. See his article, "The Holocaust and Its Survivors," in *The Nature of Man in Judaism and Social Work* (New York: Federation of Jewish Philanthropies, 1978), pp. 90–91. In addition, survivors, the majority of whom come from a traditional Jewish European background, may simply not believe in the validity and efficacy of therapy. Against this, we must consider the likelihood that those survivors who really needed help and went, did so out of desperation or were compelled by relatives or friends. When all is said and done, the 18 percent figure is low enough to require further investigation. This was, after all, a severely traumatized population. Similar results were found among respondents who attended a national gathering of survivors. Only 10 percent received regular counseling and an additional 13 percent received "some counseling." Those who sought such counseling were found (by scaling tests) to have greater psychological problems. Boaz Kahana et al., "Predictors of Psychological Well-Being," in Wilson et al., eds., *Human Adaptation,* pp. 171–92.

221 of the research to date: There is a welcome trend away from this in the more recent work, with more and more studies using control groups that are sufficiently large to be scientifically valid. It should be emphasized that there is no objection to case histories. Because of the depth of such studies, they provide crucial information and insights. It is simply that caution must be employed in generalizing too much from them.

222 Most of the research: See for example Eva Fogelman, "Intergenerational Group Therapy: Child Survivors of the Holocaust and Offspring of Survivors," *Psychoanalytic Review,* vol. 75, no. 4 (1988), pp. 619–40; Dori Laub, "Holocaust Survivors' Adaptation to Trauma," *Patterns of Prejudice,* vol. 13, no. 1 (1979), pp. 17–25; Aaron Antonovsky et al., "Twenty-Five Years Later," pp. 186–93; Gustav Bychowski, "Permanent Character Changes as an Aftereffect of Persecution," in Krystal, ed., *Massive Psychic Trauma,* pp. 75–86.

222 Other studies: Ira O. Glick, et al., *The First Year of Bereavement* (New York: John Wiley, 1974).

222 "emerge again and again": Ibid., p. 15.

222 One survey of survivors: Lore Shelley, "Jewish Holocaust Survivors' Attitudes," p. 228.

223 by a Viennese-born child survivor: EC-MK—4/10/87, Jerome Riker International Study of Organized Persecution of Children, Child Development Research, Port Washington, New York.

223 According to one study: Lore Shelley, "Jewish Holocaust Survivors' Attitudes," p. 116.

224 guilty about the death of loved ones: Gertrude Schneider, "Survival and Guilt Feelings of Jewish Concentration Camp Victims," *Jewish Social Studies,* Winter 1975, pp. 74–83; Gail Sheehy, *Spirit of Survival* (New York: William Morrow, 1986), pp. 348–49.

224 David Jagoda: MA.

224 "I didn't do anything.": Much has been written about why guilt arises in such cases. See for example Bruno Bettelheim, *The Informed*

Heart; Leo Eitinger, *Concentration Camp Survivors in Norway and Israel.*

224 In the following example: Cited in Anton Gill, *Journey Back from Hell,* p. 183.

225 "What is worse than death?": Sheila Levin, *Simple Truths* (New York: Crown Publishers, 1982), p. 83.

225 Concentration Camp Survivors Syndrome: As described in William G. Niederland, "The Psychiatric Evaluation of Emotional Disorders in Survivors of Nazi Persecution," in Krystal, ed., *Massive Psychic Trauma,* p. 8.

225 According to one study: Peter Ostwald and Egon Bittner, "Life Adjustment After Severe Persecution," pp. 1393–1400.

225 Alex Brown: Pseudonym, interview, fall 1989.

227 sensitive portrayal: Sarah Moskovitz, *Love Despite Hate.*

227 "the concept that": Ibid., p. 236.

227 "In spite of the anxiety and fear": Ibid., p. 231.

228 "Despite the severest deprivation": Ibid., p. 233.

228 Moskovitz's study is not the only one: Another interesting book about the postwar adaptation of Holocaust survivors is Judith Hemmendinger, *Survivors: Children of the Holocaust* (Bethesda: National Press, 1986). The book explores and analyzes the feelings of ninety children released from the Buchenwald concentration camp, one of whom was Elie Wiesel. See also Judith Hemmendinger, "After the Death Camps: Return to Life" (paper presented at the International Conference on the Holocaust and Genocide, Tel Aviv, June 20–24, 1982).

228 Boaz and Eva Kahana: "Coping with Extreme Trauma"; "Predictors of Psychological Well-Being."

229 Gail Sheehy: Gail Sheehy, *Spirit of Survival,* p. 354.

229 Cecilie Klein: Cecilie Klein, *Sentenced to Live,* p. 141.

230 a family that was not "affectionate": Of course, not everyone uses such excuses. Irving Louis Horowitz, who is today a world-renowned sociologist, writes in a remarkably candid memoir of how he grew up in Harlem in the 1930s under very difficult circumstances. There were serious problems in terms of relationships within the family; having little money, they were among the last whites to move out of the neighborhood. Most difficult of all, Horowitz was compelled to undergo, as a child, twenty-four separate operations for a cleft palate. Today, he is the Hannah Arendt Distinguished Professor of Sociology and Political Science at Rutgers University, the author of several dozen books, and president of Transaction Publishers. See Irving

Louis Horowitz, *Daydreams and Nightmares* (Jackson, Miss.: University of Mississippi Press, 1990).

230 "You can't tell a thing to anyone": Gail Sheehy, *Surviving,* p. 321.

230 In one survey: Lore Shelley, "Jewish Holocaust Survivors' Attitudes," p. 284.

230 This has been extensively documented: Shamai Davidson, "Human Reciprocity Among the Jewish Prisoners in the Nazi Concentration Camps" (paper presented at the Proceedings of the Fourth Yad Vashem International Historical Conference, Jerusalem, 1984), pp. 555–72; Terrence Des Pres, *The Survivor;* Hillel Klein, "Delayed Affects and After-effects of Severe Traumatisation," *Israel Annals of Psychiatry* 12 (1974), pp. 293–303.

230 As one survivor put it: Cited in Anton Gill, *Journey Back from Hell,* p. 184.

230 Thus, another survivor: Sally Frishberg, interview, December 28, 1981, Brooklyn Center for Holocaust Studies Archives.

231 Robert Lifton has explained: Robert Lifton, "The Concept of the Survivor," in Dimsdale, ed., *Survivors, Victims and Perpetrators,* pp. 120–21. As opposed to Hiroshima, the actual horror of the camps lasted for years.

231 Dori Laub: Dori Laub, "Holocaust Survivors' Adaptation to Trauma," p. 19.

231 One researcher found: Editha Sterba, "The Effect of Persecutions on Adolescents," in Krystal, ed., *Massive Psychic Trauma,* p. 60.

231 Moshe Katz: "Officer's Fists Bring Grim Reminder of Hitler's Camps," *Jewish Examiner,* November 2, 1951, p. 1.

232 The following story: A-JK, Jerome Riker International Study of Organized Persecution of Children, Child Development Research, Port Washington, New York.

232 As Lifton has observed: Robert Lifton, *Death in Life,* p. 511.

233 Responding to a questionnaire: Lore Shelley, "Jewish Holocaust Survivors' Attitudes," p. 191.

234 Livia Bitton: Interview, March 9, 1990.

234 Some researchers have noted: Peter Ostwald and Egon Bittner, "Life Adjustment After Severe Persecution," p. 1398.

234 Herbert Kalter: Interview, September 1, 1989.

234 Tom Lantos: Interview, May 10, 1990.

235 Jack Hirsch: Interview, May 21, 1989.

235 According to one woman: GB-GF—6/14/86, Jerome Riker International Study of Organized Persecution of Children, Child Development Research, Port Washington, New York.

235 Naomi Wilzig: "My Life with a Holocaust Survivor," *Martyrdom and Resistance,* September-October, 1987, p. 5.

235 Others prefer to sit: Anton Gill, *Journey Back from Hell,* p. 100.

235 the reaction is extreme: YVA, 90a.

235 Herbert Kalter: Interview, September 1, 1989.

236 "Schmuel Judkiewitz": YVA, 215.

236 Helen Lewis: Cited in Anton Gill, *Journey Back from Hell,* p. 420.

236 Ricki Bernstein: Ricki Bernstein, "Research and Methodology," pp. 6–7.

237 "rebirth fantasy": Hillel Klein, "Children of the Holocaust: Mourning and Bereavement," in Anthony and Koupernik, eds., *The Child in His Family,* p. 394.

237 Reeve Robert Brenner interviewed 708 Israeli survivors: Reeve Brenner, *The Faith and Doubt of Holocaust Survivors.* Given the lack of extensive comparative research between survivors in Israel and elsewhere in the world, it is difficult to say how unique survivors living in Israel are and this must be considered when evaluating Brenner's results with respect to American survivors. Lisa Newman has argued that for a variety of reasons survivors living in Israel adjusted better than those living in other lands. See her article "Emotional Disturbance in Children of Holocaust Survivors," *Journal of Contemporary Social Work,* January 1979, p. 49. For more on this topic see Stanley Schneider, "Attitudes Toward Death in Adolescent Offspring of Holocaust Survivors: A Comparison of Israeli and American Adolescents," *Adolescence,* vol. 23 (Fall 1988), pp. 703–10; Judith Kestenberg, "Psychoanalytic Contributions to the Problem of Children of Survivors from Nazi Persecution," *Israel Annals of Psychiatry and Related Disciplines,* vol. 10, no. 4 (1972), pp. 311–25.

237 seven out of ten survivors: Reeve Brenner, *The Faith and Doubt of Holocaust Survivors,* p. 66.

237 There was a decrease: Ibid., pp. 38–39.

238 believed in a "personal God": Ibid., pp. 90–93.

238 Another, more general study: Lore Shelley, "Jewish Holocaust Survivors' Attitudes," p. 434; a third study reported that faith weakened among 27 percent of those survivors interviewed. Barbara Burstin, *After the Holocaust,* p. 146.

238 Interestingly, Brenner also found: Reeve Brenner, *The Faith and Doubt of Holocaust Survivors,* p. 64.

238 "I got through Auschwitz": John Rosenfelder, interview, May 18, 1989.

238 Sam Halpern: Interview, February 14, 1988.

239 William Ungar: Interview, February 21, 1990.

239 As Lucy Dawidowicz wrote: Lucy Dawidowicz, *The War Against the Jews* (New York: Holt, Rinehart & Winston, 1975), p. 308.

239 Paula Gris's: Interview, May 17, 1989.

240 Faye Porter: Interview, July 26, 1989.

240 Dovid Felberbaum: Interview, March 8, 1990.

240 to question God's actions or motives: For more on the Hasidic community's attitudes toward the Holocaust, see Lloyd M. Siegel, "Holocaust Survivors in Hasidic and Ultra-Orthodox Jewish Populations," *Journal of Contemporary Psychotherapy,* vol. 11, no. 1 (1980), pp. 15–31; Peter Schindler, "Responses of Hassidic Leaders and Hassidim During the Holocaust in Europe, 1939–1945, and a Correlation Between Such Responses and Selected Concepts in Hassidic Thought" (Ed.D. diss., New York University, 1972). For a historical and sociological overview of this community, see Egon Mayer, *From Suburb to Shtetl: The Jews of Boro Park* (Philadelphia: Temple University Press, 1979).

240 Brenner's statistical finding: Reeve Brenner, *The Faith and Doubt of Holocaust Survivors,* p. 51.

240 in an article on the subject: Chaim Shapiro, "Over My Shoulder Emuna Shines Down," *Jewish Observer,* June 1989, pp. 11–16. See also William B. Helmreich, "Making the Awful Meaningful," *SOCIETY,* vol. 19, no. 6 (1982), pp. 62–66.

240 Sarah Berkowitz: Interview, September 18, 1989.

241 "Why did He forsake us?": This question is fully dealt with in Martin Buber, *Eclipse of God: Studies in the Relation Between Religion and Philosophy* (New York: Harper & Bros., 1952).

241 "A good friend of mine": As told by Benjamin Hirsch, interview, May 20, 1989.

241 One woman always places a drop: Norman Linzer, *The Jewish Family: Authority and Tradition in Modern Perspective* (New York: Human Sciences Press, 1984), p. 181.

241 Elie Wiesel expanded on this idea: Elie Wiesel, *A Jew Today* (New York: Random House, 1978), pp. 163–64.

242 Again, Wiesel: Elie Wiesel, *The Gates of the Forest* (New York: Avon, 1966), p. 196.

242 But Wiesel: Elie Wiesel, "Jewish Values in the Post-Holocaust Future: A Symposium," *Judaism,* vol. 16, no. 3 (Summer 1967), p. 287.

242 "Out from the depths": Murray J. Kohn, WOHL.

243 "Every year": YVA, 11.

243 the only tangible way: See Judith Mandel Novack, *The Lilac Bush* (New York: Shengold Books, 1989), p. 66.

243 Noach Rodzinek: Interview, September 8, 1989.

243 Vera Eden: Interview, June 22, 1989.

244 Miriam Brach: Interview, February 19, 1990.

245 Philosopher Emil Fackenheim: Emil Fackenheim, "Jewish Values in the Post-Holocaust Future: A Symposium," *Judaism,* vol. 16, no. 3 (Summer 1967), p. 272.

245 Leon Wells: Interview, January 8, 1990.

245 Abraham Kessler: Interview, August 1, 1989.

247 Another clearly blamed: Cited in Norman Linzer, *The Jewish Family,* p. 183.

247 the theologian Eliezer Berkovitz: Eliezer Berkovitz, *The Faith and Doubt of Holocaust Survivors* (New York: KTAV Publishing, 1973), pp. 4–5.

248 Alex Gross: Interview, May 17, 1989.

248 Helen Schimel: Interview, December 13, 1989.

249 Ruth Siegler: Interview, May 22, 1989.

249 Leon Gross: Interview, May 23, 1989; Dale Grisham, "1945, Gross in Death Camp, Freed by U.S.," *Tuscaloosa News,* September 16, 1979, p. C-1.

249 Livia Bitton: Interview, March 9, 1990.

250 Ina Weiss: Interview, August 25, 1989.

250 Leon Wells: Interview, January 8, 1990.

250 Manny Ragen: Interview, August 23, 1989.

250 Jack Tramiel: Interview, June 28, 1990.

252 Frances Epstein: WOHL.

252 David Honig: WOHL.

252 Livia Bitton: Interview, March 9, 1990.

252 In a statistical survey: John Sigal and Morton Weinfeld, *Trauma and Rebirth,* p. 71.

252 Abraham Krakowski: Interview, September 18, 1989.

252 Noach Rodzinek: September 8, 1989.

252 was saved by a Polish family: A study comparing attitudes toward Gentiles of survivors saved by Christians, with the views of other survivors would be interesting. For more on the ambivalence toward Christians displayed by survivors, see A-FH, Jerome Riker International Study of Organized Persecution of Children, Child Development Research, Port Washington, New York.

253 Leon Lepold: Interview, July 25, 1989.

253 The following account: Dorothy Rabinowitz, *New Lives,* pp. 213–14.

254 Sandy Mayer: Interview, January 26, 1988.

254 Joseph Eden: Interview, June 22, 1989.

254 Congressman Tom Lantos: Interview, May 10, 1990.

254 Hungary had many minorities: For more on this subject see Judith Miller, "Out of Hiding," *New York Times Magazine,* December 9, 1990, pp. 70–76.

254 General Sidney Shachnow: Interview, March 22, 1990.

254 Abe Foxman: Interview, January 10, 1990.

255 Dina Balbien: YVA.

256 reactions of Luba Bat: Luba Bat, *Phoenix.*

256 Viktor Frankl: Viktor Frankl, *Man's Search for Meaning: An Introduction to Logotherapy* (Boston: Beacon Press, 1959), pp. 3–4. Frankl, it should be noted, was not employed as a psychiatrist in the camp until the last few weeks of the war. Most of the time he was simply an ordinary worker engaged in digging and laying tracks (p. 5).

257 Des Pres concludes: Terrence Des Pres, *The Survivor,* p. 136.

257 "when you have an opportunity": Benjamin Hirsch, interview, May 20, 1989.

257 Esther Peterseil: Interview, December 26, 1990.

258 One study asked: Lore Shelley, "Jewish Holocaust Survivors' Attitudes," p. 262. The percentages presented here are rounded off.

258 In a case study: Barbara Burstin, *After the Holocaust,* p. 160.

258 Dora Zaidenweber: MA.

258 Esther Raab: Interview, June 12, 1990.

258 Marcus Tepper: Interview, April 24, 1989.

259 Herman Lewinter: Interview, July 3, 1989.

259 the social psychologists: Simon Herman and Uri Farago, "Reactions of Jews to Anti-Semitism" (American Jewish Committee, forthcoming).

260 Shirley Ragen: Interview, August 23, 1989.

260 Irena Schwarz: Interview, August 23, 1989.

261 Maury Spira: Interview, August 23, 1989.

261 those who simply preferred: It would be interesting to compare in an in-depth manner the level of satisfaction and sense of accomplishment of survivors who lived in America with those who made Israel their home. According to one researcher, Diaspora survivors in general were far more likely to believe they had become "useful members of the community than their Israeli counterparts." See Lore Shelley, "Jewish Holocaust Survivors' Attitudes," p. 313.

261 Jack Goldreich: Interview, August 20, 1989.

261 As one woman says: YVA, 90a.

262 Dovid Felberbaum: Interview, March 8, 1990.

Chapter Eight
Overcoming Tragedy

267 there has been considerable research: To take some examples, respondents who had been in concentration camps for thirty-six months or longer reported greater agreement with statements regarding psychic numbing than those imprisoned for a shorter period of time. See Lore Shelley, "Jewish Holocaust Survivors' Attitudes," p. 306. Another study found that the harder the work, the greater the long-term physical and psychological damage. See Paul Matussek, *Internment in Concentration Camps,* p. 64. Researchers have also looked at the relationship between age at the time of incarceration and aftereffects of the Holocaust. See Lore Shelley, "Jewish Holocaust Survivors' Attitudes," p. 308; and Julia Izaks, "Effects of the Holocaust on Dutch-Jewish Victims, Residents of Israel, 30 Years Afterwards," (MSW thesis, Bar-Ilan University, Israel), 1984.

268 at least some of these features: I am following here the concept of the "ideal type" as developed by the sociologist Max Weber. As such, it does not refer to a "typical survivor" but is rather a yardstick by which human behavior can be both measured and approximated. See Lewis Coser, *Masters of Sociological Thought: Ideas in Historical and Social Context,* 2nd ed. (New York: Harcourt, Brace, Jovanovich, 1977), pp. 223–24.

268 unwilling to adjust: S. N. Eisenstadt, *The Absorption of Immigrants.*

268 was *assertiveness:* Several studies have concluded that there exists a strong relationship between aggressiveness as it manifested itself during the war and successful accommodation later, noting that those who thought up escape plans and developed strategies to improve their lives during the war did better later on than those who did not. See Paul Matussek, *Internment in Concentration Camps;* Yael Danieli, "Families of Survivors of the Nazi Holocaust: Some Short- and Long-Term Effects," in Charles H. Spielberger et al., eds., *Stress and Anxiety,* vol. 13 (Washington, D.C.: Hemisphere Publishing, 1982), pp. 405–21.

269 Arthur Hertzberg: "A Lifelong Quarrel with God," *New York Times Book Review,* May 6, 1990, p. 40.

269 Elias Epstein: Interview, January 22, 1990. Viktor Frankl writes about the reaction that greeted him upon arriving in Auschwitz. Unaware of the hell he had entered, he implored another prisoner to help him keep his "scientific manuscript." The man's grin went from amused to mocking and, finally, to insulting, at which point he simply shouted "Shit!" Frankl notes, "At that moment I saw the plain truth . . . I struck out my whole former life." *Man's Search for Meaning,* p. 12. With respect to Epstein's remark, one of logotherapy's basic principles is the importance of looking to the future (p. 98).

269 Jack Tramiel: Interview, June 28, 1990.

269 Alex Gross: Interview, May 17, 1989.

270 Joseph Wind: Interview, May 23, 1989.

271 "Life has to go on.": As it happens, Leon Wells belonged to the same unit as Wind and the two men have maintained contact over the years. In his book, Wells explained how brigade members distanced themselves from what they were doing: "Everyone finally grows accustomed to the work, and on Sunday, our day off, we find ourselves some kind of job to do. In the evening we sing in the bunkers until ten o'clock. We begin to develop our own sense of humor. 'I saw a corpse today and I swear that's just how you're going to look.' 'Don't eat too much; the corpse carriers will have a hard job getting you up on the heap.' " *The Janowska Road,* pp. 180–81.

271 described by Robert Lifton: Robert Lifton, "The Concept of the Survivor," in Dimsdale, ed., *Survivors, Victims, and Perpetrators,* pp. 120–21.

271 Livia Bitton: Interview, March 9, 1990.

271 Aaron Antonovsky: Aaron Antonovsky, *Unraveling the Mystery of Health: How People Manage Stress and Stay Well* (San Francisco: Jossey-Bass, 1987), p. 175. Antonovsky presents what is known as a "salutogenic view." This is an approach that tries to explain people's good health in terms of how they manage tension or stress. People who successfully combat stress have what Antonovsky calls a high "sense of coherence."

272 Erik Erikson has observed: Erik H. Erikson, *Childhood and Society* (New York: Norton, 1963).

272 Lifton has referred to it: Robert Lifton, *Death in Life,* p. 482.

272 Gail Sheehy: Gail Sheehy, *Spirit of Survival,* p. 360.

272 an ability to translate: On this see Jerome Kagan, *The Nature of the Child* (New York: Basic Books, 1984), p. 279.

272 for going on: See Sylvia Rothchild, ed., *Voices from the Holocaust* (New York: Meridian Books, 1981), p. 450.

272 *finding meaning in one's life:* The potentially damaging effects of

meaninglessness in life are sensitively portrayed in David Grossman's novel *See Under, Love* (New York: Farrar, Straus & Giroux, 1989). See also Harold S. Kushner, *When Bad Things Happen to Good People* (New York: Schocken Books, 1981), pp. 132-48.

272 Antonovsky found: Aaron Antonovsky, *Health, Stress, and Coping,* pp. 16–18.

272 Sarah Berkowitz: Interview, September 18, 1989.

273 Alex Gross: Interview, May 17, 1989.

273 socially valued individuals: Aaron Antonovsky, *Health, Stress, and Coping,* p. 111.

276 Stories of this sort abound: See for example Leon Wells, *The Janowska Road,* p. 154.

276 In one quantitative study: Lore Shelley, "Jewish Holocaust Survivors' Attitudes," p. 427.

Index

Page numbers after 280 refer to notes.

Feuerstein, Moses, 92–93
Fifth Son, The (Wiesel), 127
Finkelstein, Barbara, 139
Fishman, Irene, 94
Fixler, Morris, 122
Florida, 167, 260
food, 71, 172, 234–35, 257
  kosher, 60, 65, 79, 101, 113, 159,
    204, 209, 241, 243
Forward, 34, 35–36, 41, 55, 70, 74,
    79–80, 82–83, 96, 142, 151, 160,
    161, 177
Foxman, Abe, 13, 27, 74, 97–98, 206,
    254–55
Frankl, Viktor, 256–57, 272, 331
Freud, Anna, 227
Frishberg, Sally, 230, 335
furriers, 99, 156

gabbai, 159
Galveston, Tx., 25
Garden Cafeteria, 74
Garfinkle, Isaac, 51
Garfinkle, Yechiel, 51
garment industry, 99, 103, 108, 115,
    156
gas chambers, 23, 32, 134, 181, 208,
    256
Gates of the Forest, The (Wiesel), 242
Geizhals, Ben, 80, 91–92, 180–81, 297
General Ballou, 19
General Black, 25, 290
General Gordon, 19
Generation After, A, 142
Germans, 125, 135, 172, 206, 224,
    232, 236, 250–52, 253, 256
Germany, Nazi, *see* Nazis
Gestapo, 224, 232
Gevirtz, Elizabeth, 23–24, 134, 309
ghettos, 17, 160, 191, 196, 231, 243,
    275–76
Giberovitch, Myra, 150, 312
Gilmer, Helen, 70, 112
Glazer, Nathan, 305
Glikman, Joseph, 136, 210
God:
  covenant of, 241, 245
  faith in, 107, 113, 149, 206, 209,
    210–11, 237–47, 256, 259, 262,
    266, 273
Goldberger, Alice, 227, 228
Golden Gate Bridge, 25
Goldhaft, Arthur, 73

Goldman, Charlie, 97
Goldman, Israel, 64
Goldman, Louis, 64, 67, 164–65
Goldreich, Jack, 261
Goldstein, Bernard, 74
Goldstein, Irving, 30, 96
Goodfriend, Isaac, 106–7
Goodman, Edward, 99–100
Gorbachev, Mikhail, 202
Great Depression, 73
Griffith, Paul, 47
Gris, Paula, 20–21, 101, 128, 239–40,
    304
grocery stores, 104–5, 108, 114–15,
    178–79, 306
Gross, Alex, 162, 198–99, 248, 269–
    270, 273
Gross, Leon, 100, 249
Grubman, Sally, 84, 298
guilt, 41, 131, 134, 142–44, 145, 188,
    224–25, 248, 257, 270
Gurevitch, Nathan, 74
Gurs concentration camp, 32
Gypsies, 14

Hadassah, 204
Haft, Harry, 13, 97
Haifa, University of, 195
Halberstam, David, 90–91
Halpern, Sam, 26, 104, 205, 238
John Hancock Building, 110
Harlem, 94
Harris, Samuel, 128–29
Hart, Kitty, 172
Hatikvah, 256
"Hava Nagila," 166
Hebrew, 67, 88, 96–97, 211
Hebrew Immigrant Aid Society
    (HIAS), 29, 30, 31, 32, 33–34,
    35, 36, 46, 47, 48–49, 50–51, 53,
    59–60, 91–92, 157, 206, 264, 277,
    288, 290, 322
Hemmendinger, Judith, 324
Hemschech, 105
Henson, Leah, 71, 275–76
Herman, Simon, 259
Hersh, Harold, 104–5, 215, 216
Herskovits, Willy, 20, 88, 134, 159,
    161, 171, 275, 309, 316
Hertzberg, Arthur, 269
Hillel Club, 77
Hillman, Sidney, 24
Hiroshima survivors, 231

About the Author

William B. Helmreich is Professor of Sociology and Judaic Studies at CUNY Graduate Center and City College of New York and is the author of eight books, including *The World of the Yeshiva* and *The Things People Say Behind Your Back: Stereotypes and the Myths Behind Them*. Dr. Helmreich lives in New York with his wife and four children.